Anonymous

Alden's Cyclopedia of Universal Literature

Presenting biographical and critical notices and specimens from the writings of eminent authors of all ages and all nations

Anonymous

Alden's Cyclopedia of Universal Literature
Presenting biographical and critical notices and specimens from the writings of eminent authors of all ages and all nations

ISBN/EAN: 9783337220181

Printed in Europe, USA, Canada, Australia, Japan

Cover: Foto ©Andreas Hilbeck / pixelio.de

More available books at **www.hansebooks.com**

ALDEN'S CYCLOPEDIA

OF

UNIVERSAL LITERATURE

PRESENTING

BIOGRAPHICAL AND CRITICAL NOTICES, AND SPECIMENS
FROM THE WRITINGS OF EMINENT AUTHORS
OF ALL AGES AND ALL NATIONS

VOL. XVIII

NEW YORK
JOHN B. ALDEN, PUBLISHER
1891

CONTENTS OF VOLUME XVIII.

CONTENTS

CONTENTS.

CYCLOPEDIA

OF

UNIVERSAL LITERATURE.

SEELEY, JOHN ROBERT, an English author, born in London, in 1834. He is the son of a London publisher, was graduated at Christ Church College, where he became a fellow in 1858, and was for several years principal classical assistant in the City of London School. In 1863 he became professor of Latin at the University College of London, and in 1869 professor of Modern History at Cambridge, which post he still holds. His books are: *Ecce Homo: The Life and Work of Jesus Christ*, published anonymously (1864), *Classical Studies as an Introduction to the Moral Sciences* (1865), *An English Primer, or Course of English Instruction for English Schools*, with E. A. Abbott 1869), republished as *English Lessons for English People*, 1869), *Roman Imperialism* (1869). *Lectures and Essays* (1870), *Life and Times of Stein* (1879), *The Expansion of England* (1883), *A Short Life of Napoleon the First* (1885). He has also published an edition of *Livy*.

THE LAW OF KINDNESS.

Philanthropy is the first and easiest lesson in positive morality. It is a duty in which all Christian sects agree and which with more or less zeal they perform. The means used may differ; the means used in this age differ widely from those used in the first ages; but the obligation which the first Christians acknowledged is substantially the same as that acknowledged now. When they visited the sick and made provision for widows and orphans and gave alms to the poor, they were doing to the best of their light and knowledge what philanthropists of the present day do when they study the science of physical well being, search into the causes of disease and suffering, and endeavor systematically to raise the standard of happiness to the highest possible point.

Did the Enthusiasm of Humanity rest content with this? It might have done so. Perhaps there are some who believe that this is in fact the substance of Christianity, and that all the rest has been overlaid upon the original system. This is not true, and it will hardly seem plausible to a reader who has given even a general assent thus far to the results of the present investigation. But we shall find it easier to understand what the substance of Christianity really is, if we consider attentively what Christianity would have been and how it would have worked if this theory of it were true. . . .

The first century, like the eighteenth, was a period of transition. It was a period when for the first time the civilized nations of the world lived together in almost unbroken peace. War had ceased to be the main business of life the support of virtue and almost the only means by which eminent virtue could show itself. In these circumstances the world was prepared for, was calling for, a theory of virtue which should be adapted to its new condition. It wanted a new pursuit in place of war, a pursuit in which, as before in war, the moral feelings might find satisfaction and in which heroism might be displayed. Christ, it may be maintained, was the social legislator who appeared in answer to this call. He induced a large number of people by his eloquence and enthusiasm to devote themselves to philanthropy. He opened their eyes to the suffering and horrors of which the world was full, and pointed out to them a noble and satisfying occupation for their energies, and a path to the truest glory in the enterprise of alleviating this misery.

There is no doubt that a philanthropic, movement such as is here supposed, were possible and would have been highly beneficial in the first century. As five centuries before, a ferment in the Greek mind, arising out of a general advance in civilization and the influence of several remarkable men, led to the appearance in the world of an entirely new character which has never since disappeared—the *sophist* or *philosopher*, so it was natural enough that in the first century of the Christian era *philanthropists* should be heard of for the first time, and that they should take their rise out of a moral ferment excited by a great preacher. A sect of philanthropists might have spread everywhere, and gradually influenced rulers, and by this means manners might have been considerably softened. The Christians were no doubt such a sect, but were they merely this? Suppose the philanthropical scheme to be far more successful than it was likely to be, suppose it to succeed perfectly in producing physical comfort everywhere, and banishing from human life all forms of pain and suffering, such a result would certainly not have been satisfactory to Christ. He described in one of his parables a man such as philanthropy might produce if it were perfectly successful, a man enjoying every physical comfort and determining to give himself up to enjoyment, but he describes him rather with horror than with satisfaction. Although much of his life was passed in relieving distress, we never find him representing physical happiness as a desirable condition ;·on the contrary most of his beatitudes are pronounced upon those who suffer.—*Ecce Homo.*

SEELYE, JULIUS HAWTRY, an American educator and author, born at Bethel, Conn., in 1824. He graduated at Amherst in 1849, studied theology at Auburn, N. Y., and at Halle, Germany, and in 1853 became pastor of the first Reformed Dutch Church in Schenectady, where he remained until 1858. From 1858 till 1875 he was professor of mental and moral philosophy at Amherst. In 1875–7 he served in Congress as a delegate from Massachusetts. From 1877 to 1890 he was President of Amherst College. In 1872 he visited India, and delivered a course of lectures. He received the degree of D. D. from Union College in 1862, and that of LL. D. from Columbia in 1876. In addition to reviews, sermons, and addresses, he has published a translation of Dr. Albert Schwegler's *History of Philosophy* (1856), *Lectures to Educated Hindus* (Bombay, 1873), republished under the title, *The Way, the Truth, and the Life* (Boston, 1873), and *Christian Missions* (1875). In 1880 he published a revised edition of Hickok's *Moral Science.*

THE LIGHT OF LIFE.

Theism speaks of God as a living spirit, to whom human souls may come and worship; but it presents no living motive thus to do. Much as we might wish it otherwise, the lamentable fact remains that men do not spontaneously come to God. Left to themselves, they seek their own ends, and turn away from him. Simple theism has nothing to reverse this tendency. Its thought of God is too vague to have personal power over men. As the sunlight, all glorious though it be, does not warm the atmosphere through which it passes till its beams have been reflected from the earth ; so the light of the knowledge of

God may shine resplendent through all our thoughts, without any vivifying warmth, till our thoughts receive it through some living reflection of him. Herein is the fitness of Jesus Christ to inspire and save men. He appears before us as the living God in human form. It is claimed of him that he is the eternal Word, which was in the beginning with God, and which was God; by whom all things were made, and without whom there was not anything made that was made. He repeatedly makes the same claim for himself. He supports this claim by his own words not only, but by a power over Nature which bore witness to his words. He showed himself to be Lord of things created; and thus he manifested forth his glory, and his disciples believed in him. Nature appears as his servant, which hears his voice, and does his will. He turns the water into wine. He speaks to the winds and waves, and they obey him. The trees of the field and the fish of the sea do his bidding. He heals diseases of every sort. He makes the blind to see and the deaf to hear, and the dead to live. Through the three years in which his public life was manifested, Nature is seen to move as responsive to his will as the pulse beats with the throbbing of the heart; and, when he was crucified, dead and buried, he rose from the sepulchre, as the Lord of life with power over death and the grave.—*The Way, the Truth, and the Life.*

THE DESIRABLE END OF PROGRESS.

Notice now the living inspiration which this truth gives to men. God's love to man, thus revealed, begets man's love to God; for "we love him because he first loved us;" and man's love to God kindles man's love to man, "for he that loveth God will love his brother also." This living germ is capable of evolving the perfect life for the individual, and the perfect social state. All the requirements of individual perfection are met in that soul where every duty and every moral precept are revealed as the righteous will of a loving Lord, in whose love the soul finds its life, and in whose service it rejoices in the liberty of the perfect love which casteth out fear. The perfect social state surely exists when society, kindled by this divine inspiration becomes knit together by that charity which seeketh not her own, and where the new life of love and purity in individual hearts works everywhere in peace and good-will. These blessings, which no other religion even proposes, and which surpass the ideal dreams of poetry or philosophy, it is not only the actual aim of Christianity to secure, but these are the actual results of this religion, in exactly the degree in which men have yielded to its sway. If it could only be everywhere accepted, if all men were true and loyal disciples of Jesus Christ, wars would cease, oppression and slavery would be no more, vice and crime of every sort would disappear; there would be purity and love universal among men, and the spiritual life which the Christian faith enkindles would furnish the unfailing impulse to all intellectual growth and all industrial activity. Not only righteousness, but knowledge, should then flow through all the earth, while the wilderness and the solitary place should be glad thereof, and the desert should rejoice and blossom as the rose. The wise man, therefore, who loves his race, will be content with nothing less than the effort to bring all nations and every heart under the living sway of Jesus Christ and his word.—*The Way, the Truth, and the Life.*

SELDEN, JOHN, an English statesmen and scholar, born in 1584; died in 1654. He studied at Oxford, then went to London to practice law; here his profound and varied learning became conspicuous. In 1623 he was returned to Parliament for Lancaster. In 1630 he was committed to the Tower on account of his opposition to the policy of the Court, and remained a prisoner for four years. In 1640 he was returned to Parliament for the University of Oxford. He opposed the admission of the bishops to seats in the House of Lords, and was one of the committee who in 1643 drew up the articles of impeachment of Archbishop Laud. He took an active part in public affiairs until the execution of Charles I., in 1648, when he retired to private life. Most of Selden's works were written in Latin. Among these are: *Jani Anglorum Facies Altera*, which has been translated into English; *De Diis Syriis; De Succesionbus in Bona Defuncti; De Successione in Pontificatum Hebræori*. In English he wrote *Titles of Honor* and a *Treatise of Tithes*. His *Table-Talk*, which is rather a Commonplace-Book, in which he was wont to jot down his thoughts, was not published until after his death. Of this work Coleridge says: "There is more weighty bullion matter in this book than I ever found in the same number of pages of any uninspired writer." The following passages are from the *Table-Talk*.

THE ADVANTAGE OF KINGS.

A king is a thing which men have made for their own sake, for quietness's sake; just as in a family one man is appointed to buy the meat. If every man should buy, or if there were many buyers, they never would agree. One would buy what the other liked not, or what the other had bought before, so there would be a confusion. But that charge being committed to one, he, according to his discretion, pleases all. If they have not what they would have to-day, they shall have it the next, or something as good.

OF HERESIES.

It is a vain thing to talk of an heretic, for a man; for his heart can think no otherwise than he does think. In the primitive times there were many opinions, nothing scarce, but some or other held. One of these opinions being embraced by some prince, and received into his kingdom, the rest were condemned as heresies: and his religion, which was but one of the several opinions, is said to be orthodox, and so to have continued from ever since the times of the Apostles.

ON EVIL-SPEAKING.

He that speaks ill of another, commonly, before he is aware, makes himself such a one as he speaks against; for if he had civility or breeding he would forbear such kind of language. A gallant man is above ill words. . . Speak not ill of a great enemy, but rather give him good words, that he may use you the better if you should chance to fall into his hands. The Spaniard did this when he was dying. His confessor told him—to work him to repentance—how the Devil tormented the wicked that went to hell. The Spaniard replied (calling the devil My Lord). "I hope, my Lord the Devil is not so cruel." His confessor reproved him. "Excuse me," said the Don, "for calling him so; I know not into what hands I may fall; and if I happen into his, I hope he will use me the better for giving him good words."

ON HUMILITY AND PRIDE.

Humility is a virtue all preach, none practice, and yet everybody is content to hear. The master thinks it good doctrine for his servant, the laity for the clergy, and the clergy for the laity.—Their is *humilitas quædam in vitio.* If a man does not take notice of that excellency and perfection that is in himself, how can he be thankful to God, who is the author of all excellency and perfection? Nay, if a man hath too mean an opinion of himself, it will render him unserviceable both to God and man.—Pride may be allowed to this or that degree, else a man cannot keep up his dignity. In gluttony there must be eating, in drunkenness there must be drinking. It is not the eating, nor is it the drinking, that is to be blamed, but the excess. So in Pride.

STRAWS SHOW WHICH WAY THE WIND BLOWS.

Though some make light of libels [placards]; yet you may see by them how the wind sits; as, take a straw and throw it up into the air, you shall see by that which way the wind is, which you shall not do as by casting up a stone. More solid things do not show the complexion of the times so well as ballads and libels.

SEVIGNE, MARIE DE RABUTIN CHANTAL DE, a French writer of charming letters, born at Paris in 1626; died in 1696. She was the daughter of Celse-Benigne de Rabutin, Baron de Chantal. Left an orphan in early childhood, she was tenderly reared by her maternal uncle, the Abbé de Coulanges, was carefully educated, and at the age of eighteen was married to the Marquis Henri de Sévigné. This unhappy marriage was terminated at the end of seven years, by the death of the dissolute husband, and Madame de Sévigné devoted herself to the education of her young son and daughter. On her return to Paris in 1654, she became, in virtue of her wit, her beauty, her tact, and her sweet disposition, the centre of a brilliant society. She was sought in marriage by several distinguished men, but her intense affection for her children, led her to reject all suitors. The marriage of her daughter to the Count de Grignan, Governor of Provence, and the consequent separation from her, was the grief of Madame de Sévigné's life. She took refuge in long letters in which she described all of the persons she met, and detailed all the events of the life around her. These *Letters*, scarcely equalled in their combination of wit, sympathy, and graceful expression, form, with letters to other friends, the foundation of Madame de Sévigné's fame.

She died of small-pox while on a visit to her daughter.

TO HER DAUGHTER.

PARIS, March 3, 1671.

If you were here, my dear child, you would certainly laugh at me. I am set down to write beforehand, but from a very different reason to that which I once gave you for writing to a person two days before I could send my letter: it was a matter of indifference to me, when I wrote, as I knew I should have no more to say to him at the two days' end than I had then. But here the case is otherwise. I do it now from the regard I have for you, and to satisfy the pleasure I take in writing to you every moment, which is the sole comfort I have now left. To-day I am shut up by myself in my room, through excess of ill-humor. I am weary of everything. . . . .

I assure you, my dear child, I am continually thinking of you: and I experience every day the truth of what you once told me, that there are certain thoughts which are not to be dwelt upon, but passed over as lightly as possible, unless we would be forever in tears. This is my case; for there is not a place in the house which does not give a stab to my heart when I see it; but your room especially deals a deadly blow from every part of it. I have placed a screen in the middle of it, that I may at least take something from the prospect. As for the window from which I saw you get into D'Hacqueville's coach, and then called you back again, I shudder every time I think how near I was throwing myself out of it after you. I was likely enough to have done it, for at times I am not in my senses. The closet where I held you last in my arms, without knowing what I did; the Capuchins, where I used to go to mass; the tears that fell so fast from my eyes that they wetted the ground, as if water had been thrown on it; Saint Mary's, Madame de la Fayette, my return to the house, your room, that night, the next morning, your first letter, and every one since, and still every day, and every conversation of those who feel with me, are so many remembrancers of my loss. Poor D'Hacqueville holds the first rank; I shall never forget the compassion he showed me. These are the thoughts incessantly uppermost; yet these are to be passed over, it seems; we are not to abandon ourselves to our thoughts, and the emotions of our heart. I had rather, however, continue my reveries on the kind of life you are leading. It occasions a sort of diversion, without making me abandon my principal, my beloved object. I do then think of you. I am always wishing for letters from you. One wish of this nature, when gratified, is followed by another continually I am in this state of expectation now, and shall go on with my letter when I have received one from you.

TO M. DE COULANGES.

PARIS, Dec. 15, 1670.

I am going to tell you a thing the most astonishing, the most surprising, the most marvellous, the most miraculous, the most magnificent, the most confounding, the most unheard of, the most singular, the most extraordinary, the most incredible, the most unforeseen, the greatest, the least, the rarest, the most common, the most public, the most private till to-day, the most brilliant, the most enviable; in short, a thing of which there is but one example in past ages, and that not an exact one either; a thing that we cannot believe at Paris; how then will it gain credit at Lyons? A thing which makes everybody cry, "Lord, have mercy upon us!" a thing which causes the greatest joy to Madame de Rohan and Madame de Hauterive; a thing, in fine, which is to happen on Sunday next, when those who are present will doubt the evidence of their senses; a thing which is to be done on Sunday, yet perhaps will not be finished on Monday. I cannot bring myself to tell it you; guess what it is. I give you three times to do it in. What, not a word to throw at a dog? Well, then, I find I must tell you. Monsieur de Lauzun is to be married next Sunday at the Louvre, to ——pray guess to whom! I give you four times to do it in, I give you six, I give you a hundred. Says Madame de Coulanges, "It is really very hard to guess; perhaps it is Madame de la Vallière." Indeed, madame, it is not. "It is Mademoiselle de Retz, then." No, nor she neither; you are extremely provincial. "Lord bless me," say you, "what stupid wretches we are! it is Mademoiselle de Colbert all the while." Nay, now you are still further from the mark. "Why then it must certainly be Mademoiselle de Crequy." You have it not yet. Well, I find I must tell you at last. He is to be married next Sunday, at the Louvre, with the king's leave, to Madêmoiselle, Mademoiselle de —Mademoiselle—guess, pray guess her name; he is to be married to Mademoiselle, the great Mademoiselle; Mademoiselle, daughter to the late Monsieur [Gaston of France, Duke of Orleans, brother of Louis XIII.]; Mademoiselle granddaughter of Henry the IVth; Mademoiselle d'Eu, Mademoiselle de Dombes, Mademoiselle de Montpensier, Mademoiselle d'Orleans, Mademoiselle, the king's cousin-german, Mademoiselle, destined to the throne, Mademoiselle, the only match in France that was worthy of Monsieur. What glorious matter for talk! If you should burst forth like a bedlamite, say we have told you a lie, that it is false, that we are making a jest of you, and that a pretty jest it is without wit or invention; in short, if you abuse us, we shall think you quite in the right; for we have done just the same things ourselves. Farewell, you will find by the letters you receive this post, whether we tell you truth or not.

TO THE SAME.

Paris, Dec. 19, 1670.

What is called "falling from the clouds," happened last night at the Tuilleries; but I must go further back. You have already shared in the joy, the transport, the ecstacies of the princess and her happy lover. It was just as I told you, the affair was made public on Monday. Tuesday was passed in talking, astonishment, and compliments. Wednesday, mademoiselle made a deed of gift to Monsieur de Lauzun, investing him with certain titles, names, and dignities, necessary to be inserted in the marriage contract, which was drawn up that day. She gave him them, till she could give him something better, four duchies; the first was that of Count d'Eu, which entitles him to rank as first peer of France; the Dukedom of Montpensier, which title he bore all that day; the Dukedom de Saint Fargeau; and the Dukedom de Châtellraut, the whole valued at twenty-two millions of livres. The contract was then drawn up, and he took the name of Montpensier. Thursday morning, which was yesterday, mademoiselle was in expectation of the king's signing the contract, as he had said that he would do; but, about seven o'clock in the evening, the queen, monsieur, and several old dotards that were about him, had so persuaded his majesty that his reputation would suffer in this affair, that sending for mademosielle and Monsieur de Lauzun, he announced to them before the prince that he forbade them to think any further of this marriage. Monsieur de Lauzun, received the prohibition with all the respect, submission, firmness, and, at the same time despair, that could be expected in so great a reverse of fortune. As for mademoiselle, she gave a loose to her feelings, and burst into tears, cries, lamentations, and the most violent expressions of grief; she keeps her bed all day long, and takes nothing within her lips but a little broth. What a fine dream is here! what a glorious subject for a tragedy or romance, but especially talking and reasoning eternally! This is what we do day and night, morning and evening, without end, and without intermission; we hope you do the same. E fra tanto vi bacio le mani; "and with this I kiss your hand."

TO THE SAME.

PARIS, Dec. 24, 1670.

You are now perfectly acquainted with the romantic story of mademoiselle and of Monsieur de Lauzun. It is a story well adapted for a tragedy, and in all the rules of the theatre; we laid out the acts and scenes the other day. We took four days instead of four and twenty hours, and the piece was complete. Never was such a change seen in so short a time; never was there known so general an emotion. You certainly never received so extraordinary a piece of intelligence before. M. de Lauzun behaved admirably; he supported his misfortune with such courage and intrepidity, and at the same time showed so deep a sorrow, mixed with such profound respect, that he has gained the admiration of everybody. His loss is doubtless great, but then the king's favor, which he has by this means preserved, is likewise great; so that, upon the whole, his condition does not seem so very deplorable. Mademoiselle, too, has behaved extremely well on her side. She has wept much and bitterly; but yesterday, for the first time, she returned to pay her duty at the Louvre, after having received the visits of every one there; so the affair is all over.

SEWARD, WILLIAM HENRY, an American statesman and author, born at Florida, N. Y., in 1801; died at Auburn, N. Y., in 1872. He entered Union College at fifteen, and after his graduation went to the South, and was for several months teacher of an Academy in Georgia. Returning to the North, he studied law, was admitted to the bar in 1822, and soon after entered upon practice at Auburn, N. Y., which was thereafter his residence. He soon began to take an active part in politics. About 1828 the "antimasonic" excitement reached its height, and Mr. Seward was elected to the State Senate as an "Antimason." In 1834 he was an unsuccessful candidate for the office of Governor of New York. In 1838 he was elected Governor by the "Whig" party. He was re-elected in 1840, but declining a re-nomination in 1842, he resumed his large legal practice at Auburn. In 1849 he was elected to the Senate of the United States, and was re-elected in 1855. He soon became a recognized leader of the political party opposed to the extension of slavery, which finally assumed the name of "Republican." In a speech, in 1849, on the admission of California as a State of the Union, he formulated what is known as "the Higher Law Doctrine." "There is," said he, "a higher law than the Constitution, which regulates the authority of congress—the law of God, and the interests of humanity."

In the Republican National Convention of 1860, Mr. Seward was apparently the foremost candidate for the presidency; but it being found impossible to concentrate upon him the votes of a majority of the delegates, the nomination was given to Abraham Lincoln, who was elected. President

Lincoln invited to his Cabinet the men who had been prominent competitors for the Presidential nomination—Mr. Seward accepting the position of Secretary of State, fulfilling its duties during Mr. Lincoln's administration. On April 14, 1865, the President was assassinated at Washington. The plot for that purpose included the assassination of Mr. Seward, who was temporarily confined to his room. The assassin penetrated the apartment, and inflicted stabs which were at first thought to be fatal, at the same time seriously wounding his son. Mr. Seward, however, recovered, and discharged the duties of secretary of state during the administration of Andrew Johnson.

In 1870 he set out upon a journey round the world, which occupied fourteen months. Crossing the continent to the Pacific ocean, he visited China, Japan, portions of British India, Egypt, and Palestine, returning by way of Europe. He had already put forth four volumes of his *Works* containing public speeches, diplomatic correspondence, several biographical sketches, and various literary addresses. He now set himself down to record the results of his observations during his recent journey. This work, entitled *William H. Seward's Travels around the World*, edited by his niece, Olive Risley Seward, was published soon after his death. He was also engaged upon a *History of his own Times*, which he left incomplete.

THE MORAL DEVELOPMENT OF THE AMERICAN PEOPLE.

Reasoning *a priori*, it is only just to infer in favor of the United States an improvement of morals from their established progress in knowledge and power; otherwise the philosophy of Society is misunderstood, and we must change all our courses, and henceforth seek safety in imbecility, and virtue in superstition and ignorance. What shall be the test of national morals? Shall it be the eccentricity of crimes? Certainly not; for then we must compare the criminal eccentricity of to-day with that of yesterday. The result of the comparison would be only this—that the crimes of society change with changing circumstances.

Loyalty to the State is a public virtue. Was it ever deeper-toned or more universal than now? I know there are ebullitions of passion and discontent, sometimes breaking out into disorder and violence; but was ever faction more disarmed and harmless than it is now? There is a loyalty which springs from affection that we bear to our native soil. This we have as strong as any people. But it is not the soil alone, nor yet the soil beneath our feet and the skies over our heads, that constitute our country. It is its freedom, equality, justice, greatness, and glory. Who among us is so low as to be insensible of an interest in them? Four hundred thousand natives of other lands every year voluntarily renounce their own sovereigns, and swear fealty to our own. Who has ever known an American to transfer his allegiance permanently to a foreign power?

The spirit of the laws, in any country, is a true index to the morals of a people, just in proportion to the power, they exercise in making them. Who complains, here or elsewhere, that crime or immorality blots our statute-books with licentious enactments? The character of a country's magistrates, legislators, and captains, chosen by its people, reflects their own. It is true that in the earnest canvassing which so frequently recurring elections require, suspicion often follows the magistrate, and scandal follows in the footsteps of the statesman. Yet when his course has been finished, what magistrate has left a name tarnished by corruption, or what statesman has left an act or an opinion so erroneous that decent charity cannot excuse, though it may disapprove? What chieftain ever tempered military triumph with so much moderation as he who, when he had placed our standard on the battlements of the capital of Mexico, not only received an offer of supreme authority from the conquered nation, but declined it?

The manners of a nation are the outward form of its inner life. Where is woman held in so chivalrous respect, and where does she deserve that eminence better? Where is property more safe, commercial honor better sustained, or human life more sacred? Moderation is a virtue in public and private life. Has not the great increase of private wealth manifested itself chiefly in widening the circle of education and elevating the standard of popular intelligence? With forces which, if combined and directed by ambition, would subjugate this continent at once, we have only made two very short wars: the one confessedly a war of defence, and the other ended by paying for peace, and for a domain already conquered.

Where lies the secret of the increase of virtue which has thus been established? I think it will be found in the entire emancipation of the consciences of men from either direct or indirect control by established ecclesiastical or political systems. Religious classes, like political parties, have been left to compete in the great work of moral education, and to entitle themselves to the confidence and affection of society by the purity of their faith and of their morals.—*Address at Yale College*, 1854.

THE PRESENT STATUS OF THE CHINESE RACE.

The Chinese, though not of the Caucasian race, have all its political, social, and moral capabilities. Long ago they reached a higher plane of civilization than most of the European states attained until a much later period. The Western nations have since risen above that plane. The whole world is anxiously inquiring whether China is to retrieve the advantages she has lost, and if she is to come within the family of modern civilized states. Mr. Burlingame's sanguine temperament and charitable disposition led him to form too favorable an opinion of the present condition of China. In his anxiety to secure a more liberal policy on the part of the Western nations toward the ancient empire, he gave us to understand that while China has much to learn from the Western nations, she is not without some peculiar institutions which they may advantageously adopt. This is not quite true. Although China is far from being a barbarous state, yet every system and institution there is inferior to its corresponding one in the West. . . . .

The long isolation of the empire, and the extirpation of native invention, have ended in reversing the position of China. From being self-sustaining and independent, as she was when found by the European states, she has become imbecile, dependent, and helpless. Without military science and art, she is at the mercy of Western nations ; without the science of political economy, the Government is incapable of maintaining an adequate system of revenue ; and without the science of Western laws and morals, it is equally incapable of maintaining an impartial and effective administration of justice. Having refused to adopt Western arts and sciences, the Government is incapable of establishing and maintaining a beneficial domestic administration. Insurrections and revolutions are therefore unavoidable, nor can the Government repress them without the aid of the Western Powers. Though China would now willingly leave all the world alone, other nations cannot afford to leave her alone. . . . .

Now for the question of the prospects of China. Before attempting to answer this, it will be well to define intelligently the present political position of China. Certainly it is no longer an absolutely sovereign and independent empire; nor has it become a protectorate of any other empire. It is, in short, a state under the constant and active surveillance of the Western maritime nations. This surveillance is exercised by their diplomatic representatives, and by their naval forces, backed by the men ace of military intervention.

In determining whether this precarious condition of China is likely to continue, and whether its endurance is desirable, it would be well to consider what are the possible alternatives. There are only three: First, absolute subjection by some foreign state; second, the establishment of a protectorate by some foreign state; third, a complete popular revolution, overthrowing not only the present dynasty, but the present forms of government, and establishing one which shall be in harmony with the interests of China and the spirit of the age.

The Chinese people, inflated with national pride, and contempt for Western sciences, arts, religions, morals, and manners, are not prepared to accept the latter alternative. The rivalry of the Western nations, with the fluctuations of the balance of their political powers, render it dangerous for any foreign state to assume a protectorate. The second alternative is therefore out of the question. We have already expressed the opinion that mankind have outlived the theory of universal empire, and certainly the absolute subjugation of China by any Western state would be a nearer approach to universal empire than Greek, or Roman, or Corsican, or Cossack ever dreamed of.

The exercise of sovereignty in China by a national dynasty, under the surveillance and protection of the maritime powers, is the condition most favorable to the country, and most desirable. The maintenance of it seems practicable so far as it depends upon the consent of the maritime surveillant powers; but how long the four hundred millions of people within the empire will submit to its continuance is a question which baffles all penetration. The present government [1871] favors, and does all it can to maintain it, Prince Kung and Wan-Sang are progressive and renovating statesmen; but a year or two hence a new emperor will come to the throne. The *literati* now less bigoted than heretofore, have an unshaken prestige among the people; and, for aught any one can judge, the first decree of the new emperor may be the appointment of a reactionary ministry, with the decapitation of the present advisers of the throne. Let it then be the policy of the Western nations to encourage and sustain the sagacious reformers of China, and in dealing with that extraordinary people to practice in all things justice, moderation, kindness, and sympathy.—*Travels around the World.*

LOYALTY TO THE UNION.

The Union IS, not because merely that men choose that it shall be, but because some government must exist here, and no other government than this can. If it could be dashed to atoms by the whirlwind, the lightning or the earthquake, to-day, it would rise again in all its just and magnificent proportions to-morrow. This nation is a globe, still accumulating upon accumulation, not a dissolving sphere.

I have heard somewhat here, and almost for the first time in my life, of divided allegiance—of allegiance to the south and to the Union—of allegiance to states severally and to the Union. . . .

But for all this I know only one country and one sovereign—the United States of America and the American People. And such as my allegiance is, is the loyalty of every other citizen of the United States. As I speak, he will speak when his time arrives. He knows no other country and no other sovereign.—*Speech on the Admission of California,* 1850.

SEWELL, ELIZABETH MISSING, an English author, born on the Isle of Wight in 1815. She is best known by her religious novels and sketches, the special aim of which is to set forth the distinctive teachings of the Anglican Church. Among these are: *Amy Herbert* (1844), *Gertrude* (1847), *Katherine Ashton* (1854), *Ursula* (1857), *Margaret Percival* (1858). At a later date she wrote many books of devotion, sketches of foreign travel, and histories among which are: *Readings for a Month Preparatory to Communion* (1859), *Grammar made Easy* (1872), *Catechism of Grecian History* (1874), *Popular History of France* (1876), *Private Devotions for Young Persons* (1881).

HELPS TO BEING GOOD.

"As for that," said Dora, "every one is vain."

"But then," said Amy, "we promised at our baptism that we would not be so; and Mamma says that persons who are vain soon become envious, and that envy leads to very great crimes; and that if we indulge in vanity we can never tell how wicked we shall become by-and-by."

"I cannot understand why you are always talking about baptism, Amy," said Dora; "it seems as if it had something to do with everything according to your notions."

"According to Mamma's notions, you mean; she reminds me of it so often that I cannot possibly forget it."

"But there is no one in the world who has kept the promise," said Dora; "and then they say we have such a wicked nature. What is the use of thinking of being good, when we have no power to be so?"

"I do not think I understand it quite," replied Amy; "and I am sure, Dora, I cannot teach you; but I could tell what Mamma tells me."

"And what is that?" asked Dora.

"Mamma says," answered Amy, "that when we are born we all have very wicked natures; but that when we are baptized God gives us a new nature which is good; and that when we grow up we can do right if we really wish to do it, because we have the Holy Spirit always to help us. And once, when I made an excuse for something I had done wrong, by saying that it was natural, and I could not help it, she told me that it might have been an excuse if I had not been baptized; but that now it was no excuse at all."

"Then what are we to do?" asked Dora. "No person really keeps their promise. How wicked we must all be."

"Mamma says we are," replied Amy, "and that we ought to be so very careful about our smallest actions, and our words and thoughts, because it is so dangerous to do wrong now."

"But," said Dora, "I cannot see why people should be baptized, if it only makes them worse off than they were before."

"Oh! but indeed, Dora," exclaimed Amy, looking rather shocked, "it makes us better off; for you know the Service about Baptism says that we are made God's children—really his children; and that when we die we shall go to heaven, if we try and do right now, and beg him to forgive us, when we do wrong, for our Saviour's sake."

"I don't understand it," said Dora; "and I never heard any one talk about it till I came to Emmerton."

"I did not understand it half as well," replied Amy, "till Mamma told me a story about Uncle Harrington's birthday, and that when we were baptized we were made heirs of heaven, just as he was heir to this place and all the property. And even now it puzzles me very much; and very often I cannot believe that it is all true; but I try to do so because Mamma says it is, and shows mee where it is written in the Bible."

"But how can we tell that we have a good nature given us at our baptism?" said Dora "I never feel it; and I don't think I do anything that is right all day long. You may have a good nature, Amy—and I think you have; but I know I have not."

"Mamma says," answered Amy, "that being sorry for our faults, and wishing to do better is a sign of it. And you know, Dora, you often tell me how much you wish to do right; and sometimes when I have had a great many wrong feelings—vain feelings, I mean—and angry and envious ones, the only thing that makes me at all happy again, is because I feel sorry for it."

Dora sighed deeply. "I wish," she said, "that the bad nature would go all at once. I am so tired of wishing to do good, and always doing wrong; and then I begin to think there is no use in trying. It would be easier if I could believe that was true about baptism, because then it would appear as if there was something to help me. But I have always heard people talk about having such a wicked nature, till at last it seemed foolish to hope to be good, as if it were impossible. Not but what I do try sometimes, Amy," she continued, with a sudden impulse to be unreserved; "I do try sometimes—though I dare say you would not believe it, because I am so cross. I meant to have tried this morning; only Lucy Cunningham made me so angry by the way she twisted her head about, and the nonsense she talked at breakfast, that I could not help becoming out of humor with every one; and when I am annoyed in the morning I go on so all day. But you cannot understand that, it is so unlike you."

"I can, though," replied Amy, "for I am very often provoked when I watch Miss Cunningham, and hear her talk. But I try not to look at her, and to think of something else." . . .

"But," said Dora, "I know very well that it is no use feeling properly only when everything goes as you like. What I wish is to have the power of being good always. There are some people who are never put out of humor—Aunt Herbert for one: I long to be like her."

"So do I!" exclaimed Amy eagerly: "but then she is so very, *very* good; I don't think it is possible to be what she is. Mrs. Walton says she never met with any one like her."

"That is what disheartens me. Good people are so set up in the clouds, where one can never get at them."

"I suppose, though," answered Amy," they were not always so good. Mamma often says she did a great many naughty things when she was my age."

"I wish she would tell me what made her better, then," said Dora. "Did she ever tell you?"

"No," replied Amy; "all that she ever told me was what I ought to do myself to cure my faults; and she said that she would pray to God to help me."

"No one will ever promise that for me," observed Dora, sighing.

"But mamma will, I am sure," exclaimed Amy. eagerly; "and I——"

"Why do you stop?" said Dora.

"Mamma tells me to mention all your names in my prayers," replied Amy; "but I don't mean that *that* would be the same as her doing so, because she is so much better."

"I cannot see what difference that can make. I should like very much to think you did it always for me. But it must be such a trouble to remember."

"Oh no, Dora; it would seem so unkind not to do it; and if I thought you cared, I never could forget. But some day or other, when I am quite good, it will be of much more use."—*Amy Herbert.*

SHAFTESBURY (ANTHONY ASHLEY COOPER), EARL of, an English statesman and author, born at London in 1671; died at Naples in 1713. He entered the House of Commons in 1693, and succeeded to the Earldom six years later. He was prominent among the statesmen and literati of his time, until impaired health compelled him to take up his residence in Italy. A complete collection of his works was published in 1716, under the title, *Characteristics of Men, Manners, Opinions, and Times.* Of the following passage, Sir James Mackintosh says: "There is scarcely any composition in our language more lofty in its moral and religious sentiments, or more exquisitely elegant and musical in its diction."

BEAUTY AND GOOD THE ORDER OF NATURE.

I have now a better idea of that melancholy you discovered; and notwithstanding the humorous turn you were pleased to give it, I am persuaded it has a different foundation from any of those fantastical causes I then assigned to it. Love is doubtless at the bottom of it, but a nobler love than such as common beauties inspire. Here, in my turn I begin to raise my voice, and imitate the solemn way you have been teaching me. Knowing as you are, well-knowing and experienced in all the degrees and orders of beauty, in all the mysterious charms of the particular forms, you rise to what is more general; and with a larger heart, and mind more comprehensive, you generously seek that which is highest in the kind. Not captivated by the lineaments of a fair face, or the well-drawn proportions of a human body, you view the life itself, and embrace rather the mind which adds the lustre, and renders chiefly amiable.

Nor is the enjoyment of such a single beauty sufficient to satisfy such an aspiring soul. It seeks how to combine more beauties, and by what coalition of these to form a beautiful society. It views communities, friendships, relations, duties; and considers by what harmony of particular minds the general beauty is composed, and common weal established. Not satisfied even with public good in one community of men, it frames itself a nobler object, and with enlarged affection seeks the good of mankind. It dwells with pleasure amidst that Reason and those orders on which this fair correspondence and goodly interest is established. Laws, constitutions, civil and religious rites; whatever civilizes or polishes rude mankind; the sciences and arts, philosophy, morals, virtue; the flourishing state of human affairs, and the perfection of human nature—these are its delightful prospects, and this the charm of beauty which attracts it.

Still ardent in this pursuit (such is its love of order and perfection), it rests not here, nor satisfies itself with the beauty of a part; but extending further its communicative bounty, seeks the good of all, and affects the interest and prosperity of the whole. True to its native world and higher country, 'tis here it seeks order and perfection, wishing the best, and hoping still to find a wise and just administration. And since all hope of this were vain and idle, if no Universal Mind presided—since without such a supreme intelligence and providential care, the distracted universe must be condemned to suffer infinite calamities—'tis here the generous mind labors to discover the healing cause by which the interest of the whole is securely established, the beauty of things, and the universal order, happily sustained.

This, Palemon, is the labor of your soul; and this its melancholy; when unsucessfully pursuing the Supreme Beauty, it meets with darkening clouds which intercept the sight. Monsters arise—not those from the Libyan deserts but from the heart of man more fertile, and with their horrid aspect cast an unseemly reflection upon Nature. She, helpless as she is thought, and working thus absurdly, is contemned, and the government of the world arraigned, and the Deity made void. Much is alleged in answer to show why Nature errs; and when she seems most ignorant or perverse in her productions, I assert her even then as wise and provident as in her goodliest works. For 'tis not then that men complain of the world's order, or abhor the face of things, when they see the various interests mixed and interfering; natures subordinate, of different kinds, opposed to one another, and in their different operations submitted the higher to the lower. 'Tis, on the contrary, from this order of inferior and superior things that we admire the world's beauty, founded thus on contrarieties; whilst from such various and disagreeing principles a universal concord is established.

Thus in the several orders of terrestrial forms a resignation is required—a sacrifice and mutual yielding of natures one to another. The vegetables by their death sustain the animals, and animal bodies dissolved enrich the earth, and raise again the vegetable world. The numerous insects are reduced by the superior kinds of birds and beasts; and these again are checked by man, who, in his turn, submits to other natures, and resigns his form—a sacrifice in common to the rest of things. And if in natures so little exalted or pre-eminent above each other the sacrifice of interests can appear so just, how much more reasonably may all inferior natures be subjected to the superior nature of the World!—that World, Palemon, which even now transported you, when the sun's fainting light gave way to those bright constellations, and left you this wide system to contemplate.

Here are those Laws which ought not nor can submit to anything below. The central powers which hold the lasting orbs in their just poise and movement, must not be controlled to save a fleeting form, and rescue from the precipice a puny animal whose brittle frame, however protected, must of itself so soon dissolve. The ambient air, the inward vapors, the impending meteors, or whatever else is nutrimental or preservative of this earth, must operate in a natural course; and other good constitutions must submit to the good habit and constitution of the all-sustaining globe. Let us not wonder, therefore, if by earthquakes, storms, pestilential blasts, nether or upper fires, or floods, the animal kinds are oft afflicted, and whole species perhaps involved at once in common ruin. Nor need we wonder if the interior form, the soul and temper, partakes of this occasional deformity, and sympathizes often with its close partner. Who is there that can wonder either at the sicknesses of sense or the depravity of minds enclosed in such frail bodies and dependent on such pervertible organs?

Here, then, is that solution you require; and hence those seeming blemishes cast upon Nature. Nor is there aught in this beside what is natural and good. 'Tis good which is predominant, and every corruptible and mortal nature, by its mortality and corruption, yields only to some better, and all in common to that best and highest nature which is incorruptible and immortal.

SHAIRP, JOHN CAMPBELL, an English author, born at Linlithgow, Scotland, in 1836; died in London in 1885. He was educated at the Glasgow University and at Oxford, was assistant master at Rugby, Professor of Humanity at the United College of St. Andrews in 1861, and became its principal in 1868. In 1877 he was made Professor of Poetry at Oxford, which post he held at the time of his death. He is the author of *Kilmahoe, a Highland Pastoral* (1864), *Studies in Poetry and Philosophy* (1868), *Lectures on Culture and Religion* (1870), *Life of James Forbes* (1873), *The Poetic Interpretation of Nature* (1877), and *Aspects of Poetry* (1881).

THE LITERARY THEORY OF CULTURE.

Mr. Arnold sets before us a lofty aim,—he has bid us seek our good in something unseen, in a spiritual energy. In doing this he has done well. But I must hold that he has erred in his estimate of what that spiritual energy is, and he has missed, I think, the true source from which it is to be mainly derived. For in his account of it he has placed that as primary which is secondary and subordinate, and made that secondary which by right ought to be supreme. You will remember that when describing his idea of perfection to be aimed at, he makes religion one factor in it,—an important and powerful factor no doubt, still but one element out of several, and that not necessarily the ruling element, but a means towards an end, higher, more supreme, more all-embracing than itself. The end was a many-sided, harmonious development of human nature, and to this end religion was an important means.

In thus assigning to religion a secondary, however important place, this theory as I conceive, if consistently acted on, would annihilate religion. There are things which are either ends in themselves or they are nothing; and such, I conceive, religion is. It either is supreme, a good in itself and for its own sake, or not at all. The first and great commandment must either be so set before us as to be obeyed, entered into, in and for itself, without any ulterior view, or it cannot be obeyed at all. It cannot be made subservient to any ulterior purpose. And herein is instanced "a remarkable law of ethics, which is well known to all who have given their minds to the subject." I shall give it in the words of one who has expressed it so well in his own unequalled language that it has been proposed to name it after him, Dr. Newman's law:—"All virtue and goodness tend to make men powerful in the world; but they who aim at the power have not the virtue." Again "Virtue is its own reward, and brings with it the truest and highest pleasures; but they who cultivate it for the pleasure-sake are selfish, not religious, and will never gain the pleasure, because they never can have the virtue."

Apply this to the present subject. They who seek religion for culture-sake are æsthetic, not religious, and will never gain that grace which religion adds to culture, because they never can have the religion. To seek religion for the personal elevation or even for the social improvement it brings, is really to fall from faith which rests in God and the knowledge of Him as the ultimate good, and has no by-ends to serve. And what do we see in actual life? There shall be two men, one of whom has started on the road of self-improvement from a mainly intellectual interest, from the love of art, literature, science, or from the delight these give, but has not been actuated by a sense of responsibility to a Higher than himself. The other has begun with some sense of God, and of his relation to Him, and starting from this centre has gone on to add to all the moral and mental improvement within his reach, feeling that, beside the pleasure these things give in themselves, he will thus best promote the good of his fellow-men, and attain the end of his own existence. Which of these two will be the highest man, in which will be gathered up the most excellent graces of character, the truest nobility of soul? You cannot doubt it. The sense that a man is serving a Higher than himself, with a service which will become ever more and more perfect freedom, evokes more profound, more humbling, more exalted emotions than anything else in the world can do. The spirit of man is an instrument which cannot give out its deepest finest tones except under the immediate hand of the Divine Harmonist. That is, before it can educe the highest capacities of which human nature is susceptible, culture must cease to be merely culture, and pass over to religion. And here we see another aspect of that great ethical law already noticed as compassing all human action, whereby "the abandoning of some lower object in obedience to a higher aim is made the very condition of securing the said lower object." According to this law it comes that he will approach nearer to perfection, or (since to speak of perfection in such as we are sounds like presumption) rather let us say, he will reach further, will attain to a truer, deeper, more lovely humanity who makes not culture, but oneness with the will of God, his ultimate aim. The ends of culture, truly conceived, are best attained by forgetting culture and aiming higher. And what is this but translating into modern and less forcible language the old words, whose meaning is often greatly misunderstood, "Seek ye first the kingdom of God. and all these things will be added unto you?" But by seeking the other things first, as we naturally do, we miss not only the kingdom of God, but those other things also which are only truly attained by aiming beyond them.

Another objection to the theory we have been considering remains to be noted. Its starting-point is the idea of perfecting self;

and though, as it gradually evolves, it tries to forget self, and to include quite other elements, yet it never succeeds in getting clear of the taint of self-reference with which it set out. While making this objection, I do not forget that Mr. Arnold, in drawing out his view, proposes as the end of culture to make reason and the kingdom of God prevail; that he sees clearly, and insists strongly, that an isolated self-culture is impossible, that we cannot make progress towards perfection ourselves unless we strive earnestly to carry our fellow-men along with us. Still may it not with justice be said that these unselfish elements—the desire for others' good, the desire to advance God's kingdom on earth—are in this theory awakened, not simply for their own sakes, not chiefly because they are good in themselves, but because they are clearly discerned to be necessary to our self-perfection—elements apart from which this cannot exist? And so it comes that culture, though made our end never so earnestly, cannot shelter a man from thoughts about himself, cannot free him from that which all must feel to be fatal to high character,—continual self-consciousness. The only forces strong enough to do this are great truths which carry him out of and beyond himself, the things of the spiritual world sought, not mainly because of their reflex action on us, but for their own sakes, because of their own inherent worthiness. There is perhaps no truer sign that a man is really advancing than that he is learning to forget himself, that he is losing the natural thoughts about self in the thought of One higher than himself, to whose guidance he can commit himself and all men.—*Culture and Religion.*

SHAKSPEARE, WILLIAM, an English dramatist, born at Stratford-on-Avon perhaps on April 23, 1564; died there, April 23, 1616. The precise day of his birth is not fixed with certainty, but as he was baptized on April 26, the date traditionally assigned is at least approximately correct. The authenticated facts in the life of Shakspeare may be very briefly told. His father was an apparently well-to-do tradesman—a wool-comber or glover, but there is evidence that he fell into reduced circumstances while his son was yet a boy. William Shakspeare, the eldest son who survived childhood, was sent to the grammar-school at Stratford, where, according to Ben Jonson, he acquired "small Latin and less Greek." There is no evidence that he was ever able to read easily or speak any language except his own. Tradition says that he was for a time an assistant in his father's shop. But of the youth and early manhood of Shakspeare nothing is known except that six months before he had entered upon his nineteenth year he was hastily married to Anne Hathaway, a woman some seven years his senior; that a child was soon born to them and christened less then six months after the marriage; and that within eighteen months a boy and a girl, twins, were born to them.

When about twenty-three Shakspeare left Stratford for London. Tradition says that this departure was somehow connected with his having been arrested for deer-stealing in the park of Sir Thomas Lucy. He soon became connected with the metropolitan theatre. One tradition has it that he got his living for a while by holding the horses of gentlemen at the door of the theatre; another has it that he was for a while stage-prompter. There is good reason to believe that these stories are entire fabrications; for within less than half-a-dozen years we find incidental mention made of him showing that he was already known as a man of parts, and of good social repute. His connection with the London theatre could hardly have been a merely accidental one. The London players were wont to visit Stratford: Thomas Green, one of the best of them, was a native of the town; and Richard Burbage, afterwards the friend of Shakspeare—the original Richard III., Hamlet, and Othello—was from the same part of the country. We cannot doubt that Shakspeare had become favorably known to them, and that he went up to London upon no uncertain adventure. At all events it was not long before he was regularly installed as "playwright" to the company. A part of his duty was undoubtedly that of "touching up" the works of others; but it was not long before he began to produce original dramas. He also bore a part in the representation of his own plays; the part of "the ghost" in *Hamlet* being especially mentioned as one of those which were enacted by him. That he throve in a pecuniary point of view is clear. As early as 1597, when he was thirty-three, we find him with money which he could afford to invest in landed property in his native place. In that year he paid about $1,500 (we reduce the sums approximately to their present equivalent in purchasing power) for the "New Place" at Stratford; in 1602 he paid $8,000 for 107 acres of land adjoining his place: in 1605 he paid $11,000 for the lease of the titles at Stratford. All these were permanent investments, from accumulations from his income; for he still retained his large proprietary interest in the London theatre. He was evidently a shrewd man of business, farming his own lands, disposing of their product, and looking to it that the purchasers paid what they owed: for in 1604 we find him bringing action against one Philip Rogers for about $45 for "malt sold and delivered to him." Up to about 1612 he continued to reside mainly in London. Then having sold out his interest in the theatre, he retired, with an ample competence, to his native Stratford. Of the remaining four years of his life next to nothing is authentically recorded. It has been conjectured that he busied himself in the revisal of his plays, and preparing them for the press; but of this there is no positive proof. He died somewhat suddenly of a fever, and was buried in the parish church, where a contemporary bust of him still exists, which must be regarded as the best-authenticated likeness of the poet. His wife survived him seven years. His only son, Hamnet, died at the age of twelve; his two daughters, Susanna and Judith, both married, and one of them had three sons, but they all died without issue, so that a quarter of a century after his death there was living no descendant of Shakspeare.

Apart from his dramas Shakspeare claims a high place—after Spenser perhaps the very highest—among the poets who were his contemporaries. His poems, beside their intrinsic merits, have much biographical interest. They are: *Venus and Adonis*, first printed in 1593, *The Rape of Lucrece*, in 1594, and the *Sonnets*, in 1609.

The *Venus and Adonis* is dedicated to "the right Honorable Henry Wriothesly, Earl of Southampton, and Baron of Tichfield." Shakspeare styles it "the first heir of my invention," and promises—"if your Honor seem but pleased, I account myself highly praised, and vow to take advantage of all idle hours till I have honored you with some graver invention." The poem was printed when Shakspeare was in his twenty-ninth year; and it is not probable that it was written much earlier. It displays a mastery of versification which one would not expect from a very young man. Here commendation must end; for the glowing pictures are inextricably interwoven with wanton lasciviousness.

The poem was immensely popular in the days of Elizabeth. The first edition of 1592 was followed by others in 1594, 1596, 1600, and 1602. A single extract must here suffice.

THE STEED OF ADONIS.

Look, when a painter would surpass the life,
　　In limning out a well-proportioned steed,
His art with nature's workmanship at strife
　　As if the dead the living should exceed;
So did this horse excel a common one,
In shape, in courage, color, pace, and bone.

Round-hoof'd, strong-jointed, fetlocks shag and long,
　Broad breast, full eye, small head, and nostril wide,
High crest, short ears, straight legs and passing strong,
　Thin mane, thick tail, broad buttock, tender hide,

Look, what a horse should have he did not lack,
Save a proud rider on so proud a back.

Sometimes he scuds far off, and there he stares;
 Anon he starts at stirring of a feather;
To bid the wind abase he now prepares,
 And whether he run or fly, they know not whether;
For through his mane and tail the high wind sings,
Fanning the hairs, who wave like feathered wings.

The *Rape of Lucrece*, printed in 1594, is also dedicated to the Earl of Southampton and may be regarded as a fulfillment of his promise of "Some graver invention." Shakspeare says, in the dedication: "The warrant I have of your honorable disposition, not the worth of my untutored lines, makes it assured of acceptance. What I have done is yours: what I have to do is yours; being part in all I have devoted yours. Were my worth greater, my duty would show greater." The poem is a grave and solemn one, and the theme which might have been loosely handled, is treated without pruriency. It is worth noting that this poem did not achieve the immediate popularity of *Venus and Adonis*. It was four years before a second edition was called for. We give the concluding stanzas:

BRUTUS, OVER THE BODY OF LUCRECE.

Brutus, who plucked the knife from Lucrece's side,
 Seeing such emulation in their woe,
Began to clothe his wit in state and pride,
 Burying in Lucrece's wound his folly's show.
 He with the Romans was esteemed so

As silly-jeering idiots are with kings,
For sportive words and uttering foolish things.

But now he throws that shallow habit by,
Wherein deep policy did him disguise,
And arm'd his long-hid wits advisedly,
To check the tears in Collatinus's eyes.
"Thou wronged lord of Rome," quoth he, "arise!
Let my unsounded self, supposed a fool
Now set thy long experienced wit to school.

"Why, Collatine, is woe the cure for woe?
Do wounds help wounds, or grief help grievous deeds?
Is it revenge to give thyself a blow
For his foul act by whom thy fair wife bleeds?
Such childish humor from weak minds proceeds;
Thy wretched wife mistook the matter so,
To slay herself, that should have slain her foe.

"Courageous Roman, do not steep thy heart
In such relenting dew of lamentation;
But kneel with me and help to bear thy part
To rouse our Roman gods with invocations,
That they will suffer these abominations—
Since Rome herself in them doth stand disgraced—
By our strong arms from forth her fair streets chased.

"Now, by the Capitol that we adore,
And by this chaste blood so unjustly stain'd,
By heaven's fair sun that breeds the fat earth's store,
By all our country's rights in Rome maintain'd,
And by chaste Lucrece's soul that late complain'd
Her wrongs to us, and by this bloody knife,
We will revenge the death of this true wife."

This said, he struck his hand upon his breast,
And kiss'd the fatal knife, to end his vow;

And to his protestations urged the rest,
  Who, wondering at him, did his words allow;
  Then jointly to the ground their knees they bow,
And that deep vow, which Brutus made before,
He doth again repeat, and that they swore.

When they had sworn to this advised doom,
  They did conclude to bear dead Lucrece thence;
To show her bleeding body through Rome,
  And so to publish Tarquin's foul offence,
  Which being done with speedy diligence,
The Romans plausibly did give consent
To Tarquin's everlasting banishment.

The special biographical interest of the *Venus and Adonis* and the *Rape of Lucrece* lies in the proof they give of the high place which the young Shakspeare had already attained in the esteem of the Earl of Southampton, one of the most accomplished noblemen of the Court of Elizabeth, and a munificent patron of men of genius. It is said, though not upon the best authority, that he once made Shakspeare a present of £1.000 (equivalent to $25,000 in our day). It is certain that not long after the publication of *Venus and Adonis* he was the means of procuring for "William Kempe, William Shakspeare, and Richarde Burbage, servauntes to the Lord Chamberleyne," an invitation to present before the Court "twoe severall comedies or enterludes," for which they received £20 ($500).

Of far higher import are the *Sonnets* of Shakspeare. These so-called "Sonnets," are really a love-poem, or rather an amatory correspondence, consisting of 154 fourteen-lined stanzas. Of these 126 are clearly addressed to a man, 26 to a woman, and the concluding two form a sort of epilogue to those which had gone before. Commentators have made sad work in dealing with this poem. With almost unanimous consent they look upon it as a personal confession by Shakspeare, as penitential as the confessions of Augustine or Bunyan. "He laments," says one, "his errors with deep and penitential sorrow, summoning up things past 'to the sessions of sweet silent thought,' and exhibiting the depths of a spirit 'solitary in the very vastness of its sympathies.'" "His excessive and elaborate praise of youthful beauty in a man seems derogatory to his genius, and savors of adulation; and when we find him excuse this friend for robbing him of his mistress, and subjecting his noble spirit to all the pangs of jealousy, of guilty love, and blind, misplaced attachment, it is painful and difficult to believe that all this weakness and folly can be associated with the name of Shakspeare; and still more that he should record it in verse which he believed would descend to future ages."

To all which, and much more of like purport, there is this adequate reply: These 126 amatory sonnets which purport to be addressed to a man purport just as clearly to be addressed *by* a woman. They are such verses as Helen might have written to Paris, or Aspasia to Pericles. The briefer replies from Him to Her are of like tenor.

A word as to the bibliography of the *Sonnets* is in place. The volume was first published in 1609—after Shakspeare had acquired fame and fortune—by Thomas

Thorpe, a London printer. To it is prefixed this dedication, not by the author but by the printer: "To the Onlie Begetter of these insuing Sonnets Mr W H all Happinesse and that Eternitie promised by our ever-living Poet wisheth the will-wishing Adventurer in setting forth T T." There is not the slightest clue as to this "Onlie Begetter" of these Sonnets. It has been guessed that "Mr. W. H." was William Herbert, afterwards Earl of Pembroke, who was certainly a patron of Shakspeare. It has also been suggested that by reversing the order of these initials we shall have those of that Henry Wriothesly, Earl of Southampton, to whom Shakspeare, in his dedication of *Lucrece*, had wished "long life, still lengthened with all happiness."

The whole series of Sonnets is evidently a correspondence carried on for a considerable time, and it would not be difficult to arrange the epistles in their approximate chronological order.

Nothing surely could be farther from the truth than to consider these Sonnets to be in any sense an autobiography of Shakspeare. True, they were written by him; so were *Macbeth* and *Hamlet*: and it would be no more absurd to say that when Macbeth sets forth his own dishonored name and hopeless future, it is Shakspeare himself bewailing his own irremediable past and inevitable doom; or when Claudius speaks of that rank offence of his that "smells to heaven," it is really Shakspeare confessing to the world that he has been guilty of incest and fratricide. The truth is—as is apparent on every page—the poem is a purely imaginative one, with which the personality of the poet had. nothing more to do than that of Pope with the letters of Heloise to Abelard. The poem was written during the very brightest years of Shakspeares's bright and joyous life, at the very summit of his powers; and in it he gives utterance to not a little of his deepest thought and brightest poesy. Not a few of these Sonnets are even finer when detached from their context and considered as independent poems. Thus read the following Sonnets, not as parts of a series of love-letters from an imaginary erring man and woman, but as so many separate poems, to which we have ventured to affix titles.

POETICAL IMMORTALITY.

Who will believe my verse in time to come,
  If it were filled with your most high deserts?
Though yet, heaven knows, it is but as a tomb
  Which hides your life, and shows not half your parts.
If I could write the beauty of your eyes,
  And in fresh numbers number all your graces,
The age to come would say, "This poet lies;
  Such heavenly touches ne'er touch'd earthly faces."
So should my papers, yellow'd with their age,
  Be scorn'd like old men of less truth than tongue,
And your true rights be term'd a poet's rage
  And stretchéd metre of an antique song.
But were some child of yours alive that time,
You should live twice: in it and in my rhyme.

Shall I compare thee to a summer's day?
  Thou art more lovely and more temperate;
Rough winds do shake the darling buds of May,
  And summer's lease hath all too short a date.
Sometimes too hot the eye of heaven shines,
  And often is his gold complexion dimm'd;

And every fair from fair sometimes declines
By chance or nature's changing course untrimm'd.
But thy eternal summer shall not fade,
Nor lose possession of that face thou owest;
Nor shall Death brag thou wander'st in his shade,
When in eternal lines to time thou growest.
So long as men can breathe or eyes can see,
So long lives this, and this gives life to thee.
Sonnets XVII., XVIII.

FORECAST AND RETROSPECT.

Let those who are in favor with their stars
Of public honor and proud titles boast,
Whilst I, whom fortune of such honors bars,
Unlook'd for joy in that I honor most.
Great princes' favorites their fair leaves spread
But as the marigold at the sun's eye,
And in themselves their pride lies buried,
For at a frown they in their glory die.
The painful warrior famousèd for fight,
After a thousand victories once foil'd,
Is from the book of honor razèd quite,
And all the rest forgot for which he toil'd.
Then happy I, that love and am beloved
Where I may not remove or be removed.

When to the sessions of sweet silent thought
I summon up remembrance of things past,
I sigh the lack of many things I sought,
And with old woes now wail my dear times waste:
Then can I drown an eye, unused to flow,
For precious friends hid in death's dateless night,
And weep afresh love's long since cancell'd woe,
And moan the expense of many a vanish'd sight:
Then can I grieve at grievances foregone,
And heavily from woe to woe tell o'er
The sad accounts of fore-bemoanèd moan,
Which I now pay as if not paid before.

But if the while I think on thee, dear friend,
All losses are restored and sorrows end
Sonnets. XXV., XXX.

TIME, THE DESTROYER.

When I have seen by Time's fell hand defaced
The rich proud cost of outworn buried age;
When sometimes lofty towers I see down-razed,
And brass eternal slave to mortal rage;
When I have seen the hungry ocean gain
Advantage on the kingdom of the shore,
And the firm soil win of the watery main,
Increasing store with loss and loss with store;
When I have seen such interchange of state,
Or state itself confounded to decay;
Ruin hath taught me thus to ruminate,
That Time will come and take my love away.
This thought is as a death, which cannot choose
But weep to have that which it fears to lose.

Since brass, nor stone, nor earth, nor boundless sea,
But sad mortality o'ersways their power,
How with this rage shall beauty hold a plea,
Whose action is no stronger than a flower?
O, how shall summer's honey breath hold out
Against the wreckful siege of battering days,
When rocks impregnable are not so stout,
Nor gates of steel so strong, but Time decays?
O fearful meditation! where alack,
Shall Time's best jewel from Time's chest lie hid?
Or what strong hand can hold his swift foot back?
Or who his spoil of beauty can forbid?
O, none, unless this miracle have might,
That in black ink my love may still shine bright.
Sonnets LXIV., LXV.

THE ENDURING MONUMENT.

Not marble, nor the gilded monuments
Of princes, shall outlive this powerful rhyme;
But you shall shine more bright in these contents
Than unswept stone besmear'd with sluttish time.
When wasteful war shall statues overturn,
And broils root out the work of masonry,
Nor Mars's sword nor war's quick fire shall burn,
The living record of your memory.
'Gainst death and all-oblivious enmity
Shall you pace forth; your praise shall still find room
Even in the eyes of all posterity,
That wear this world out to the ending doom.
So, till the judgment that yourself arise,
You live in this, and dwell in lovers' eyes.

Sonnet LV.

That Shakspeare had written more or less before he went up to London is altogether probable; that *Venus and Adonis* was "the first fruits of his invention" in any other sense than that of being the first to be printed, is not probable. That he was certainly employed as playwright or adapter of dramas for the stage before this time is unquestionable, and it is most likely that as a poet he had attracted the notice of the author of the *Faerie Queene*, who was his senior by eleven years. In his pastoral of *Colin Clout*, published not long after Shakspeare's first poem, Spenser commemorates, under fictitious names, Raleigh, Sidney, and other contemporary poets, and adds:

And then—though last, not least—is Aëtion:
"A gentler shepherd may nowhere be found,
Whose muse, full of high thoughts' invention,
Doth like his name, heroically sound."

We know of no other poet than Shakspeare who fits this description; his name does certainly heroically sound, and his muse was "full of high thoughts' invention." Astrophel is not more like Sidney, than the "gentle shepherd." Aëtion is like Shakspeare. The productive literary life of Shakspeare, as far as we can date it, covers the twenty years preceding 1612, when at the age of forty-eight he retired to his native Stratford-upon-Avon, after which we have no proof that he wrote anything.

Shakspeare's dramas, according to the all but universally accepted canon, number thirty-seven. There is no good reason to suppose that any of his plays have been lost; or that he had any considerable share in the composition of any others. He undoubtedly availed himself somewhat of the works of earlier playwrights; and in his historical plays made large use of the chroniclers, from whom he took not merely the historical outlines, but page after page of their very words, only throwing into dramatic form the continuous narrative of his authorities. Scene after scene in *Macbeth*, is to be found in the *Chronicles* of Holinshed, themselves a translation from the Latin of Hector Boece, which had been published only a few years; and some of the most dramatic scenes in *Richard III.* are reproductions from *The Union of the Two Noble and Illustr Families of Lancastre and Yorke*, by Edward Hall. In all of Shakspeare's dramas there are few passages so thoroughly Shakspearean as the delineation of Wolsey, in *Henry VIII.*, put into the mouths of Queen Katharine and her attendant, Griffith; this passage is taken bodily from Holingshed, with only an occasional verbal change.

The dates of the production of the dramas are mainly conjectural; although it is pretty well settled that *Pericles, Prince of Tyre*, was one of the earliest, and *The Tempest* one of the latest; that *Romeo and Juliet* was an early play and *Cymbeline* a late one. In 1598 Francis Meres speaks of the great excellence of Shakspeare both in tragedy and comedy, making special of the following plays as already well known: *All's Well that Ends Well, Comedy of Errors, Henry IV., King John, Love's Labor's Lost, Merchant of Venice, Midsummer Night's Dream, Richard II., Richard III., Romeo and Juliet, Titus Andronicus, Two Gentlemen of Verona.* These twelve plays at least, and doubtless several others, had been produced before Shakspeare reached his thirty-fourth year. His greatest works are of later date. *Hamlet* was certainly produced as early as 1604, and *Macbeth* previous to 1610.

About a dozen of the plays of Shakspeare seem to have been printed during his lifetime, probably not by his procurement. The entire plays were first put forth in a folio volume in 1623, seven years after his death. It has a preface and dedication by his fellow-players Heminge and Condell, and was undoubtedly printed from the stage-copies, which could hardly have failed to have been sanctioned by Shakspeare. This "first folio" is the *textus receptus*, for the "second folio" of 1632 contains many palpable errors. Critical editions are numerous; but we hold that all the work of commentators, besides a glossary of words and phrases which time has rendered obsolete, is worse than useless. The best edition is that which is encumbered by the fewest "critical aids." We know of no more sound and sober estimate of Shakspeare than this of Mr. George Saintsbury:

"I do not know an unnatural character or an unnatural scene in Shakspeare, even among those which have most evidently been written to the gallery. Everything in him passes, in some mysterious way, under and into that "species of eternity" which transforms all the great works of Art, which at once prevents them from being mere copies of Nature, and excuses whatever there is of Nature in them that is not beautiful or noble. If this touch is wanting anywhere (and it is wanting very seldom), that, I take it, is the best—indeed the only sign that that passage is not Shakspeare's—that he had either made use of some other man's work, or that some other man had made use of his. If such passages were of more frequent occurrence, this argument might be called a circular one. But the proportion of such passages as I at least should exclude is so small, and the difference between them and the rest is so marked, that no improper begging of the question can properly be charged. The plays, in "The Globe Edition" contain just a thousand closely printed pages. I do not think that there are fifty in all, perhaps not twenty—putting scraps and patches together—in which the Shakspearean touch is wanting; and I do not think that the touch appears, outside of the covers of the volume, once in a thousand pages of all the rest of English literature. The finest things of other men—of Marlowe, of Fletcher, of Webster (who no doubt comes nearest to the Shakspearean touch, infinitely as he falls short of the Shakspearean range)—might conceivably be the work of others. But the famous passages of Shakspeare, too numerous and too well known to quote, could be no one else's. It is to this point that æsthetic criticism of Shakspeare is constantly coming round with an almost monotonous repetition. As great as all others in their own points of greatness; holding points of greatness which no others even approach: such is Shakspeare."

While the noblest and finest passages in the dramas of Shakspeare are far finer and nobler when taken in their connection with the characters a part of whose utterances they are; still there is no other author in any language who presents anything like so many passages of every length which may well stand by themselves as quotations. There are phrases which have come to be proverbial; there are snatches of exquisite song; there are minute pictures of character; there are grave and extended musings on man, on nature, and on human life. Yet few men could ever have seen less of the world than Shakspeare saw. He never passed the boundaries of England. From Stratford to London is barely a hundred miles; and there is no evidence that he was ever fifty miles from the highway between these two points. A single moderate bookshelf would hold all the books which he ever read.

AT JULIET'S BALCONY.

Romeo.—But soft, what light through yonder window breaks?
It is the east, and Juliet is the sun!—
Arise, fair sun, and kill the envious moon,
Who is already sick and pale with grief,
That thou her maid, art far more fair than she:
Be not her maid, since she is envious;
Her vestal livery is but sick and green,
And none but fools do wear it; cast it off.
It is my lady, O, it is my love!
O that she knew she were!

She speaks, yet she says nothing: what of that?
Her eye discourses; I will answer it.
I am too bold, 'tis not to me she speaks.
Two of the fairest stars in all the heaven,
Having some business, do entreat her eyes
To twinkle in their spheres till they return.
What if her eyes were there, they in her head?
The brightness of her cheek would shame those stars,
As daylight doth a lamp; her eyes in heaven
Would through the airy region stream so bright
That birds would sing, and think it were not night.
See how she leans her cheek upon her hand!
O, that I were a glove upon that hand,
That I might touch her cheek.

Jul. (*above*).— Ay me!

Rom.— She speaks:
O, speak again, bright angel! for thou art
As glorious to this night, being o'er my head,
As is a winged messenger of heaven
Unto the white-upturned wondering eyes
Of mortals that fall back to gaze on him
When he bestrides the lazy-pacing clouds
And sails upon the bosom of the air.

Jul.—O Romeo, Romeo! wherefore art thou Romeo?
Deny thy father and refuse thy name:
Or, if thou wilt not, be but sworn my love,
And I'll no longer be a Capulet.

Rom. (*aside*).—Shall I hear more, or shall I speak at this?

Jul.—'Tis but thy name that is my enemy;
Thou art thyself, though not a Montague.
What's Montague? it is nor hand, nor foot,
Nor arm, nor face, nor any other part
Belonging to a man. O, be some other name!
What's in a name? that which we call a rose
By any other name would smell as sweet;
So Romeo would, were he not Romeo call'd,
Retain that dear perfection which he owes
Without that title. Romeo, doff thy name,
And for that name which is no part of thee
Take all myself.

Rom.— I take thee at thy word :
Call me but love, and I'll be new-baptized ;
Henceforth I never will be Romeo.
Jul.—What man art thou that thus be-screen'd in night
So stumblest on my counsel ?
Rom.— By a name
I know not how to tell thee who I am :
My name, dear saint, is hateful to myself,
Because it is an enemy to thee ;
Had I it written I would tear the word.
Jul.—My ears have not yet drunk a hundred words
Of that dear tongue's utterance, yet I know the sound :
Art thou not Romeo, and a Montague ?
Rom.—Neither, fair saint, if either thee dislike.
Jul.—How camest thou hither, tell me, and wherefore ?
The orchard walls are high and hard to climb,
And the place death, considering who thou art,
If any of my kinsmen find thee here.
Rom.—With love's light wings did I o'er-perch these walls
For stony limits cannot hold love out,
And what love can do that dares love attempt ;
Therefore thy kinsmen are no let to me.
Jul.—If they do see thee, they will murder thee.
Rom.—Alack, there lies more peril in thine eye
Than twenty of their swords : look thou but sweet,
And I am proof against their enmity.
Jul.—I would not for the world they saw thee here.
Rom.—I have night's cloak to hide me from their sight ;
And but thou love me, let them find me here :
My life were better ended by their hate,
Than death prorogued, wanting of thy love.
Romeo and Juliet. II, 2.

SHYLOCK AND ANTONIO.

Bassanio.—This is Signior Antonio.
Shylock (*aside*).—How like a fawning publican he looks!
I hate him for he is a Christian;
But more for that in low simplicity
He lends out money gratis and brings down
The rate of usance here with us in Venice.
If I can catch him once upon the hip,
I will feed fat the ancient grudge I bear him.
He hates our sacred nation, and he rails,
Even there where merchants most do congregate,
On me, my bargains and my well-won thrift,
Which he calls interest. Cursed be my tribe,
If I forgive him. . . .
Antonio.—Shylock, although I neither lend nor borrow
By taking nor by giving of excess,
Yet, to supply the ripe wants of my friend,
I'll break a custom. . . .
Shy.—Methought you said you neither lend nor borrow
Upon advantage.
Ant.— I do never use it.
Shy.—When Jacob grazed his uncle Laban's sheep. . . .
Ant.—And what of him? did he take interest?
Shy.—No, not take interest, not, as you would say,
Directly interest: mark what Jacob did. . . .
This was a way to thrive, and he was blest:
And thrift is blessing, if men steal it not. . . !
Ant.— Mark you this, Bassanio,
The devil can cite Scripture for his purpose.
An evil soul producing holy witness
Is like a villain with a smiling cheek,
A goodly apple rotten at the heart. . . .
Shy.—Signior Antonio, many time and oft
In the Rialto you have rated me
About my money and my usances:
Still have I borne it with a patient shrug,

For sufferance is the badge of all our tribe.
You call me misbeliever, cut-throat dog,
And spit upon my Jewish gaberdine,
And all for use of that which is mine own.
Well then, it now appears you need my help:
Go too then; you come to me, and you say,
"Shylock, we would have moneys:" you say
so;
You that did void your rheum upon my beard,
And foot me as you spurn a stranger cur
Over your threshold: moneys is your suit.
What should I say to you? Should I not say,
"Hath a dog money? is it possible
A cur can lend three thousand ducats?" or
Shall I bend low, and in a bondman's key,
Say this: "Fair Sir, you spit on me on Wed-
nesday last;
You spurn'd me such a day; another time
You called me dog; and for these courtesies
I'll lend you thus much moneys?"
Ant.—I am as like to call thee so again,
To spit on thee again, to spurn thee too.
If thou wilt lend this money, lend it not
As to thy friends; for when did friendship
take
A breed for barren metal of his friend?
But lend it rather to thine enemy.
Who, if he break, thou mayest with better face
Exact the penalty.
Shy.— Why, look you, how you storm!
I would be friends with you and have your love,
Forget the shames that you have stain'd me
with,
Supply your present wants and take no doit
Of usance for my moneys' and you'll not hear
me:
This is kind I offer.
Bass.—This were kindness.
Shy.— This kindness will I show.
Go with me to a notary, seal me there
Your single bond; and in a merry sport,
If you repay me not on such a day,
In such a place, such sum or sums as are
Express'd in the condition, let the forfeit

Be nominated for an equal pound
Of your fair flesh, to be cut off and taken
In what part of your body pleaseth me.
Ant.—Content i' faith: I'll seal to such a bond,
And say there is much kindness in the Jew.
Bass.—You shall not sign to such a bond for me.
I'll rather dwell in my necessity.
Ant.—Why, fear not man; I will not forfeit it:
Within these two months,—that's a month before
This bond expires,—I do expect return
Of thrice three times the value of this bond.
Shy.—O father Abram, what these Christians are,
Whose own hard dealings teaches them suspect
The thoughts of others! Pray you, tell me this?
If he should break his day, what should I gain?
A pound of man's flesh taken from a man
Is not so estimable, profitable neither,
As flesh of muttons, beefs, or goats. I say
To buy his favor, I extend this friendship:
If he will take it, so; if not, adieu:
And, for my love, I pray you wrong me not.
Ant.—Yes, Shylock, I will seal unto this bond.
Shy.—Then meet me henceforth at the notary's;
Give him directions for this money bond,
And I will go and purse the ducats straight;
See to my house, left in the fearful guard
Of an unthrifty knave, and presently
I will be with you.
Ant.—Hie thee, gentle Jew,
The Hebrew will turn Christian: he grows kind.

Merchant of Venice, I. 3.

IN PRAISE OF ROSALIND.

Why should this a desert be?
  For it is unpeopled? No;
Tongues I'll hang on every tree,
  That shall civil sayings show:
Some, how brief the life of man
  Runs his erring pilgrimage,
That the stretching of a span
  Buckles in his sum of age;
Some of violated vows
  'Twixt the souls of friend and friend.
But upon the fairest boughs,
  Or at every sentence end,
Will I Rosalinda write,
  Teaching all that read to know
That the quintessence of every sprite
  Heaven would in little show.
Therefore Heaven Nature charged
  That one body should be fill'd
With all graces wide enlarged:
  Nature presently distill'd
Helen's cheek, but not her heart,
  Cleopatra's majesty,
Atalanta's better part,
  Sad Lucretia's modesty.
Thus Rosalind of many parts
  By heavenly synod was devised,
Of many faces, eyes and hearts
  To have the touches dearest prized.
Heaven would that she these gifts should have,
  And I to live and die her slave.

As You Like It, III. 2.

DIRGE FOR IMOGEN.

Fear no more the heat o' the sun,
  Nor the furious winter's rages;
Thou thy worldly task hast done,
  Home art gone and ta'en thy wages
Golden lads and girls all must,
As chimney-sweepers, come to dust.

Fear no more the frown o' the great,
  Thou art past the tyrant's stroke;
Care no more to clothe and eat;

To thee the reed is as the oak:
The sceptre, learning, physic, must
All follow this, and come to dust.

Fear no more the lightning-flash,
Nor the all-dreaded thunder-stone;
Fear not slander, censure rash;
Thou hast finished joy and moan:
All lovers young, all lovers must,
Consign to thee, and come to dust.

No exorciser harm thee!
Nor no witchcraft charm thee!
Ghost unlaid forbear thee!
Nothing ill come near thee!
Quiet consummation have;
And renownèd be thy grave!

Cymbeline, v.

CARDINAL WOLSEY.

Griffith.—About the hour of eight, which he himself
Foretold should be his last, full of repentance,
Continual meditations, tears and sorrows,
He gave his honors to the world again,
His blessed part to heaven, and slept in peace.
Kath.—So may he rest; his faults lie gently on him.
Yet thus far, Griffith, give me leave to speak him,
And yet with charity. He was a man
Of an unbounded stomach, ever ranking
Himself with princes; one that, by suggestion,
Tied all the kingdom; simony was fair play;
His own opinion was his law; i' the presence
He would say untruths; and be ever double
Both in his words and meaning; he was never,
But where he meant to ruin, pitiful.
His promises were, as he then was, mighty;
But his performance, as he is now, nothing.
Of his own body he was ill, and gave
The clergy ill-example.
Grif.— Noble madam,
Men's evil manners live in brass; their virtues
We write in water. May it please your highness,

To hear me speak his good now?
Kath.—Yes, good Griffith;
I were malicious else.
Grif—This Cardinal
Though from an humble stock, undoubtedly
Was fashioned to much honor from his cradle.
He was a scholar, and a ripe and good one;
Exceeding wise, fair-spoken, and persuading;
Lofty and sour to them that loved him not;
But to those that sought him sweet as summer.
And though he were unsatisfied in getting,
Which was a sin, yet in bestowing, madam,
He was most princely: ever witness for him
Those twins of learning that he raised in you,
Ipswich and Oxford! one of which fell with him,
Unwilling to outlive the good that did it;
The other, though unfinished yet so famous,
So excellent in art, and still so rising,
That Christendom shall ever speak his virtue.
His overthrow heap'd happiness upon him;
For then—and not till then, he felt himself,
And found the blessedness of being little.
And, to add greater honors to his age
Then man could give him, he died fearing God.
Kath.—After my death I wish no other herald,
No other speaker of my living actions,
To keep mine horror from corruption,
But such an honest chronicler as Griffith.
Whom I most hated living, thou hast made me,
With thy religious truth and modesty,
Now in his ashes honor. Peace be with him!
Patience, be near me still; and set me lower;
I have not long to trouble thee. Good Griffith,
Cause the musicians play me that sad note
I named my knell, whilst I sit meditating
On that celestial harmony I go to.
Henry VIII., IV. 2

KING LEAR AND HIS DAUGHTERS.

Lear.—Give me the map there. Know that we have divided
In three our kingdom: and 'tis our fast intent

To shake all cares and business from our age,
Conferring them on younger strengths, while we
Unburthen'd crawl toward death.—Our son of Cornwall,
And you, our no less loving son of Albany,
We have this hour a constant will to publish
Our daughters' several dowers, that future strife
May be prevented now. The princes, France and Burgundy,
Great rivals in our youngest daughter's love
Long in our court have made their amorous sojourn,
And here are to be answer'd. Tell me, my daughters—
Since now we will divest us both of rule,
Interest of territory, cares of state—
Which of you shall we say doth love us most?
That we our largest bounty may extend
Where nature doth with merit challenge. Goneril,
Our eldest-born, speak first.

Gon.—Sir, I love you more than words can wield the matter;
Dearer than eyesight, space and liberty;
Beyond what can be valued, rich or rare;
No less than life, with grace, health, beauty, honor;
As much as child e'er loved or father found;
A love that makes breath poor, and speech unable:
Beyond all manner of so much I love you.

Cordelia (*aside*).—What shall Cordelia do? Love and be silent.

Lear.—Of all these bounds, even from this line to this,
With shadowy forests and with champains rich'd,
With plenteous rivers and wide-skirted meads,
We make thee lady: to thine and Albany's issue
Be this perpetual.—What says our second daughter,
Our dearest Regan wife to Cornwall? Speak.

Regan.— Sir, I am made
Of the self-same metal that my sister is,
And prize me at her worth. In my true heart
I find she names my very deed of love;
Only she comes too short: that I profess
Myself an enemy to all other joys
Which the most precious square of sense possesses;
And find I am alone felicitate
In your dear highness's love.
Cor. (*aside*).— Then poor Cordelia
And yet not so; since, I am sure, my love's
More richer than my tongue.
Lear.—To thee and thine hereditary ever
Remain this ample third of our fair kingdom;
No less in space, validity, and pleasure
Than that conferred on Goneril. Now, our joy,
Although the last, not least; to whose young love
The vines of France and milk of Burgundy
Strive to be interess'd; what can you say to draw
A third more opulent than your sisters? Speak.
Cor.—Nothing, my lord.
Lear.— Nothing!
Cor.— Nothing.
Lear—Nothing will come of nothing: Speak again.
Cor.—Unhappy that I am, I cannot heave
My heart into my mouth: I love your Majesty
According to my bond; nor more nor less.
Lear.—How, how, Cordelia; mend your speech a little,
Lest you mar your fortunes.
Cor.— Good my lord,
You have begot me, bred me, loved me: I
Return those duties back, as are right fit,
Obey you, love you, and most honor you.
Why have my sisters husbands, if they say
They love you all? Haply, when I shall wed
That lord whose hand must take my plight shall carry
Half my love with him, half my care and duty.

Sure I shall never marry like my sisters
To love my father all.
Lear.—But goes thy heart with this?
Cor.— Ay, good my lord.
Lear.—So young, and so untender?
Cor.— So young, my lord, and true.
Lear—Let it be so; thy truth, then, be thy dower.
For, by the sacred radiance of the sun,
The mysteries of Hecate, and the night,
By all the operations of the orbs
From which we do exist and cease to be,
Here I disclaim all my paternal care,
Propinquity and property of blood,
And as a stranger to my heart and me
Hold thee, from this, forever. The barbarous Scythian,
Or he that makes his generation messes
To gorge his appetite, shall to my bosom
Be as well neighbored, pitied, and relieved,
As thou my sometime daughter.
Kent.— Good my liege—
Lear.— Peace, Kent!
Come not between the dragon and his wrath:
I loved her most, and sought to set my rest
On her kind nursery. Hence, and avoid my sight!
So be my grave my peace, as here I give
Her father's heart from her! Call France: who stirs?
Call Burgundy. Cornwall and Albany,
With my two daughters' dowers digest this third:
Let pride, which she calls plainness, marry her.
I do invest you jointly with my power,
Pre-eminence, and all the large effects
That troop with majesty. Ourself, by monthly course,
With reservation of an hundred knights,
By you to be sustain'd, shall our abode
Make with you by due turns. Only we still retain
The name, and all the additions to a king;
The sway, revenue, execution of the rest,

Beloved sons, be yours: which to confirm,
This coronet part betwixt you.
King Lear, I.

MACBETH AT BAY.

Macbeth.—Hang out your banners on the outward walls,
The cry is still, "They come!" Our castle's strength
Will laugh a siege to scorn: here let them lie
Till famine and the ague eat them up.
Were they not forced with those that should be ours,
We might have met them dareful, beard to beard,
And beat them backward home.—What is that noise?
Seyton.—It is the cry of women, my good lord. [*Exit.*]
Macb.—I have almost forgot the taste of fears:
The time has been, my senses would have cool'd
To hear a night-shriek; and my fell of hair
Would at a dismal treatise rise and stir
As life were in it. I have supp'd full with horrors;
Direness, familiar to my slaughterous thoughts,
Cannot once start me. [*Re-enter* SEYTON.]
Wherefore was that cry?
Sey.—The queen, my lord, is dead.
Macb.— She should have died hereafter;
There would have been a time for such a word.
To-morrow, and to-morrow, and to-morrow,
Creeps in this petty pace from day to day
To the last syllable of recorded time,
And all our yesterdays have lighted fools
The way to dusty death. Out, out, brief candle!
Life's but a walking shadow, a poor player
That struts and frets his hour upon the stage,
And then is heard no more. It is a tale
Told by an idiot, full of sound and fury,
Signifying nothing. [*Enter a* Messenger.]

Thou comest to use thy tongue: thy story
quickly!
Mess.— Gracious my lord,
I should report that which I say I saw,
But know not how to do it.
Macb.— Well, say, sir.
Mess.—As I did stand my watch upon the
hill
I looked toward Birnam, and anon, methought,
The wood began to move.
Macb.— Liar and slave!
Mess.—Let me endure your wrath, if't be
not so:
Within this three mile may you see it coming;
I say, a moving grove.
Macb.— If thou speak'st false,
Upon the next tree shalt thou hang alive,
Till famine cling thee. If thy speech be
sooth,
I pull in resolution and begin
To doubt the equivocation of the fiend
That lies like truth: "Fear not, till Birnam
wood
Do come to Dunsinane:" and now a wood
Comes toward Dunsinane. Arm, arm, and out!
If this which he avouches does appear,
There is no flying hence nor tarrying here.
I 'gin to be a-weary of the sun.
And wish the estate o' the world were now un-
done.
Ring the alarum bell! Blow wind! come wrack!
At least we'll die with harness on our back.

Macbeth, v. 5.

POLONIUS'S COUNSEL TO HIS SON.

Pol.— There; my blessing with thee!
And these few precepts in thy memory
Look thou character: Give thy thoughts no
tongue,
Nor any unproportioned thought his act.
Be thou familiar but by no means vulgar.
Those friends thou hast, and their adoption
tried,

Grapple them to thy soul with hooks of steel;
But do not dull thy palm with entertainment
Of each unhatch'd, unfledg'd comrade. Beware
Of entrance to a quarrel, but being in,
Bear't that the opposèd may beware of thee.
Give every man thy ear, but few thy voice.
Take each man's censure, but reserve thy judgment.
Costly thy habit as thy purse can buy,
But not express'd in fancy; rich not gaudy;
For the apparel oft proclaims the man,
And they in France of the best rank and station
Are most select and generous, chief in that.
Neither a borrower nor a lender be;
For loan oft loses both itself and friend,
And borrowing dulls the edge of husbandry.
This above all: To thine own self be true,
And it must follow, as the night the day,
Thou canst not then be false to any man.
Farewell: my blessing season this in thee!

Hamlet, I. 3.

PROSPERO'S VALEDICTION.

Prospero.— Go release them, Ariel:
My charms I'll break, their senses I'll restore,
And they shall be themselves.
Ariel.— I'll fetch them, sir. [*Exit.*
Pros.—Ye elves of hills, brooks, standing lakes and groves,
And ye that on the sands with printless foot
Do chase the ebbing Neptune, and do fly him
When he comes back; you demi-puppets that
By moonshine do the green-sour ringlets make,
Whereof the ewe not bites, and you whose pastime
Is to make midnight mushrooms, that rejoice
To hear the solemn curfew; by whose aid,
Weak masters though ye be, I have bedimm'd
The noontide sun, call'd forth the mutinous winds,
And 'twixt the green sea and the azured vault,
Set roaring war; to the dread rattling thunder
Have I given fire, and rifted Jove's stout oak
With his own bolt; the strong-based promontory

Have I made shake, and by the spurs pluck'd
up
The pine and cedar; graves at my command
Have waked their sleepers, opéd, and let 'em
forth
By my so potent act. But this rough magic
I here abjure, and when I have required
Some heavenly music, which even now I do,
To work mine end upon their senses that
This airy charm is for, I'll break my staff,
Bury it certain fathoms in the earth,
And deeper than did ever plumet sound
I'll drown my book. . . . .
Our revels now are ended. These our actors,
As I foretold you, were all spirits, and
Are melted into air, into thin air:
And, like the baseless fabric of this vision,
The cloud-capp'd towers, the gorgeous palaces,
The solemn temples, the great globe itself,
Yea, all which it inherits, shall dissolve,
And, like this unsubstantial pageant faded,
Leave not a rack behind. We are such stuff
As dreams are made of, and our little life
Is rounded with a sleep.

Tempest, v. 1.

SHEA, JOHN GILMARY, an American author, born in New York in 1824. He was educated for the law, and was admitted to the bar, but preferred to devote himself to literature. From 1859 to 1865 he edited the *Historical Magazine*, and was many years editor-in-chief for the Frank Leslie publishing house. He has given much time to the study of the history and languages of the North American Indians, and has published a series of *Grammars* and *Dictionaries* of the Indian languages in fifteen volumes (1860–1874). He is a member of many historical societies in the United States, and of the Royal Academy of History of Madrid, Spain. Besides contributing largely to periodicals and to publications of historical societies, he has translated Charlevoix's *History and General Description of New France* (1866-72), Le Clercq's *Establishment of the Faith*, Perralosa's *Expedition to Quivira*, and other works; has edited the Cramoisy series of *Relations and Documents in French Bearing on the Early History of the French-American Colonies* (20 vols., 1857–68), *Washington's Private Diary* (1861), Colden's *History of the Five Indian Nations*, edition of 1727 (1866), Alsop's *Maryland* (1869). Among his works are *The Discovery and Exploration of the Mississippi Valley* (1853), *History of French and Spanish Missions among the Indian Tribes of the United States* (1854), *The Fallen Brave* (1861), *Early Voyages up and down the Mississippi*, and *Novum-Belgium; an Account of New Netherlands in* 1643–4 (1862), *The Story of a Great Nation* (1886), *History of the Catholic Church in the United*

States (1886–88), and a *Life of Archbishop Hughes* in the *American Religious Leaders* series (1889).

THE EXPEDITION OF FATHER MARQUETTE.

The French Government in Canada at last resolved to send out an expedition of discovery. In November, 1672, Frontenac wrote to Colbert, the great prime minister of France: "I have deemed it expedient for the service to send the Sieur Jolliet to the country of the Maskoutens, to discover the South Sea (Pacific Ocean), and the great river called Mississippi, which is believed to empty into the gulf of California." One single man with a bark canoe was all the Provincial Government could afford; but Jolliet had evidently planned his course. Like the Sulpitians he proceeded to a Jesuit mission, to that of Father James Marquette, who had so long been planning a visit to the country of the Illinois, and who, speaking no fewer than six Indian languages, was admirably fitted for such an exploration. That missionary received permission or direction from his superiors to join Jolliet on his proposed expedition, and there are indications that the venerable Bishop Laval, to accredit him to the Spanish authorities whom he might encounter, made him his Vicar-General for the lands into which they were to penetrate.

Jolliet reached Michilimackinac on the 8th of December, 1672, the Feast of the Immaculate Conception, and the pious missionary with whom he was to make the exploration, thenceforward made the Immaculate Conception the title of his discovery and mission. They spent the winter studying their projected route by way of Green Bay, acquiring from intelligent Indians all possible knowledge of the rivers they should meet, and the tribes they would encounter. All this information they embodied on a sketch-map, both possessing no little topographical skill. On the 17th of May, 1673, Father Marquette and Jolliet, with five men in two canoes, set out, taking no provision but some Indian corn and some dried meat. Following the western shore of Lake Michigan, they entered Green Bay, and ascended Fox River undeterred by the stories of the Indians who warned them of the peril of their undertaking. Guided by two Miamis whom they obtained at the Maskoutens' town, they made the portage to the Wisconsin, and then reciting a new devotion to the Blessed Virgin, they paddled down amid awful solitudes, shores untenanted by any human dwellers. Just one month from their setting out their canoes glided into the Mississippi, and the hearts of all swelled with exultant joy. The dream of Father Marquette's life was accomplished: he was on the great river of the West, to which he gave the name of the Immaculate Conception. On and on their canoes kept while they admired the game and birds, the fish in the river, the changing character of the shores. More than a week passed before they met with the least indication of the presence of man. On the 25th they saw foot-prints on the western shore, and an Indian trail leading inland. The missionary and his fellow-explorer leaving the canoes followed it in silence. Three villages at last came in sight. Their hail brought out a motley group, and two old men advanced with calumets. When near enough to be heard, Father Marquette asked who they were. The answer was: "We are Illinois." The missionary was at the towns of the nation he had for years yearned to visit. The friendly natives escorted them to a cabin, where another aged Indian welcomed them: "How beautiful is the sun, O Frenchman, when thou comest to visit us! All our town awaits thee and thou shalt enter all our cabins in peace." These Illinois urged the missionary to stay and instruct them, warning him against the danger of descending the river, but they gave him a calumet and an Indian boy. He promised these Illinois of the Peoria and Moingona bands to return the next year and abide with them. Having announced the first gospel tidings to the tribe, the missionary with his associate was escorted to their canoes by the warriors. Past the Piesa, the painted rock which Indian superstition invested with terror and awe ; past the turbid Missouri, pouring its vast tide into the Mississippi ; past the unrecognized mouth of the Ohio coming down from the land of the Senecas, the explorers glided along, impelled by the current and their paddles. At last the character of the country changed, canebrakes replaced the forest and prairie, and swarms of mosquitoes hovered over land and water. After leaving the Illinois, they had encountered only one single Indian band, apparently stragglers from the East, who recognized the dress of the Catholic priest. To them he spoke of God and eternity. But as the canoes neared the Arkansas river, the Metchigameas on the western bank came out in battle array, a band of the Quappa confederation of Dakotas. Hemming in the French above and below, they filled the air with yells. The missionary held out his calumet of peace, and addressed them in every Indian language he knew. At last an old man answered him in Illinois. Then Father Marquette told of their desire to reach the sea and of his mission to teach the red men the ways of God. All hostile demonstrations ceased. The French were regaled and referred to the Arkansas, the next tribe below. This more friendly nation, then on the eastern shore, was soon reached. The explorers had solved the great question and made it certain that the Mississippi emptied into the Gulf of Mexico. The Jesuit Father had published the gospel as well as he could to the nations he had met, and opened the way to future missions. *History of the Catholic Church in the United States.*

SHEDD, WILLIAM GREENOUGH THAYER, an American theologian, born at Acton, Mass., in 1820. He graduated at the University of Vermont in 1839; at Andover Theological Seminary in 1843, and became pastor of a Congregational church at Brandon, Vt. In 1845 he was chosen Professor of English Literature in the University of Vermont, and prepared an excellent edition, with Introductory, Essays, of the *Works of Samuel T. Coleridge*. In 1852 he became Professor of Sacred Rhetoric in Auburn Theological Seminary; in 1854 Professor of Church History in Auburn Theological Seminary; in 1863 Professor of Biblical Literature, and in 1874 Professor of Systematic Theology in the Union Theological Seminary, New York. He has prepared several works in Scriptural exegeses and commentary. Among his other works are *Lectures on the Philosophy of History* (1856), *Manual of Church History* (1857), *History of Christian Doctrine* (1863), *Homiletics and Pastoral Theology* (1867), *Sermons to the Practical Man* (1871), *Theological Essays* (1877), *Literary Essays* (1878), *Sermons to the Spiritual Man* (1884), *The Doctrine of Endless Punishment* (1885), *Dogmatic Theology* (1887).

THE FOUNDATION OF LITERARY STYLE.

Having a distinctively clear apprehension of truth, the mind utters its convictions with all that simplicity and pertinence of language which characterizes the narrative of an honest eye-witness. Nothing intervenes between thought and expression. The clear, direct view instantaneously becomes the clear, direct statement. And when the clear conception is thus united with the profound intention, thought assumes its most perfect form. The form in which it appears is full and round with solid truth, and yet distinct and transparent. The immaterial principle is embodied in just the right amount of matter; the former does not overflow, nor does the latter overlay. The discourse exhibits the same opposite and counterbalancing excellences which we see in the forms of nature—the simplicity and richness, the negligence and the niceness, the solid opacity and the aeriel transparence.

It is rare to find such a union of the two main elements of culture, and consequently rare to find them in style. A profoundly contemplative mind is often mystic and vague in its discourse, because it has not come to a clear as well as profound consciousness: because distinctness has not gone along with depth of apprehension. The discourse of such a man is thoughtful and suggestive, it may be, but is lacking in that scientific, logical power which penetrates and illumines. It has warmth and glow, it may be, but it is the warmth of the stove (to use the comparison of another)—warmth without light.

On the other hand, it often happens that the culture of the mind is clear but shallow. In this case, nothing but the merest commonplace is uttered; in a manner intelligible and plain enough, but without depth or weight or even genuine force of style. Shallow waters show a very clear bottom, and but little intensity of light is needed in order to display the pebbles and clear sand. That must be a "purest ray serene"—a pencil of strongest light—which discloses the black, rich, wreck-strewn depths. For the clearness of depth is very different from the clearness of shallowness. The former is a positive quality. It is the positive irradiation of that which is solid and dark by that which is ethereal and light. The latter is a negative quality. It is the mere absence of darkness, because there is no substance to be dark—no *body* in which (if the expression be allowed) the darkness can inhere. Nothing is more luminous than solid fire; nothing is more flashing than an ignited void.

These two fundamental characteristics of mental culture lie at the foundation of style. Even if the secondary qualities of style could exist without the weightiness and clearness of manner that spring from the union of profound with distinct apprehension, they would exist in vain. The ornament is worthless if there is nothing to sustain it. The bas-relief is valueless without the slab to support it. But these secondary qualities of style—the beauty and the elegance, and the harmony—derive all their charm from springing out of the primary qualities, and in this way, ultimately, out of the deep and clear culture of the mind itself—from being the white flower of the black root.

Style, when having this mental and natural origin, is to be put into the first class of fine forms. It is the form of thought, and, as a piece of art, is as worthy of study and admiration as those glorious material forms which embody the ideas of Phidias, Michael Angelo, and Raphael. It is the form in which the human mind manifests its freest, purest, and most mysterious activity—its thinking. There is nothing mechanical in its origin, or stale in its nature. It is plastic and fresh as the immortal energy of which it is the air and bearing.—*Literary Essays.*

SHELLEY, MARY WOLLSTONECRAFT (GODWIN), an English author, born at London in 1797; died there in 1851. She inherited much of the genius of her mother, Mary Wollstonecraft, and of her father, William Godwin, and imbibed many of their theories upon social subjects. The circumstances of her connection with Percy Bysshe Shelley will be found in the succeeding sketch of the poet. Her most distinctive work is the wild romance *Frankenstein* written in her eighteenth year. After the death of Shelley she edited his works, and wrote several novels, among which are: *Valperga*, *The Last Man*, *Lodore*, *The Fortunes of Perkin Warbeck*, and a volume of *Rambles in Italy and Germany*. The plot of Frankenstein runs thus: Frankenstein, who tells the story, is a German student of the occult sciences. He succeeds in creating a living being in the human form, but having the most diabolical instincts. This monster becomes a torment to his own creator, whom he haunts like a spell for years; and finally extorts from him a promise to create a mate like unto himself.

THE MONSTER CREATED BY FRANKENSTEIN.

It was on a dreary night of November that I beheld the accomplishment of my toils. With an anxiety that almost amounted to agony I collected the instruments of life around me that I might infuse a spark of being into the lifeless thing that lay at my feet. It was already one in the morning; the rain pattered dismally against the panes, and my candle was nearly burnt out, when by the glimmer of the half-extinguished light I saw the dull yellow eye of the creature open. It breathed hard, and a convulsive motion agitated its limbs.

How can I describe my emotions at this catastrophe, or how delineate the wretch whom with such infinite pains and care I had endeavored to form? His limbs were in proportion, and I had selected his features as beautiful. Beautiful! Great God! His yellow skin scarcely covered the work of muscles and arteries beneath; his hair was of a lustrous black, and flowing; his teeth of a pearly whiteness; but these luxuriances only formed a more horrid contrast with his watery eyes, that seemed of almost the same color as the dun white sockets in which they were set, his shrivelled complexion, and straight black lips.

I had worked hard for nearly two years for the sole purpose of infusing life into an inanimate body. For this I had deprived myself of rest and health. I had desired it with an ardor that far exceeded moderation; but now that I had finished, the beauty of the dream vanished, and breathless horror and disgust filled my heart. Unable to endure the aspect of the being I had created, I rushed out of the room; and continued a long time traversing my bedchamber, unable to compose my mind to sleep. At length lassitude succeeded to the tumult I had before endured, and I threw myself on the bed in my clothes, endeavoring to seek a few moments of repose. But it was in vain; I slept indeed, but I was disturbed by the wildest dreams.

I started from my sleep with horror; a cold dew covered my forehead; my teeth chattered, and every limb became convulsed, when by the dim and yellow light of the moon, as it forced its way though the window-shutters, I beheld the wretch—the miserable Monster whom I had created. He held up the curtain of the bed, and his eyes—if eyes they may be called—were fixed on me. His jaws opened, and he muttered some inarticulate sounds, while a grin wrinkled his cheeks. He might have spoken, but I did not hear. One hand was stretched out as if to detain me; but I escaped, and rushed downstairs. I took refuge in the courtyard belonging to the house which I inhabited, where I remained during the rest of the night, walking up and down in the greatest agitation, listening attentively, catching and fearing each sound as if it were to announce the approach of the demoniacal corpse to which I had so miserably given life. Oh! no mortal could support the horror of that countenance. A mummy again endued with animation could not be so hideous as that wretch. I had gazed on him while unfinished. He was ugly then; but when those muscles and joints were rendered capable of motion, it became a thing such as even Dante could not have conceived.

I passed the night wretchedly. Sometimes my pulse beat so quickly and hardly that I felt the palpitation of every artery; at others I nearly sank to the ground through languor and extreme weakness. Mingled with this horror I felt the bitterness of disappointment; dreams that had been my food and pleasant cost for so long a space were now become a hell to me: and the change was so rapid, the overthrow so complete.

Morning, dismal and wet, at length dawned, and discovered to my sleepless eyes the church of Ingolstadt, its white steeple and clock, which indicated the sixth hour. The porter opened the gates of the court which had that night been my asylum, and I issued into the streets, pacing them with quick steps, as if I sought to avoid the wretch whom I feared every turning of the street would present to my view. I did not dare to return to the apartment which I inhabited, but felt impelled to hurry on, although wetted by the rain, which poured from a black and comfortless sky. I continued walking in this manner for some time, endeavoring by bodily exercise to ease the load that weighed upon my mind. I traversed the streets without any clear conception of where I was or what I was doing. My heart palpitated with fear, and I hurried on with irregular steps, not daring to look about me.

SHELLEY, Percy Bysshe, an English poet, born in 1792; drowned in the Bay of Spezzia, near Leghorn, Italy, in 1822. His father, Timothy Shelley, of Field Place, Sussex, was the eldest son and heir of Sir Bysshe Shelley, a wealthy baronet, to whose title and family estates he ultimately succeeded. At thirteen Percy was sent to Eton, where he remained four years, during which time he wrote two novels, *Zastrozzi* and *St. Irvyne.* In 1810 he was matriculated at University College. He brought from Eton a good acquaintance with Latin and Greek, but gave little attention to the presented college course: he was fond of dabbling in chemical experiments; his favorite authors were Locke and the French materialistic philosophers. Early in 1811, when he had just entered upon his nineteenth year, he put forth anonymously a little brochure, *The Necessity of Atheism*, an abstract of the current arguments against the existence of a Deity. He was summoned before the College authorities, and asked whether he was the author of the tractate; he refused to answer, and was expelled from the University. His father was highly incensed, forbade him to return to his home, and made him a very small allowance, which was eked out by what his young sisters could save from their pocket-money. They were at school at Clapham, near London, and among their schoolmates was Harriet Westbrook, the daughter of a retired publican. Shelley became acquainted with her; they ran away to Scotland, and were married, after the Scottish fashion. This marriage proved an uncongenial one. Harriet bore him two children, and a third was expected when he abandoned his wife and children. He had formed an attachment for Mary Godwin, daughter of William Godwin and Mary Wollstonecraft, and in the summer of 1814 they set out upon a jaunt through France to Switzerland, but were compelled by lack of money to return in six weeks. Up to this time Shelley's income had been small; but Sir Bysshe died early in 1815, and Timothy Shelley succeeded to the baronetcy and large estates. Percy was the next heir, and could easily have raised money upon his "expectations." To prevent this Sir Timothy settled an allowance of £4,000 a year upon his son.

In May, 1815, Shelley and Mary again went to Switzerland, taking with them their infant son. They were accompanied by Jane Clermont, the daughter of a widow whom Godwin had married after the death of Mary Wollstonecraft. She was about the same age as Mary Godwin, had imbibed romantic notions; called herself Claire Clermont; wished to go upon the stage, and sought the aid of Byron. The result was a liaison, which seems to have begun not long after the marriage of Byron and Miss Milbanke, and was continued until their separation. The reported conduct of Byron which led to the separation aroused a howl of popular indignation before which he quailed, and he left England never to return. He found the Shelleys at Geneva; and his liaison with Jane Clermont was renewed. Byron and Shelley took neighboring villas, and the two households became almost as one. The poets sailed together on the lake, made excursions among the Alps, and planned poems and tales. This way of life lasted five months, when it came to a sudden end. Byron crossed the Apennines, and went to Italy, bringing up at Venice. Shelley and his companions returned to England. Jane Clermont's child, Allegra, was born at Shelley's house in the ensuing February. Harriet Westbrook, deserted by Shelley, had formed an intimacy with another man; was abandoned by him, and committed suicide in November, 1816. On the last day of the next month Mary Godwin became the wife of Shelley. Soon afterward Shelley attempted to regain charge of his children, who had been left with their maternal grandfather. A Chancery suit was instituted, but Lord Eldon, before whom the cause was tried, decided that Shelley had forfeited all his paternal rights, and ordered that he should pay £200 a year for the maintenance of the children, who were placed under the charge of a clergyman to be religiously brought up.

In the spring of 1818 Shelley left England for the last time. Jane Clermont and Allegra went with them. Circumstances rendered it advisable that the child should be committed to the care of her father. Shelley took her to Byron at Venice; and the intimacy between the two poets was renewed, continuing during the remaining four years of Shelley's life. To this period belong the best of Shelley's longer poems; notably *Prometheus Unbound*, *The Cenci*, and *Adonais;* the finest of his Odes and Lyrics; the translation of the Homeric *Hymn to Mercury*, from the *Magico Prodigioso* of Calderon, and the *Faust* of Goethe.

In April, 1822, Shelley hired the Villa Magni, on the Gulf of Spezzia, near Lerici. On July 1, Shelley sailed for Leghorn to greet Leigh Hunt who had just joined Byron there. On the afternoon of the 20th, Shelley, Williams, and Charles Vivian, a sailor, sailed from Leghorn in the *Don Juan*, an open boat belonging to Shelley. Before long a sea-fog arose, and shut out all view from the shore: then came a sharp squall, with wind, rain, and thunder, lasting not more than twenty minutes. When the fog lifted, there were no traces of the *Don Juan*. Nothing was known of the fate of those on board until July 18, when two bodies were found cast upon the shore, about four miles apart. One was that of Williams, the other that of Shelley. By the laws of Tuscany all bodies cast on shore must be burned. The bodies were buried in the sand: and it was not until August 6 that permission was gained to disinter them for cremation. This took place in the presence of Trelawney, Byron, and Leigh Hunt. The scene is thus described by Trelawney:

THE CREMATION OF SHELLEY.

The work went silently on in the deep and unresisting sand. Not a word was spoken. We were startled and drawn together by a dull, hollow sound that followed the blow of a mattock. The iron had struck a skull, and the body was soon uncovered. . . . After the fire was well kindled more wine was poured over Shelley's dead body than he had ever consumed during his life. The fire was so fierce as to produce a white heat on the iron, and to reduce its contents to gray ashes. The only portions that were not consumed were some fragments of bones, the jaw, and the skull; but what surprised us all was that the heart remained entire. In snatching this relic from the fiery furnace my hand was severely burnt, and had any one seen me do the act, I should have been put into quarantine.

The heart was given to Hunt, who was subsequently, and not without difficulty, persuaded to resign it to Mrs. Shelley, and it was taken to England. The ashes were taken to Rome, and buried in the Protestant Cemetery there, not far from those of Keats.

The following are approximately the dates of the composition of Shelley's principal poems; but some of them were not printed until long after his death: *Queen Mab* (1813), *Alastor* (1815), *The Revolt of Islam*, which originally bore the title of *Laon and Cythna* (1816), *Prince Athanase* (1817), *Rosalind and Helen* (1818), *Prometheus Unbound* (1819), *The Cenci* (1819), *Julian and Maddalo* (1819), *Masque of Anarchy* (1820), *The Witch of Atlas* (1820), *Adonais* (1821), *Epipsychidion* (1821), *The Triumph of Life* (1822), *Hellas* (1822). *Queen Mab* was completed when Shelley had just reached his twenty-first year, and was dedicated to Harriet Westbrook, his wife of about a year. He had only a few copies of it printed for private circulation, and we may well regret that it was not consigned to that oblivion to which he wished to consign it, notwithstanding the high poetic beauty which abounds in it. But as it has not been suffered to die, it must be read by all who wish to understand the character of the poet. Milton proposed as the theme of *Paradise Lost*, to "justify the ways of God to man." Shelley proposed in *Queen Mab* to denounce those ways, as he believed them to be set forth in the Bible and formulated by theologians.

Shelley's longest poem, the *Revolt of Islam* was written not long after his marriage with Mary Godwin. As originally published it bore the title *Laon and Cythna.* The poem, as it came to stand, depicts the kindling of a great nation at the cry of Laon, the temporary triumph of the cause of liberty, then the overthrow of the good cause and the immolation of Laon and Cythna. The poem *Adonais*, an Elegy upon the death of John Keats, is the poem upon which Shelley most counted for a place among the immortals of Song. "Keats," says Shelley, "died at Rome in his twenty-fourth year, and was buried in the romantic and beautiful cemetery of the Protestants in that city, under the pyramid which is the tomb of Cestius, and the many walls and towers, now mouldering and desolate, which formed the circuit of ancient Rome. The cemetery is an open space among the ruins, covered in winter with violets and daisies. It might make one in love with death, to think that one should be buried in so sweet a place." Milton's *Lycidas*, written at about the same age, is the only poem in English with which *Adonais* can be compared.

A LAMENT FOR ADONAIS.

I.

I weep for Adonais—he is dead
  Oh, weep for Adonais, though our tears
Thaw not the frost which binds so dear a head;
  And thou, sad hour, selected from all years
  To mourn our loss, rouse thy obscure compeers,

And teach them thine own sorrow! Say, "With me
Died Adonais! Till the Future dares
Forget the Past, his fate and fame shall be
An echo and a light unto eternity."

IV.

Most musical of mourners, weep again!
Lament anew Urania! He died,
Who was the sire of an immortal strain,
Blind, old, and lonely, when his country's pride,
The priest, the slave, and the liberticide,
Trampled and mocked with many a loathed rite
Of lust and blood; he went unterrified
Into the gulf of death; but his clear Sprite
Yet reigns o'er earth; the third among the sons of light.

VI.

But now thy youngest, dearest one, has perished—
The nursling of thy widowhood, who grew
Like a pale flower by some sad maiden cherished,
And fed with true love-tears, instead of dew;
Most musical of mourners, weep anew!
Thy extreme hope, the loveliest and the last,
The bloom whose petals, nipt before they blew,
Died on the promise of the fruit, is waste;
The broken lily lies—the storm is overpast.

VII.

To that high Capital where kingly death
Keeps his pale court in beauty and decay,
He came; and bought, with price of purest breath,
A grave among the eternal.—Come away!
Haste, while the vault of blue Italian day
Is yet his fitting charnel-roof! While still
He lies, as if in dewy sleep he lay:
Awake him not! surely he takes his fill
Of deep and liquid rest, forgetful of all ill.

XLI.

He lives, he wakes—'tis Death is dead, not he;
Mourn not for Adonais! Thou young Dawn,
Turn all thy dew to splendor, for from thee
The spirit thou lamentest is not gone;
Ye caverns and ye forests, cease to moan!
Cease ye faint flowers and fountains, and thou Air,
Which like a mourning veil thy scarf hadst thrown
O'er the abandoned Earth, now leave it bare
Even to the joyous stars which smile on its despair.

XLII.

He is made one with Nature: there is heard
His voice in all her music, from the moan
Of thunder, to the song of night's sweet bird;
He is a presence to be felt and known
In darkness and in light, from herb and stone,
Spreading itself where'er that Power may move
Which has withdrawn his being to its own;
Which wields the world with never-wearied love,
Sustains it from beneath, and kindles it above.

XLIII.

He is a portion of the loveliness
Which once he made more lovely; he doth bear
His part, while the one Spirit's plastic stress
Sweeps through the dull dense world, compelling there
All new successions to the forms they wear;
Torturing the unwilling dross that checks its flight
To its own likeness, as each mass they bear;
And bursting in its beauty and its might
From trees and beasts and men into the Heaven's light.

XLV.

The inheritors of unfulfilled renown
Rose from their thrones, built beyond mortal thought,
Far in the Unapparent. Chatterton
Rose pale, his solemn agony had not
Yet faded from him; Sidney, as he fought
And as he fell, and as he lived and loved,
Sublimely mild, a spirit without spot,
Arose; and Lucan, by his death approved:
Oblivion as they rose shrank like a thing reproved.

XLVI.

And many more, whose names on earth are dark,
But whose transmitted effluence cannot die
So long as fire outlives the parent spark,
Rose, robed in dazzling immortality.
"Thou art become as one of us," they cry;
"It was for thee yon kingless sphere has long
Swung blind in unascended majesty,
Silent alone amid a Heaven of Song:
Assume thy wingèd throne, thou Vesper of our throng!"

LV.

The breath whose might I have invoked in song
Descends on me; my spirit's bark is driven
Far from the shore, far from the trembling throng
Whose sails were never to the tempest given;
The massy earth and sphered skies are riven!
I am borne darkly, fearfully afar;
Whilst burning through the inmost veil of Heaven
The soul of Adonais, like a star,
Beacons from the abode where the Eternal are.

Of the lost drama, *Prometheus Unbound*, produced by Æschylus, we are told little, except that in it Zeus, the oppressor of mankind, and Prometheus, the champion of humanity, are reconciled. To Shelley such a reconciliation was impossible unless one or the other should change his character. The foul dominion of Zeus must come to an end. In his poem of the same title the destined hour arrives; and the freed earth bursts into jubilation.

PROMETHEUS TO ZEUS.

Monarch of Gods and Demons, and all spirits
But one, who throng these bright and rolling
worlds
Which Thou and I alone of living things
Behold with sleepless eyes; regard this Earth
Made multitudinous with thy slaves, whom
thou
Requitest for knee-worship, prayer, and praise,
With toil and hecatombs of broken hearts,
With fear and self-contempt and barren hope;
Whilst me, who am thy foe, eyeless in hate,
Hast thou made reign and triumph, to thy
scorn,
Over my misery and thy vain revenge.
Three thousand years of sleep-unsheltered
hours,
And moments aye divided by keen pangs
Till they seemed years, torture and solitude,
Scorn and despair—these are mine empire,
More glorious far than that which thou surveyest
From thine unenvied throne, O Mighty God!
Almighty, had I deigned to share the shame
Of thine ill tyranny, and hung not here
Nailed to this wall of eagle-baffling mountain,
Black, wintry, dead, unmeasured; without
herb,
Insect, or beast, or shape or sound of life.
Ah me! alas, pain, pain ever, forever! . . . .
The crawling glaciers pierce me with the spears
Of their moon-freezing crystals, the bright
chains
Eat with their burning cold into my bones.

Heaven's winged hound, polluting from thy
lips
His beak in poison not his own, tears up
My heart; and shapeless sights come wandering by,
The ghastly people of the land of dreams,
Mocking me; and the earthquake-fiends are
charged
To wrench the rivets from my quivering
wounds
When the rocks split and close again behind;
While from their loud abysses howling throng
The genii of the storm, urging the rage
Of whirlwind, and afflict me with keen hail.
And yet to me welcome is Day and Night,
Whether one breaks the hoar-frost of the
morn,
Or, starry, dim, and slow, the other climbs
The leaden-colored east; for then they lead
The wingless, crawling Hours, one among
whom
As some dark Priest hales the reluctant
victim—
Shall drag thee, cruel king, to kiss the blood
From these pale feet, which then might trample
thee
If they disdained not such a prostrate slave.
Disdain! Ah no! I pity thee. What ruin
Will hunt thee undefended through the wide
Heaven!
How wilt thy soul, cloven to its depths with
terror,
Gape like a hell within! I speak in grief,
Not exultation, for I hate no more,
As then, ere misery made me wise.

Prometheus Unbound.

FINAL PÆAN FOR PROMETHEUS.

This is the day, which down the void abysm
At the Earth-born's spell yawns for Heaven's
despotism,
And Conquest is dragged captive through the
deep;
Love from its awful throne of patient power

In the wise heart, from the last giddy hour
  Of dead endurance, from the slippery, steep,
And narrow verge of crag-like agony, springs,
And folds over the world its healing wings.

Gentleness, Virtue, Wisdom, and Endurance,
These are the seals of that most firm assurance
  Which bars the pit over Destruction's strength;
And if, with infirm hand, Eternity,
Mother of many acts and hours, should free
  The serpent that would clasp her with his length,
  These are the spells by which to re-assume
An empire o'er the disentangled gloom.

To suffer woes which Hope thinks infinite;
To forgive wrongs darker than death or night;
  To defy Power which seems omnipotent,
To love and bear; to hope till Hope creates
From its own wreck the thing it contemplates;
  Neither to change, nor flatter, nor repent:—
This like thy glory, Titan, is to be
Good, great, and joyous, beautiful, and free:
This is alone Life, Joy, Empire, and Victory.

Prometheus Unbound, IV. 2.

INVOCATION TO NATURE.

Mother of this unfathomable world!
Favor my solemn song, for I have loved
Thee ever, and thee only; I have watched
Thy shadow, and the darkness of thy steps,
And my heart ever gazes on the depth
Of thy deep mysteries. I have made my bed
In charnels and on coffins, where black Death
Keeps record of the trophies won from thee,
Hoping to still these obstinate questionings
Of thee and thine, by forcing some lone ghost,
Thy messenger, to render up the tale
Of what we are. In lone and silent hours,
When night makes a weird sound of its own stillness,
Like an inspired and desperate alchymist,
Staking his life on some dark hope,

Have I mixed awful talk and asking looks
With my most innocent love, until strange
tears
Uniting with these breathless kisses, made
Such magic as compels the charmed night
To render up thy charge.
And though never yet
Thou hast unveiled thy inmost sanctuary,
Enough from incommunicable dream,
And twilight phantasms, and deep noonday
thought
Has shone within me, that serenely now,
And moveless as a long-forgotten lyre
Suspended in the solitary dome
Of some mysterious and deserted fane,
I wait thy breath, Great Parent, that my strain
May modulate with murmurs of the air,
And motions of the forests and the sea,
And voice of living beings, and the woven
hymns
Of Night and Day, and the deep heart of Man.

Alastor.

HYMN TO INTELLECTUAL BEAUTY.

The awful shadow of some unseen Power
Floats, though unseen, among us; visiting
This various world with as inconstant wing
As summer winds that creep from flower to
flower;
Like moonbeams that behind some puny mountain shower,
It visits with inconstant glance
Each human heart and countenance;
Like hues and harmonies of evening,
Like clouds in starlight widely spread,
Like memory of music fled,
Like aught that for its grace may be
Dear, and yet dearer for its mystery.

Spirit of Beauty that dost consecrate
With thine own hues all thou dost shine
upon
Of human thought or form, where art thou
gone?

Why dost thou pass away and leave our state,
This dim, vast vale of tears, vacant and desolate?
Ask why the sunlight, set forever,
Weaves rainbows o'er yon mountain river;
Why aught should fail and fade that once is shown;
Why fear and dream and death and birth
Cast on the daylight of this earth
Such gloom; why man has such a scope
For love and hate, despondency and hope?

No voice from some sublimer world hath ever
To sage or poet these responses given;
Therefore the names of Demon, Ghost, and Heaven,
Remain the records of their vain endeavor:
Frail spells, whose uttered charm might not avail to sever
From all we hear and all we see,
Doubt chance, and mutability.
Thy light alone, like mist o'er mountains driven,
Or music by the night-wind sent
Through strings of some still instrument,
Or moonlight on a midnight stream,
Gives grace and truth to life's unquiet dream.

Love, Hope, and Self-esteem, like clouds, depart
And come, for some uncertain moments lent.
Man were immortal and omnipotent
Didst thou, unknown and awful as thou art,
Keep with thy glorious train firm state within his heart.
Thou messenger of sympathies
That wax and wane in lovers' eyes;
Thou, that to human thought art nourishment,
Like darkness to a dying flame,
Depart not as thy shadow came;
Depart not, lest the grave should be,
Like life and fear, a dark reality.

While yet a boy I sought for ghosts, and sped
Through many a listening chamber, cave, and ruin,

And starlight wood, with fearful steps pursuing
Hopes of high talk with the departed dead.
I called on poisonous names with which our youth is fed:
I was not heard ; I saw them not.
When musing deeply on the lot
Of life, at that sweet time when winds are wooing
All vital things that wake to bring
News of birds and blossoming,
Sudden thy shadow fell on me :
I shrieked, and clasped my hands in ecstasy.

I vowed that I would dedicate my powers
To thee and thine : have I not kept the vow ?
With beating heart and streaming eyes, even now
I call the phantoms of a thousand hours
Each from his voiceless grave: they have in visioned bowers
Of studious zeal or love's delight
Outwatched with me the envious night:
They know that never joy illumed my brow,
Unlinked with hope that thou would'st free
This world from its dark slavery ;
That thou, O awful Loveliness,
Wouldst give whate'er these words cannot express.

The day becomes more solemn and serene
When noon is past ; there is a harmony
In autumn, and a lustre in its sky,
Which in the summer is not felt or seen
As if it could not be, as if it had not been.
Thus let thy power which, like the truth
Of nature, on my passive youth
Descended, to my outward life supply
Its calm, to one who worships thee,
And every form containing thee ;
Whom, Spirit fair, thy spell did bind
To fear himself, and love all human kind.

SHELTON, FREDERICK WILLIAM, an American clergyman and author, born at Jamaica, N. Y., in 1814; died at Carthage Landing, on the Hudson, in 1881. He graduated at Princeton in 1834, and studied for the Presbyterian ministry. In 1847 he took orders in the Episcopal Church, and was thereafter Rector at Fishkill, N. Y., and Montpelier, Vt., finally making his residence at Carthage Landing, where he was occupied in literary pursuits. Among his works are: *Salander and the Dragon* (1851), *Up the River* (1853), *The Rector of St. Bardolph's* (1853), *Crystalline* (1854), *Peeps from a Belfry* (1855).

A BURIAL AMONG THE MOUNTAINS.

It was in the month of January when the boreal breath is so keen, after a walk to the summit of the mountain, that I returned at nightfall to my chamber, with my cloak and hat completely covered with snow.

Scarce had I disposed myself for an evening's work, when I was called on with a request to perform funeral services on the next day over the body of a poor Irish laborer killed suddenly on the line of the railroad by the blasting of rocks. The priest was absent; for although there was a numerous body of Irish Catholics in that vicinity, he came only once in six weeks. During the interval those poor people were left without any shepherd; and as they had a regard for the decencies of Christian burial, they sometimes, as on this occasion, requested the Church clergyman to be at hand. I willingly consented to do what appeared to be a necessary charity, although I apprehended, and afterwards learned that the more rigid and disciplined of the faith were indignant, and kept away from the funeral rites, which they almost considered profane. Nor could I disrespect their scruples, considering the principles whence they grew.

The snow fell all night to the depth of several inches, and when the morrow dawned the wind blew a hurricane, filling the air with fine particles of snow, and making the cold intense. Muffling myself as well as possible, I proceeded two miles to the Irish shanty where the deceased lay, which was filled to the utmost capacity with a company of respectable friends and sincere mourners. It was indeed a comfortless abode; but for the poor man who reposed there in his pine coffin it was as good a tenement as the most sumptuous palace ever reared. When I see the dead going from an abode like this, the thought comes up that perhaps they have lost little, and are gaining much, that the grave over which the grass grows, and the trees wave, and the winds murmur, is after all a peaceful haven and a place of rest. But when they go from marble halls and splendid mansions, the last trappings appear a mockery, and I think only of what they have left behind.

Standing in one corner of that small cabin among the sorrowing relatives, while the winds of winter howled without their requiem of the departed year, I began to read the Church's Solemn Office for the Dead: "I am the Resurrection and the Life, saith the Lord." Having completed the reading of these choral words, and the magnificent and inspiring words of St. Paul, the procession was formed at the door of the hovel, and we proceeded on foot.

The wind-storm raged violently, so that you could scarce see by reason of the snowy pillar, while the drifts were sometimes up to your knees. The walk was most dreary. On either hand the mountains lifted their heads loftily, covered to the summit with snow; the pine-trees and evergreens which skirted the highway presented the spectacle of small pyramids; every weed which the foot struck was glazed over; and the bushes, in the faint beams of the struggling light, sparkled with gems. In a wild Titanic defile gigantic icicles hung from the oozing rocks, and as we passed a mill-stream we had the sight of a frozen water-fall, arrested in its descent, and with all its volume, spray, and mist, as if by the hand of some enchanter, changed into stone.

At last we arrived at the place of graves. It was an acclivity of the mountain; a small field surrounded by a fence, in one corner of which were erected many wooden crosses; and a pile of sand, or rather of sandy, frozen clods, dug out with a pick-axe and cast upon the surrounding snow, indicated the spot of this new sepulture. There was not a single marble erected, not a monument of brown stone; or epitaph; but the emblem of the cross denoted that it was the resting-place of the lowliest of the lowly—of the poor sons of Erin, the hewers of wood and the drawers of water, who had from time to time, in these distant regions, given up their lives to toil, to suffering, or to crime. But the mountain in which they were buried was itself a monument which, without any distinction, in a spot where all were equal, was erected equally for all? There is no memorial, even of the greatest, so good as the place in which they repose; and when I looked upon the Sinai-like peak which rose before us, I thought that these poor people had, in the depth of poverty, resorted to the very God of Nature to memorize their dead.

But I must not forget to notice by way of memorial, the history of that poor man. He was one of those who lived by the sweat of the brow. By digging and delving in the earth, by bearing heavy burdens, and performing dangerous work, he obtained a living by hard labor, "betwixt daylight and dark;" and while the famine was raging in his own land—like many of his race, who exhibit the same noble generosity and devotion—he had carefully saved his earnings, and transmitted them to his relatives. They arrived too late. His father and mother had already died of starvation; but his only sister had scarcely reached the doors of this poor man's hovel, after so long a journey, when, as she awaited anxiously his return that evening from his daily work, the litter which contained his body arrived at the door.

I reflected upon this little history as we approached the grave upon the mountain side; and melancholy as the scene was, with the snow drifting upon our uncovered heads, I would not have exchanged the good which it did my soul for the warmest and best-lighted chamber where revelry abounds. I thought that the surrounding gloom was of itself suggestive of hope to the Christian soul. In a few months more the mountains would again be clothed in verdure, and the little hills would rejoice on every side. As the winds died away into vernal gales, as the icicles fell from the rocks, as the snows vanished, they would be succeeded by the voice of the blooming and beautiful earth, with all its forest choirs prolonging the chant of thanksgiving. How much more should the body of him, which now lay cold in its grave, with the clods and the snows of the mountains piled upon it, awake to a sure, and, it was to be hoped, a joyous resurrection. With such cheering thoughts we hurried away from the spot, when the services were ended, humbly praying that a portion of consolation might be conveyed to the heart of her who, in a strange land, mourned the loss of an only brother.—*Peeps from a Belfry.*

SHENSTONE WILLIAM, an English poet, born in 1714; died in 1763. He studied at Pembroke College, Oxford, but did not take a degree. At the age of thirty the paternal estate of Leasowes came into his hand, and, as Johnson says, "he began to point his prospects, to diversify his surface, to entangle his walks, and to wind his waters." The property, however, was worth not more than £300 a year, and Shenstone devoted so much of his means to the embellishment of the grounds that he had to live in a dilapidated old house, hardly rain-proof. He is known almost wholly by his poem. *The Schoolmistress*, consisting of nearly forty stanzas in the Spenserian measure. This poem was published in 1742, and so was written while he was a student at Oxford. The following extract contains some of the opening stanzas of the poem, which are better than the later portions.

THE DAME AND HER SCHOOL.

Ah me! full sorely is my heart forlorn
  To think how modest worth neglected lies,
While partial Fame doth with her blasts adorn
  Such deeds alone as pride and pomp disguise;
  Deeds of ill sorts and mischievous emprise.—
Lend me thy clarion, goddess! let me try
  To sound the praise of merit ere it dies,
Such as I oft have chancèd to espy
Lost in the dreary shades of dull obscurity.
In every village marked with humble spire,
  Embowered in trees, and hardly known to fame,
There dwells, in lowly shades and mean attire,
  A matron old, whom we Schoolmistress name,
  Who boasts unruly brats with birch to tame;
They grieven sore, in piteous durance pent,
  Awed by the power of this relentless dame,

And ofttimes on vagaries idly bent,
For unkempt hair, or task unconned, are sorely
spent.

And all in sight doth rise a birchen tree,
Which Learning near her little dome did show;
Whilom a twig of small regard to see,
Though now so wide its waving branches
flow,
And work the simple vassals' mickle woe;
For not a wind might curl the leaves that blew,
But their limbs shuddered, and their pulse
beat low; [grew,
And as they looked, they found their horror
And shaped it into rods, and tingled at the
view. . . . .

Her cap, far whiter than the driven snow,
Emblem right meet of decency doth yield;
Her apron, dyed in grain, as blue, I trow,
As is the harebell that adorns the field;
And in her hand, for sceptre, she does wield
Tway birchen sprays, with anxious fear en-
twined,
With dark mistrust and sad repentance filled,
And steadfast hate and sharp affliction joined,
And fury uncontrolled, and chastisement un-
kind. . . . .

Right well she knew each temper to descry;
To thwart the proud, and the submiss to raise;
Some with vile copper prize exalt on high,
And some entice with pittance small of praise;
And other some with baleful sprig she 'frays:
E'en absent, she the reins of power doth hold,
While with quaint arts the giddy crowd she
sways;
Forewarned, if little bird their pranks behold,
'Twill whisper in her ear, and all the scene
unfold.

Lo! now with state she utters the command:
Eftsoons the urchins to their task repair;
Their books, of stature small, they take in hand,
Which with pellucid horn securèd are
To save from fingers wet the letters fair;

The work so gay that on their back is seen
  Saint George's high achievements does declare,
On which thilk wight that has y-gazing been,
Kens the forthcoming rod—unpleasing sight, I ween.

Ah, luckless he, and born beneath the beam
  Of evil star! It irks me while I write;
As erst the bard by Mulla's silver stream,
  Oft as he told of deadly, dolorous plight,
  Sighed as he sung, and did in tears indite.
For, brandishing the rod, she doth begin
  To loose the brogues, the stripling's late delight!
And down they drop: appears his dainty skin,
  Fair as the furry coat of whitest ermelin.

The Schoolmistress.

MUCH TASTE AND LITTLE ESTATE.

See yonder hill, so green and round,
Its brow with ambient beeches crowned!
'Twould well become thy gentle care
To raise a dome to Venus there:
Pleased would the Nymphs thy zeal survey,
And Venus in their arms repay.
'Twas such a shade, near such a brook,
From such a rocky fragment springing,
That famed Apollo chose to sing in.
  There let an altar wrought with art
Engage thy tuneful patron's heart:
How charming there to muse and warble
Beneath his bust of breathing marble!
With laurel wreath and mimic lyre,
That crown a poet's vast desire.
Then near it scoop the vaulted cell,
Where Music's charming maids may dwell,
Prone to indulge thy tender passion,
And make thee many an assignation.
Deep in the grove's obscure retreat
Be placed Minerva's sacred seat;
There let her awful turrets rise
(For Wisdom flies from vulgar eyes);
There her calm dictates thou shalt hear

Distinctly strike thy listening ear:
And who would shun the pleasing labor,
To have Minerva for his neighbor?
  But did the Muses haunt his cell?
Or in his dome did Venus dwell?
Did Pallas in his counsels share?
The Delian god reward his prayer?
Or did his zeal engage the fair?
When all the structure shone complete—
Not much convenient, wondrous neat—
Adorned with gilding, painting, planting,
And the fair guests alone were wanting;
Ah, me! ('twas Damon's own confession),
Came Poverty, and took possession.

The Progress of Taste.

SHERIDAN, RICHARD BRINSLEY, a British politician and dramatist, born at Dublin in 1751; died at London in 1815. He was educated at Harrow School, and in 1773 commenced the study of law at the Middle Temple, London. In 1780 he was returned to Parliament, and for many years took a prominent part in the political movements of the time. In 1787 he was chosen as one of the managers of the impeachment of Warren Hastings. His opening speech on the articles committed to his charge was deemed a masterpiece of eloquence. When he closed, the excitement was so great that no other speaker could obtain a hearing, and the House adjourned. Mr. Fox, long afterwards, pronounced it to be the best speech ever made in the House of Commons. Before twenty-four hours had passed. Sheridan was offered a thousand pounds for the copyright of the speech, if he would himself prepare it for the press; this was never done, and we have only an inadequate report of the great speech. We need not follow his political and personal career. What with extravagant living, enormous losses at the gaming table, and the burning, in 1809, of the Drury Lane Theatre, he was reduced to great pecuniary straits. He was enfeebled in health, was harassed by his creditors, imprisoned for debt, and the bailiffs were with difficulty prevented from dragging him from his death-bed to a spunging-house. He died deserted by all but a few of his former friends and associates, but he was honored with a tomb in the Poets' Corner of Westminster Abbey.

Sheridan's claim to a place in literature rests almost wholly on his comedies—the best of which are, *The Rivals*, *The School for Scandal*, and *The Critic*. *The Life of Sheridan* has been written by Thomas Moore (1825). His *Dramatic Works*, with a *Memoir* by James Brown, were published in 1873, and a collection of his entire *Works and Remains*, edited by F. Stainbull, in 1874.

A SCENE FROM "THE CRITIC."

[*Enter* SERVANT *to* DANGLE, MRS. DANGLE, *and* SNEER.]

Servant.—Sir Fretful Plagiary, Sir.

Dangle.—Beg him to walk up. [*Exit Servant.*] Now, Mrs. Dangle, Sir Fretful Plagiary is an author to your own taste.

Mrs. Dangle.—I confess he is a favorite of mine, because everybody else abuses him.

Sneer.—Very much to the credit of your charity, Madam, if not of your judgment.

Dangle.—But, egad! he allows no credit to any author but himself; that's the truth on't, though he is my friend.

Sneer.—Never. He is as envious as an old maid verging on the desperation of six-and-thirty; and then the insidious humility with which he seduces you to give a free opinion on any of his works can be exceeded only by the petulant arrogance with which he is sure to reject your observations.

Dan.—Very true, egad! though he's my friend.

Sneer.—Then his affected contempt of all newspapers strictures; though, at the same time, he is the poorest man alive, and shrinks like a scorched parchment from the fiery ordeals of true criticism. Yet he is so covetous of popularity that he had rather be abused than not mentioned at all.

Dan.—There's no denying it; though he is my friend.

Sneer.—You have read the tragedy he has just finished, haven't you?

Dan.—Oh, yes· he sent it to me yesterday.

Sneer.—Well, and you think it execrable, don't you?

Dan.—Why, between ourselves, egad! I must own—though he's my friend—that it is one of the most——he's here [*Aside.*] finished and most admirable perform——

Sir Fretful [*Without.*].—Mr. Sneer with him, did you say?

[*Enter* SIR FRETFUL PLAGIARY.]

Dan.—Ah, my dear friend!' Egad! We were just speaking of your tragedy. Admirable, Sir Fretful, admirable!

Sneer.—You never did anything beyond it, Sir Fretful; never in your life.

Sir Fretful.—You make me extremely happy; for, without a compliment, my dear Sneer, there isn't a man in the world whose judgment *I* value as I do yours, and Mr. Dangle's.

Mrs. Dangle.—They are only laughing at you, Sir Fretful; for it was but just now that——

Dan.—Mrs. Dangle!—Ah, Sir Fretful, you know Mrs. Dangle. My friend Sneer was rallying just now. He knows how she admires you, and——

Sir Fretful.—O Lord! I am sure that Mr. Sneer has more taste and sincerity than to—— [*Aside.*] A double-faced fellow!

Dan.—Yes, yes; Sneer will jest; but a better-humored——.

Sir Fret.—Oh, I know.

Dan.—He has a ready turn for ridicule; his wit costs him nothing.

Sir Fret.—No, egad! [*Aside.*] Or I should wonder how he came by it.

Mrs. Dan.—Because his jest is always at the expense of his friend.

Dan.—But, Sir Fretful, have you sent your play to the managers yet? or can I be of any service to you?

Sir Fret.—Sincerely, then, do you like the piece?

Sneer.—Wonderfully.

Sir Fret.—But, come, now, there must be something that you think might be mended, eh! Mr. Dangle, has nothing struck you?

Dan.—Why, faith, it is but an ungracious thing for the most part to——

Sir Fret.—With most authors it is so, indeed; they are in general strangely tenacious. But, for my part, I am never so well pleased as when a judicious critic points out any defect to me; for what is the purpose of showing a work to a friend if you don't mean to profit by his opinion?

Sneer.—Very true. Why, then, though I seriously admire the piece upon the whole, yet there is one small objection which, if you'll give me leave, I'll mention.

Sir Fret.—Sir, you can't oblige me more.

Sneer.—I think it wants incident.

Sir Fret.—Good God! you surprise me! wants incident!

Sneer.—Yes, I own I think the incidents are too few.

Sir Fret.—Good God! Believe me, Mr. Sneer, there is no person for whose judgment I have a more implicit deference; but I protest to you, Mr. Sneer, I am only apprehensive that the incidents are too crowded.—My dear Dangle, how does it strike you?

Dan.—Really, I can't agree with my friend Sneer. I think the plot quite sufficient; and the first four acts by many degrees the best I ever read or saw in my life. If I might venture to suggest anything, it is that the interest rather falls off in the fifth——

Sir Fret.—Rises, I believe you mean, Sir.

Dan.—No; I don't, upon my word.

Sir Fret.—Yes, yes, you do, upon my soul. It don't certainly fall off, I assure you, no, no, it don't fall off.

Dan.—Mrs. Dangle, didn't you say it struck you in the same light!

Mrs. Dan.—No, indeed, I did not. I did not see any fault in any part of the play from beginning to end.

Sir Fret.—Upon my soul, the women are the best judges, after all!

Mrs. Dan.—Or if I made any objection, I am sure it was to nothing in the piece; but I was afraid it was, on the whole, a little too long.

Sir Fret.—Pray, Madam, do you speak as to duration of time? or do you mean that the story is tediously spun out?

Mrs. Dan.—O no. I speak only with reference to the usual length of acting pieces.

Sir Fret.—Then I am very happy—very happy indeed; because the play is a short play, a remarkable short play. I should not venture to differ with a lady on a point of taste; but on these occasions the watch you know, is the critic.

Mrs. Dan.—Then I suppose it must have been Mr. Dangle's drawling manner of reading it to me.

Sir Fret.—Oh, if Mr. Dangle read it, that's quite another affair. But I assure you, Mrs. Dangle, the first evening you can spare me three hours and a half, I'll undertake to read you the whole from beginning to end, with the Prologue and the Epilogue, and allow time for the music between the Acts.

Mrs. Dan.—I hope to see it on the stage next.

Dan.—Well, Sir Fretful, I wish you may be able to get rid as easily of the newspaper criticisms as you do of ours.

Sir Fret.—The newspapers! Sir, they are the most villainous, licentious, abominable, infernal—not that I ever read them; no, I make it a rule never to look into a newspaper.

Dan.—You are quite right; for it certainly must hurt an author of delicate feelings to see the liberties they take.

Sir Fret.—No; quite the contrary; their abuse is, in fact, the best panegyric; I like it of all things. An author's reputation is only in danger from their support.

Sneer.—Why, that's true; and that attack, now, on you the other day——

Sir Fret.—What? Where?

Dan.—Ay, you mean in a paper of Thursday; it was completely ill-natured, to be sure.

Sir. Fret.—Oh, so much the better. Ha, ha, ha! I wouldn't have it otherwise.

Dan.—Certainly, it is only to be laughed at, for——

Sir Fret.—You don't happen to recollect what the fellow said, do you?

Sneer.—Pray, Dangle; Sir Fretful seems a little anxious——

Sir Fret.—O lud, no! Anxious, not I, not in the least—I—but one may as well hear, you know.

Dan.—Sneer, do *you* recollect? [*Aside.*] Make out something.

Sneer.—I will. [*To Dangle*]. Yes, yes, I remember perfectly.

Sir Fret.—Well, and pray now—not that it signifies—what might the gentleman say?

Sneer.—Why, he roundly asserts that you have not the slightest invention or original genius whatever, though you are the greatest traducer of all authors living.

Sir Fret.—Ha, ha, ha! Very good!

Sneer.—That as to comedy, you have not one idea of your own, he believes, even on your commonplace-book, where stray jokes and pilfered witticisms are kept with as much method as the ledger of the Lost and Stolen Office.

Sir Fret.—Ha, ha, ha! Very pleasant!

Sneer.—Nay, that you are so unlucky as not to have the skill even to steal with taste; but that you glean from the refuse of obscure volumes, where more judicious plagiarists have been before you; so that the body of your work is a composition of dregs and sediments, like a bad tavern's worst wine.

Sir Fret.—Ha, ha!

Sneer.—In your more serious efforts, he says, your bombast would be less intolerable if the thoughts were ever suited to the expressions; but that the homeliness of the sentiment stares through the fantastic encumbrance of its fine language, like a clown in one of the new uniforms.

Sir Fret.—Ha, ha !

Sneer.—That your occasional tropes and flowers suit the general coarseness of your style, as tambour-sprigs would a ground of linsey-woolsey ; while your imitations of Shakspeare resemble the mimicry of Falstaff's page, and are about as near the standard of the original.

Sir Fret.—Ha !——

Sneer.—In short, that even the finest passages of your steal are of no service to you ; for the poverty of your own language prevents their assimilating, so that they lie on the surface like heaps of marl on a barren moor, encumbering what it is not in their power to fertilize !

Sir Fret.—[*After great agitation.*] Now another person would be vexed at this.

Sneer.—Oh, but I would not have told you, only to divert you.

Sir Fret.—I know it. I *am* diverted—ha, ha, ha. Not the least invention ! ha, ha, ha ! Very good, very good !

Sneer.—Yes ; no genius ! ha, ha, ha !

Dan.—A severe rogue, ha, ha, ha ! But you are quite right, Sir Fretful, never to read such nonsense.

Sir Fret.—To be sure ; for if there is anything to one's praise, it is a foolish vanity to be gratified at it ; and if it is abuse, why, one is always sure to hear of it from one d—d good-natured friend or another.

SHERLOCK, THOMAS, an English bishop and author, born at London in 1678; died there in 1761. He was educated at Eton and Cambridge; became Master of the Temple in 1704, Vice-chancellor of his college in 1714, Dean of Chichester in 1716, and Prebendary of Norwich in 1719. He was made Bishop of Bangor in 1728, was transferred to the see of Salisbury in 1734, and to that of London in 1748, having declined the Archbishopric of Canterbury. His principal works are: *The Use and Intent of Prophecy* (1725), *The Trial of the Witnesses to the Resurrection of Jesus* (1729), Discourses at the Temple Church, London (4 vols., 1754–1758).

RELIGION AND ETERNAL LIFE.

Religion is founded in the principles of sense and nature; and without supposing this foundation it would be as rational an act to preach to horses as to men. A man who has the use of reason cannot consider his condition and circumstances in this world, or reflect on his notions of good and evil, and the sense he feels in himself that he is an accountable creature for the good or the evil he does, without asking himself how he came into this world, and for what purpose, and to whom it is that he is, or possibly may be, accountable.

When, by tracing his own being to the original, he finds that there is one supreme all-wise cause of all things; when by experience he sees that this world neither is nor can be the place for taking a just and adequate account of the actions of men; the presumption that there is another state after this, in which men shall live, grows strong and almost irresistible. When he considers further that the fears and hopes of nature with respect to futurity, the fear of death common to all, the desire of continuing in being, which never forsakes us; and reflects for what use and purpose these strong impressions were given us by the Author of our nature—he cannot help concluding that man was made not merely to act a short part upon the stage of this world, but that there is another and more lasting state to which he bears relation. And from hence it must necessarily follow that his religion must be formed on a view of securing a future happiness.

Since, then, the end that men propose to themselves by religion is such, it will teach us wherein the true excellency of religion consists. If eternal life and future happiness are what we aim at, that will be the best religion which will most certainly lead us to eternal life and future happiness; and it will be to no purpose to compare religions together in any other respects which have no relation to this end. Let us, then, by this rule examine the pretensions of revelation; and, as we go along, compare it with the present state of natural religion, that we may be able to judge "to whom we ought to go."

Eternal life and happiness are out of our power to give ourselves or to obtain by any strength and force, or any policy or wisdom. Could our own arm rescue us from the jaws of death and the powers of the kingdom of darkness; could we set open the gates of heaven for ourselves, and enter in to take possession of life and glory, we should want no instructions or assistances from religion; since what St. Peter said of Christ, every man might apply to himself, and say, "I have the words, or means, of eternal life."

But since we have not this power of life and death, and since there is One above us who has—who governeth all things in heaven and earth, who is over all God blessed for evermore—it necessarily follows that either we must have no share or lot in the glories of futurity, or else that we obtain them from God, and receive them as His gift and favor; and consequently if eternal life be the end of religion, and likewise the gift of God, religion can be nothing else but the means of obtaining eternal life; and if eternal life can only be had from the gift of God, religion must be the means of obtaining this gift of God.

And thus far all religions that have ever appeared in the world have agreed. The question has never been made by any whether God is to be applied to for eternal happiness or no; but every sect has placed its excellency in this—that it teaches the properest and most effectual way of making this application. Even natural religion pretends to no more than this. It claims not eternal life as the right of nature, but the right of obedience—and of obedience to God, the Lord of nature; and the dispute between natural and revealed religion is not whether God is to be applied to for eternal happiness; but only whether nature or revelation can best teach us how to make this application.

Prayers, and praises, and repentance for sins past, are acts of devotion which nature pretends to direct us in. But why does she teach us to pray, to praise, or to repent, but that she esteems one to be the proper method of expressing our wants; the other of expressing our gratitude, and the third for making atonement for iniquity and offences against God? In all these acts reference is had to the overruling power of the Almighty; and they amount to this confession, that the upshot of all religion is to please God in order to make ourselves happy.—*Discourses.*

SHERLOCK, WILLIAM, an English divine, born in 1641; died in 1707. He became Prebendary of St. Paul's in 1681; Master of the Temple in 1684; Dean of St. Paul's in 1691. He was the author of numerous pamphlets against Romanism, several works in dogmatic theology, and many sermons. His *Practical Discourses concerning Death* (1689) passed through about twenty editions in thirty years.

OUR IGNORANCE OF THE TIME OF DEATH.

For a conclusion of this argument I shall briefly vindicate the wisdom and goodness of God in concealing from us the time of our death. We are very apt to complain that our lives are so very uncertain, that we know not to-day but what we may die to-morrow; and we would be mighty glad to meet with any one who would certainly inform us in this matter how long we are to live. But if we think a little better of it, we shall be of another mind.

For *First:* Though I presume many of you would be glad to know that you shall certainly live twenty, or thirty, or forty years longer, yet would it be any comfort to know that you must die to-morrow, or some few months, or a year or two hence?—which may be your case for aught you know; and this, I believe you are not very desirous to know—for how would this chill your blood and spirits; how would it overcast all the pleasures and comforts of life! You would spend your days like men under sentence of death, while the execution is suspended.

Did all men who must die young certainly know it, it would destroy the industry and improvements of half mankind; which would half destroy half the world, or be an insupportable mischief to human societies; for what man who knows that he must die at twenty, or five-and-twenty—a little sooner or later—would trouble himself with ingenious or gainful arts;

or concern himself any more with this world than just to live so long in it? And yet how necessary is the service of such men in the world! What great things do they many times do; and what great improvements do they make! How pleasant and diverting is their conversation while it is innocent! How do they enjoy themselves, and give life and spirit to the graver age! How thin would our schools, our shops, our universities, and all places of education be, did they know how little time many of them had to live in the world! For would such men concern themselves to learn the arts of living, who must die as soon as they have learnt them? Would the father be at a great expense in educating his child, only that he might die with a little Latin and Greek, logic and philosophy? No: half the world must be divided into cloisters, and nunneries, and nuseries for the grave.

Well, you'll say: suppose that, and is not this an advantage above all the inconveniences you can think of to secure the salvation of so many thousands who are now eternally ruined by youthful lusts and vanities, but who would spend their days in piety and devotion, and make the next world their only care, if they knew how little while they were to live here? —Right; I grant this might be a good way to correct the heat and extravagance of youth; and so it would be to show them heaven and hell. But God does not think fit to do either, because it offers too much force and violence to men's minds; it is no trial of their virtue, of their reverence for God, of their conquests and victory over this world by the power of faith; but makes religion a matter of necessity, not of choice. Now, God will force and drive no man to heaven; for the gospel dispensation is the trial and dispensation of ingenuous spirits; and if the certain hopes and fears of another world, and the uncertainty of our living here, will not conquer these flattering temptations, and make men sincerely religious, as those who must certainly die and go into another world—and they know not how soon—God will not try whether the certain knowledge of the time of their death will make them religious. That they may die young, and that thousands do so, is reason enough to engage young men to expect death, and prepare for it. If they will venture, they must take their chances, and not say they had no warning of dying young, if they eternally miscarry by their wilful delays.

And besides this, God expects our youthful service and obedience, though we were to live on till old age. That we may die young is not the proper, much less the only reason why we should remember our Creator in the days of our youth; but because God has a right to our youthful strength and vigor. And if this will not oblige us to an early piety, we must not expect that God will set death in our view, to fright and terrify us. . . .

Secondly: Though I doubt not but that it would be a great pleasure to you to know that you should live to old age; yet consider a little with yourselves, and then tell me whether you yourselves can judge it wise and fitting for God to let you know this. I observed to you before, what danger there is in flattering ourselves with the hopes of long life; that it is apt to make us too fond of this world when we expect to live so long in it, that it weakens the hopes and fears of the next world, by removing it at too great a distance from us; that it encourages men to live in sin, because they have time enough before them to indulge their lusts, and to repent of their sins, and make their peace with God before they die. And if the uncertain hope of this undoes so many men, what would the certain knowledge of it do? Those who are too wise and considerate to be imposed on by such uncertain hopes, might be conquered by the certain knowledge of a long life.

SHERMAN, FRANK DEMPSTER, an American poet, born at Peekskill, N. Y., in 1860. He was educated in his native town and at Columbia College, of which he was made a Fellow in 1887, and with which he is now connected as instructor in architecture. He has achieved fame as a writer of graceful, piquant verses. He contributes frequently to the *Century* and other magazines, and has published *Madrigals and Catches* (1887), *Lyrics for a Lute* (1890), and *New Waggings of Old Tales*, in collaboration with John Kendrick Bangs.

PEPITA.

Up in her balcony where
  Vines through the lattices run
Spilling a scent on the air,
  Setting a screen to the sun,
Fair as the morning is fair,
  Sweet as a blossom is sweet,
  Dwells in her rosy retreat
    Pepita.

Often a glimpse of her face
  When the wind rustles the vine
Parting the leaves for a space
  Gladdens this window of mine,—
Pink in its leafy embrace,
  Pink as the morning is pink,
Sweet as a blossom I think
    Pepita.

I, who dwell over the way,
  Watch where Pepita is hid—
Safe from the glare of the day
  Like an eye under its lid:
Over and over I say,—
  Name like the song of a bird,
  Melody shut in a word,—
    "Pepita."

Look where the little leaves stir!
  Look the green curtains are drawn!

Therein a blossoming blur
  Breaks a diminutive dawn ;—
Dawn and the pink face of her,—
  Name like the lisp of the south,
  Fit for a rose's small mouth—,
      Pepita.

BACKLOG DREAMS.

Above the glowing embers
  I hear the backlog sing
The music it remembers
  Of some remembered spring ;
Back to the branch forsaken
  Return the jocund choir,
And in the chimney waken
  A melody of fire.

The sparks' red blossoms glisten
  And flash their glances brief
At me, who lean and listen
  And dream I hear a leaf
On some May-morning sunny,
  Low lisping in the tree,—
Or, in his haunt of honey,
  A bloom-enamored bee :

Or 'tis the soft wind blowing
  Its sweetness from the South,—
A fragrant kiss bestowing
  Upon the rose's mouth ;
And ere the spell is broken,
  Or darkness o'er it slips,
I see the scarlet token
  Of love upon her lips.

Without, the wind is bitter,
  The snowflakes fill the night ;
Within, the embers glitter
  And gild the room with light ;
And in the fireplace gleaming
  The backlog sings away,
And mingles all my dreaming
With birds, and blooms, and May !

TWO VALENTINES.

Love, at your door young Cupid stands
　　And knocks for you to come ;
The frost is in his feet and hands,
　　His lips with cold are numb.
Grant him admittance, sweetheart mine,
　　And by your cheering fire
His lips shall loosen as with wine
　　And speak forth my desire.

He left me not an hour ago,
　　And when the rascal went
Barefooted out into the snow
　　I asked him whither bent.
Quoth he : " To her whose face is like
　　A garden full of flowers,
To her whose smiles like sunlight strike
　　Across the winter hours."

No more he said, nor need of more
　　Had I to know. I knew
His path lay straight unto your door—
　　That face belongs to you.
" Godspeed ! " I cried, " and give her this
　　When you her face shall see ; "
And on his lips I set a kiss
　　A Valentine from me !

SHILLABER, BENJAMIN PENHALLOW, an American humorist, born at Portsmouth, N. H., in 1814, died in 1890. He received a district school education and entered a printing-office in 1830. He removed to Boston in 1832. From 1840 till 1850 he was editor of the Boston *Post*, and in 1851–3, he edited a comic paper called *The Carpet Bag*. From 1856 till 1866 he conducted *The Saturday Evening Gazette*. His *Life and Sayings of Mrs. Partington* (1854) gave him fame, and the book was widely quoted. His other works are: *Rhymes with Reason and Without* (1853), *Knitting Work* (1857), *Partingtonian Patchwork* (1873), *Lines in Pleasant Places* (1875), *The Ike Partington Juvenile Series* (1879), *Ike and his Friends* (1879), *Cruises with Captain Bob* (1881), *The Doublerunner Club* (1882), and *Wide-Swath*, a collection of verses (1882), and *Mrs. Partington's New Gripsack filled with Fresh Things* (1890).

DECIDED OPINIONS.

"Are you in favor of the prohibitic laws, or the license law?" asked her opposite neighbor of the relict of P. P., corporal of the Bloody 'Leventh.

She carefully weighed the question, as though she were selling snuff, and answered—"Sometimes I think I am, and then again I think I am not."

Her neighbor was surprised, and repeated the question, varying it a little.

Have you seen the "Mrs. Partington Twilight Soap?" she asked.

"Yes," was the reply, "everybody has seen that; but why?"

"Because," said the dame, "it has two sides to it, and it is hard to choose between 'em. Now here are my two neighbors, contagious to me on both sides—one goes for probation, t'other for licentiousness; and I think the best thing for me is to keep nuisance."

She meant neutral, of course. The neighbor admired and smiled, while Ike lay on the floor with his legs in the air, trying to balance Mrs. Partington's fancy waiter on his toes.

"I've always noticed," said Mrs. Partington on New Year's Day, dropping her voice to the key that people adopt when they are disposed to be philosophical or moral: "I've always noticed that every year added to a man's life is apt to make him older, just as a man who goes a journey finds, as he jogs on, that every mile he goes brings him nearer where he is going, and farther from where he started. I am not so young as I was once, and I don't believe I shall ever be if I live to the age of Samson, which heaven knows as well as I do, I don't want to, for I wouldn't be a centurion, or an octagon, and survive my factories, and become idiomatic by any means. But then there is no knowing how a thing will turn out till it takes place, and we shall come to an end some day, though we may never live to see it."

"Mrs. Partington *et als!*" said Mrs. Partington, as Ike read eulogistic notice of herself and retinue thus headed. "Is that so Isaac?"

"'T'ain't nothing else," replied he, thrusting the cat's head through the paper which served as an elaborate choker.

"Et als!" mused she, "I never eat als in my life that I know of, though there is so many dishes with new names that one might forget 'em all, unless he is an epicac."

She turned everything in her mind to remember what she had eaten,—her mind an oven full of turnovers,—but it refused to come to her; and she made a memorandum of tying a knot in her handkerchief to call on the editor and find out about it.—*Partingtonian Patchwork.*

SHIRLEY, James, an English dramatist born at London in 1594; died there in 1666. He studied at Oxford and Cambridge, took orders, and obtained a curacy; which he had to give up on going over to the Roman Catholic Church. He then set up a school, which, proving unsuccessful, he went to London, and took to writing for the stage. Play-acting being prohibited during the Commonwealth and the Protectorate, he opened another school, and put forth several text-books, among which is an *Essay towards an Universal and Rational Grammar.* He was driven from his home by the Great Fire in London, and shortly afterwards he and his wife died on the same day, from the exposure to which they had been subjected, He produced in all about forty dramas, and some separate poems. The best of the poems are lyrics introduced into one and another of his dramas. A complete edition of his *Works* edited by Willam Gifford was published in 1833.

A LULLABY.

Cease, warring thoughts, and let us here
No more discord entertain;
But be smooth and calm again.
Ye crystal rivers that are nigh,
As your streams are passing by,
Teach your numbers harmony.
Ye winds that wait upon the Spring,
And perfume to flowers do bring,
Let your amorous whispers here
Breathe soft murmurs to his ear.
Ye warbling nightingales, repair
From every wood to charm the air,
And with the wonders of your breast
Each striving to excel the rest;

When it is time to wake him, close your parts,
And drop down from the tree with broken
hearts.

From the Triumph of Beauty.

THE MIGHT OF DEATH.

Victorious men of earth, no more
Proclaim how wide your conquests are:
Though you bind in every shore,
And your triumphs reach as far
As night or day,
Yet you, proud monarchs, must obey,
And mingle with forgotten ashes, when
Death calls ye to the crowd of common men.

Devouring famine, plague, and war,
Each able to undo mankind,
Death's servile emissaries are;
Nor to these alone confined,
He hath at will
More quaint and subtle ways to kill:
A smile or kiss, as he will use his art,
Shall have the cunning skill to break a heart.

From Cupid and Death.

THE VICTORY OF DEATH.

The glories of our birth and state
Are shadows, not substantial things;
There is no armor against fate;
Death lays his iron hand on kings;
Sceptre and crown
Must tumble down,
And in the dust be equal made
With the poor crooked scythe and spade.

Some men with swords may reap the field,
And plant fresh laurels where they kill;
But their strong nerves at last must yield—
They tame but one another still;
Early or late,
They stoop to fate,
And must give up their murmuring breath
When they, pale captives, creep to death.

The garlands wither on your brow—
Then boast no more your mighty deeds;

Upon Death's purple altar, now,
    ee where the victor victim bleeds !
        All heads must come
        To the cold tomb :
Only the actions of the just
    Smell sweet, and blossom in the dust.

From the Contention between Ajax and Ulysses.

FERNANDO'S DESCRIPTION OF HIS MISTRESS'S CHARMS.

Her eye did seem to labor with a tear,
Which suddenly took birth but over-weighed
With its own swelling, dropt upon her bosom,
Which, by reflection of her light appeared
As nature meant her sorrow for an ornament.
After, her looks grew cheerful, and I saw
A smile shoot graceful upward from her eyes,
As if they had gained a victory over grief ;
And with it many beams twisted themselves,
Upon whose golden threads the angels walk
To and again from heaven.

SHORTHOUSE, JOSEPH HENRY, an English author, born at Birmingham in 1834. He was educated at private schools, and is now (1890) engaged in the manufacture of chemicals in Lansdowne, where his books have been written. His philosophical romance, *John Inglesant* (1882), brought him fame and lifted him into the first rank of modern writers. His style is pure and artistic, and there is a quaint, picturesque, and old-fashioned grace in the color of his fancy. His other books are: *The Platonism of Wordsworth* (1881), *Preface to George Herbert's Temple* (1882). *Little Schoolmaster Mark, and Other Stories* (1883), *Sir Percival* (1886). *A Teacher of the Violin, and Other Stories* (1887), *The Countess Eve* (1888).

THE HEART OF THE CITY.

The narrow streets through which Inglesant's chair passed terminated at last in a wide square. It was full of confused figures, presenting to the eye a dazzling movement of form and color, of which last, owing to the evening light, the prevailing tint was blue. A brilliant belt of sunset radiance, like molton gold along the distant horizon, threw up the white houses into strong relief. Dark Cypress trees rose against the glare of the yellow sky, tinged with blue from the fathomless azure above. The white spray of fountains flashed high over the heads of the people in the four corners of the square, and long lance-like gleams of light shot from behind the Cypresses and the white houses, refracting a thousand colors in the flashing water. A murmur of gay talk filled the air; and a constant change of varied form perplexed the eye.

Inglesant alighted from his chair, and directing his servants to proceed at once to the Cardinal's, crossed the square on foot. Following so closely on his previous dreamy thoughts, he was intensely interested and touched by this living pantomime. Human life had never before seemed to him so worthy of regard, whether looked at as a whole, inspiring noble and serious reflections, or viewed in detail, when each separate atom appears pitiful and often ludicrous. The infinite distance between these poles, between the aspirations and the exhortations of conscience, which have to do with humanity as a whole, and the actual circumstances and capacities of the individual, with which satirists and humorists have ever made free to jest,—this contrast, running through every individual life as well as through the mass of existence, seemed to him to be the true field of humor, and the real science of those "Humanities," which the schools pedantically professed to teach.

Nothing moved in the motley crowd before him but what illustrated this science,—the monk, the lover, the soldier, the improvisatore, the matron, the young girl : here the childish hand brandishing its toy, there the artisan, and the shop-girl, and the maid-servant, seeking such enjoyment as their confined life afforded ; the young boyish companions with interlaced arms, the benignant priest, every now and then the stately carriage slowly passing by to its place on the Corso, or to the palace or garden to which its inmates are bound.

Wandering amid this brilliant phantasia of life, Inglesant's heart smote him for the luxurious sense of pleasure which he found himself taking in the present movement and aspect of things. Doubtless this human philosophy, if we may so call it, into which he was drifting has a tendency, at least, very different from much of the teaching which is the same in every school of religious thought.

But if a man does not desire a perfect world, what part can he have in the Christian warfare ? It is true that an intimate study of a world of sin and of misfortune throws up the sinless character of the Saviour into strong relief ; but the student accepts this Saviour's character and mission ás part of the phenomena of existence, not as an irreconcilable crusade and battle-cry against the powers of the world on every hand. The study of life is indeed possible to both schools; but the pleased acquiescence in life as it is, with all its follies and fantastic pleasures, is surely incompatible with following the footsteps of the Divine Ascetic who trod the winepress of the wrath of God. With all their errors, they who rejected the world and all its allurements, and taught the narrow life of painful self-denial, must be more nearly right than this.

Nevertheless, even before this last thought was completely formed in his mind, the sight of the moving people and of the streets of the wonderful city opening out on every side, full of palaces and glittering shops and stalls, and crowded with life and gaiety, turned his halting choice back again in the opposite direction, and he thought something like this:—"How useless and even pitiful is the continued complaint of moralists and divines, to whom none lend an ear whilst they endeavor, age after age, to check youth and pleasure, and turn the current of life and nature backward on its course. For how many ages in this old Rome, as in every other city since Terence gossiped of the city life, has this frail faulty humanity for a few hours sunned itself on warm afternoons in sheltered walks and streets, and comforted itself into life and pleasure, amid all its cares and toils and sins. Out of this shifting phantasmagoria comes the sound of music, always pathetic and sometimes gay; amid the roofs and belfries peers the foliage of the public walks, the stage upon which in every city, life may be studied and taken to heart; not far from these walks is, in every city, the mimic stage, the glass in which, in every age and climate, human life has seen itself reflected, and has delighted, beyond all other pleasures, in pitying its own sorrows, in learning its own story; in watching its own fantastic developments, in foreshadowing its own fate, in smiling sadly for an hour over the still more fleeting representation of its own fleeting joys. Forever without any change, the stream flows on, in spite of moralist and divine, the same as when Phædra and Thais loved each other in old Rome. We look back on these countless ages of city life, cooped in narrow streets and alleys and paved walks, breathing itself in fountained courts and shaded arcades, where youth and manhood and old age have sought their daily sustenance not only of bread but of happiness, and have with difficulty and toil enough found the one and caught fleeting glimpses of the other, between the dark thunder clouds, and under the weird, wintry sky of many a life. Within such a little space how much life is crowded, what high hopes, how much pain! From those high windows behind the flower-pots young girls have looked out upon life, which their instincts told them was made for pleasure, but which year after year convinced them was, somehow or other, given over to pain. How can we read this endless story of humanity with any thought of blame? How can we watch this restless, quivering human life, this ceaseless effort of a finite creature to attain to those things which are agreeable to its created nature, alike in all countries, under all climates and skies, and whatever change of garb or semblance the long course of years may bring, with any other thought than that of tolerance and pity,—tolerance of every sort of city existence, pity for every kind of toil and evil, year after year repeated, in every one of earth's cities, full of human life and handicraft, and thought and love and pleasure, as in the streets of that old Jerusalem over which the Saviour wept?"—*John Inglesant.*

SIDNEY, ALGERNON, an Englisy patriot, grand-nephew of Sir Philip Sidney and son of the Earl of Leicester, born in 1622; executed at London in 1683. He served in Ireland, where his father was Lord Lieutenant, and in 1646 was made Governor of Dublin; next year, having received the thanks of the House of Commons, he was made Governor of Dover. He held republican views, and favored the substitution of a republic in place of the exisiting monarchy. He fell under the suspicion of the Government, and, upon the discovery of the Rye House plot in 1683, was arrested, together with Lord William Russell, and brought to trial before Judge Jeffrey for high treason. "Russel," says Macaulay, "who appears to have been guilty of no offense falling within the definition of high treason, and Sidney, of whose guilt no legal evidence could be produced, were beheaded in defiance of law and justice. Russell died with the fortitude of a Christian, Sidney with the fortitude of a Stoic." Six years afterwards, when William and Mary had come to the throne of England, the judgment against Sidney was annulled. His *Discourses Concerning Government*, were published in 1698.

GOVERNMENT AND LIBERTY.

Such as enter into society must in some degree diminish their liberty. Reason leads them to this. No one man or family is able to provide that which is requisite for their convenience or security; whilst every one has an equal right to everything, and none acknowledges a superior to determine the controversies that upon such occasions must continually arise, and will probably be so great that mankind cannot bear them. Therefore, though I do not believe what Bellarmine said, that a commonwealth could not exercise its power; for he could not be ignorant that Rome and Athens did exercise theirs, and that all regular kingdoms of the world are commonwealths; yet there is nothing of absurdity in saying that man cannot continue in the perpetual and entire fruition of the liberty that God hath given him. The liberty of one is thwarted by that of another, and whilst they are all equal none will yield to any, otherwise than by a general consent. This is the ground of all just governments; for fraud or violence can create no rights, and the same consent gives the form to them all.

Some small numbers of men, living within the precincts of one city, have, as it were, cast into a common stock the right which they had of governing themselves and children, and by common consent joining in one body, exercised such power over every single person as seemed beneficial to the whole; and this men call perfect Democracy. Others chose to be governed by a select number of such as most excelled in wisdom and virtue, and this, according to the signification of the word, was called Aristocracy; or when one man excelled all others, the government was put into his hands, under the name of Monarchy. But the wisest, best, and far the greatest part of mankind rejecting these simple species, did form governments mixed or composed of the three—as shall be proved hereafter—which commonly received their respective denomination from the part that prevailed, and did deserve praise or blame as they were well or ill proportioned.

It were a folly hereupon to say that the liberty for which we contend is of no use to us, since we cannot endure the solitude, barbarity, weakness, want, misery, and dangers that accompany it whilst we live alone, nor can enter into society without resigning it; for the choice of that society, and the liberty of framing it according to our own wills, for our own good, is all we seek. This remains to us, whilst we form governments that we ourselves are judges how far it is good for us to recede from our natural liberty; which is of so great importance that from thence only can we know whether we are freemen or slaves; and the difference between the best government and the worst doth wholly depend on a right or wrong exercise of that power. If men are naturally free, such as have wisdom and understanding will always frame good government. But if they are born under the necessity of a perpetual slavery, no wisdom can be of use to them; but all must forever depend upon the will of their lords, how cruel, mad, proud, or wicked soever they be. . . . .

We may conclude that no privilege is peculiarly annexed to any form of government; but that all magistrates are equally the ministers of God, who perform the work for which they are instituted; and that the people which institutes them may proportion, regulate, and terminate their power as to time, measure, and number of persons, as seems most convenient to themselves—which can be no other than their own good. For it cannot be imagined that a multitude of people should send for Numa, or any other person to whom they owed nothing, to reign over them, that he might live in glory and pleasure; or for any other reason than that it might be good for them and their posterity. This shows the work of all magistrates to be always and everywhere the same—even the doing of justice, and procuring the welfare of them that create them. This we learn from common sense. Plato, Aristotle, Cicero, and the best human authors, lay it down as an immovable foundation, upon which they build their arguments relating to matters of that nature.—*Discourses upon Government.*

SIDNEY, Sir Philip, an English author born at Penshurst, Kent, in 1554; died at Arnheim, Holland, in 1586. His father, Sir Henry Sidney, was President of Wales and Lord Deputy of Ireland, under Queen Elizabeth. In 1568 he entered Christ Church, Oxford; from 1572 to 1575 he travelled on the Continent, being at Paris at the time of the St. Bartholomew massacre. In 1577 he was sent to Prague as ambassador to the Emperor Rudolph II. The next year he incurred the displeasure of the Queen by an outspoken letter which he addressed to her, dissuading her from a projected marriage with the Duke of Anjou, and retired for some years to his estate, where most of his works appear to have been written, although they were not printed until after his death. In 1584 he was appointed Governor of Flushing, in Holland: and was wounded in the thigh at the battle of Zutphen, September 22, 1586. "As he was borne from the field," writes his friend and biographer, Lord Brooke, "being thirsty with excess of bleeding, he called for a drink, which was presently brought him; but as he was putting the bottle to his mouth he saw a poor soldier carried along, ghastly, casting up his eyes at the bottle; which Sir Philip perceiving, he took it from his head before he drank, and delivered it to the poor man with these words: 'Thy necessity is greater than mine.'" He lingered in great agony for several weeks, solacing even his last hours with literary composition. His body was taken to London and interred in St. Paul's Cathedral, the day being observed as one of general mourning. The principal works of Sir Philip Sidney are:

A Metrical Version of the Psalms, made in conjunction with his sister, the Countess of Pembroke; *Astrophel and Stella*, a series of more than a hundred sonnets; *Arcadia*, a prose romance, with poems interspersed through it; *The Apologie for Poesie*.

DESCRIPTION OF ARCADIA.

There were hills which garnished their proud heights with stately trees; humble valleys whose base estate seemed comforted with the refreshing of silver rivers; meadows enamelled with all sorts of eye-pleasing flowers; thickets, which being lined with most pleasant shade, were witnessed so too by the cheerful disposition of many well-tuned birds; each pasture stored with sheep, breeding with sober security, while the pretty lambs, with bleating oratory, craved the dam's comfort. Here a shepherd's boy piping as though he should never be old; there a young shepherdess knitting and singing withal; and it seemed that her voice comforted her hands to work, and her hands kept time to her voice-music.—*Arcadia.*

AN ARCADIAN LOVE-LETTER.

Most blessed paper, which shall kiss that hand whereto all blessedness is in nature a servant, do not disdain to carry with thee the woeful words of a miser [wretch] now despairing; neither be afraid to appear before her, bearing the base title of the sender; for no sooner shall that divine hand touch thee but that thy baseness shall be turned to most high preferment. Therefore, mourn boldly, my ink; for while she looks upon you your blackness will shine: cry out boldly, my lamentation; for while she reads you your cries will be music. Say, then, O happy messenger of a most unhappy message that the too soon born and too late dying creature, which dares not speak—no, not look—no, not scarcely think, as from his miserable self, unto her heavenly highness, only presumes to desire thee, in the times that her eyes and voice do exalt thee, to say, and in this manner to say, not from him —oh, no; that were not fit—but of him, thus much unto her sacred judgment:—O you, the only honor to women, to men the only admiration; you that, being armed by love defy him that armed you, in this high estate wherein you have placed me, yet let me remember him to whom I am bound for bringing me to your presence; and let me remember him who, since he is yours, how mean soever he be, it is reason you have an account of him. The wretch—yet your wretch—though with languishing steps, runs fast to his grave; and will you suffer a temple—how poorly built soever, but yet a temple of your deity—to be razed? But he dieth, it is most true, he dieth; and he in whom you live to obey you dieth. Whereof though he plain, he doth not complain; for it is a harm, but no wrong, which he hath received. He dies, because, in woeful language, all his senses tell him that such is your pleasure; for, since you will not that he live, alas! alas! what followeth—what followeth of the most ruined Dorus but his end? End, then, evil-destined Dorus, end; and end thou woeful letter, end; for it sufficeth her wisdom to know that her heavenly will shall be accomplished.

IN PRAISE OF POESIE.

Learned men have learnedly thought that where reason hath so much over-mastered passion, that the mind hath a free desire to do well, the inward light each man hath in himself is as good as a philosopher's book; since in Nature we know it is well to do well, and what is well and what is evil, although not in the words of art which philosophers bestow upon us; for out of natural conceit the philosophers drew it. But to be moved to do that which we know, or to be moved with desire to know, *hoc opus hic labor est.*

Now, therein, of all sciences—I speak of

human, and according to human conceit—is our poet the monarch. For he doth not only show the way but giveth so sweet a prospect into the way as will entice any man to enter into it. Nay, he doth—as if your journey should lie through a fair vineyard—at the very first give you a cluster of grapes, that full of that taste you may long to pass further. He beginneth not with obscure definitions, which must blur the margin with interpretations, and load the memory with doubtfulness; but he cometh to you with words set in delightful proportion, either accompanied with or prepared for the well-enchanting skill of music. And with a tale forsooth, he cometh unto you —with a tale which holdeth children from play, and old men from the chimney corner; and, pretending no more, doth intend the winning of the mind from wickedness to virtue; even as the child is often brought to take most wholesome things by hiding them in such other as have a pleasant taste; which, if any one should begin to tell them of the nature of the aloes or rhubarbum they should receive, would sooner take their physic at their ears than at their mouth. So is it in men—most of whom are childish in their best things till they be cradled in their graves.—*Defence of Poesie.*

TRUE BEAUTY VIRTUE IS.

It is most true that eyes are formed to serve
  The inward light, and that the heavenly part
Ought to be King, from whose rules who do 'swerve,
  Rebels to Nature, strive for their own smart.
  It is most true, what we call Cupid's dart
An image is which for ourselves we carve,
  And, fools, adore in temple of our heart,
Till that good god make Church and Churchmen starve.
  True, that True Beauty Virtue is indeed,
Whereof this Beauty can be but a shade
  Which elements with mortal mixtures breed.

True, that on earth we are but pilgrims made,
And should in soul up to our country move:
True; and yet true—that I must Stella love.
Astrophel and Stella.

ETERNAL LOVE.

Leave me, O Love which reachest but to dust,
And thou, my Mind, aspire to higher things;
Grow rich in that which never taketh rust:
Whatever fades, but fading pleasure brings.
Draw in thy beams, and humble all their might
To that sweet yoke where lasting freedoms be,
Which breaks the clouds, and opens forth the light
That doth both shine and give us light to see!
Oh, take fast hold; let that light be thy guide
In this small course which birth draws out to death;
And think how evil becometh him to slide,
Who seeketh heaven and comes of heavenly breath.
Then farewell, world! thy uttermost I see:
Eternal Love, maintain thy Life in me!
Astrophel and Stella.

TO SLEEP.

Come Sleep, O Sleep, the certain knot of peace,
The baiting-place of wit, the balm of woe,
The poor man's wealth, the prisoner's release,
The indifferent judge between the high and low!
With shield of proof shield me from out the prease
Of those fierce darts, Despair at me doth throw;
Oh, make in me those civil wars to cease,
I will good tribute pay if thou do so.
Take thou of me smooth pillows, sweetest bed,
A chamber deaf to noise and blind to light;
A rosy garland and a weary head.
And if these things, as being thine by right,

Move not thy heavy grace, thou shalt in me,
Lovelier than elsewhere, Stella's image see.
Astrophel and Stella.

INVOCATION TO NIGHT.

O Night! the ease of care, the pledge of pleasure,
Desire's best mean, harvest of hearts affected,
The seat of peace, the one which is erected
Of human life to be the quiet measure;
Be victor still of Phœbus's golden treasure,
Who hath our sight with too much sight infected;
Whose light is cause we have our time neglected,
Turning all Nature's course to self-displeasure.
These stately stars, in their now shining faces,
With sinless Sleep, and Silence—Wisdom's mother—
Witness this wrong, which by thy help is easèd.
Thou art, therefore, of these our desert places
The sure refuge; by thee, and by no other,
My soul is blest, sense joyed, and fortune raisèd.
Arcadia.

SIGOURNEY, LYDIA (HUNTLY), an American author, born at Norwich, Conn., in 1791; died at Hartford in 1865. In 1819 she was married to Charles Sigourney, a merchant of Hartford. She commenced her career of authorship with a volume of *Moral Pieces in Prose and Verse*. Her subsequent works in prose and verse, many of them juveniles, number more than sixty. Among them are: *Traits of the Aborigines* (1822), *Sketch of Connecticut* (1824), *Biography of Females* (1829), *How to be Happy* (1833), *Pleasant Memories of Pleasant Lands* (1842), *The Sea and the Sailor* (1845), *Whisper to a Bride* (1849), *Past Meridian* (1854), *Lucy Howard's Journal* (1857), *The Man of Uz* (1862), *Letters of Life*, a posthumous volume (1866).

INDIAN NAMES.

Ye say they all have passed away—that noble race and brave;
That their light canoes have vanished from off the crested wave:
That 'mid the forests where they roamed there rings no hunter's shout:—
But their name is on your waters—ye may not wash it out.

'Tis where Ontario's billow, like ocean's surge is curled;
Where strong Niagara's thunders wake the echo of the world;
Where red Missouri bringeth rich tribute from the west,
And Rappahannock sweetly sleeps on green Virginia's breast.

Ye say their cone-like cabins, that clustered o'er the vale,
Have fled away like withered leaves before the autumn's gale:—

But their memory liveth on your hills, their baptism on your shore;
Your everlasting rivers speak their dialect of yore.

Old Massachusetts wears it upon her lordly crown,
And broad Ohio bears it amid her young renown;
Connecticut hath wreathed it where her quiet foliage waves,
And bold Kentucky breathes it hoarse through all her ancient caves.

Wachusetts hides its lingering voice within his rocky heart,
And Alleghany graves its tone throughout his lordly chart;
Monadnock on his forehead hoar doth seal the sacred trust:
Your mountains build their monument, though ye destroy their dust.

Ye call these red-browed brethren the insects of an hour,
Crushed like the noteless worm amid the regions of their power;
Ye drive them from their fathers' lands, ye break of faith the seal;
But can ye from the court of heaven exclude their last appeal?

Ye see their unresisting tribes, with toilsome step and slow,
On through the trackless desert pass—a caravan of woe:—
Think ye the Eternal Ear is deaf? By sleepless vision dim?
Think ye the soul's blood may not cry from that far land to Him?

THE BLESSED RAIN.

I marked at morn the thirsty earth,
  By lingering drought oppressed,
Like sick man in a fever heat,
  With panting brow and breast;

But evening brought a cheering sound
  Of music o'er the pane:
The voice of heavenly showers that said,
  "Oh, blessed, blessed rain!"

The pale and suffocating plants,
  That bowed themselves to die,
Imbibed the pure, reprieving drops—
  Sweet gift of a pitying sky;
The fern and heath upou the rock,
  And the daisy on the plain,
Each whispered to their new-born buds,
  "Oh, blessed, blessed rain!"

The herds that o'er the wasted fields
  Roamed with dejected eye,
To find their verdant pasture brown,
  Their crystal brooklet dry,
Rejoiced within the mantling pool
  To stand refreshed again,
Each infant ripple leaping high,
  To meet the blessed rain.

The farmer sees his crisping corn,
  Whose tassels swept the ground,
Uplift once more a stately head,
  With hopeful beauty crowned;
While the idly lingering water-wheel,
  Where the miller ground his grain,
Turns gayly round, with a dashing sound,
  At the touch of the blessed rain.

Lord, if our drooping souls too long
  Should close their upward wing,
And the adhesive dust of earth
  All darkly round them cling,
Send Thou such showers of quickening grace
  That the angelic train
Shall to our grateful shout respond,
  "Oh, blessed, blessed rain!"

SILL, EDWARD ROWLAND, an American poet, born at Windsor, Conn., in 1841; died at Cleveland, Ohio, in 1887. He was graduated at Yale in 1861, and went to the Pacific coast. Returning in 1866, he studied theology at Harvard. Subsequently he taught in Ohio, and in 1871 became principal of the high school at Oakland, Cal. From 1874 till 1882 he was Professor of English Language and Literature at the University of California, and afterwards devoted himself to literary work at his home at Cuyahoga Falls. His early poems were published collectively, in 1868. Since his death two other collections have been put forth by his friends: *Poems by Edward Rowland Sill* (1888), and *The Hermitage, and Later Poems* (1890).

SPRING TWILIGHT.

Singing in the rain, robin?
  Rippling out so fast
All thy flute-like notes, as if
  This singing were thy last!

After sundown, too, robin?
  Though the fields are dim,
And the trees grow dark and still,
  Dripping from leaf and limb.

'Tis heart-broken music—
  That sweet, faltering strain,—
Like a mingled memory,
  Half ecstasy, half pain.

Surely thus to sing, robin,
  Thou must have in sight
Beautiful skies behind the shower,
  And dawn beyond the night.

Would thy faith were mine, robin!
  Then though night were long,
All its silent hours should melt
  Their sorrow into song.

SERVICE.

Fret not that the day is gone,
And thy task is still undone.
'Twas not thine, it seems, at all:
Near to thee it chanced to fall,
Close enough to stir thy brain,
And to vex thy heart in vain,
Somewhere, in a nook forlorn,
Yesterday a babe was born:
He shall do thy waiting task;
All thy questions he shall ask,
And the answers will be given,
Whispered lightly out of heaven.
His shall be no stumbling feet,
Falling where they should be fleet;
He shall hold no broken clue;
Friends shall unto him be true;
Men shall love him; falsehood's aim
Shall not shatter his good name.
Day shall nerve his arm with light,
Slumber soothe him all the night;
Summer's peace and winter's storm
Help him all his will perform.
'Tis enough of joy for thee
His high service to foresee.

A MORNING THOUGHT.

What if some morning, when the stars are paling,
And the dawn whitened, and the East was clear,
Strange peace and rest fell on me from the presence
Of a benignant Spirit standing near:

And I should tell him, as he stood beside me,
"This is our Earth—most friendly Earth, and fair;
Daily its sea and shore through sun and shadow
Faithful it turns, robed in its azure air:

"There is blest living here, loving and serving,
And quest of truth, and serene friendships dear;

But stay not, Spirit! Earth has one destroyer—
His name is Death: flee, lest he find thee here!'

And what if then, while the still morning brightened,
And freshened in the elm the Summer's breath,
Should gravely smile on me the gentle angel
And take my hand and say, "My name is Death."

OPPORTUNITY.

This I beheld, or dreamed it in a dream:—
There spread a cloud of dust along a plain;
And underneath the cloud, or in it, raged
A furious battle, and men yelled, and swords
Shocked upon swords and shields. A prince's banner
Wavered, then staggered backward, hemmed by foes.
A craven hung along the battle's edge,
And thought, "Had I a sword of keener steel—
That blue blade that the king's son bears,—but this
Blunt thing—!" he snapt and flung it from his hand,
And lowering crept away and left the field.
Then came the king's son, wounded, sore bestead
And weaponless, and saw the broken sword,
Hilt-buried in the dry and trodden sand,
And ran and snatched it, and with battle-shout
Lifted afresh he hewed his enemy down
And saved a great cause that heroic day.

SILLIMAN, BENJAMIN, an American scientist, born at Trumbull, Conn., in 1779; died at New Haven in 1864. He graduated at Yale in 1796; became tutor in the College in 1799, and in 1804 was made Professor of Chemistry, Mineralogy, and Geology. He visited Europe in 1805 for the purpose of procuring books and apparatus, and published a *Journal of Travels*, describing this visit. Nearly fifty years afterwards he again went to Europe, and published *A Visit to Europe in* 1851. In 1818 he founded *The American Journal of Science and Arts*, which he conducted for nearly thirty years. In 1853 he resigned his professorship at Yale, and received the honorary title of "Professor Emeritus." His principal work is *Elements of Chemistry in the Order of the Lectures in Yale College* (1830). He wrote largely upon scientific topics in his own *Journal* and in other periodicals, and delivered courses of popular lectures in all the principal cities in the United States.

THE NATURE OF GEOLOGICAL EVIDENCE.

Geological evidence is the same which is readily admitted as satisfactory in the case of historical antiquities. When, in 1738, the workmen, in excavating a well, struck upon the theatre of Herculaneum, which had reposed for more than sixteen centuries beneath the lava of Vesuvius —when, in 1748, Pompeii was disencumbered of its volcanic ashes and cinders, and thus two buried cities were brought to light—had history been quite silent respecting their existence, would not observers say, and have they not actually said, here are the works of man—his temples, his forums, his amphitheatres, his tombs, his shops of traffic and of arts, his houses, furniture, pictures, and personal ornaments; here are his streets, with their pavements and wheel-ruts worn in the solid stone, his coins, his grinding-mills, his wine, food, and medicines; here are his dungeon and stocks, with the skeletons of the prisoners chained in their awful solitudes; and here and there are the bones of a victim who, although at liberty, was overtaken by the fiery storm. while others were quietly buried in their domestic retreats. The falling cinders and ashes copied, as they fell, even the delicate outlines of the female form, as well as the head and helmet of a sentinel; and having concreted, they thus remain true volcanic casts, to be seen by remote generations, as now, in the Museum of Naples.

Because the soil had formed, and grass and trees had grown, and successive generations of men had unconsciously walked, tilled the ground, or built their houses over the entombed cities, and because they were covered by volcanic cinders, ashes, and projected stones, does any one hesitate to admit that they were once real cities; that at the time of their destruction they stood upon what was then the upper surface; that their streets once rang with the noise of business, their halls and theatres with the voice of pleasure; that in an evil time they were overwhelmed by a volcanic tempest from Vesuvius, and their name and place for more than seventeen centuries blotted out from the earth and forgotten? The tragical story is legibly perused by every observer, and all alike, whether learned or unlearned, agree in the conclusions to be drawn.

SIMMONS, BARTHOLOMEW, a British poet, born in County Cork, Ireland, in 1811; died in 1850. In 1837, and for ten years subsequently, he was a frequent contributor to *Blackwood's Magazine.* He held a situation in the Excise Office of London, which was for many years his residence. A collection of his *Legends, Lyrics, and Other Poems* was published in 1843.

THE MOTHER OF KINGS.

[*A Lady who visited "Madame Letitia," the mother of Napoleon, then in her eighty-fourth year, describes her as lying on her bed, the room being hung around with portraits of her children.*]

Strange looked that lady old, reclined
  Upon her lonely bed
In that vast chamber, echoing not
  To page or maiden's tread;
And stranger still the gorgeous forms,
  In portrait, that glanced round
From the high walls, with cold, bright looks
  More eloquent than sound.

They were her children: never yet,
  Since, with the primal beam,
Fair Painting brought on rainbow wings
  Its own immortal beam,
Did one fond mother give such race
  Beneath its smile to glow,
As they who now back on her brow
  Their pictured glories throw.

Her daughters there—the beautiful!
  Looked down in dazzling sheen:
One lovelier than the Queen of Love,
  One crowned an earthly Queen.
Her sons—the proud—the Paladins—
  With diadem and plume,
Each leaning on his sceptred arm,
  Made empire of that room. . . . .

But right before her couch's foot
  One mightier picture blazed,

One form august, to which her eyes
  Incessantly were raised;
A monarch's too—and monarch-like
  The artist's hand had bound him,
With jewelled belt, imperial sword,
  And ermined purple round him.

One well might deem, from the white flags
  That o'er him flashed and rolled,
Where the puissant lily laughed
  And waved its bannered gold,
And from the Lombard's iron crown
  Beneath his hand which lay,
That Charlemagne had burst Death's reign
  And leaped again to day.

How gleamed that awful countenance,
  Magnificently stern!
In its dark smile and smiting look
  What destiny we learn!
The laurel simply wreathes that brow,
  While nations watch its nod,
As though he scoffed all pomp below,
  The thunderbolt of God.

Such was the scene—the noontide hour—
  Which, after many a year,
Had swept above the memory
  Of his meteor-like career—
Saw the mother of the mightiest—
  Napoleon's mother—lie,
With the living dead around her,
  With the Past before her eye.

SIMMS, WILLIAM GILMORE, an American novelist and poet, born at Charleston, S. C., in 1806; died there in 1870. He was for a time a clerk in a drug-store; afterwards studied law, and was admitted to the bar, but did not enter upon regular practice. In 1827 he put forth a volume of *Lyrical and Other Poems*, which was followed from time to time by other volumes of verse, among which are: *The Vision of Cortes* (1829), *Atlantis* (1832), *Southern Passages and Pictures* (1839), *Areytos* (1846), *Lays of the Palmetto* (1848), and a fresh collection of *Poems* (1854). He wrote biographies of *Francis Marion* (1844), *Captain John Smith* (1846), and *Nathanael Greene* (1849), and edited a volume of *The War Poetry of the South* (1867). The greater part of his works consist of novels, of which he wrote about thirty, among which are: *Martin Faber* (1833), *Guy Rivers* (1834), *Pelayo* (1838), *The Yemassee* (1840), *The Scout* (1845), *Katherine Walton* (1851), *Charlemont* (1856), *The Cassique of Kiawah* (1860). An edition of the novels by which he set most store was published in 1859, in nineteen volumes. His *Life* has been written by George W. Cable in the "American Men of Letters," series (1888).

FASCINATED BY A RATTLESNAKE.

Before the maiden rose a little clump of bushes—bright tangled leaves flaunting wide in the glossiest green, with vines trailing over them, thickly decked with blue and crimson flowers. Her eyes communed vacantly with these; fastened by a star-like shining glance, a subtle ray that shot out from the circle of green leaves, seeming to be their very eye, and sending out a fluid lustre that seemed to stream across the space between, and find its way into her own eyes. Very piercing was that beautiful and subtle brightness,—of the sweetest, strangest power. And now the leaves quivered, and seemed to float away only to return; and the vines waved and swung around in fantastic mazes, unfolding ever-changing varieties of form and color to her gaze; but the one star-like eye was ever steadfast, bright, and gorgeous, gleaming in their midst, and still fastened with strange fondness upon her own. How beautiful, with wondrous intensity, did it gleam and dilate, growing larger and more lustrous with every ray which it sent forth!

And her own glance became intense; fixed also, but with a dreaming sense that conjured up the wildest fancies, terribly beautiful, that took her soul away from her, and wrapt it about as with a spell. She would have fled, she would have flown; but she had not power to move. The will was wanting to her flight. She felt that she could have bent forward to pluck the gem-like thing from the bosom of the leaf in which it seemed to grow, and which it irradiated with its bright gleam, but even as she aimed to stretch forth her hand and bend forward, she heard a rush of wings and a shrill scream from the tree above her—such a scream as the mocking-bird makes, when angrily it raises its dusky crest and flaps its wings furiously against its slender sides. Such a scream seemed like a warning, and though yet unawakened to full consciousness, it startled her, and forbade her effort.

More than once, in her survey of this strange object, had she heard that shrill note, and still had it carried to her ear the same note of warning, and to her mind the same vague consciousness of an evil presence. But the star-like eye was yet upon her own: a small, bright eye, quick, like that of a bird; now steady in its place and observant seemingly of hers, now darting forward with all the clustering leaves about it, and shooting up towards her, as if wooing her to seize. At another moment, invited to the vine which lay around it, it would whirl round and round, dazzlingly bright and beautiful, even as a torch waving hurriedly by night in the hands of some playful boy. But in all this time the glance was never taken from her own; there it grew fixed—a very principle of light—and such a light—a subtle, burning, piercing, fascinating gleam, such as gathers in vapor above the old grave, and binds us as we look—shooting, darting, directly into her eye, dazzling her gaze, defeating its sense of discrimination, and confusing strangely that of perception. She felt dizzy; for, as she looked, a cloud of colors, bright, gay, various colors, floated and hung, like so much drapery, around the single object that had so secured her attention and spell-bound her feet. Her limbs felt momently more and more insecure; her blood grew cold, and she seemed to feel the gradual freeze of vein by vein throughouth er person.

At that moment a rustling was heard in the branches of the tree beside her; and the bird, which had repeatedly uttered a single cry above her, as if it were of warning, flew away from his station with a scream more piercing than ever. This movement had the effect, for which it really seemed intended, of bringing back to her a portion of the consciousness she seemed so totally to have been deprived of before. She strove to move from before the beautiful but terrible presence, but for a while she strove in vain. The rich, star-like glance still riveted her own, and the subtle fascination kept her bound. The mental energies, however, with the moment of their greatest trial, now gathered suddenly to her aid, and with a desperate effort, but with a feeling still of most annoying uncertainty and dread, she succeeded partially in the attempt, and threw her arms backwards, her hands grasping the neighboring tree, feeble, tottering, and depending upon it for that support which her own limbs almost entirely denied her.

With that movement, however, came the full development of the powerful spell and dreadful mystery before her. As her feet receded, though but for a single pace, to the tree against which she now rested, the audibly-articulated ring—like that of a watch when wound up, but with the verge broken—announced the nature of that splendid yet dangerous presence, in the form of the monstrous rattlesnake, now but a few feet before her, lying coiled at the bottom of a beautiful shrub, with which, to her dreaming eye, many of its own glorious hues had become associated. She was at length conscious enough to perceive and to feel all her danger; but terror had denied her the strength necessary to fly from her dreadful enemy. There still the eye glared beautifully bright and piercing upon her own; and seemingly in a spirit of sport, the insidious reptile slowly unwound itself from his coil, but only to gather himself up again into his muscular rings, his great flat head rising in the midst, and slowly nodding, as it were, towards her, the eye still peering deeply into her own, the rattle still slightly ringing at intervals and giving forth that paralyzing sound which, once heard, is remembered forever.

The reptile all this while appeared to be conscious of and to sport with, while seeking to excite her terrors. Now, with its flat head, distended mouth, and curving neck, would it dart forward its long form towards her; its fatal teeth, unfolding on either side of its upper jaw, seeming to threaten her with instantaneous death; while its powerful eye shot forth glances of that fatal power of fascination, malignantly bright, which, by paralyzing with a novel form of terror and of beauty, may readily account for the spell it possesses of binding the feet of the timid, and denying to fear even the privilege of flight. Could she have fled? She felt the necessity; but the power of her limbs was gone. And there it still lay, coiling and uncoiling, its arched neck glittering like a ring of brazed copper, bright and lurid; and the dreadful beauty of its eye still fastened, eagerly contemplating the victim, while the pendulous rattle still rang the death-note, as if to prepare the conscious mind for the fate which is momently approaching to the blow.

Meanwhile the stillness became deathlike, with all surrounding objects. The bird had gone with its scream and rush. The breeze was silent; the vines ceased to wave; the leaves faintly quivered on their stems. The serpent once more lay still; but the eye was never once turned away from the victim. Its corded muscles are all in coil; they have but to unclasp suddenly, and the dreadful folds will be upon her; its full length, and the fatal teeth will strike, and the deadly venom which they secrete will mingle with the life-blood in her veins.

The terrified damsel—her full consciousness restored, but not her strength—feels all her danger. She sees that the sport of the terrible reptile is at an end. She cannot now mistake the horrid expression of its eye. She strives to scream, but the voice dies away, a feeble gurgling in her throat. Her tongue is paralyzed; her lips are sealed; once more she strives for flight, but her limbs refuse their office. She has nothing left of life but its fearful consciousness. It is in her despair that—a last effort —she succeeds to scream—a single wild cry, forced from her by the accumulated agony. She sinks down upon the grass before her enemy, her eyes, however, still open, and still looking upon those which he directs forever upon them. She sees him approach; now advancing, now receding; now swelling in every part with something like anger, while his neck is arched beautifully, like that of a wild horse under the curb; until at length, tired as it were of play, like the cat with its victim, she sees the neck growing larger, and becoming completely bronzed, as about to strike—the huge jaws unclosing almost directly above her, the long tubulated fang, charged with venom, protruding from the cavernous mouth—and she sees no more. Insensibility came to her aid, and she lay almost lifeless under the very folds of the monster.

In that moment the copse parted, and an arrow piercing the monster through and through the neck, bore his head forward to the ground, alongside the maiden; while his spiral extremities, now unfolding in his own agony, were actually in part writhing upon her person. The arrow came from the fugitive Occonestoga, who had fortunately reached the spot in season on his way to the Block House. He rushed from the copse as the snake fell, and with a stick fearlessly approached him where he lay tossing in agony upon the grass.

Seeing him advance, the courageous reptile made an effort to regain his coil, shaking the fearful rattle violently at every evolution which he took for that purpose; but the arrow, completely passing through his neck, opposed an unyielding obstacle to his endeavor; and finding it hopeless, and seeing the new enemy about to assault him—with something of the spirit of the white man under like circumstances —he turned desperately round, and striking his charged fangs, so that they were riveted in the wound they made, into a susceptible part of his own body, he threw himself over with a single convulsion and a moment after lay dead beside the nearly unconscious maiden.—*The Yemassee.*

SIMONIDES, a Greek lyric poet, born on the island of Cos, in 556 B. C., died at Syracuse in 469 B. C. Shortly before the Persian War he went to Athens, where he wrote numerous epigrams, elegies, and dirges in connection with that memorable contest. In 477 B. C. he was for the fifty-sixth time victor in a poetical contest at Athens. Towards the close of his life he took up his residence at the Court of Hiero, ruler of Syracuse, on the island of Sicily. Many of his pieces relating to the Persian War have been handed down in the "Greek Anthology."

EPIGRAMS, EPITAPHS, AND ELEGIES.

Go, passer-by, to Lacedæmon tell,
That here, obedient to her laws, we fell.
Of those at famed Thermopylæ who lie,
Glorious the fortune, bright their destiny.
Their tomb an altar is; their noble name
A fond remembrance of ancestral fame;
Their death a song of triumph. Neither rust,
Nor time that turns all mortal things to dust,—
Shall dim the splendor of that holy shrine,
Where Greece forever sees her native virtues shine.

Nobly to die! if that be Virtue's crown,
Fortune to us her bounty well displayed.
Striving to make Greece free, we gained renown
That shrouds us where we lie, and ne'er can fade.

DANAË.

Whilst, around her lone ark sweeping,
  Wailed the winds and waters wild,
Her wan cheeks all wan and weeping,
  Danaë clasped her sleeping child.

And, "Alas," cried she, "my dearest,
  What deep wrongs, what woes are mine!
But not woes nor wrongs thou fearest,
  In that sinless rest of thine.

Faint the moonbeams break above thee,
And within here, all is gloom;
But wrapt fast in arms that love thee,
  Little reck'st thou of thy doom.

"Not the rude spray round thee flying
  Has ever damped thy clustering hair,
On thy purple mantlet lying,
  O mine Innocent, my Fair!
Yet, to thee were Sorrow sorrow,
  Thou would'st lend thy little ear,
And this heart of mine might borrow
  Haply yet a moment's cheer.

"But no. Slumber on, Babe, slumber;
Slumber, Ocean-waves; and you,
My dark troubles without number,
  Oh! that ye would slumber too!
Though with wrongs they've brimmed my
    chalice,
  Grant, Jove, that in future years
This boy may defeat their malice,
  And avenge his mother's tears!"

Transl. of William Peters.

SISMONDI, Jean Charles Leonard Simonde, de. a Swiss historian, born at Geneva in 1773; died there in 1842. At an early age he was placed in a mercantile house at Geneva. But the storms of the French Revolution compelled the family to take refuge in England. In 1795 his father bought a small farm in Tuscany, and the young man had leisure for the pursuit of literature. When peace was finally restored to Europe, Sismondi returned to his native city, where he devoted himself to historical composition. His principal works are: *History of the Italian Republics*, *Literature of the South of Europe*; *Fall of the Roman Empire* and *History of France*. This last enormous work was begun in 1819, and though he labored steadily upon it, it was not fully completed at his death in 1842.

THE OVERTHROW OF THE OLD CIVILIZATION.

The longest, the most universal, the most important of all the convulsions to which the human race has been exposed is that which destroyed the whole fabric of ancient civilization, and prepared the elements out of which the structure of modern life is composed. It found men at the highest point of perfection which they had as yet attained to, whether in the career of social organization and of legislation, or in those of philosophy, literature, or art; and hurried them down by reiterated shocks, each more terrific than the last, into the deepest night of barbarism.

Its influence embraced all that portion of the human race which had any consciousness of its present condition, any power of preserving the memory of its past existence; consequently all that portion whose thoughts have come down to us by means of written records. Dating its commencement from the reign of the Antonines

—the period at which the human race seemed to have reached its highest point of prosperity —and having its progress, through each succeeding shock, to the almost total dissolution of all the old-established associations of men, and to the reconstruction of society from its very foundations, this revolution continued through at least eight centuries.

The Roman Empire, which then extended over the whole of what was then believed to be the habitable earth, was invaded, ravaged, depopulated, dismembered, by the various tribes of barbarians who rushed in upon all its borders. The conquering nations which had possessed themselves of its ruins made repeated attempts to found monarchies upon its antique soil. All, after two or three generations, vanished; then imperfect and barbarous institutions were insufficient to the preservation of national life. Two great men arose—Mohammed in the East, Charlemagne in the West—each of whom tried to put himself at the head of a new order of society. Each of them founded an empire which for a time rivalled the ancient power of Rome. But the moment of reorganization was not yet come. The throne of the Khaliphs, the empire of the Carlovingians, soon crumbled into dust.

The nations of the earth then seemed in a state of general dissolution; the various races of men were intermingled; a violent and short-lived power was seized by Kings, Dukes, Emirs, who were not Chiefs of the People, but accidental masters of a fraction of territory whose boundaries were marked by chance alone. No man could feel that he was bound to any land, as a son to a mother; no man could feel himself the lawful subject of any Government. Society could no longer afford protection to its members, and could no longer claim their allegiance in return. At length the moment arrived in which the proprietors of land built themselves strongholds; in which cities surrounded themselves with walls; in which all men armed for their own defence. Each individual was compelled to take a share of the government into his own hands, and thus to begin society anew from its very foundations.

Such was the tremendous revolution which took place between the third and the tenth centuries of our era; and yet from its very universality and duration it is impossible to find one common name under which to designate it. If we would grasp one comprehensive idea of this gigantic catastrophe we must, so to speak, collect its several incidents into one focus; we must reject all those circumstances which dissipate the attention; we must confine ourselves to the grand movements of each people and of each age; we must show the co-operation of the barbarian conquerors, who were themselves unconscious that they acted in concert. We must trace the moral history of the world, regardless of the details of wars and of crimes. We must seek in an enlightened appreciation of causes that unity of design which it were impossible to find in a scene so full of rapid and various movement. The earlier half of the Middle Ages appears to our eye like a chaos; but this chaos conceals beneath its ruins most important subjects for reflection.—*Preface to Fall of the Roman Empire.*

THE TENTH CENTURY: ANTICIPATED END OF THE WORLD.

At the close of the tenth century an almost universal expectation was entertained of the approaching end of the world. So strong was this belief that it led the greater part of the contemporary writers to lay down the pen. For a while silence was complete; for historians cared not to write for a posterity whose existence was so doubtful. Pious persons who had endeavored to understand the Apocalypse, and to determine the time of the accomplishment of its prophecies, had been particularly struck with the twentieth chapter, where it is announced that after the lapse of a thousand years. Satan would be let loose to deceive the nations; but that after a little season God would cause a fire to come down from heaven and devour him. The accomplishment of all the awful prophecies contained in this book appeared therefore to be at hand; and the end of the world was supposed to be indicated by the devouring fire and by the first resurrection of the dead. The nearer the thousandth year from the birth of Christ approached, the more did terror take possession of every mind. The archives of all countries contain a great number of charters of the tenth century, beginning with these words—*Appropinquante fine Mundi.* "As the end of the world is approaching." . .

We are struck with a sort of affright at the idea of the state of disorganization into which the belief of the imminent approaching end of the world must have thrown society. All the ordinary motives of action were suspended, or superseded by contrary ones; every passion of the mind was hushed, and the Present was lost in the appalling Future. The entire mass of the Christian nations seemed to feel that they stood in the situation of a condemned criminal, who had received his sentence, and counted the hours which still separated him from eternity. Every exertion of mind or body was become objectless, saving the labors of the faithful to secure their salvation; any provision for an earthly futurity must have appeared absurd; any monument erected for an age which was never to arrive would have been a contradiction; any historical records written for a generation never to arrive would have betrayed a want of faith.

It is almost a matter of surprise that a belief so general as this would appear to have been, did not bringabout its own dreaded fulfilment; that it did not transform the West into one vast convent; and by causing a total cessation of labor, deliver up the human race to universal and hopeless famine. But doubtless the force of habit was still stronger with many than the disease of the imagination. Besides, some uncertainty as to chronology had caused hesitation between two or three different periods; and though many charters attest "certain and evident signs," which left no room for doubt of the rapid approach of the end of the world, yet the constant order of the seasons, the regularity of Nature, the beneficence of Providence, which continued to cover the earth with its wonted fruits, raised questions even in the most timid minds. At last the extreme period fixed by the prophecies was past; the end of the world had not arrived; the terror was gradually but entirely dissipated; and it was universally acknowledged that on this subject the language of the sacred Scriptures had been misunderstood.—*Fall of the Roman Empire.*

THE IMPROVVISATORE.

He would not be an improvvisatore if he did not entirely abandon himself to the impression of the moment, or if he trusted more to his memory than to his feelings. After having been informed of his subject, the improvvisatore remains a moment in meditation, to view it in its various lights, and to shape out a plan of the little poem which he is about to compose. He then prepares the eight first verses, that his mind during the recitation of them may receive the proper impulse, and that he may awaken that powerful emotion, which makes him, as it were, a new being. In about seven or eight minutes he is fully prepared, and commences his poem, which often consists of five or six hundred verses. His eyes wander around him, his features glow, and he struggles with the prophetic spirit which seems to animate him. Nothing in the present age can represent in so striking a manner the Pythia of Delphos, when the god descended and spoke by her mouth. —*Historical View of the Literature of the South of Europe.*

SMILES, SAMUEL, a British author, born at Haddington, Scotland, in 1816. He studied surgery, practised for some time at Leeds, and afterwards became editor of the *Leeds Times*. In 1845 he became Secretary of the Leeds and Thirsk Railway, and seven years later of the Southeastern Railway, holding that position until 1866. The greater portion of his works are biographical, relating especially to men who have borne an important part in invention and industrial operations. Among these works are: *The Life of George Stephenson* (1857), *Self-Help* (1859), *Lives of the Engineers* (1861), *Industrial Biography* (1863), *The Huguenots in England and Scotland* (1867), *Character* (1871), *The Huguenots in France* (1874), *Duty* (1880), *Life and Labor* (1887).

OLD INVENTIONS REVIVED.

Steam-locomotion, by sea and land, had long been dreamt of and attempted. Blasco de Garay made his experiment in the harbor of Barcelona as early as 1543; Denis Papin made a similar attempt at Cassel in 1707; but it was not until Watt had solved the problem of the steam-engine that the idea of the steamboat could be developed in practice, which was done by Miller of Dalswinton, in 1788. Sages and poets have frequently foreshadowed inventions of great practical moment. Thus Dr. Darwin's anticipation of the locomotive, in his *Botanic Garden*, published in 1791, before any locomotive had been invented, might almost be regarded as prophetic:—

> "Soon shall thine arm, unconquered steam, afar
> Drag the slow barge, and drive the rapid car."

Denis Papin first threw out the idea of atmospheric locomotion; and Gauthery, another Frenchman, in 1782, projected a method of conveying parcels and merchandise by subterranean tubes. . . . .

Even the reaping-machine is an old invention revived. Thus Barnabas Googe, the translator of a book from the German, entitled *The Whole Arte and Trade of Husbandrie*, published in 1577, speaks of the reaping-machine as a worn-out invention—a thing "which was woont to be used in France. The device was a lowe kind of carre with a couple of wheeles, and the front armed with sharp syckles, which forced by the beaste through the corne did cut al before it. This tricke might be used in levell and champion countreys; but with us it wolde make but ill-favored woorke." . . .

There is every reason to believe that the Romans knew of gunpowder, though they only used it for purposes of fireworks; while the secret of the destructive Greek fire has been lost altogether. When gunpowder came to be used for purposes of war, invention busied itself upon instruments of destruction. When recently examining the Museum of the Arsenal at Venice, we were surprised to find numerous weapons of the fifteenth and sixteenth centuries embodying the most recent English improvements in arms, such as revolving pistols, rifled muskets, and breech-loading cannon. The latter, embodying Sir William Armstrong's modern idea, though in a rude form, had been fished up from the bottom of the Adriatic, where the ship armed with them had been sunk hundreds of years ago. Even Perkins's steam-gun was an old invention revived by Leonardo da Vinci, and by him attributed to Archimedes. The Congreve rocket is said to have an Eastern origin, Sir William Congreve having observed its destructive effects when employed by the forces under Tippoo Saib in the Mahratta war; on which he adopted and improved the missile, and brought out the invention as his own. . . .

The use of ether as an anæsthetic was known to Albertus Magnus, who flourished in the thirteenth century; and in his works he gives a recipe for its preparation. In 1681 Denis Papin published his *Traité des Opéra-*

tions sans Douleur, showing that he had discovered methods of deadening pain. But the use of anæsthetics is much older than Albertus Magnus or Papin; for the ancients had their *nepenthe* and *mandragora;* the Chinese their *mayo*, and the Egyptians their *hachish*—both preparations of *Cannabis Indica*—the effects of which in a great measure resemble those of chloroform.

What is perhaps still more surprising is the circumstance that one of the most elegant of recent inventions—that of sun-painting by the daguerreotype —was in the fifteenth century known to Leonardo da Vinci, whose skill as an architect and engraver, and whose accomplishments as a chemist and natural philosopher, have been almost entirely overshadowed by his genius as a painter. The idea thus early born lay in oblivion until 1760, when the daguerreotype was again clearly indicated in a book published in Paris, written by a certain Tiphanie de la Roche, under the anagrammatic title of *Giphantie*. Still later, at the beginning of the present century, we find Josiah Wedgwood, Sir Humphry Davy, and James Watt making experiments on the action of light upon nitrate of silver; and only within the last few months a silvered copperplate has been found amongst the old household lumber of Matthew Boulton, Watt's partner, having on it a representation of the old premises at Soho, apparently taken by some such process.—*Industrial Biography.*

SMITH, ADAM, a Scottish philosopher, born at Kirkcaldy in 1723; died at Edinburgh in 1790. He studied for three years at the University of Glasgow, then for seven years at Oxford. In 1748 he took up his residence at Edinburgh, where he lectured on rhetoric and belles-lettres. In 1752 he was made Professor of Moral Philosophy in the University of Glasgow, holding that position for nearly twelve years. In 1759 he published his *Theory of the Moral Sentiments*, the cardinal idea of which is that the emotions and moral distinctions spring from sympathy. In 1766 he resigned his professorship, and travelled for two years on the Continent. He then took up his residence with his mother at his native Kirkcaldy, where for ten years he devoted himself to the study of social science. The result was his *Inquiry into the Nature and Causes of the Wealth of Nations*, which was published in 1776, and is conceded to be the first systematic statement of the fundamental principles of political economy, though many of the views of Smith have been called in question by later writers. In 1778 he was appointed one of the Commissioners of Customs for Scotland, a position which gave him a large income, the surplus of which was devoted to charitable purposes. In 1787 he was elected Lord Rector of the University of Glasgow.

ADVANTAGES OF THE DIVISION OF LABOR.

Observe the accommodation of the most common artificer or day-laborer in a civilized and thriving country, and you will perceive that the number of people of whose industry a part —though but a small part—has been employed in procuring him this accommodation, exceeds all computation. The woollen coat, for example, which covers the day-laborer, as coarse and rough as it may appear, is the produce of the joint labor of a great number of workmen. The shepherd, the sorter of the wool, the woolcomber or carder, the dyer, the scribbler, the spinner, the weaver, the fuller, the dresser, with many others, must all join their different arts in order to complete even this homely production. How many merchants and carriers, besides, must have been employed in transporting the materials from some of the workmen to others, who live in a very distant part of the country. How much commerce and navigation, in particular; how many shipbuilders, sailors, sail-makers, rope-makers, must have been employed to bring together the different drugs made use of by the dyer, which often come from the remotest parts of the world. To say nothing of such complicated machines as the ship of the sailor, the mill of the fuller, or even the loom of the weaver, let us consider only what a variety of labor is requisite in order to form that very simple machine, the shears with which the shepherd clips the wool. The miner, the builder of the furnace for smelting the ore, the feller of the timber, the burner of the charcoal to be made use of in the smelting-house, the brick-maker, the bricklayer, the workmen who attend the furnace, the millwright, the forger, the smith, must all of them join their different arts in order to produce them.

Were we to examine in the same manner all the different parts of his dress and household furniture—the coarse linen shirt which he wears next his skin, the shoes which cover his feet, the bed which he lies on, and all the different parts which compose it, the kitchen-grate at which he prepares his victuals, the coals which he makes use of for that purpose, dug from the bowels of the earth, and brought to him, perhaps, by a long sea and a long land-carriage; all the other utensils of his kitchen, all the furniture of his table, the knives and forks, the earthen and pewter plates upon which he serves up and divides his victuals; the different hands employed in preparing his bread and his beer, the glass window which lets in the heat and the light, and keeps out the wind and the rain; with all the knowledge and art requisite for preparing that beautiful and happy invention without which these northern parts of the world could scarce have afforded a very comfortable habitation, together with the tools of the different workmen employed in producing these conveniences: if we examine, I say, all of these things, and consider what a variety of labor is employed about each of them, we shall be sensible that, without the assistance and co-operation of many thousands, the very meanest person in a civilized country could not be provided, even according to what we very falsely imagine the easy and simple manner in which he is commonly accommodated. Compared indeed with the more extravagant luxury of the great, his accommodation must no doubt appear extremely simple and easy; and yet it may be true, perhaps, that the accommodation of a European prince does not always so much exceed that of an industrious and frugal peasant, as the accommodation of the latter exceeds that of many an African king, the absolute master of the lives and liberties of ten thousand naked savages.—*The Wealth of Nations.*

SMITH, ALEXANDER, a Scottish author, born in 1830; died in 1867. He began life as a designer of patterns for a lace-factory in Glasgow. In 1853 he published *A Life-Drama*, a poem which met with immediate attention, and in the following year he received the appointment of Secretary of the University of Edinburgh, a position which he held until his death. His subsequent poems are: *Sonnets of the War*, written in conjunction with Sydney Dobell (1855), *City Poems* (1857), *Edwin of Deira* (1861). In prose he wrote, *Dreamthorp* (1863), *A Summer in Skye* (1865) *Alfred Hagart's Household* (1866), *Miss Oona McQuarrie* (1866). A posthumous volume, entitled *Last Leaves* with a *Memoir*, was published in 1868.

UNREST AND CHILDHOOD.

Unrest! unrest! The passion-haunted sea
Watches the unveiled beauty of the stars
Like a great hungry soul. The unquiet clouds
Break and dissolve, then gather in a mass,
And float like mighty icebergs through the blue.
Summers, like blushes, sweep the face of earth;
Heaven yearns in stars. Down comes the frantic rain;
We hear the wail of the remorseful winds
In their strange penance. And this wretched orb
Knows not the taste of rest; a maniac world,
Homeless and sobbing through the deep she goes.

[*A child runs past.*]

Oh thou bright thing, fresh from the hand of God!
The motions of thy dancing limbs are swayed
By the unceasing music of thy being!
Nearer I seem to God when looking on thee,
'Tis ages since He made his youngest star:
His hand was on thee as 'twere yesterday,

Thou later revelation! Silver stream,
Breaking with laughter from the lake divine,
Whence all things flow. Oh, bright and singing babe,
What will thou be hereafter?

A Life-Drama.

A SPRING DAY.

The lark is singing in the blinding sky,
Hedges are white with May. The bridegroom sea
Is toying with the shore, his wedded bride.
And, in the fullness of his marriage joy,
He decorates her tawny brow with shells,
Retires a space to see how fair she looks,
Then, proud, runs up to kiss her. All is fair,
All glad, from grass to sun.

A Life-Drama.

A SUMMER DAY.

Each leaf upon the trees doth shake with joy,
With joy the white clouds navigate the blue,
And on his painted wings the butterfly—
Most splendid masker in this carnival—
Floats through the air in joy. Better for man,
Were he and Nature more familiar friends.

AT CHRISTMAS TIME.

Sheathed is the river as it glideth by,
Frost-pearled are all the boughs in forests old,
The sheep are huddling close upon the wold,
And over them the stars tremble on high.
Pure joys these winter nights around me lie:
'Tis fine to loiter through the lighted streets
At Christmas time, and guess from brow and pace
The doom and history of each one we meet,
What kind of heart beats in each dusky case;
Whiles startled by the beauty of a face
In a shop-light a moment. Or instead,
To dream of silent fields where calm and deep
The sunshine lieth like a golden sleep—
Recalling sweetest looks of Summers dead.

ALEXANDER SMITH.—3

THE PHILOSOPHY OF MONTAIGNE.

The Essays contain a philosophy of life, which is not specially high, yet which is certain to find acceptance more or less with men who have passed out beyond the glow of youth, and who have made trial of the actual world. The essence of his philosophy is a kind of cynical common sense. He will risk nothing in life; he will keep to the beaten track: he will not let passion blind or enslave him; he will gather around him what good he can, and will therewith endeavor to be content. He will be as far as possible self sustained; he will not risk his happiness in the hands of man or woman either. He is shy of friendship, he fears love, for he knows that both are dangerous. He knows that life is full of bitters, and he holds it wisdom that a man should console himself, as far as possible, with its sweets, the principal of which are peace, travel, leisure, and the writing of essays. He values obtainable Gascon bread and cheese more than the unobtainable stars. He thinks crying for the moon the foolishest thing in the world. He will remain where he is. He will not deny that a new world may exist beyond the sunset, but he knows that to reach the new world there is a troublesome Atlantic to cross; and he is not in the least certain that, putting aside the chance of being drowned on the way, he will be one whit happier in the new world than he is in the old. For his part he will embark with no Columbus. He feels that life is but a sad thing at best; but as he has little hope of making it better, he accepts it, and will not make it worse by murmuring. When the chain galls him, he can at least revenge himself by making jests on it.

He will temper the despotism of nature by epigrams. He has read Æsop's fable, and is the last man in the world to relinquish the shabbiest substance to grasp at the finest shadow.—*Dreamthorp.*

SMITH, ELIZABETH OAKES (PRINCE), an American author; born at North Yarmouth, Maine, in 1806. At the age of seventeen she married Seba Smith (born in 1792, died in 1868), a journalist of Portland. In 1839 they removed to New York, where he acquired reputation as a journalist, especially by his "Jack Downing Letters." In 1876 she removed to North Carolina, where she has since resided. Besides numerous occasional poems and books for the young, Mrs. Smith wrote *The Sinless Child and Other Poems* (1841), *Stories for Children* (1847), *The Roman Tribute*, a tragedy (1850), *Woman and her Needs* (1851), *Hints on Dress and Beauty* (1852), *Jacob Leister*, a tragedy (1853), *Bald Eagle* (1867), *The Two Wives*, *Kitty Howard's Journal*, *Destiny*, a tragedy.

THE WIFE.

All day, like some sweet bird, content to sing
  In its small cage, she moveth to and fro:
And ever and anon will upward spring
  To her sweet lips fresh from the fount below—
The murmured melody of pleasant thought,
  Unconscious uttered, gentle-toned and low.
Light household duties, evermore inwrought
  With placid fancies of one trusting heart
That lives but in her smile, and ever turns
  From life's cold seeming and the busy mart,
With tenderness, that heavenward ever yearns
To be refreshed where one pure altar burns.
  Shut out from hence the mockery of life,
  Thus liveth she content, the meek, fond, trusting wife.

THE UNATTAINED.

And is this life? and are we born for this?—
  To follow phantoms that elude the grasp,
  Or whatsoe'er secured, within our clasp,

To withering lie, as if each earthly kiss
Were doomed Death's shuddering touch alone to meet.
O Life! hast thou reserved no cup of bliss?
Must still the Unattained beguile our feet?
The Unattained with yearnings fill the breast,
That rob for aye the Spirit of its rest?
Yes, this is life; and everywhere we meet.
Not victor crowns, but wailings of defeat.
Yet faint thou not: thou dost apply a test,
That shall incite thee onward, upward still,
The Present cannot sate, nor e'er thy Spirit fill.

FAITH.

Beware of doubt! Faith is the subtle chain
Which binds us to the Infinite; the voice
Of a deep life within, that will remain
Until we crowd it thence. We may rejoice
With an exceeding joy, and make our life—
Ay, this external life—become a part
Of that which is within, o'erwrought and rife
With Faith, that childlike blessedness of heart;
The order and the harmony inborn
With a perpetual hymning crown our way,
Till callousness and selfishness and scorn
Shall pass as clouds where scathless lightnings play!
Cling to thy Faith! 'tis higher than the thought
That questions of thy Faith—the cold, external doubt.

STRENGTH FROM THE HILLS.

Come up unto the hills! thy strength is there:
Oh, thou hast tarried long,
Too long amid the bowers and blossoms fair,
With notes of summer song.
Why dost thou tarry there? what though the bird
Pipes matin in the vales,
The ploughboy whistles to the loitering herd,
As the red daylight fails.

Yet come unto the hills—the old strong hills—
And leave the stagnant plain ;
Come to the gushing of the new-born rills,
As sing they to the main ;
And thou with denizens of power shalt dwell
Beyond demeaning care ;
Composed upon his rock, 'mid storm and fell,
The eagle shall be there.

Come up unto the hills ! The shattered tree
Still clings unto the rock,
And flingeth out his branches wild and free,
To dare again the shock.
Come where no fear is known : the sea-bird's
nest
On the old hemlock swings ;
And thou shalt taste the gladness of unrest,
And mount upon thy wings.

Come up unto the hills ! The men of old—
They of undaunted wills—
Grew jubilant of heart, and strong, and bold
On the enduring hills ;
Where came the soundings of the sea afar,
Borne upward to the ear,
And nearer grew the moon and midnight star,
And God himself more near.

SMITH, GOLDWIN, an English essayist and historical writer, born at Reading in 1823. He was educated at Eton, and Oxford; took his degree of B. A. at Magdalen College, Oxford, in 1845; became Fellow and Tutor in the University; and was called to the bar in 1850. He did not enter upon legal practice; but became a member of several Educational Commissions. In 1856 he was made Regius Professor of Modern History at Oxford. In 1868 he came to the United States, having been elected Professor of Constitutional History in Cornell University, Ithaca, N. Y. This position he resigned in 1871. He then removed to Canada where he was appointed a member of the Senate of the University of Toronto.

He has been a frequent contributor to periodical literature, and has delivered numerous lectures upon social, and political topics. Most of his lectures have been published. Among his works are: *The Study of History*, delivered at Oxford (1861), *Irish History and Irish Character* (1861), *Three English Statesmen* (Pym, Cromwell, and Pitt): *a Course of Lectures on the Political History of England* (1867), *The Civil War in America; A Short History of England, down to the Reformation* (1869), *William Cowper* (1880), *False Hopes* (1883), *Life of Jane Austen* (1890).

MARCUS CATO.

Marcus Cato was the one man whom, living and dead, Cæsar evidently dreaded. The Dictator even assailed his memory in a brace of pamphlets entitled *Anti-Cato*, of the quality of which we have one or two specimens in Plutarch, from which we should infer that they were scurrilous and scandalous in the last degree: a proof even that Cæsar could feel fear, and that in Cæsar too, fear was mean. Of the two court-poets of Cæsar's successor, one makes Cato preside over the spirits of the good in the Elysian fields, while the other speaks, at all events, of the soul which remained unconquered in a conquered world. Patercules an officer of Tiberius, and a thorough Cæsarian, calls Cato a man of "ideal virtue," who did right not for appearance's sake, but because it was not in his nature to do wrong.

When the victor is thus overawed by the shade of the vanquished, the vanquished could have hardly been a "fool." Contemporaries may be mistaken as to the merits of a character, but they cannot well be mistaken as to the space which it occupied in their own eyes. Sallust, the partisan of Marius and Cæsar, who had so much reason to hate the Senatorial party, speaks of Cæsar and Cato as the two mightiest opposites of his time; and in an elaborate parallel ascribes to Cæsar the qualities which secure the success of the adventurer; to Cato those which make up the character of the patriot.

It is a mistake to regard Cato the Younger as merely an unseasonable parody of Cato the Elder. His inspiration came not from a Roman Forum, but from a Greek School of Philosophy, and from that School which, with all its errors and absurdities, and in spite of the hypocrisy of its professors, really aimed high in the formation of character; and the practical teachings and aspirations of which, embodied in the *Reflections* of Marcus Aurelius, it is impossible to study without profound respect for the force of moral insight which they sometimes display. Cato went to Greece to sit at the feet of a Greek teacher, in a spirit very different from the national pride of his ancestor. It is this which makes his character interesting—that it was an attempt at all events to grasp and hold fast by the high rule of life, in an age when the whole moral world was sinking into a vortex of scoundrelism, and faith in morality, public or private, had been lost.

Of course, the character is formal, and in some respects even grotesque. But you may trace formalism, if you look close enough, in every life led by a rule; in everything between the purest spiritual impulse on the one side, and abandoned sensuality on the other. Attempts to revive old Roman simplicity of dress and habits in the age of Lucullus, were no doubt futile enough; but after all, this is the symbolical garb of the Hebrew prophet. We are in ancient Rome, not in the smoking-room of the House of Commons. We are among the countrymen, too, of Savonarola. The character, as painted by Plutarch—who seems to have drawn from contemporaries—is hard, of course, but not cynical. Cato was devoted to his brother Cæpio; and when Cæpio died, forgot all his Stoicism in the passionate indulgence of his grief, and all his frugality in lavishing gold and perfumes on the funeral. . . . .

Cato's resignation of his fruitful wife to a childless friend—revolting as it is to our sense—betokens less any brutality in him than the coarseness of the conjugal relations at Rome. Evidently the man had the power of touching the hearts of others. His soldiers—though he gave them no largesses, and indulged them in no license—when he leaves them, strew their garments under his feet. His friends at Utica linger, at the peril of their lives to give him a sumptuous funeral. . . . .

Impracticable, of course, in a certain sense he was. But his part was that of a reformer; and to compromise with the corruption with which he was contending would have been to lose the only means of influence which—having no military force and no party—he possessed: that of the perfect integrity of his character.

SMITH, HORACE, an English author, born at London in 1779, died there in 1849. His literary and personal life was closely connected with that of his brother, JAMES SMITH (1775–1839), and they were joint authors of the *Rejected Addresses*. Horace Smith accumulated an ample fortune as a member of the Stock Exchange. In 1820 he retired from active business, after which he wrote several novels, among which are: *Brambletye House*, *Tor Hill*, *Reuben Apsley*, *Jane Lomax*, and *The New Forest*. In 1812 the rebuilding of Drury Lane Theatre, which had been destroyed by fire, led to the offering of a prize for an opening address. None of those offered were accepted, and Byron was asked to produce one, which was pronounced. The brothers Smith thereupon put forth a small volume entitled *Rejected Addresses*, purporting to have been written by several of the most distinguished living poets. In these the manner of the respective authors is cleverly imitated and sometimes travestied. Perhaps the cleverest of these imitations are that of Crabbe by James Smith and that of Scott by Horace. Besides his contributions to the *Rejected Addresses*, James Smith published anonymously articles in the *New Monthly Magazine* and other periodicals, and wrote the greater part of *The Country Cousins*, *Trip to France*, and *Trip to America*, highly successful pieces at the English Opera House.

A TALE OF DRURY LANE. BY W. G.

As Chaos which, by heavenly doom,
Had slept in everlasting gloom,
Startled with terror and surprise
When light first flashed upon her eyes,
So London's sons in night-cap woke,
   In bed-gown woke her dames;

For shouts were heard 'mid fire and smoke,
"The play-house is in flames!"
And lo! where Catherine Street extends,
A fiery tale its lustre lends
To every window-pane.
Blushes each spout in Martlet Court,
And Barbican—moth-eaten fort,
And Covent Garden Kennels spout
A bright ensanguined drain.
Meux's new brew-house shows the light,
And Rowland Hill's chapel, and the height
Where patent shot they sell.

The Tennis Court, so fair and tall,
Partakes the ray, with Surgeons' Hall;
The ticket-porter's house of call,
Old Bedlam, close by London Wall,
Wright's shrimp and oyster-shop withal,
And Richardson's Hotel.
Nor these alone, but far and wide,
Across the Thames's gleaming tide,
To distant fields the blaze was borne,
And daisy white and hoary thorn
In borrowed lustre seemed to sham
The rose or red Sweet-Wil-li-am.
To those who on the hills around
Beheld the flames from Drury's mound,
As from a lofty altar rise,
It seemed that nations did conspire
To offer to the God of Fire
Some vast, stupendous sacrifice!

The summoned firemen woke at call,
And hied them to their stations all.
Starting from bed and broken snooze,
Each sought his ponderous hobnailed shoes;
But first his worsted hosen plied;
Plush breeches next, in crimson dyed,
His nether limbs embraced;
Then jacket thick, of red or blue,
Whose massy shoulders gave to view
The badge of each respective crew,
In tin or copper traced.
The engines thundered through the street,

Fire-hook, pick, bucket, all complete,
And torches glared, and clattering feet
Along the pavement paced. . . . .

E'en Higginbottom now was posed,
For sadder sight was ne'er disclosed:
Without, within, in hideous show,
Devouring flames resistless glow,
And blazing rafters downward go,
And never halloo, "Heads below!"
Nor notice give at all.
The firemen, terrified, are slow
To bid the pumping torrent flow,
For fear the roof should fall.
"Back, Robbins, back!" "Crump, stand aloof!'
"Whitford, keep near the walls!"
"Huggins, regard your own behoof!"
For lo! the blazing racking roof
Down, down, in thunder falls.

An awful pause succeeds the stroke,
And o'er the ruin's volumed smoke,
Rolling around its pitchy shroud,
Concealed them from the astonished crowd;
When lo! amid the wreck upreared
Gradual a moving head appeared,
And eagle firemen knew
'Twas Joseph Muggins—name revered—
The foreman of their crew.
Loud shouted all, in signs of woe,
"A Muggins to the rescue, ho!"
And poured the hissing tide.
Meanwhile the Muggins fought amain,
And strove and struggled all in vain,
For rallying but to fall again,
He tottered, sunk, and died.

Did none attempt, before he fell,
To succor one they loved so well?
Yes, Higginbottom did aspire;
His fireman's soul was all on fire
His brother-chief to save.
But ah! his reckless, generous ire
Served but to share his grave!

'Mid blazing beams and scalding streams,
Through fire and smoke he dauntless broke,
Where Muggins broke before;
But sulphurous stench and boiling drench,
Destroying sight, o'erwhelmed him quite—
He sunk to rise no more.
Still o'er his head, while fate he braved,
His whizzing water-pipe he waved:
"Whitford and Mulford, ply your pumps!
You, Clutterbuck, come, stir your stumps!
Why are you in such doleful dumps?
A fireman, and afraid of bumps!
What are they feared on? fools, 'od rot em!"
Were the last words of Higginbottom.

HORACE SMITH.

TO THE MUMMY IN BELZONI'S EXHIBITION.

And hast thou walked about (how strange a story!)
In Thebes's streets three thousand years ago,
When the Memnonium was in all its glory,
And time had not begun to overthrow
Those temples, palaces, and piles stupendous,
Of which the very ruins are tremendous!

Speak! for thou long enough hast acted dummy:
Thou hast a tongue—come, let us hear its tune;
Thou'rt standing on thy legs above-ground, Mummy,
Revisiting the glimpses of the moon!
Not like thin ghosts or disembodied creatures,
But with thy bones and flesh and limbs and features.

Tell us—for doubtless thou canst recollect—
To whom we should assign the Sphinx's fame.
Was Cheops or Cephrenes architect
Of either pyramid that bears his name?
Is Pompey's Pillar really a misnomer?
Had Thebes a hundred gates, as sung by Homer?

Perhaps thou wert a mason, and forbidden
By oath to tell the secrets of thy trade;
Then say, what secret melody was hidden
In Memnon's statue, which at sunrise played?
Perhaps thou wert a priest; if so, my struggles
Are vain, for priestcraft never owns its juggles.

Perchance that very hand, now pinioned flat,
Has hob-a-nobbed with Pharaoh, glass to glass,
Or dropped a half-penny in Homer's hat,
Or doffed thine own to let Queen Dido pass,
Or held, by Solomon's own invitation,
A torch at the great Temple's dedication.

I need not ask thee if that hand, when armed,
Has any Roman soldier mauled and knuckled;
For thou wert dead and buried and embalmed
Ere Romulus and Remus had been suckled:
Antiquity appears to have begun
Long after thy primeval race was run.

Thou couldst develop, if that withered tongue
Might tell us what those sightless orbs have seen,
How the world looked when it was fresh and young,
And the great deluge still had left it green;
Or was it then so old that history's pages
Contained no record of its early ages?

Still silent, incommunicative elf!
Art sworn to secrecy? then keep thy vows;
But prithee tell us something of thyself;
Reveal the secrets of thy prison-house.
Since in the world of spirits thou hast slumbered,
What hast thou seen—what strange adventures numbered?

Since first thy form was in this box extended,
We have, above-ground, seen some strange mutations:
The Roman Empire has begun and ended;

New worlds have risen, we have lost old nations,
And countless kings have into dust been humbled,
While not a fragment of thy flesh has crumbled.

Didst thou not hear the pother o'er thy head,
When the great Persian conqueror, Cambyses,
Marched armies o'er thy tomb with thundering tread,
O'erthrew Osiris, Orus, Apis, Isis,
And shook the pyramids with fear and wonder
When the gigantic Memnon fell asunder?

If the tomb's secrets may not be confessed,
The nature of thy private life unfold:
A heart has throbbed beneath that leathern breast;
And tears adown that dusky cheek have rolled;
Have children climbed those knees and kissed that face?
What was thy name and station, age and race?

Statue of flesh! immortal of the dead!
Imperishable type of evanescence!
Posthumous man, who quit'st thy narrow bed,
And standest undecayed within our presence!
Thou wilt hear nothing till the Judgment morning,
When the great trump shall thrill thee with its warning.

Why should this worthless tegument endure,
If its undying guest be lost forever?—
Oh, let us keep the soul embalmed and pure
In living virtue, that when both must sever,
Although corruption may our frame consume,
The immortal spirit in the skies may bloom.

Horace Smith.

THE THEATRE. BY G. C.

'Tis sweet to view, from half-past five to six,
Our long wax-candles, with short cotton wicks,

Touched by the lamplighter's Promethean art,
Start into light, and make the lighter start;
To see red Phœbus through the gallery-pane
Tinge with his beam the beams of Drury Lane;
While gradual parties fill our widened pit,
And gape and gaze and wonder ere they sit.
At first, while vacant seats give choice and ease,
Distant or near, they settle where they please;
But when the multitude contracts the span,
And seats are rare, they settle where they can.
Now the full benches to late-comers doom
No room for standing, miscalled *standing room.*
Hark! the check-taker moody silence breaks,
And bawling "Pit full!" gives the check he takes;
Yet onward still the gathering numbers cram,
Contending crowders shout the frequent damn,
And all is bustle, squeeze, row, jabbering, and jam.
See, to their desks Apollo's sons repair,—
Swift rides the rosin o'er the horse's hair!
In unison their various tones to tune,
Murmurs the hautboy, growls the hoarse bassoon;
In soft vibrations sighs the whispering lute,
Tang goes the harpsichord, too-too the flute,
Brays the loud trumpet, squeaks the fiddle sharp,
Winds the French horn, and twangs the tingling harp;
Till, like great Jove, the leader, figuring in,
Attunes to order the chaotic din.
Now all seems hushed,--but, no, one fiddle will
Give, half ashamed, a tiny flourish still.
Foiled in his crash, the leader of the clan
Reproves with frowns the dilatory man;
Then on his candlestick thrice taps his bow,
Nods a new signal, and away they go. . . .
What various swains our motley walls contain!—
Fashion from Moorfields, honor from Chick Lane;
Bankers from Paper Buildings here resort,

Bankrupts from Golden Square and Riches
Court;
From the Haymarket canting rogues in grain,
Gulls from the Poultry, sots from Water Lane;
The lottery-cormorant, the auction-shark,
The full-price master and the half-price clerk;
Boys who long linger at the gallery door,
With pence twice five,—they want but two-
pence more;
Till some Samaritan the twopence spares,
And sends them jumping up the gallery stairs.
Critics we boast who ne'er their malice balk,
But talk their minds,—we wish they'd mind
their talk;
Big-worded bullies, who by quarrels live,—
Who give the lie, and tell the lie they give;
Jews from St. Mary Axe, for jobs so wary,
That for old clothes they'd even axe St. Mary;
And bucks with pockets empty as their pate,
Lax in their gaiters, laxer in their gait;
Who oft, when we our house lock up, carouse
With tippling tipstaves in a lock-up house.
Yet here, as elsewhere, Chance can joy
bestow,
For scowling fortune seemed to threaten woe.
John Richard William Alexander Dwyer
Was footman to Justinian Stubbs, Esquire;
But when John Dwyer listed in the Blues,
Emanuel Jennings polished Stubb's shoes.
Emanuel Jennings brought his youngest boy
Up as a corn-cutter,—a safe employ;
In Holy-well Street, St. Pancras, he was bred
(At number twenty-seven, it is said),
Facing the pump, and near the Granby's
Head;
He would have bound him to some shop in
town,
But with a premium he could not come down.
Pat was the urchin's name,—a red-haired youth,
Fonder of purl and skittle grounds than truth.

Silence ye gods! to keep your tongues in
awe,
The Muse shall tell an accident she saw.

Pat Jennings in the upper gallery sat,
But, leaning forward, Jennings lost his hat:
Down from the gallery the beaver flew,
And spurned the one to settle in the two.
How shall he act? Pay at the gallery-door
Two shillings for what cost, when new, but
four?
Or till half-price, to save his shilling, wait,
And gain his hat again at half-past eight?
Now, while his fears anticipate a thief,
John Mullens whispers, "Take my handker-
chief."
"Thank you," cries Pat; "but one won't
make a line."
"Take mine," cried Wilson; and cried Stokes,
"Take mine."
A motley cable soon Pat Jennings ties,
Where Spitalfields with real India vies.
Like Iris' bow, down darts the painted clew,
Stained, striped, and spotted, yellow, red, and
blue,
Old calico, torn silk, and muslin new.
George Green below, with palpitating hand,
Loops the last kerchief to the beaver's band,—
Upsoars the prize! The youth with joy un-
feigned
Regained the felt, and felt what he regained;
While to the applauding galleries grateful Pat
Made a low bow, and touched the ransomed
hat.

JAMES SMITH.

SMITH, SAMUEL FRANCIS, an American clergyman and author, born at Boston in 1808. He graduated at Harvard in 1829, Oliver Wendell Holmes and James Freeman Clarke being among his classmates; studied theology at Andover, and in 1834 became pastor of a Baptist church at Waterville, Maine, and Professor of Modern Languages in the college there. In 1842 he became pastor of a church at Newton, Mass., and was also for seven years editor of the *Christian Review*. He subsequently devoted himself to private teaching and to literary work, making music a specialty. Of his "National Hymn" he says: "It was written at Andover in 1831 or 1832; was first used at a children's Fourth of July celebration at the Park Street Church, and made a National Hymn, without my planning or seeking for such a distinction; because the people, unasked, took it up, and *would* sing it."

"MY COUNTRY, 'TIS OF THEE."

My Country, 'tis of thee,
Sweet land of Liberty,
Of thee I sing:
Land where my fathers died,
Land of the Pilgrim's pride,
From every mountain-side
Let Freedom ring!

My Native Country, thee,—
Land of the noble, free—
Thy name I love!
I love thy rocks and rills,
Thy woods and templed hills;
My heart with rapture thrills,
Like that above.

Let music swell the breeze,
And ring from all the trees,
Sweet Freedom's song;

Let mortal tongues awake,
Let all that breathe partake,
Let rocks their silence break;
The sounds prolong.

Our fathers' God! to Thee,
Author of Liberty,
To Thee I sing.
Long may our land be bright
With Freedom's holy light;
Protect us by thy might,
Great God our King!

THE MORNING LIGHT.

The morning light is breaking;
The darkness disappears!
The sons of earth are waking
To penitential tears;
Each breeze that sweeps the ocean
Brings tidings from afar,
Of nations in commotion,
Prepared for Zion's war.

See heathen nations bending
Before the God we love,
And thousand hearts ascending
In gratitude above;
While sinners, now confessing,
The gospel call obey,
And seek the Saviour's blessing—
A nation in a day.

Blest river of salvation!
Pursue thine onward way;
Flow thou to every nation,
Nor in thy richness stay:
Stay not till all the lowly
Triumphant reach their home:
Stay not till all the holy
Proclaim—"The Lord is come!"

SMITH, SYDNEY, an English clergyman and author, born at Woodford, Essex, in 1771; died at London in 1845. He studied at Oxford, where he gained a Fellowship; took orders, and in 1794 became a curate on Salisbury Plain. In 1797 he went to Edinburgh as private tutor to a young gentleman, where he became intimate with the rising young men. In 1802, Jeffrey, Brougham, Smith, and others, projected the *Edinburgh Review*, Smith undertaking the editorship of the first number, and thereafter contributing largely for a quarter of a century. About 1804 he went to London, where he became a popular preacher, and delivered a series of lectures on Moral Philosophy, which were not published until after his death. In 1806 he was presented to the living of Forton-le-Clay, situated in a wild part of Yorkshire, "twelve miles from a lemon," and worth £500 a year. Preferment came slowly to him; but in 1828 he was made a canon of Bristol, and soon afterward rector of Combe-Florey in Somersetshire. In 1831 he was made Canon Residentiary of St. Paul's, London, his residence being thereafter in the metropolis. Besides his contributions to the *Edinburgh Review*, he commenced in 1807 a series of "Letters on the subject of the Catholics to my Brother Abraham who lives in the Country, by Peter Plymley." In the *Plymley Letters* the current political topics of the day were treated in a manner which justifies Macaulay's dictum that "he was a great reasoner, and the greatest master of ridicule that has appeared among us since Swift." He performed his clerical duties in a conscientious manner; but he was especially noted as a conversationalist. By the death of a brother in 1843 he came into possession of a considerable fortune, much of which he invested in the purchase of the public stock of Pennsylvania. The failure of that State to make provision for the payment of the interest on her bonds gave occasion for his caustic *Petition to Congress* and *Letters on American Debts.* A collection of his miscellaneous writings, in four volumes, was published in 1840. After his death were published a volume of *Sermons* preached at St. Paul's, and *Lectures on Moral Philosophy.* In 1856 appeared the *Memoirs of Sydney Smith* by his daughter, the wife of Sir Henry Holland. The *Wit and Wisdom of Sydney Smith*, with a *Memoir* by E. A. Duyckinck, was published in 1856.

MAKING HASTE SLOWLY.

There is something extremely fascinating in quickness; and most men are desirous of appearing quick. The great rule for becoming so is, *by not attempting to appear quicker than you really are;* by resolving to understand yourself and others, and to know what *you* mean, and what *they* mean, before you speak or answer. Every man must submit to be slow before he is quick; and insignificant before he is important. The too early struggle against the pain of obscurity, corrupts no small share of understandings. Well and happily has that man conducted his understanding, who has learned to derive from the exercise of it, regular occupation and rational delight; who, after having overcome the first pain of application, and acquired a habit of looking inwardly upon his own mind, perceives that every day is multiplying the relations, confirming the accuracy, and augmenting the number of his ideas; who feels that he is rising in the scale of intellectual beings, gathering new strength with every new difficulty which he subdues, and enjoying to-day as his pleasure, that which yesterday he labored at as his toil. There are many consolations in the mind of such a man, which no common life can ever afford; and many enjoyments which it has not to give! It is not the mere cry of moralists, and the flourish of rhetoricians; but it is *noble* to seek truth, and it is *beautiful* to find it. It is the ancient feeling of the human heart,—that knowledge is better than riches; and it is deeply and *sacredly true!*

To mark the course of human passions as they have flowed on in the ages that are past; to see why nations have risen, and why they have fallen; to speak of heat, and light, and winds; to know what man has discovered in the heavens above, and in the earth beneath; to hear the chemist unfold the marvelous properties that the Creator has locked up in a speck of earth; to be told that there are worlds so distant from our sun, that the quickness of light traveling from the world's creation, has never yet reached us, to wander in the creations of poetry, and grow warm again, with that eloquence which swayed the democracies of the old world; to go up with great reasoners to the First Cause of all, and to perceive in the midst of all this dissolution and decay, and cruel separation, that there *is* one thing unchangeable, indestructible, and everlasting;—it is worth while in the days of our youth to strive hard for this great discipline; to pass sleepless nights for it, to give up to it laborious days; to spurn for it present pleasures; to endure for it afflicting poverty; to wade for it through darkness, and sorrow, and contempt, as the great spirits of the world have done in all ages and all times.—*Moral Philosophy.*

TALENT AND COURAGE.

A great deal of talent is lost to the world for the want of a little courage. Every day sends to their graves a number of obscure men who have only remained obscure because their timidity has prevented them from making a first effort; and who, if they could only have been induced to begin, would in all probability have gone great lengths in the career of fame.

The fact is, that in order to do anything in this world worth doing, we must not stand shivering on the bank, and thinking of the cold and the danger, but jump in and scramble through as well as we can. It will not do to be perpetually calculating risks, and adjusting nice chances: it did all very well before the flood, when a man could consult his friends upon an intended publication for a hundred and fifty years, and then live to see its success for six or seven centuries afterward; but at present a man waits, and doubts, and hesitates and consults his brother, and his uncle, and his first cousins, and his particular friends, till one fine day he finds that he is sixty-five years of age —that he has lost so much time in consulting first cousins and particular friends, that he has no more time to follow their advice. There is such little time for over-squeamishness at present, the opportunity so easily slips away, the very period of life at which a man chooses to venture, *if ever,* is so confined, that it is no bad rule to preach up the necessity, in such instances, of a little violence done to the feelings, and of efforts made in defiance of strict and sober calculation.—*Moral Philosophy.*

SMOLLETT, TOBIAS GEORGE, a British author, born in Dumbartonshire, Scotland, in 1721; died at Leghorn, Italy, in 1771. He was of an ancient family, received a good education, and was apprenticed to a surgeon. After acting as surgeon's mate in the navy, he betook himself to London, and authorship. His writings included compositions of almost every kind. He wrote novels, plays, poems, travels and histories; translated *Don Quixote*, from the Spanish, and *Gil-Blas* and *Telemachus* from the French. He wrote a *Complete History of England to* 1748, in four quarto volumes; compiled a *Compendium of Authentic and Entertaining Voyages*, in seven volumes; and became editor of the *Critical Review*. His best works are his novels, among which are: *Roderick Random* (1748), *Peregrine Pickle* (1751), *Ferdinand, Count Fathom* (1752), *Sir Lancelot Graves* (1762), *Humphrey Clinker* (1771), The following account of a "Modern Feast in the Ancient Manner," is here considerably abridged by omitting the numerous ludicrous mishaps which befel one another of the guests at this repast.

THE DOCTOR'S CLASSICAL DINNER.

Peregrine Pickle, by his insinuating behavior, acquired the full confidence of the Doctor; who invited him to an entertainment which he intended to prepare in the manner of the ancients. Pickle, struck with this idea, eagerly embraced the proposal, which he honored with many encomiums, as a plan in all respects worthy of his genius and apprehension; and the day was appointed at some distance of time, that the treater might have leisure to compose certain pickles and confections which were not to be found among the culinary preparations of these degenerate days. With a view of rendering the physican's taste more conspicuous, and extracting from it the more diversion, Peregrine proposed that some foreigners should partake of the banquet; and the task being left to his care and discretion, he actually bespoke the company of a French Marquis, an Italian Count, and a German Baron, whom he knew to be egregious coxcombs.

The mutual compliments that passed on this occasion were scarce finished, when a servant, coming into the room, announced dinner; and the entertainer led the way into another apartment, where they found a long table—or rather two boards joined together—and furnished with a variety of dishes, the steams of which had such evident effect upon the nerves of the company, that the Marquis made frightful grimaces under pretence of taking snuff, the Italian's eyes watered, the German's visage underwent several distortions of feature. Our hero found means to exclude the odor from his sense of smelling by breathing only through his mouth; and the poor painter, running into another room, plugged his nostrils with tobacco.

The Doctor himself, who was the only person then present whose organs were not discomposed, pointing to a couple of couches placed on each side of the table, told his guests that he was sorry he could not procure the exact *triclinia* of the ancients, which were somewhat different from these conveniences, and desired that they would have the goodness to repose themselves without ceremony, each in his respective couchette, while he and his friend Mr. Pallet would place themselves upright at the ends, that they might have the pleasure of serving those that lay along. This disposition, of which the strangers had no previous idea, disconcerted and perplexed them in a most ridiculous manner. The Marquis and Baron stood bowing to each other on pretense of disputing the lower seat: but, in reality, with a view of profiting by the example of the other, for neither of them understood the manner in which they were to loll. In this disagreeable and ludicrous suspense, they continued acting a pantomime of gesticulations, until the Doctor earnestly entreated them to waive all compliment and form, lest the dinner should be spoiled before the ceremonial could be concluded. . . . .

This misfortune being repaired as well as the circumstances of the occasion would permit, and every one settled according to the arrangement which had been made, the Doctor graciously undertook to give some account of the dishes as they occurred, that the company might be directed in their choice; and with an air of infinite satisfaction thus began:

"This here, gentlemen, is a boiled goose, served up in a sauce composed of pepper, lovage, coriander, mint, rues, anchovies, and oil. I wish, for your sakes, gentlemen, it was one of the geese of Ferrara, so much celebrated for the magnitude of their livers, one of which is said to have weighed two pounds. With this food, exquisite as it was, did the tyrant Heliogabalus regale his hounds. But I beg pardon; I had almost forgot the soup, which I hear is so necessary at all tables in France. At each end are dishes of the *salacacabia* of the Romans. One is made of parsley, pennyroyal, cheese, pine-tops, honey, vinegar, brine, eggs, cucumbers, onions, and hen-livers; the other is much the same as the *soup-maigre* of this country. Then there is a loin of boiled veal with fennel and caraway-seed, on a potage composed of pickle, oil, honey, and flour; and a curious hashis of the lights, liver, and blood of a hare, together with a dish of roasted pigeons. Monsieur le Baron, shall I help you to a plate of this soup?"

The German, who did not at all disapprove of the ingredients, assented to the proposal, and seemed to relish the composition; while the Marquis, being asked by the painter which of the silly-kickabys he chose, was, in consequence of his desire accommodated with a portion of the *soup-maigre*; and the Count, in lieu of spoon-meat, of which he said he was no great admirer, supplied himself with a pigeon; therein conforming to the choice of our young gentleman, whose example he determined to follow through the whole course of the entertainment.

The various dishes affected the eaters in various unpleasant ways—literally *ad nauseam*—which are fully narrated. The whole table was thrown into confusion.

The Doctor finding that it would be impracticable to re-establish the order of the banquet by presenting again the dishes which had been discomposed, ordered everything to be removed, a clean cloth to be laid, and the dessert to be brought in. Meanwhile he regretted his incapacity to give them a specimen of the *alicus*, or fish-meals of the ancients: such as the jusdiabaton, the conger-eel, which, in Galen's opinion, is hard of digestion; the cornuta or gurnard, described by Pliny in his *Natural History*, who says that the horns of many of them were a foot and a half in length; the mullet and the lamprey, that were in the highest estimation of old, of which Julius Cæsar borrowed six thousand at one triumphal supper. He observed that the manner of dressing them was described by Horace in the account he gives of the entertainment to which Mæcenas was invited by the epicure Nasiedenus; and told them that they were commonly eaten with the *Chus syriacum*—a certain anodyne and astringent seed which qualified the purgative nature of the fish.

Finally this learned physician gave them to understand that though this was reckoned a luxurious dish in the zenith of the Roman taste, it was by no means comparable in point of expense to some preparations in vogue about the time of that absurd voluptuary Heliogabalus, who ordered the brains of six hundred ostriches to be compounded in one mess.—*Peregrine Pickle.*

SNIDER, DENTON JAQUES, an American author, born in Mt. Gilead, Ohio, in 1841. After graduation at Oberlin in 1862, he engaged in teaching, and is now a lecturer on general literature. He has published: *A System of Shakespeare's Dramas* (1877), *Delphic Days* (1880), *A Walk in Hellas* (1882), *Agamemnon's Daughter*, a poem (1885), *An Epigrammatic Voyage* (1886), *Commentary on Goethe's Faust* (1886), and *Commentary on Shakespeare's Tragedies* (1887).

IPHIGENIA AT AULIS.

Still the Euboic hills detained the sun,
Who threw upon their peaks his last of light
For that one day, and then his course was done;
In silence flew the silken wings of night,
To brush out of the skies the cloudlets bright,
And tinted films hung high on heaven's way;
Then sank into the mist the mountain height,
And twilight poured its flood on Aulis' bay.

Meantime, they bore the Maiden to the shrine,
Which lay upon a knoll within a wood;
There Calchas led her through a weeping line
Of massive men, who round her pathway stood.
To see the highest worth of womanhood;
The hearts of all burst out in tearful rue,
As they beheld in her what was the good,
And made the vow to her they would be true.

The fair white fane of marbled Artemis
A smile into the twilight seemed to throw;
From its fond pillars flowed a silent kiss
Which showered love around the deed of woe,
As there in flight of stone she grasped her bow
To save a fleeing fawn from savage chase;

She touched the arrow in a sacred glow,
The very marble lit up in her face.

Within the door the maiden disappears,
A cloud descends and fills the holy space,
And for a moment sheds its gentle tears,
Till every leaf and grass-blade in the place
Hath on it one pure drop of sorrow's grace,
And bends to let it fall upon the ground,
Which swallows it at once and shows no trace,
Though leaf and grass, freed from the weight, rebound.

But soon with ragged rent is pierced the cloud,
And through it looks the silver-shining moon,
Which softly strokes the melancholy crowd
And to a music sweet doth them attune,
While they quite sink away into its swoon;
It drives far off the night with the dark cloud,
And out the air into her lunar noon
The Goddess stepped at once and spake aloud:

"Thy time is full, thee have I come to save,
As promised in Mycenæ from my shrine;
Men say I in revenge thy life must have,
Because thy father slew with heart malign
The guiltless fawn he knew I loved as mine;
But no! the Goddess must not vengeance pay,
Not death for death can be the law divine,
Though he slay mine, his shall I never slay.

The Gods must not revengeful be to man.
Else they will not escape his penalty:
The Gods must also learn, and learn they can,
To give up hate, and turn to charity.
Whereby alone we Gods are whole and free.
The Greeks shall deem the dead, with grief be racked.
But sacrifice they shall hereafter see,
And find the richer blessing for thine act.

But to myself I shall now rescue thee,
I, the mild Goddess, dare not take thy blood;

Thee shall I bear away to Barbary,
  There in a land remote to do the Good,
  Anew the offering for a multitude
Vaster than all on earth, to be now found;
  The world, all time thy deed will yet include,
Far wilt thou pass beyond the Grecian bound.

This hour auspicious gales begin to blow,
  Helen, the erring one, is to return,
The armament shall crush the Trojan foe
  Through deed of thine to-day, which men
    will burn
  To imitate, and from a maiden learn
To offer life for land and family;
  With Helen home, thou too wilt homeward
    turn,
And Greece once saved, is saved again by
    thee."

The moon has fled with night, and timid rays
  Of rosy dawn into the heavens rise;
While in the woods a godlike presence prays,
  Soft hymns of triumph float up to the skies,
  Bearing aloft a world of harmonies;
The Greeks rush to the fane to hear the word,
  The axe unbloody on the altar lies,
The maid is gone, and naught of her is heard.

Astonied they all stand at plan divine,
  But see, there is another wonder new:
The fawn that dead was lying at the shrine,
  Rose up to sudden life before their view,
  And to its perfect strength at once it grew;
Unharmed through all the gazing crowd it flees
  No stains upon the grass it now doth strew,
  And soon from sight is lost amid the trees.

Agamemnon's Daughter.

SOCRATES, a Greek philosopher, born at Athens in 470 B. C.; died there in 399 B. C. He was the son of a sculptor, to whose profession he was brought up, and which he exercised for a while with good success; but gave it up in order to become what we may call a "private lecturer" on ethics, in obedience to what he esteemed a divine monition. It was his wont to frequent work-shops and public places, discoursing to any one who would listen to him. His favorite method of disputation was to assume the attitude of a learner, put a series of artful questions until his interlocutor had involved himself, in some self-contradiction or manifest absurdity, and then bear down upon him with the keenest ridicule.

Though he set up no school, had no fixed place of instruction, and even disclaimed the appellation of a teacher, there gathered around him in time a group of men who may properly be called his disciples. Among these were two young men, Plato and Xenophon, from whom we learn nearly all that we know about Socrates and his teaching. For more than sixty years he seems to have been an Athenian citizen of good repute. But towards the close of his life he incurred the disfavor of the party which had obtained the political ascendancy. In his seventieth year he was indicted upon charges that he was "guilty, firstly, of denying the gods recognized by the state, and introducing new divinities; secondly, of corrupting the young." The tribunal before which he was arraigned consisted of 500 "judges." He was found guilty by a vote of 280 to 220; and was sentenced to die by drinking a decoction of the poisonous "hemlock," a species of cicuta. Thirty days intervened between the sentence and its execution. During this period he was kept in prison, securely bound; but his friends were allowed free access to him, and he discoursed to them upon the loftiest themes, as is recorded by Plato, especially in the Phædo.

Socrates committed none of his teachings to writing. It is not altogether certain how far the words which Plato puts into the mouth of Socrates were actually spoken by him. But there can be little question that the *Apologia*, or "Defense," of Socrates is substantially the speech which he made at his trial. After having defended himself against the special charges made against him, and apparently after the vote had been taken, but before the sentence had been pronounced, Socrates turned to his friends among the "judges," and discoursed upon the question of the moment.

THE PROBLEM OF LIFE AND DEATH.

Friends, who would have acquitted me, I would like to talk with you about this thing which has happened, before I go to the place at which I must die. Stay then awhile, for we may as well talk with one another while there is time.* You are my friends, and I should like to show you the meaning of this event which has happened to me. O my judges—for so I may truly call you, I should like to tell you of a wonderful circumstance:—

Hitherto the familiar oracle within me has constantly been in the habit of opposing me, even in trifles, if I was going to make a slip or err in any matter; and now, as you see, there has come upon me the last and worst evil. But

* Socrates supposed that the execution would take place, on that day, according to Athenian usage. The delay of thirty days happened unexpectedly by reason of the occurrence of a religious festival.

the oracle made no sign of opposition, either as I was leaving my house and going out in the morning, or while I was speaking, at anything which I was going to say; and yet I have often been stopped in the middle of a speech; but now in nothing that I either said or did touching this matter has the oracle opposed me. What do I take to be the explanation of this? I will tell you. I regard this as a great proof that what has happened to me is a good; and that those who think that death is an evil are in error. For the customary sign would surely have opposed me had I been going to evil and not to good.

Let us reflect in another way, and we shall see that there is great reason to hope that death is a good. For one of two things—either death is a state of nothingness; or, as men say, there is a change and migration of the soul from this world to another.

Now if you suppose that there is no consciousness, but a sleep like the sleep of him who is undisturbed even by the sight of dreams, death will be an unspeakable gain. For if a person were to select the night in which his sleep was undisturbed even by dreams, and were to compare this with the other days and nights of his life; and then were to tell us how many days and nights he had passed in the course of his life better and more pleasantly than this one. I think this man—I will not say a private man, but even the great king—will not find many such days or nights, when compared with others. Now if death is like this I say that to die is gain; for eternity is then only a single night.

But if death is the journey to another place —and there, as men say, all the dead are— what good can be greater than this? If, indeed, when the pilgrim arrives in the world below, he is delivered from the professors of justice in this world, and finds the true judges who are said to give judgment there—Minos, and Rhadamanthus, and Æacus, and Triptolemus, and other sons of God who were righteous in their own life—that pilgrimage will be worth making.

Above all, I shall then be able to continue my search into true and false knowledge, as in this world, so also in that. And I shall find out who is wise, and who pretends to be wise and is not. What would not a man give to be able to examine the leader of the Trojan expedition; or Odysseus, or Sisyphus, or numberless others—men and women too! What infinite delight would there be in conversing with them and asking questions!—in another world they do not put a man to death for asking questions; assuredly not. For besides being happier in that world than in this, they will be immortal, if what is said be true. Wherefore, be of good cheer about death, and know of a certainty that no evil can happen to a good man, either in this life or after death. He and his are not neglected by the gods, nor has my own approaching end happened by mere chance. But I see clearly that to die and be released was better for me; and therefore the oracle gave no sign.

For which reason, also I am not angry with my condemners or with my accusers. They have done me no harm, although they did not mean to do me any good: and for this I may gently blame them. Still I have a favor to ask of them. When my sons grow up, I would ask you, my friends, to punish them. And I would have you trouble them, as I have troubled you, if they seem to care about riches, or anything more than about virtue. Or if they pretend to be something when they are really nothing, then reprove them, as I have reproved you, for not caring about that for which they ought to care, and thinking that they are really something when they are really nothing. And if you do this, I and my sons will have received justice at your hands.

The hour of my departure has arrived, and we go our ways—I to die, and you to live. Which is better, God only knows.—*Tranls. of* Jowett.

SOMERVILLE, Mary (Fairfax), a British author, born at Jedburgh, Scotland, in 1780; died at Naples, Italy, in 1872. She was the daughter of Vice-Admiral Sir William Fairfax. She was married in 1804 to Samuel Greig, then Russian consul in London. She was left a widow in 1807. Five years later she was married, in 1812, to Dr. William Somerville. In 1816 he was appointed a member of the army medical board, and removed to London, where Mrs. Somerville attracted attention by her experiments on the magnetic influence of the violet rays in the solar spectrum. Her results were published in the *Philosophical Transactions* (1826). She prepared a Summary of Laplace's *Méchanique Celeste* for the *Library of Useful Knowledge*, which proved too large for its purpose, and was published under the title of *Mechanism of the Heavens* (1831). This led to her election to the Royal Astronomical Society. She was a member of other distinguished societies, and received many honors. Her last years were spent in Italy. Mrs. Somerville's works are: *The Connection of the Physical Sciences* (1834; 9th ed., 1858), *Physical Geography* (2 vols., 1848; 6th ed., 1870), *Molecular and Microscopic Science* (2 vols., 1869). Her life has been written by her daughter, Martha Somerville.

WAVES.

The friction of the wind combines with the tides in agitating the surface of the ocean, and, according to the theory of undulations, each produces its effect independently of the other; wind, however, not only raises waves, but causes a transfer of superficial water also. Attraction between the particles of air and water, as well as the pressure of the atmosphere, brings its lower stratum into adhesive contact with the surface of the sea. If the motion of the wind be parallel to the surface, there will still be friction, but the water will be smooth as a mirror; but if it be inclined, in however small a degree, a ripple will appear. The friction raises a minute wave, whose elevation protects the water beyond it from the wind, which consequently impinges on the surface at a small distance beyond; thus, each impulse, combining with the other, produces an undulation which continually advances.

Those beautiful silvery streaks on the surface of a tranquil sea called Cats-paws by sailors, are owing to a partial deviation of the wind from a horizontal direction. The resistance of the water increases with the strength and inclination of the wind. The agitation at first extends little below the surface, but in long-continued gales even the deep water is troubled; the billows rise higher and higher, and, as the surface of the sea is driven before the wind, their "monstrous heads," impelled beyond the perpendicular, fall in wreathes of foam. Sometimes several waves overtake one another, and form a sublime and awful sea. The highest waves known are those which occur during a northwest gale off the Cape of Good Hope, aptly called by the ancient Portuguese navigators the Cape of Storms. Cape Horn also seems to be the abode of the tempest. The sublimity of the scene, united to the threatened danger. naturally leads to an over-estimate of the magnitude of the waves, which appear to rise mountain-high, as they are proverbially said to do: there is, however, reason to doubt if the highest waves off the Cape of Good Hope exceed forty feet from the hollow trough to the summit. The waves are short and abrupt in small shallow seas, and on that account are more dangerous than the long rolling billows of the wide ocean. . . . .

The waves raised by the wind are altogether independent of the tidal waves; each maintains its undisturbed course; and as the inequalities of the coasts reflect them in all directions, they modify those they encounter and offer new resistance to the wind, so that there may be three or four systems or series of co-existing waves, all going in different directions, while the individual waves of each maintain their parellelism.

The undulation called a ground-swell, occasioned by the continuance of a heavy gale, is totally different from the tossing of the billows, which is confined to the area vexed by the wind; whereas the ground-swell is rapidly transmitted through the ocean to regions far beyond the direct influence of the gale, that raised it, and it continues to heave the smooth and glassy surface of the deep, long after the wind and the billows are at rest. In the South Pacific, billows which must have travelled one thousand miles against the trade-wind from the sea to the storm, expend their fury on the lee-side of the many coral islands which bedeck that sunny sea. A swell sometimes comes from a quarter in direct opposition to the wind, and occasionally from various points of the compass at the same time, producing a vast commotion even in a dead calm, without ruffling the surface.—*Physical Geography.*

SOPHOCLES, a Greek dramatic poet, born at Colonus, a village near Athens, in 495 B. C., died in 405 B. C. He was of good family, inherited a competent estate, and received the best education of his time. He was noted for the beauty of his person the amenity of his manners, and the amiability of his disposition. Aristophanes, who caricatured Socrates, and girded at Æschylus and Euripides, has only praise for Sophocles. He was a contemporary of Æschylus and Euripides, being thirty years younger than the former, and fifteen years older than the latter. At twenty-six he came forward as a competitor for the dramatic prize at the great festival of Bacchus, Æschylus being one of his rivals. The first prize—a simple wreath of wild olives—was awarded to Sophocles. He continued to exhibit plays for more than forty years, sometimes gaining the first place, and never falling to the third. He produced more than a hundred dramas, of which only the seven following have come down to us: *Œdipus the King*, *Œdipus at Colonus* *Antigone*, *The Death of Ajax*, *The Maidens of Trachis*, *Philoctetes*, *Electra*. Sophocles was pre-eminently a religious poet. The gods of his country were with him objects of profound veneration. His dramas abound in passages which might have been written by the most sincere Christian of any age.

A BLAMELESS LIFE.

Speak thou no word of pride, nor raise
A swelling thought against the Gods on high;
For Time uplifteth and Time layeth low
All human things; and the great gods above
Abhor the wicked as the good they love. . . .

Be blameless in all duties toward the gods,
For God the Father in compare with this
Lightly esteemeth all things else; and so
Thy righteousness shall with thee to the end
Endure, and follow thee beyond the grave.
Philoctetes.—Transl. of D' ARCY THOMPSON.

The dialogue, which with Sophocles sometimes becomes a trilogue—or spoken part of his tragedies—is often of very high dramatic power; but the "Chorus," or lyrical part is their most distinguishing feature. We give several of these.

MAN'S DOMINION OVER NATURE.

Many the things that strange and wondrous are;
None stranger and more wonderful than Man:
He dares to wander far,
With stormy blast across the hoary sea,
Where naught his eyes can scan
But waves still surging round unceasingly;
And Earth, of all the gods
Mightiest, unwearied, indestructible,
He weareth year by year, and breaks her clods,
While the keen ploughshare makes her furrows well,
Still turning to and fro;
And still he bids his steeds
Through daily task-work go.
Antigone.—Transl. of PLUMPTRE.

THE FINAL DOOM OF GUILT.

Shall Judgment be less strong than Sin?
Shall man o'er Jove dominion win?—
No! Sleep beneath his leaden sway
May hold but things that know decay.
The unwearied months with godlike vigor move,
Yet cannot change the might of Jove.
Compassed with dazzling light,
Throned on Olympus's height,
His front the eternal God uprears,
By toils unwearied, and unaged by years.

Far back through seasons past,
  Far on through times to come,
Has been, and still must last
  Sin's never-failing doom:
Doom, whence with countless sorrows rife
Is erring man's tumultuous life.
Some, heeding Hope's beguiling voice
  From Virtue's pathway rove;
And some, deluded, make their choice
  The levities of Love.
For well and wisely was it said,
That all, by Heaven to sorrows led,
Perverted by delirious mood,
Deem Evil wears the shape of Good;
Chase the fair phantom, free from fears,
And waken to a life of tears.

Antigone.—Transl. of ANSTICE.

SUPPLICATION OF THEBAN CITIZENS.

Lord of the starry heaven,
Grasping the terrors of the burning levin!
Let thy fierce bolt descend,
Scathe the Destroyer's might, and suffering
    Thebes befriend.
Speed thou here, Lycæan King—
Archer from whose golden string
Light the unerring arrows spring—
    Apollo, lend thine aid!
And come, ye beams of the wreathed light,
Glancing on the silent night,
In mazy dance, on Lycia's height,
    When roves the Huntress Maid.
Thou, the golden chaplet fair
Braiding 'mid thy clustering hair,
To thy native haunts repair,
    Thy name that gave.
Thou, whose brow the vineless stain,
Thou, to whom on starlit plain
"Evoë!" sing the frenzied train—
    Bacchus the brave!
With thy torch of pine defy
(Hated by the powers on high)
War's unhallowed deity:
    Haste thee to save!

Œdipus the King.—Transl. of ANSTICE.

THE MADNESS OF AJAX.

Tecmessa.—Sons of Erectheus, of Athenian race,
Ye brave companions of the valiant Ajax,
Oppressed with grief behold a wretched woman,
Far from her native soil, appointed here
To watch your hapless lord, and mourn his fate.

Chorus.—What new misfortune hath the night brought forth?
Say, daughter of Teleutas, for with thee,
His captive bride, the noble Ajax deigns
To share the nuptial bed, and therefore thou
Canst best inform us.

Tec.— How shall I declare
Sadder than death th' unutterable woe!
This night, with madness seized, hath Ajax done
A dreadful deed; within thou mayst behold
The tents o'erspread with bloody carcasses
Of cattle slain, the victims of his rage.

Chor.—Sad news indeed thou bringst of that brave man:
A dire disease! and not by human aid
To be removed; already Greece hath heard
And wond'ring crowds repeat the dreadful tale;
Alas! I fear th' event! I fear me much,
Lest, with their flocks and herds the shepherds slain,
Against himself he lift his murth'rous hand.

Tec.—Alas! this way he led his captive spoils,
And some he slew, and others tore in sunder;
From out the flock two rams of silver hue
He chose, from one the head and tongue divided,
He cast them from him; then the other chained
Fast to the pillar, with a double rein
Bore cruel stripes, and bitterest execrations,
Which not from mortal came, but were inspired

By that avenging god who thus torments
him.
Chor.—Now then, my friends (for so the
time demands),
Each o'er his head should cast the mournful
veil,
And instant fly, or to our ships repair,
And sail with speed; for dreadful are the
threats
Of the Atridæ; death may be our lot,
And we shall meet an equal punishment
With him whom we lament, our frantic lord.
Tec.—He raves not now, but like the south-
ern blast,
When lightnings cease and all the storm is
o'er,
Grows calm again; yet to his sense restored,
He feels new griefs, for oh! to be unhappy,
And know ourselves alone the guilty cause
Of all our sorrows, is the worst of woes.
Chor.—Yet if his rage subside we should re-
joice;
The ill removed, we should remove our care.
Tec.—Hadst thou then rather, if the choice
were given,
Thyself at ease, behold thy friend in pain,
Than with thy friend be joined in mutual
sorrow?
Chor.—The double grief is sure the most
oppression.
Tec.—Therefore, though not distempered, I
am wretched.
Chor.—I understand thee not.
Tec.— The noble Ajax,—
Whilst he was mad, was happy in his frenzy,
And yet the while affected me with grief
Who was not so; but now his rage is o'er,
And he hath time to breathe from his mis-
fortune,
Himself is almost dead with grief, and I
Not less unhappy than I was before;
Is it not double then?
Chor.— It is indeed;
And much I fear the wrath of angry heaven,

If from his madness ceased he yet receive
No kind relief.

Tec.— 'Tis so; and 'twere most fit
You knew it well.

Chor.— Say, then, how it began;
For like thyself we feel for his misfortunes.

Tec.—Since you partake the sorrows of a friend,
I'll tell you all. Know, then, at dead of night,
What time the evening taper was expired,
Snatching his sword, he seemed as if he meant
To roam abroad. I saw and chid him for it;
What wouldst thou do, I cried, my dearest Ajax?
Unasked, uncalled for, whither wouldst thou go?
No trumpet sounds to battle, the whole host
Is wrapped in sleep. Then did he answer me
With brief but sharp rebuke, as he was wont:
"Woman, thy sex's noblest ornament
Is silence." Thus reproved, I said no more.
Then forth he rushed alone, where and for what,
I knew not; but returning he brought home
In chains the captive herd, in pieces some
He tore, whilst others bound like slaves he lashed
Indignant; then out at the portal ran,
And with some shadow seemed to hold discourse
Against th' Atridæ, and Ulysses oft
Would he inveigh; or laughing loud, rejoice
That he had ta'en revenge for all his wrongs;
Then back he came. At length, by slow degrees,
His fury ceased; when, soon as he beheld
The tents o'erwhelmed with slaughter, he cried out,
And beat his brains; rolled o'er the bloody heaps
Of cattle slain, and tore his clotted hair,
Long fixed in silence: then, with horrid threats
He bade me tell him all that had befallen
And what he had been doing. I obeyed,
Trembling with fear, and told him all I knew.
Instant he poured forth bitt'rest lamentations,

Such as I ne'er had heard from him before,
For grief like that, he oft would say, betrayed
A weak and little mind, and therefore ever
When sorrow came refrained from loud complaint,
And like the lowing heifer, inly mourned.
But sinking now beneath this sore distress,
He will not taste of food or nourishment;
Silent he sits, amid the slaughtered cattle,
Or if he speaks, utters such dreadful words
As shows a mind intent on something ill.
Now then my friends, for therefore came I hither,
Oh! if ye have the power, assist me now;
Perhaps ye may; for oft the afflicted man
Will listen to the councils of a friend.

Ajax.

THE SUPPLICATION FOR DEJANIRA.

Thou flaming Sun! whom spangled Night,
Self-destroying, brings to light,
  Then lulls to sleep again;
Bright Herald, girt with beaming rays,
Say, where Alemena's offspring strays:
  Say, lurks he on the main?
Or lays his head to rest
On Europe's or on Asia's breast?
  In pity deign reply,
  Thou of the lordly eye.
His bride, erst won by desperate fray,
Muses where lies his dangerous way;
Like some sad bird, her soul is set
On constancy and vain regret.
Sleep never seals those eyes, where woe
Lies all too deep for tears to flow,
While thought and boding Fancy's dread
Flit ever round her lonely bed.
  Oft when the northern blast,
Or southern winds unwearied rave,
  Ye see the ocean cast
In quick succession wave on wave;
So to whelm old Cadmus's son,
Rush redoubled labors on,
Thick as round the Cretan shore

The swoln and turbid billows roar;
Yet his step from Pluto's halls
Still some unerring god recalls. . . .
Grief and delight, in endless change,
Round man in many circles range,
Like never-setting stars that roll
In endless courses round the pole.
Soon spangled night must turn to day,
Soon wealth, soon trouble, flits away;
In turn—so fixed the eternal plan—
Bliss and bereavement wait on man.
My queen! on hope thy soul be stayed,
Nor yield thee to despair:
When hath not Jove his children made
His providential care?

The Maidens of Trachis.—Transl. of ANSTICE.

THE CHARIOT-RACE.—REPORTED DEATH OF ORESTES.

They took their stand where the appointed judges
Had cast their lots and ranged the rival cars.
Rang out the brazen trump! Away they bound,
Cheer the hot steeds, and shake the slackened reins;
As with a body the large space is filled
With the huge clangor of the battling cars.
High whirl aloft the dust-clouds; blent together,
Each presses each, and the lash rings: and loud
Snort the wild steeds, and from their fiery breath
Along their manes and down the circling wheels
Scatter the foam. . . . .

[The narrator goes on to relate how the goal was six times rounded; but then the horses of one chariot became unmanageable, and the chariot dashed against another.—The whole story is, however, a fabricated one. Orestes has not been killed; but lives to kill Clytemnestra, his adulterous mother, and Ægsithus, her paramour.]

. . . . Then order changed to ruin;
Car crashed on car; the wide Circæan plain

Was sea-like strewed with wrecks. The
Athenian saw, [marge,
Slackened his speed, and wheeling round the
Left the wild tumult of that tossing storm.
Behind, Orestes, hitherto the last,
Had yet kept back his courses for the close.
Now one sole rival left, on, on he flew,
And the sharp sound of the impelling scourge
Rang in the keen ears of the flying steeds.
He hears, he reaches; they are side by side;
Now one—the other—by a length the victor.
The courses all are past—the wheels erect—
All safe; when, as the hurrying courses round
The fatal pillar dashed, the wretched boy
Slackened the left rein; on the column's edge
Crashed the frail axle; headlong from the car,
Caught, and all meshed within the reins he
fell;
And masterless the mad steeds raged along.
Loud from that mighty multitude arose
A shriek—a shout! But yesterday such deeds,
To-day such doom! Now whirled upon the
earth,
Now his limbs dashed aloft, they dragged him
—those
Wild horses—till all gory from the wheels
Released: and no man, not his nearest friend,
Could in that mangled corpse have traced
Orestes.
They laid the body on the funeral pyre;
And, while we speak, the Phocian strangers
bear,
In a small brazen melancholy urn,
That handful of cold ashes to which all
The grandeur of the Beautiful hath shrunk.
Hither they bear him, in his father's land
To find that heritage—a tomb!

Electra.—Transl of LORD LYTTON.

ELECTRA, CLYTEMNESTRA AND THE CHORUS.

Electra.—A cry goes up within: friends, hear ye not?

Chorus.—I heard what none should hear—ah, misery!—

And shuddered listening.
Clytem.—(*Within.*)—Ah me! ah me! Woe, woe!
Ægisthus, where art thou?
Electra.— Her! List again,
I hear a bitter cry.
Clytem.—(*Within.*)— My son,
Have pity on thy mother!
Electra.— Thou hadst none
On him, nor on the father that begat him.
Clytem.—(*Within.*)— Ah, I am smitten!
Electra.— Smite her yet again,
If thou hast strength for it.
Clytem.—(*Within.*)—Ah! blow on blow!
Electra.—Would that Ægis thus shared them!
Chorus.— Yes; the curse
Is now fulfilled. The buried live again;
For they who died long since now drain in him
The blood of those that slew them.

Electra.—Transl. of PLUMPTRE.

SOTHEBY, William, an English poet, born at London in 1757; died in 1833. He was educated at Harrow School; entered the army at seventeen; resigned his commission in 1780, and purchased an estate near Southampton. He wrote many poems, the most ambitious of which is *Saul;* and produced several tragedies, among which is *Orestes*, constructed on the ancient Greek model. Byron said of him that "he imitated everybody, and occasionally surpassed his models." He is, however, best known by his translations, which rank among the best in our language. Among these are the *Oberon* of Wieland (1798), the *Georgics* of Virgil (1800), the *Iliad*, and *Odyssey* of Homer, began about 1827, when he had reached his seventieth year.

STAFFA AND IONA.

Staffa, I scaled thy summit hoar
  I passed beneath thy arch gigantic,
Whose pillared caverns swell the roar,
When thunders on thy rocky shore
  The roll of the Atlantic.

That hour the wind began to roar,
  The surge forgot its motion,
And every pillar in thy cave
Slept in its shadow on the wave,
  Unrippled by the ocean.

Then the past age before me came,
  When 'mid the lightning's sweep,
Thy isle with its basaltic frame,
And every column wreathed with flame
Burst from the boiling deep.

When 'mid Iona's wrecks meanwhile
  O'er sculptured graves I trod,
Where time had strewn each mouldering aisle
O'er saints and kings that reared the pile,
  I hailed the eternal God.
Yet, Staffa, more His presence in thy cave
Than where Iona's cross rose o'er the western
    wave.

SOUTH, Robert, an English clergyman and author, born at London in 1633; died in 1716. He was educated at Christ Church, Oxford, where he received his first degree in 1655; took orders in 1658, and two years later was made University Orator. He became a Canon of Christ Church in 1670; and in 1680 the rectory of Islip was conferred upon him, and he was made Chaplain in Ordinary to Charles II. He was a staunch adherent of the Church of England, and a determined opponent of every form of dissent. His voluminous writings, consisting mainly of sermons, have been several times reprinted in Great Britain and America. Of these sermons Henry Rogers says, in the *Edinburgh Review*, "Of all the English preachers, South seems to us to furnish, in point of style, the truest specimens of the most effective species of pulpit eloquence."

RELIGION NOT HOSTILE TO PLEASURE.

That pleasure is man's chiefest good—because indeed, it is the perception of good that is properly pleasure—is an assertion most certainly true; though, under the common acceptation of it, not only false but odious. For, according to this, pleasure and sensuality pass for terms equivalent; and therefore he that takes it in this sense, alters the subject of the discourse. Sensuality is indeed a part—or, rather, one part—of pleasure, such an one as it is. For pleasure, in general, is the consequent apprehension of a suitable object suitably applied to a rightly disposed faculty; and so must be conversant both about the faculties of the body and of the soul respectively, as being the result of fruitions belonging to both.

Now, amongst those many arguments used to press upon men the exercise of religion, I know none that are like to be so successful as those that answer and remove the prejudices that generally possess and bar up the hearts of men against it; amongst which there is none so prevalent in truth, though so little owned in pretence, as that it is an enemy to men's pleasures; that it bereaves them of all the sweets of converse; dooms them to an absurd and perpetual melancholy, designing to make the world nothing else but a great monastery; with which notion of religion nature and reason have great reason to be dissatisfied.

For since God never created any faculty, either in soul or body, but withal prepared for it a suitable object, and that in order to its gratification, can we think that religion was designed only for a contradiction to nature, and with the greatest and most irrational tyranny in the world, to tantalize and tie men up from enjoyment, in the midst of all the opportunities of enjoyment? To place men with the most furious affections of hunger and thirst in the very bosom of plenty, and then to tell them that the envy of Providence has sealed up everything that is suitable, under the character of unlawful? For certainly first to frame appetites to receive pleasure, and then to interdict them with a "Touch not, taste not," can be nothing else than only to give them occasion to devour and prey upon themselves, and so to keep men under the perpetual torment of an unsatisfied desire: a thing hugely contrary to the natural felicity of the creature; and consequently to the wisdom and goodness of the great Creator.

He, therefore, that would persuade men to religion, both with art and efficacy, must found the persuasion of it on this. That it interferes not with any rational pleasure; that it bids nobody to quit the enjoyment of any one thing that his reason can prove to him ought to be enjoyed.

SOUTHEY, Robert, an English author, born at Bristol in 1774; died at Keswick in 1843. Having been left an orphan at an early age, he was placed by a maternal uncle in Westminster School, where he remained four years, and was then expelled for publishing a paper satirizing corporal punishment. In 1793 he was entered at Balliol College, Oxford. He was destined for the Church; but he had embraced Unitarian views in religion—as did Coleridge, with whom he here became intimate; both however, before long, became High Churchmen in the Anglican faith. He left Oxford after a year's residence. He had become dazzled with the democratic theories engendered by the French Revolution; and he, with Coleridge and Robert Lovell, formed a scheme for emigrating to America and establishing upon the banks of the Susquehanna a "Pantisocracy," or ideal community, in which all the members were to be on a perfect equality. All were to be married, the women to perform the domestic duties, and the men to cultivate literature, "with neither king nor lord nor priest to mar their felicity." To raise the requisite funds, Southey and Coleridge each undertook to deliver a course of lectures, and in conjunction wrote *The Fate of Robespierre*, a drama of which two-thirds were by Southey, who had already published *Wat Tyler*, a poem that attracted sufficient attention to be denounced in the House of Commons as seditious. The pantisocratic scheme was abandoned in consequence of some disagreement among the projectors. In 1795 Southey wrote *Joan of Arc;* an epic poem, for which Cottle, a Bristol publisher, paid him fifty guineas. He also engaged to publish all the poems that Coleridge had written, and all that he should thereafter write. In 1795 Southey married Miss Edith Fricker of Bristol, her sister Sara becoming the wife of Coleridge. A third sister was already married to Lovell.

In 1797, Southey, who had outgrown his radical views in religion and politics, accompanied his uncle, Mr. Herbert Chaplain to the "factory" at Lisbon, Portugal; here he remained six months, and laid the foundation for that intimate acquaintance with the Portuguese and Spanish languages, which afterwards served him in good stead. Returning to England he went to London with the design of studying law; but he devoted himself mainly to literary labor. In 1804 he took up his residence at Greta Hall, near Keswick, in the Lake Region. Coleridge was then domiciled there, and Wordsworth lived a few miles distant. These three poets, so dissimilar in genius, came to be popularly designated as "the Lake Poets." From this time the life of Southey consisted mainly of his numerous works in prose and verse. A few events in his external life are to be noted: In 1813 he succeeded James Pye as. Poet Laureate; and was himself succeeded by Wordsworth, and he by Tennyson. In 1835 he was offered a baronetcy, which he declined, for the reason that his means were not adequate to maintain the dignity. In 1837 his wife died, having been for three years in a state of mental imbecility. Eighteen months afterward he married Caroline Bowles, herself a poet of considerable ability, and a friend of many years' standing. But

Southey's own mental powers had begun to fail. He had scarcely brought his wife to their home when his mind gave way entirely. Memory failed utterly. He would wander among his books, taking them down and opening them mechanically, but he was wholly incapable of understanding them. It was a relief rather than a sorrow when, after three such years, the end came. For many years Southey's house was the home of the widow of Lovell, and of the wife and children of Coleridge, who had practically abandoned them. Southey left about £12,000 to his children; he had gradually collected a valuable library, "more ample," he says, "than was ever before possessed by one whose whole estate was in his inkstand."

There is scarcely a department in literature in which Southey was not more or less eminent. Besides translations from the Portuguese and Spanish, frequent contributions to the *Quarterly Review*, which had been established to oppose the Whig teachings of the *Edinburgh Review*, and editing the poems of Henry Kirke. White and the works of Cowper, and others, his principal prose works are: *History of Brazil* (1810–1819) *Life of Nelson* (1813), *Life of John Wesley* (1820), *History of the Peninsular War* (1820--1832). *Book of the Church* (1824), *Sir Thomas More, or Colloquies on Society*, trenchantly criticised by Macaulay (1829), *Life of John Bunyan* (1834), *Essays, Moral and Political* (1832), *The Doctor*, a curious melange written and put forth in separate volumes, and never publicly acknowledged by Southey (1834—1837). His principal poems are: *Joan of Arc* (1796), *Thalaba, the Destroyer* (1801), *Madoc* (1805), *Metrical Tales, and Other Poems* (1805), *The Curse of Kehama* (1810), *Roderick the Last of the Goths* (1814), *A Pilgrimage to Waterloo* (1816). *A Vision of Judgment*, eulogizing George III. (1821), *A Pilgrimage to Compostella* (1839). Southey's *Common-Place Book*, edited by his son-in-law, John Wood Warter, was published in 1849, and his *Life and Correspondence*, edited by his son, the Rev. Charles Cuthbert Southey, in 1850. A succinct *Life of Southey*, by E. Dowden, forms a volume of the "English Men of Letters" series (1886).

THE DEATH OF NELSON AT TRAFALGAR.

It had been part of Nelson's prayer that the British fleet might be distinguished by humanity in the victory which he expected. Setting the example himself, he twice gave orders to cease firing upon the *Redoubtable*, supposing that she had struck, because her great guns were silent; for, as she carried no flag, there was no means of instantly ascertaining the fact. From this ship, which he had twice spared, he received his death. A ball fired from her mizzen-top which, in the then situation of the two vessels, was not more than fifteen yards from that part of the deck where he was standing, struck the epaulette on his left shoulder, about a quarter after one, just in the heat of the action. He fell upon his face, on the spot which was covered with his poor secretary's blood. Captain Hardy, who was but a few steps from him, turning round saw three men raising him up. "They have done for me at last, Hardy!" said he. "I hope not," cried Hardy. "Yes," he replied; "my backbone is shot through."

Yet even now, not for a moment losing his presence of mind, as they were carrying him down, he observed that the tiller-ropes, which had been shot away, had not been replaced; he ordered that new ones should be rove immediately; then, that he might not be seen by the crew, he took out his handkerchief, and covered his face and his stars. Had he but concealed these badges of honor from the enemy, England perhaps would not have had cause to receive with sorrow the news of the battle of Trafalgar. The cockpit was crowded with wounded and dying men, over whose bodies he was with some difficulty conveyed, and laid upon a pallet in the midshipmen's berth. It was soon perceived that the wound was mortal. This, however, was concealed from all but Captain Hardy, the chaplain, and the medical attendants. He himself being certain, from the sensation in his back, and the gush of blood he felt momently in his breast, that no human care could avail him, insisted that the surgeon should leave him, and attend to those to whom he might be useful; "for," said he, "you can do nothing for me." All that could be done was to fan him with paper, and frequently to give him lemonade to alleviate his intense thirst.

He was in great pain, and expresed much anxiety for the event of the action, which now began to declare itself. As often as a ship struck, the crew of the *Victory* hurrahed; and at every hurrah a visible expression of joy gleamed in the eye and marked the countenance of the dying hero. But he became impatient to see Captain Hardy; and as that officer, though frequently sent for, could not leave the deck, Nelson feared that some fatal cause prevented him, and repeatedly cried, "Will no one bring Hardy to me? He must be killed!" An hour and ten minutes elapsed from the time when Nelson received his wound before Hardy could come to him. They shook hands in silence; Hardy in vain struggling to suppress the feelings of that most painful and yet sublimest moment.

"Well, Hardy," said Nelson, "how goes the

day with us?"—"Very well," replied Hardy; "ten ships have struck, but five of the van have tacked, and show an intention to bear down upon the *Victory*. I have called two or three of our fresh ships round, and have no doubt of giving them a sound drubbing."—"I hope," said Nelson, "none of our ships have struck!" Hardy answered, "There is no fear of that." Then, and not till then, Nelson spoke of himself. "I am a dead man, Hardy," said he; "I am going fast; it will all be over with me soon. Come nearer to me. Let my dear Lady Hamilton have my hair and all other things belonging to me." Hardy observed, that he hoped Mr. Beatty could yet hold out some prospect of life. "Oh, no!" he replied; "it is impossible. My back is shot through; Beatty will tell you so." Captain Hardy then once more shook hands with him, and, with a heart almost bursting, hastened upon deck. By this time all feeling below the breast was gone; and Nelson, having made the surgeon ascertain this, said to him, "You know I am gone. I feel something rising in my breast which tells me so." And upon Beatty's inquiring whether his pain was very great, he replied, so great that he wished that he was dead. "Yet," said he, in a lower voice, "one would like to live a little longer too!" And after a few minutes, in the same undertone, he added, "What would become of poor Lady Hamilton if she knew my situation?" Next to his country she occupied his thoughts.

Captain Hardy, some fifty minutes after he had left the cockpit, returned: and, again taking the hand of his dying friend and commander, congratulated him on having gained a complete victory. How many of the enemy were taken he did not know, as it was impossible to perceive them distinctly; but fourteen or fifteen at least. "That is well," said Nelson; "but I bargained for twenty." And then, in a stronger voice, he said, "Anchor, Hardy, anchor!" Hardy upon this hinted that Admiral Collingwood would take upon himself the direction of affairs. "Not while I live," said the dying Nelson, ineffectually endeavoring to raise himself from the bed; "do you anchor." Presently calling Hardy back, he said to him in a low voice, "Dont throw me overboard!" and desired that he might be buried by his parents, unless it should please the king to order otherwise. Then, reverting to his private feelings: "Take care of poor Lady Hamilton. Kiss me, Hardy," said he. Hardy stood over him in silence for a moment or two, then knelt again and kissed him on his forehead. "Who is that?" said Nelson; and being informed, he replied, "God bless you, Hardy!" And then Hardy left him forever.

Nelson now desired to be turned upon his right side, and said, "I wish I had not left the deck; for I shall soon be gone." Death was indeed rapidly approaching. He said to the chaplain, "Doctor, I have not been a very great sinner;" and after a short pause, "Remember that I leave Lady Hamilton as a legacy to my country." His articulation now became difficult; but he was distinctly heard to say, "Thank God, I have done my duty!" These words he repeatedly pronounced; and they were the last words which he uttered. He expired at thirty minutes after four—three hours and a quarter after he had received his wound.

IMMORTALITY OF LOVE.

They sin who tell us Love can die.
With life all other passions fly,
All others are but vanity:
In heaven Ambition cannot dwell,
Nor Avarice in the vaults of hell;
Earthly these passions of the earth,
They perish where they have their birth:
But Love is indestructible;
Its holy flame forever burneth,
From heaven it came, to heaven returneth.
Too oft on earth a troubled guest,
At times deceived, at times oppressed,

It here is tried and purified,
Then hath in heaven its perfect rest.
It soweth here with toil and care,
But the harvest-time of Love is there.
Oh! when a mother meets on high
The babe she lost in infancy,
Hath she not then, for pains and fears,
The day of woe, the watchful night,
For all her sorrow, all her tears,
An over-payment of delight?

Kehama.

THE MAGIC THREAD.

He found a woman in the cave,
A solitary woman,
Who by the fire was spinning,
And singing, as she spun.
The pine-boughs were cheerfully blazing,
And her face was bright with the flame,
Her face was as a damsel's face,
And yet her hair was gray.
She bade him welcome with a smile,
And still continued spinning,
And singing as she spun.

The thread she spun it gleamed like gold
In the light of the odorous fire;
Yet was it so wondrously thin,
That, save when it shone in the light,
You might look for it closely in vain.
The youth sate watching it,
And she observed his wonder,
And then again she spake,
And still her speech was song:—
"Now twine it round thy hands, I say,
Now twine it round thy hands I pray:
My thread is small, my thread is fine,
But he must be
A stronger than thee,
Who can break this thread of mine!"

And up she raised her bright blue eyes,
And sweetly she smiled on him,
And he conceived no ill;
And round and round his right hand,

And round and round his left,
He wound the thread so fine.
And then again the woman spake,
And still her speech was song :—
"Now thy strength, O stranger, strain!
Now then break this slender chain!"

Thalaba strove, but the thread
By magic hands was spun;
And in his cheek the flush of shame
Arose, commixed with fear.
She beheld, and laughed at him,
And then again she sung :—
"My thread is small, my thread is fine,
But he must be
A stronger than thee,
Who can break this thread of mine!"

And up she raised her bright blue eyes,
And fiercely she smiled on him :—
I thank thee, I thank thee, Hodeirah's son!
I thank thee for doing what can't be undone,
For binding thyself in the chain I have spun!"
Then from his head she wrenched
A lock of his raven hair,
And cast it into the fire,
And cried aloud as it burnt,
"Sister, Sister! hear my voice!
Sister! Sister! come and rejoice!
The thread is spun, the prize is won,
The work is done,
For I have made captive Hodeirah's son!"

Thalaba.

THE FATE OF THE LAST OF THE GOTHS.

The evening darkened, but the avenging sword
Turned not away its edge till night had closed
Upon the field of blood. The chieftain then
Blew the recall; and from their perfect work
Returned rejoicing, all but he for whom
All looked with most expectance. - He full sure
Had thought upon that field to find his end
Desired, and with Florinda in the grave
Rest, in indissoluble union joined.
But still where through the press of war he
went

Half-armed, and like a lover seeking death,
The arrows passed him by to right and left;
The spear-point pierced him not, the scimitar
Glanced from his helmet. He, when he beheld
The rout complete, saw that the shield of Heaven
Had been extended over him once more,
And bowed before its will. Upon the banks
Of Sella was Orelio found, his legs
Incarnadined, his poitral smeared
With froth and foam and gore; his silver mane
Sprinkled with blood, which hung on every hair,
Aspersed like dew-drops. Trembling there he stood
From the toil of battle, and at times sent forth
His tremulous voice, far-echoing loud and shrill,
A frequent, anxious cry, with which he seemed
To call the master whom he loved so well,
And who had thus again forsaken him.
Silverian's helm and cuirass on the grass
Lay near; and Julian's sword, its hilt and chain
Clotted with blood. But where was he whose hand
Had wielded it so well that glorious day? . . . . .
Days, month, and years, and generations passed,
And centuries held their course, before far-off
Within a hermitage near Viseu's walls
A humble tomb was found, which bore inscribed
In ancient characters King Roderick's name.

Roderick.

THE BATTLE OF BLENHEIM.

It was a summer evening,
Old Kaspar's work was done,
And he before his cottage door
Was sitting in the sun;
And by him sported on the green
His little grandchild Wilhelmine.

She saw her brother Peterkin
Roll something large and round,

Which he beside the rivulet,
 In playing there, had found;
He came to ask what he had found,
That was so large, and smooth and round.

Old Kaspar took it from the boy,
 Who stood expectant by;
And then the old man shook his head,
 And with a natural sigh,
"'Tis some poor fellow's skull," said he,
"Who fell in the great victory.

"I find them in the garden,
 For there's many here about;
And often, when I go to plough,
 The ploughshare turns them out;
For many thousand men," said he,
"Were slain in that great victory."

"Now tell us what 'twas all about,"
 Young Peterkin he cries;
While little Wilhelmine looks up,
 With wonder-waiting eyes;
"Now tell us all about the war,
And what they killed each other for."

"It was the English," Kaspar cried,
 "Who put the French to rout;
But what they killed each other for
 I could not well make out;
But everybody said," quoth he,
"That 'twas a famous victory.

"My father lived at Blenheim then,
 Yon little stream hard by;
They burned his dwelling to the ground,
 And he was forced to fly;
So with his wife and child he fled,
Nor had he where to lay his head.

"With fire and sword the country round
 Was wasted far and wide;
And many a childing mother then
 And new-born baby died:
But things like these, you know, must be
At every famous victory.

"They say it was a shocking sight
After the field was won;
For many a thousand bodies here
Lay rotting in the sun;
But things like that, you know must be
After a famous victory.

Great praise the Duke of Marlbro' won,
And our good Prince Eugene."—
"Why 'twas a very wicked thing!"
Said little Wilhelmine.—
"Nay, nay, my little girl," quoth he,
"It was a famous victory.

And everybody praised the Duke
Who this great fight did win."
"And what good came of it at last?"
Quoth little Peterkin.
"Why, that I cannot tell," said he;
"But 'twas a famous victory."

THE HOLLY-TREE.

O reader! hast thou ever stood to see
The Holly-tree?
The eye that contemplates it well perceives
Its glossy leaves,
Ordered by an intelligence so wise
As might confound the Atheist's sophistries.

Below, a circling fence, its leaves are seen,
Wrinkled and keen;
No grazing cattle through their prickly round
Can reach to wound,
But as they grow where nothing is to fear,
Smooth and unarmed the pointless leaves appear.

I love to view these things with curious eyes,
And moralize;
And in this wisdom of the Holly-tree
Can emblems see
Wherewith perchance to make a pleasant rhyme—
One which may profit in the after time.

Thus, though abroad perchance I might appear
Harsh and austere,

To those who on my leisure would intrude,
　　Reserved and rude,
Gentle at home amid my friends I'd be,
Like the high leaves upon the Holly-tree.

And should my youth—as youth is apt, I know—
　　Some harshness show,
All vain asperities I day by day
　　Would wear away,
Till the smooth temper of my age should be
Like the high leaves upon the Holly-tree.

And as, when all the summer trees are seen
　　So bright and green,
The Holly-leaves a sober hue display
　　Less bright than they;
But when the bare and wintry woods we see,
What then so cheerful as the Holly-tree.

So serious should my youth appear among
　　The thoughtless throng;
So would I seem amid the young and gay
　　More grave than they,
That in my age as cheerful I might be
As the green winter of the Holly-tree.

IN MY LIBRARY.

My days among the dead are past;
　Around me I behold,
Where'er these casual eyes are cast,
　The mighty minds of old.
My never-failing friends are they,
With whom I converse day by day.

With them I take delight in weal,
　And seek relief in woe;
And while I understand and feel
　How much to them I owe,
My cheeks have often been bedewed
With tears of thoughtful gratitude. . .

My hopes are with the dead. Anon
　With them my place will be;
And I with them shall travel on
　Through all futurity;
Yet leaving here a name, I trust,
That will not perish in the dust.

SPARKS, Jared, an American biographer and historical writer, born at Willington, Conn., in 1789; died at Cambridge, Mass., in 1866. He graduated at Harvard in 1815. In 1817 he was appointed tutor in mathematics and natural philosophy in the college; in 1819 he was ordained pastor of a new Unitarian church at Baltimore. He took part in the theological controversies of the time, and in 1821 was chosen chaplain to the House of Representatives. In 1823 he resigned his pastorate, and became editor of the *North American Review*, which he had aided in establishing, and to which he had been a frequent contributor. In 1839 he became Professor of Ancient and Modern History at Harvard; and in 1849 was made President of the College, but resigned the presidency in 1853 on account of impaired health. Mr. Sparks commenced his biographical work by the *Life of John Ledyard* (1828). In 1830 he originated the *American Almanac and Repository of Useful Knowledge*, the early volumes of which were edited by him. In 1832 he published the Life of Governeur Morris. In 1834 he projected the *Library of American Biography*, which reached twenty-five volumes (1834–1848), containing sixty biographies, of which those of Ethan Allen, Benedict Arnold, Marquette, De la Salle, Pulaski, Ribault, Charles Lee, and Ledyard were by Sparks. As early as 1826 he began the preparatory labor on what proved to be the main work of his life, and which was carried on with the direct aid of Congress. These works are: the *Writings of George Washington* (10 vols., 1834–1838), the *Diplomatic Correspondence of the American Revolution*

(12 vols., 1829-30), the *Works of Benjamin Franklin* (10 vols.,) 1836-1840), the *Correspondence of the American Revolution* (4 vols., 1854). At the time of his death he was engaged upon a *History of the American Revolution.* The *Memoirs of Jared Sparks* have been best written by George E. Ellis (1869).

WASHINGTON'S DOCUMENTS.

The large mass of papers accumulated in the hands of Washington during the long period of his public life, as well as those of a private nature, were carefully preserved by him at Mount Vernon. By his will he left his estate at Mount Vernon and all his papers to his nephew, Bushrod Washington, who was for many years one of the associate justices of the Supreme Court of the United States. These manuscripts were placed in my possession by Judge Washington for the purpose of preparing for the press and publishing the work which is now brought to a conclusion and submitted to the public.

The original papers, including Washington's own letters and those received by him, and amounting to more than two hundred folio volumes, have recently been purchased by Congress and are deposited in the archives of the Department of State. With these materials it will readily be supposed that the work might have been extended to a much larger number of volumes. The task of selection has not been without its difficulties. I feel bound to say, however, that any errors in this respect should be attributed to defects of judgment, and not to carelessness or negligence. . . . .

It was Washington's custom, in all his letters of importance first to write drafts which he transcribed. In making the transcripts he sometimes deviated from the drafts—omitting, inserting, and altering parts of sentences; nor did he always correct the drafts so as to make them accord with the letters as sent to his correspondents. These imperfect drafts were laid aside, and from time to time copied by an amanuensis into letter-books. Hence the drafts, as now recorded, do not in all cases agree precisely with the originals which were sent away. My researches have brought under my inspection many of these original letters. Regarding them as containing the genuine text, I have preferred it to that in the letter-books; and it has accordingly been adopted whenever it could be done. But the discrepancies are of little moment, relating to the style, not to the substance.

For the most part I have been obliged to rely upon the letter-books; and, for the reasons here mentioned, it is probable that the printed text may not in every particular be the same as in the originals—that is, the corrected copies which were sent to his correspondents. These remarks apply chiefly to private letters, written when Washington was at Mount Vernon, and to those written during the French War. In the période of the Revolution, and during the Presidency, much more exactness was observed; and as far as my observation has extended, there is generally a literal accordance between the original letters and the transcripts in the letter-books.—*Preface to Writings of Washington.*

THE STATESMEN OF THE REVOLUTION.

The acts of the Revolution derive dignity and interest from the character of the actors and the nature and magnitude of the events. Statesmen were at hand who, if not skilled in the art of governing empires, were thoroughly imbued with the principles of just government, intimately acquainted with the history of former ages and, above all, with the condition, sentiments, and feelings of their countrymen. If there were no Richelieus nor Mazarins, no Cecils nor Chathams in America, there were men who, like Themistocles, knew how to raise a small state to glory and greatness.

The eloquence and the internal counsels of the Old Congress were never recorded; we know them only by their results. But that assembly, with no other power than that conferred by the suffrage of the people, with no other influence than that of their public virtue and their talents, unsupported even by the arm of the law or of ancient usages—that assembly levied troops, imposed taxes, and for years not only retained the confidence and upheld the civil existence of a distracted country, but carried through a perilous war, under its most aggravated burdens of sacrifice and suffering. Can we imagine a situation in which were required higher moral courage, more intelligence and talent, a deeper insight into human nature and the principles of social and political organizations, or, indeed, any of those qualities which constitute greatness of character in a statesman?

See, likewise, that work of wonder, the Confederation—a union of Independent States, constructed in the very heart of a desolating war, but with a beauty and strength, imperfect as it was, of which the ancient leagues of the Amphictyons, the Achæans, the Lycians and the modern confederacies of Germany, Holland. Switzerland afford neither exemplar nor parallel. In their foreign affairs these same statesmen showed no less sagacity and skill, taking their stand boldly in the rank of nations, maintaining it there, competing with the tactics of practiced diplomacy, and extorting from the Powers of the Old World not only the homage of respect but the proffers of friendship.

The instructive lesson of history, teaching by example, can nowhere be studied with more profit, or with a better promise, than in this Revolutionary period of America; and especially by us, who sit under the tree our fathers have planted, enjoy its shade, and are nourished by its fruits.—*The Men of the Revolution.*

SPEDDING James, an English biographer, born in 1808; died in 1881. In 1870, he put forth, in conjunction with R. L. Ellis and D. D. Heath, an edition of the *Works of Francis Bacon*. As a supplement to this, Mr. Spedding published in 1874 the *Letters and Life of Francis Bacon*, in seven volumes. Upon the preparation of these works was lavished the labor of nearly a score of years. Mr. Spedding announces that his object was "to enable posterity to form a true conception of the kind of man Bacon really was." While the fact of Bacon's having accepted bribes in his judicial capacity is admitted, his biographer does the best that could be done to palliate the enormity of his guilt.

BACON AND HIS CRIME.

I know nothing more inexplicable than Bacon's unconsciousness of the nature of his own case, unless it be the case itself. That he, of all men, whose fault had always been too much carelessness about money, who though always too ready to borrow, to give, to lend, and to spend; had never been either a bargainer, or a grasper, or a hoarder; and whose professional experience must have continually reminded him of the peril of meddling with anything that could be construed into corruption; that he should have allowed himself on any account to accept money from suitors, while their cases were before him is wonderful. That he should have done it without feeling at the time that he was laying himself open to what in law would be called bribery, is more wonderful still. That he should have done it often, and not have lived under an abiding sense of insecurity—from the consciousness that he had secrets to conceal, of which the disclosure would be fatal to his reputation, yet the safe-keeping of which did not rest wholly with himself—is most wonderful of all.

Give him credit for nothing more than ordinary intelligence and ordinary prudence—wisdom for a man's self—and it seems almost incredible. And yet I believe it was the fact. The whole course of his behavior, from the first rumor to the final sentence, convinces me that not the discovery of the thing only, but the thing itself, came upon him as a surprise; and that if anybody had told him the day before that he stood in danger of a charge of taking bribes, he would have received the suggestion with unaffected incredulity. How far I am justified in thinking so, the reader shall judge for himself, for the impression is derived solely from the tenor of the correspondence.

DEATH OF THE DUKE OF WELLINGTON.

A public funeral was of course decreed, and never in any country was such a solemnity celebrated. The procession was planned, marshalled, and carried out, with a discretion, a judgment, and a good taste which reflected the highest honor on the civil and military authorities by whom it was directed. Men of every arm and of every regiment in the service, for the first and last time in the history of the British army, marched together on this occasion. But what was more admirable still was the conduct of the incredible mass of sympathetic spectators who had congregated from all parts of the kingdom, and who formed no insignificant proportion of its population. From Grosvenor Gate to St. Paul's Cathedral there was not one foot of unoccupied ground; not a balcony not a window, that was not filled, and as far as could be observed, every face amidst that vast multitude wore an expression of respectful sorrow. And unbroken silence was maintained as the funeral cortège moved slowly and solemnly forward to the mausoleum prepared to receive the remains of England's greatest warrior in the central of the stupendous masterpiece of Wren's architectural genius. —*History of England.*

SPEKE, John Hanning, an English explorer in Africa, born in Devonshire in 1827; died near Bath, in 1864. At seventeen he was commissioned as ensign in the Bengal Native Infantry, served in the war of the Punjaub, and rose to the rank of lieutenant. In 1854 he accompanied Captain Burton in an exploration in Eastern Africa, and two years afterward in an expedition to ascertain the character of the great lakes supposed to exist in the interior, and especially whether they were connected with the basin of the Nile. In this expedition Lake Tanganyike was discovered. In 1858 Speke traveled northward and reached the southern end of the great lake now designated as the Victoria Nyanza, which he, in contradiction to the views of Burton, thought was the true source of the Nile. To settle this question, Speke, who was now accompanied by Captain James Grant, headed another expedition which set out in 1860. He traversed a region hitherto unvisited by Europeans, reached the kingdom of Uganda, near the northern end of the Victoria Nyanza, discovered the outlet of the lake, which he afterwards showed to be the real source of the Nile or rather of that branch of it, known as the "White Nile." This he descended as far as its junction with the "Blue Nile," which rises among the mountains of Abyssinia. He was the first to ascertain practically the true character of the Nile. Returning to England, he put forth in 1863 his *Journal of the Discovery of the Source of the Nile*, which was followed by a supplementary work, *What Led to the Discovery of the Sources of the Nile*. He was killed on the 15th of September

1864, by the accidental discharge of his own gun.

INTRODUCTION TO THE COURT OF UGANDA.

The mighty King was now reported to be sitting on his throne in the state-hut. I advanced, hat in hand, with my guard of honor following, formed in open ranks, who, in their turn were followed by the bearers carrying the presents. I did not walk straight up to him as if to shake hands, but went outside of the ranks to a three-sided square of squatting Wakungu, all habited in skins—mostly cow-skins; some few of them had in addition leopard-skins girt around the waist—the sign of royal blood. Here I was desired to halt and sit in the glaring sun; so I donned my hat, mounted my umbrella—a phenomenon which set them all wondering and laughing; ordered the guard to close ranks, and sat gazing at the novel spectacle.

A more theatrical sight I never saw. The King—a good-natured, well-figured young man of twenty-five—was sitting on a red blanket spread upon a square platform of royal grass, incased in tiger grass reeds, scrupulously well-dressed mbugu. The hair of his head was cut short excepting on the top, where it was combed up to a high ridge, running from stem to stern, like a cock's-comb. On his neck was a very neat ornament—a large ring of beautifully worked beads, forming elegant patterns by their various colors. On one arm was another bead ornament, prettily devised, and on the other a wooden charm, tied by a string, covered with snake-skin. On every finger and every toe he had alternate brass and copper rings; and above the ankles, half-way up to the calf, a stocking of very pretty beads. Everything was light, neat, and elegant in its way; not a fault could be found with the taste of his "getting-up." For a handkerchief he had a well-folded piece of bark, and a piece of gold-embroidered silk, which he constantly employed to hide his large mouth when laughing, or to wipe it after a drink of plantain-wine, of which he took constant and copious draughts from neat little gourd-cups, administered by his ladies-in-waiting, who were at once his sisters and wives. A white dog, spear, shield, and woman—the Uganda cognizance—were by his side, as also a knot of staff-officers with whom he kept up a brisk conversation, on one side; and on the other was a band of Wachwézi, or lady sorcerers.

I was now asked to draw nearer within the hollow-square of squatters, where leopard-skins strewed upon the ground, and a large copper kettle-drum, surmounted with brass bells on arching wires, with two other smaller drums covered with cowrie-shells and beads of color worked into patterns, were placed. I now longed to open conversation, but knew not the language, and no one near me dared speak, or even lift his head, from fear of being accused of eying the women; so the King and myself sat staring at one another for full an hour; I mute, and he pointing and remarking to those around him on the novelty of my guard and general appearance, and requiring to see my hat lifted, the umbrella shut and opened, and the guards face about and show off their red cloaks; for such wonders had never been seen in Uganda.

Then, finding the day waning, he sent Maula on an embassy to ask me if I had seen him; and on receiving my reply, "Yes, for full an hour," I was glad to see him rise, spear in hand, lead his dog, and walk unceremoniously away through the inclosure into the fourth tier of huts; for this being a pure levée-day, no business was transacted. The King's gait on retiring was intended to be very majestic, but did not succeed in conveying to me that impression. It was the traditional walk of his race, founded on the step of the lion; but the outward sweep of the legs, intended to represent the stride of the noble beast, appeared to me to realize only a very ludicrous kind of waddle. —*Source of the Nile.*

SPENCER, HERBERT, an English author, born at Derby in 1820. At the age of seventeen he became a civil engineer; but abandoned that profession after about eight years, and devoted himself to studying the problems of social life, contributing largely to perodicals. His principal works are: *The Proper Sphere of Government* (1842), *Over-Legislation* (1854), *Principles of Psychology* (1855), *Education: Intellectual, Moral, and Physical* (1861), *Principles of Biology* (1863), *Essays: Scientific, Political, and Speculative* (1858-1863), *The Study of Sociology* (1872), *The Principles of Sociology*, vol. I. (1876), *Classification of the Sciences* (1874), *Sins of Trade and Commerce* (1875), *The Data of Ethics* (1879), *Ceremonial Institutions* (1879), *Political Institutions* (1882), *Ecclesiastical Institutions* (1885), *Man versus the State* (1884), *The Facts of Organic Evolution* (1887), *An Epitome of Synthetic Philosophy* (1889). His works have passed through numerous editions, and many of them have been translated into more than one language, that on Education being rendered into all of the European languages including Greek, and into Japanese and Chinese.

THE STUDY OF LANGUAGES AND OF THE SCIENCES.

One advantage claimed for that devotion to language-learning which forms so prominent a feature in the odinary *curriculum* is that the memory is thereby strengthened; and it is apparently assumed that this is an advantage peculiar to the study of words. But the truth is that the sciences afford far wider fields for the exercise of memory. It is no slight task to remember all the facts ascertained respecting our solar system, much more to remember all that is known concerning the structure of our galaxy. The new compounds which chemistry daily accumulates are so numerous that few save professors know the names of them all: and to recollect the atomic constitutions and affinities of all these compounds is scarcely possible without making chemistry the occupation of life. So vast is the accumulation of facts which men of science have before them. that only by dividing and subdividing their labors can they deal with it. To a complete knowledge of his own division each adds but a general knowledge of the rest. Surely, then, science, cultivated even to a very moderate extent, affords adequate exercise for memory. To say the very least, it involves quite as good a training for this faculty as language does.

But now mark, that while for the training of mere memory, science is as good as, if not better than language. it has an immense superiority in the kind of memory it cultivates. In the acquirement of a language. the connections of ideas to be established in the mind correspond to facts that are in great measure accidental; whereas in the acquirement of science the connections of ideas to be established in the mind correspond to facts that are mostly necessary. It is true that the relations of words to their meaning is in one sense natural. and that the genesis of these relations may be traced back to a certain distance, though very rarely to the beginning: to which let us add the remark that the laws of this genesis form a branch of mental science—the science of philology. But since it will not be contended that in the acquisition of languages, as ordinarily carried on, these natural relations between words and their meanings are habitually traced, and the laws regulating them explained. it must be admitted that they are commonly learned as fortuitous relations. On the other hand, the relations which science presents are casual relations; and when properly taught are understood as such. Instead of being practically accidental, they are necessary; and, as such, give exercise to the reasoning faculties. While language familiarizes with non-rational relations, science familiarizes with rational relations. While the one exercises memory only, the other exercises both memory and understanding.

Observe next that a great superiority of science over language as a means of discipline is that it cultivates the judgment. As Professor Faraday well remarks, the most common intellectual fault is deficiency of judgment. He contends that "Society, speaking generally, is not only ignorant as respects education of the judgment, but is ignorant of its ignorance." And the cause to which he ascribes this state is want of scientific culture. The truth of his conclusion is obvious. Correct judgment with regard to all surrounding things, events, and consequences becomes possible only through knowledge of the way in which surrounding phenomena depend on each other. No extent of acquaintance with the meaning of words can give the power of forming correct inferences respecting causes and effects. The constant habit of drawing conclusions from data, and then of verifying those conclusions by observation and experiment, can alone give the power of judging. And that it necessitates this habit is one of the immense advantages of science.

Not only, however, for intellectual discipline is science the best, but also for *moral* discipline. The learning of language tends, if anything, further to increase the already undue respect for authority. Such and such are the meanings of these words, says the teacher or the dictionary. So and so is the rule in this case, says the grammar. By the pupil these dicta are received as unquestionable. His constant attitude of mind is that of submission to dogmatic authority; and a necessary result is a tendency to accept without inquiry, whatever is established.

Quite opposite is the attitude of mind generated by the cultivation of science. By science constant appeal is made to individual reason. Its truths are not accepted upon authority alone; but all are at liberty to test them; nay, in many cases, the pupil is required to think out his own conclusions. Every step in a scientific conclusion is submitted to his judgment. He is not asked to admit it without seeing it to be true. And the trust in his own powers thus produced is further increased by the constancy with which Nature justifies his conclusions when they are correctly drawn. From all which there flows that independence which is a most valuable element in character. Nor is this the only moral benefit bequeathed by scientific culture. When carried on, as it should always be, as much as possible under the form of independent research, it exercises perseverance and sincerity.—*Education, Intellectual, Moral and Physical.*

SELF-EDUCATION.

In education the process of self-development should be encouraged to the fullest extent. Children should be led to make their own investigations, and to draw their own inferences. They should be *told* as little as possible, and induced to *discover* as much as possible. Humanity has progressed solely by self-instruction; and that to achieve the best results, each mind must progress somewhat after the same fashion, is continually proved by the marked success of self-made men. Those who have been brought up under the ordinary school-drill, and have carried away with them the idea that education is practicable only in that style, will think it hopeless to make children their own teachers. If, however, they will call to mind that the all-important knowledge of surrounding objects which a child gets in its early years is got without help—if they will remember that the child is self-taught in the use of its mother tongue—if they will estimate the amount of that experience of life, that out-of-school wisdom, which every boy gathers for himself—if they will mark the unusual intelligence of the uncared-for London *gamin*, as shewn in all the directions in which his faculties have been tasked—if, further, they will think how many minds have struggled up unaided, not only through the mysteries of our irrationally-planned *curriculum*, but through hosts of other obstacles besides; they will find it a not unreasonable conclusion, that if the subjects be put before him in right order and right form, any pupil of ordinary capacity will surmount his successive difficulties with but little assistance. Who indeed can watch the ceaseless observation, and inquiry, and inference going on in a child's mind, or listen to its acute remarks on matters within the range of its faculties, without perceiving that these powers which it manifests, if brought to bear systematically upon any studies *within the same range*, would readily master them without help? This need for perpetual telling is the result of our stupidity, not of the child's. We drag it away from the facts in which it is interested, and which it is actively assimilating of itself; we put before it facts far too complex for it to understand, and therefore distasteful to it; finding that it will not voluntarily acquire these facts, we thrust them into its mind by force of threats and punishment; by thus denying the knowledge it craves, and cramming it with knowledge it cannot digest, we produce a morbid state of its faculties, and a consequent disgust for knowledge in general; and when, as a result partly of the stolid indolence we have brought on, and partly of still continued unfitness in its studies, the child can understand nothing without explanation, and becomes a mere passive recipient of our instruction, we infer that education must necessarily be carried on thus. Having by our method induced helplessness, we straightway make the helplessness a reason for our method.—*Education.*

SPENSER, Edmund, an English poet, born at London in 1553, died there in 1599. In 1569 he was entered at Pembroke Hall, Cambridge, where he took his first degree in 1572. In 1580 he was appointed Secretary to Lord Grey of Wilton, the Queen's deputy in Ireland. In 1586 he received a grant of 3,000 acres of land in the County of Cork. In 1590 he was visited by Sir Walter Raleigh, who took him to England, and presented him to Queen Elizabeth. In 1594 he married, and his *Epithalamion* was written to welcome his bride to their Irish home. In 1598 he was made Sheriff of Cork. His office rendered him obnoxious to the disaffected Irish, who attacked and burned his residence of Kilcolman Castle, his wife and infant son perishing in the flames. He returned to London, where he soon died, and at his own request was buried in Westminster Abbey, close by the tomb of Chaucer. The principal poems of Spenser are: *The Shepherd's Calendar* (1579), the *Epithalamion* (1594), *The Faerie Queene*, the first two books of which appeared in 1590, and three others in 1595. There were to have been six more books, of which only one canto, and a fragment of another exists. In 1590 appeared a collection of his lesser poems, entitled *Complaints;* and in 1596 four *Hymns*, celebrating the Platonic doctrine of Beauty. He also wrote, in prose, a *View of Ireland.*

AT THE ALTAR.

Open the temple gates unto my love,
Open them wide that she may enter in,
And all the posts adorn as doth behove,
And all the pillars deck with garlands trim,
For to receive this saint with honour due,
   That cometh in to you.

With trembling steps, and humble reverence,
She cometh in, before the Almighty's view;
Of her ye virgins, learn obedience,
When so ye come into those holy places,
To humble your proud faces:
Bring her up to the high altar, that she may
The sacred ceremonies there partake,
The which do endless matrimony make;
And let the roaring organs loudly play
The praises of the Lord in lively notes
The whiles, with hollow throats,
The choristers with joyous anthem sing,
That all the woods may answer, and their echo
ring.

Behold, whiles she before the altar stands,
Hearing the holy priest that to her speaks,
And blesseth her with his two happy hands,
How the red roses flush up in her cheeks,
And the pure snow, with goodly vermeil stain,
Like crimson dyed in grain;
That even the angels, which continually
About the sacred altar do remain,
Forget their service, and about her fly,
Oft peeping in her face, that seems more fair,
The more they on it stare.
But her sad eyes, still fastened on the ground,
Are governéd with goodly modesty,
That suffers not one look to glance awry,
Which may let in a little thought unsound.
Why blush ye, love, to give to me your hand
The pledge of all our band?
Sing, ye sweet angels, alleluja sing,
That all the woods may answer, and your echo
ring. *The Epithalamion.*

UNA AND THE LION.

One day, nigh weary of the irksome way,
From her unhasty beast she did alight;
And on the grass her dainty limbs did lay
In secret shadow, far from all men's sight;
From her fair head her fillet she undight,
And laid her stole aside; her angel's face,

As the great eye of heaven, shined bright,
And made a sunshine in the shady place;
Did never mortal eye behold such heavenly
grace.

It fortunéd, out of the thickest wood
A ramping lion rushéd suddenly,
Hunting full greedy after salvage blood.
Soon as the royal virgin he did spy,
With gaping mouth at her ran greedily,
To have at once devoured her tender corse;
But to the prey when as he drew more nigh,
His bloody rage assuagéd with remorse,
And, with the sight amazed, forgot his furious
force.

Instead thereof he kissed her weary feet,
And licked her lily hands with fawning
tongue,
As he her wrongéd innócence did weet.
Oh, how can beauty master the most strong,
And simple truth subdue avenging wrong!
Whose yielded pride and proud submission,
Still dreading death, when she had markéd
long,
Her heart 'gan melt in great compassion;
And drizzling tears did shed for pure affection.

"The lion, lord of every beast in field,"
Quoth she, "his princely puissance doth
abate,
And mighty proud to humble weak doth yield,
Forgetful of the hungry rage which late
Him pricked, in pity of my sad estate.
But he, my lion, and my noble lord,
How does he find in cruel heart to hate
Her that him loved, and ever most adored
As the god of my life? Why hath he me ab-
horred?"

Redounding tears did choke th' end of her
plaint,
Which softly echoed from the neighbor wood;
And, sad to see her sorrowful constraint,
The kingly beast upon her gazing stood:
With pity calmed, down fell his angry mood.

At last, in close heart shutting up her pain,
  Arose the virgin born of heavenly brood,
And to her snowy palfrey got again,
To seek her strayéd champion if she might
    attain.

The lion would not leave her desolate,
  But with her went along, as a strong guard
Of her chaste person, and a faithful mate
  Of her sad troubles and misfortunes hard.
  Still when she slept he kept both watch and
    ward;
And when she waked he waited diligent
  With humble service to her will prepared.
From her fair eyes he took commandément,
And ever by her looks conceivéd her intent.
Faerie Queene, Book I., Canto 3.

THE MINISTRY OF ANGELS.

And is there care in heaven? And is there
    love
  In heavenly spirits to these creatures base,
That may compassion of their evils move?—
  There is:—else much more wretched were the
    case
  Of men than beasts. But oh! the exceeding
    grace
Of mighty God, that loves his creatures so.
  And all his works with mercy doth embrace,
That blesséd angels He sends to and fro,
To serve the wicked man—to serve his wicked
    foe!

How oft do they their silver bowers leave
  To come to succor us that succor want!
How oft do they with golden pinions cleave
  The flitting skies, like flying pursuivant,
  Against foul fiends to aid us militant!
For us they fight, they watch and duly ward,
  And their bright squadrons round about us
    plant;
And all for love, and nothing for reward.
Oh, why should heavenly God to men have such
    regard?
Faerie Queene, Book II., Canto 8.

HEAVENLY AND EARTHLY BEAUTY.

Rapt with the rage of mine own ravished
thought,
Through contemplation of those goodly sights
And glorious images in heaven wrought,
Whose wondrous beauty, breathing sweet
delights,
Do kindle love in high-conceited sprites,
I fain to tell the things that I behold,
But feel my wits to fail, and tongue to fold.

Vouchsafe then, O thou most Almighty Sprite,
From whom all gifts of wit and knowledge
flow,
To shed into my breast some sparkling light
Of Thine eternal truth, that I may show
Some little beams to mortal eyes below
Of that Immortal Beauty there with Thee
Which in my weak distraughted mind I see;

That with the glory of so goodly sight
The hearts of men, which fondly here admire
Fair seeming shows, and feed on vain delight,
Transported with celestial desire
Of these fair forms, may lift themselves up
higher,
And learn to love, with zealous, humble duty,
The eternal fountain of that Heavenly Beauty.

Ne from thenceforth doth any fleshly sense
Or idle thought of earthly things remain;
But all that erst seemed sweet seems now
offence,
And all that pleaséd erst now seems to pain.
Their joy, their comfort, their desire, their gain
Is fixed all on that which now they see;
All other sights but feignéd shadows be.

And that fair lamp which useth to inflame
The hearts of men with self-consuming fire,
Thenceforth seems foul, and full of sinful
blame;
And all that pomp to which proud minds
aspire
By name of honor, and so much desire,

Seems to them baseness, and all riches dross,
And all mirth sadness, and all lucre loss.

So full their eyes are of that glorious sight,
And senses fraught with such satiety,
That in nought else on earth they can delight
But in th' aspect of that felicity,
Which they have written in their inward eye,
On which they feed, and in their fastened mind
All happy joy and full contentment find.

And then, my hungry soul, which long hast fed
On idle fancies of my foolish thought,
And, with false Beauty's flattering bait misled,
Hast after vain, deceitful shadows sought,
Which all are fled, and now have left thee nought
But late repentance through thy folly's prief,
Ah! cease to gaze on matter of thy grief;

And look at last up to that sovereign light
From whose pure beams all perfect Beauty springs,
That kindleth love in every godly sprite—
Even the Love of God, which loathing brings
Of this vile world and these gay-seeming things;
With whose sweet pleasures being so possessed,
Thy straying thoughts henceforth forever rest.

From Hymn of Heavenly Beauty.

WEDLOCK A FREE BONDAGE.

The doubt which ye misdeem, fair love, is vain,
That fondly fear to lose your liberty;
When, losing one, two liberties ye gain,
And make him bound that bondage erst did fly.
Sweet be the bonds the which true love doth tye,
Without constraint or dread of any ill.
The gentle bird feels no captivity
Within her cage; but sings and feeds her fill;
There Pride dare not approach, nor Discord spill

The league 'twixt them that loyal love hath bound;
But simple truth, and mutual good-will,
Seeks, with sweet peace, to salve each other's wound;
There Faith doth fearless dwell in brazen tower,
And spotless Pleasure builds her sacred bower.

EASTER MORNING.

Most glorious Lord of Life, that on this day
Didst make thy triumph over Death and Sin,
And, having harrowed Hell, didst bring away
Captivity thence captive, us to win;
This day, dear Lord, with joy begin;
And grant that we, for whom Thou diddest die,
Being with thy dear blood clean washed from sin,
May live forever in felicity;
And that thy love we weighing worthily
May likewise love Thee for the same again.
And for thy sake, that all like dear didst buy,
With love may one another entertain.
So let us love, dear Love, like as we ought:
Love is the lesson which the Lord us taught.

SPIELHAGEN, FRIEDRICH, a German novelist, born at Magdeburg, in 1829. He is the son of a German official, was educated at the University of Berlin, studied law in Bonn, and in 1854 went to Leipsic where he taught in the Gymnasium. Devoting himself to literature, he has gained a foremost place among modern German novelists. His works are: *Clara Vere* (1854), *On the Downs* (1858), *Problematical Characters* (1861), *Through Night to Light*, a sequel (1862), *At the Twelfth Hour* (1863), *The Rose of the Court* (1864), *The Hohensteins* (1864), *Rank and File* (1866), *Hans and Margaret* (1868), *The Village Coquette* (1869), *Hammer and Anvil* (1869), *German Pioneers* (1870), *Ever Forward* (1872), *What the Swallows Sang* (1873), *Ultimo* (1873), *Love for Love* (1875), *Storm-Floods* (1878), *Low Land* (1879), *The Skeleton in the House* (1879). *Quisisana* (1880), *Angela* (1881), *Uhlenhanns* (1803) and *A New Pharaoh* (1888), *Hans and Margaret* was dramatized as a comedy in 1876.

AMONG UNSEEN FOES.

They left the grotto and looked around. They could not see much as yet. A dense fog floated in waving masses over the meadows, now allowing green islands to rise from the gray sea, and then swallowing them up again. The forest from which they had come was lost to sight. Munzer thought it was on one side, Antonia on the other; they went first in this direction, then in that, and still the pine-trees which they sought would not show themselves. At last they saw them at some distance; but a brook, which had changed the meadow into a swamp, prevented the wanderers from approaching in a straight line. They turned aside, and instantly the wood was lost again in the mist. All of a sudden they found themselves near the stump on which they had been sitting last night. To the left of it, about a hundred yards farther on the edge of the wood, the little path led to the camp of the corps.

"All is right now," said Munzer, "but it was high time. What is that?"

A peculiar noise of bushes being trod down, and then again a low sound as of many men marching with equal step on a soft ground, and, between, every now and then, a word of command—thus it came up the hill.

They stood still and listened, breathless, into the mist.

"The enemy!" whispered Munzer, taking down his rifle.

"What are you going to do?"

"Give a warning before it is too late!" He fired; almost at the same instant several shots fell, which had been fired at hap-hazard by the approaching troops, and Munzer fell at Antonia's feet.

With a wild cry she sank down by his side and raised his bleeding head. She thought he had been killed, but she soon perceived that the ball had only glanced along the temple. and that all hope was not lost. She pressed her handkerchief on the gaping wound; she tore her silk fichu from her neck and bound it around his head. In vain! The blood but ran all the faster over her trembling hands. She loosened her belt, tore off her blouse, and wrapped it around him; she sat down on the grass and placed the dear head on her lap; she saw nothing but the flowing blood, nothing but the fading face. What did it matter to her that gray forms slipped by her on all sides, that soon the firing became more serious, large masses being engaged, and that at last the mist rose, and so deprived her of the only protection which had concealed her until now, as by a miracle, from the eyes of the attacking party. One company after another came up, sharp-shooters on the flanks, at the beat of the drum, charging the edge of the wood, which it seemed was held by the revolutionary troops, and obstinately defended. Again and again the bugle gave the signal for retreat. At last, however, they had apparently succeeded in gaining a hold on the forest; for the trees now resounded with the cheers of the soldiers and the crack of the rifles. A new battalion came to the support of the troops who were already engaged in the forest. The sharp-shooters deploying in line, approached the spot where Antonia was sitting motionless, with her terrible burden.

"There are some more dogs of republicans!" cried one, aiming at Antonia.

"Save your cartridge, my man!" said an officer, knocking up the barrel of the gun with his sword.

Lieutenant Todwitz had seen that the man who was lying on the ground, with his head in the lap of the handsome young woman, was either dead or grievously wounded: the sight had excited his pity. He rushed up to the group. Antonia looked at him with fixed, imploring eyes. She knew the young officer well; she had danced with him often enough in the city.

"Save him, Baron Todwitz!" she cried, forgetting everything else.

The officer was petrified. Was this Antonia?—The brilliant Antonia Hohenstein?—In this costume?—In such a position?

Nevertheless he was a good fellow, and not so hardened against the impulse of doing a heroic thing, that he was not touched by what he saw.

"I will do what I can," he said, "but I fear that will be little enough."—*The Hohensteins.*—*Transl. of* ACHELE DE VERE.

SPINOZA, BARUCH, a Dutch philosopher, of Jewish parentage, born at Amsterdam in 1632; died at the Hague in 1677. He Latinized his name of Baruch into BENEDICTUS, by which he is usually designated. He received a careful Rabbinical training; but at an early age he began to hold heterodox opinions, and was repeatedly summoned before a Rabbinical Council. As he failed to appear, the *anathema maranatha* was pronounced against him in 1656. At the urgency of the Rabbins he was banished from Amsterdam, and finally took up his residence at the Hague, where he devoted himself to speculative philosophy. He had learned the art of grinding lenses for optical instruments, by the exercise of which craft he supported himself, though poorly, for for most of his time was devoted to study. In 1673 he was offered a professorship in the University of Marburg, on condition that he would teach nothing opposed to the established religion; this he declined. A suggestion was made to him that he should dedicate some work to Louis XIV. of France, in the expectation of being rewarded by a pension; he replied that he had nothing to dedicate to that monarch. During his lifetime Spinoza put forth several profound treatises, but he withheld several of his most notable works, which were not published until after his death. Among these are the *Ethica*, the *Tractatus de Intellectus Emendatione*, the *Tractatus Theologico-Politicus*. Our extracts from his writings are given in the translation of J. A. Froude. The First Book of his *Ethica* contains a series of "Definitions" and "Axioms," which may be regarded as the basis of his philosophical system.

PHILOSOPHICAL DEFINITIONS.

(1.) By a thing which is *causus sui*—its own cause—I mean a thing the essence of which involves the existence of it, or a thing which cannot be conceived except as existing.—(2.) I call a thing finite, *suo genere*, when it can be limited by another (or others) of the same nature. For example, a given body is called finite, because we can always conceive another body enveloping it; but body is not limited by thought, nor thought by body.—(3.) By substance I mean what exists in itself, and is conceived by itself; the conception of which, that is, does not involve the conception of anything else as the cause of it.—(4.) By attribute I mean whatever the intellect perceives of substance as constituting the essence of substance. —(5.) Mode is an affection of substance, or is that which is in something else, by and through which it is conceived.—(6.) God is a being absolutely infinite; a substance consisting of infinite attributes, each of which expresses His eternal and infinite essence.

PHILOSOPHICAL AXIOMS.

(1.) All things that exist, exist either themselves or in virtue of something else.—(2.) What we cannot conceive of as existing in virtue of something else, we must conceive through and in itself.—(3.) From a given cause an effect necessarily follows, and if there be no cause, no effect can follow.—(4.) Things which have nothing in common with each other cannot be understood through one another; that is, the conception of one does not involve the conception of the other.—(5.) To understand an effect implies that we understand the cause of it.—(6.) A true idea is one which corresponds with its *ideate*—(7.) The essence of anything which can be conceived as non-existent does not involve existence.

SUBSTANCE AN ETERNAL VERITY.

If any one affirms that he has a clear, distinct—that is to say, a true—idea of substance, but that nevertheless he is uncertain whether any such substance exists, it is the same as if he were to affirm that he had a true idea, but yet was uncertain whether it was not false. Or if he says that substance can be created, it is like saying that a false idea can become a true idea; as absurd a thing as it is possible to conceive. And therefore the existence of substance, as well as the essence of it, must be acknowledged as an eternal verity.

THE BODY AND THE MIND.

What Body can or cannot do, no one has yet determined; Body, that is, by the law of its own nature and without any assistance from Mind. No one has so probed the human frame as to have detected all its functions, and exhausted the list of them. There are powers exhibited by animals far exceeding human sagacity; and, again, feats are performed by somnambulists on which in the waking state the same persons would never venture—itself a proof that Body is able to accomplish what Mind can only admire.

Men *say* that Mind moves Body; but how it moves it they cannot tell, or what degree of motion it can impart to it; so that, in fact, they do not know what they say, and are only confessing their own ignorance in specious language. They will answer me that whether or not they understand how it can be, yet they are assured by plain experience that unless Mind could perceive, Body would be altogether inactive; they know that it depends on the Mind whether the tongue speaks or is silent. But do they not equally experience that if their bodies are paralyzed their minds cannot think? that if their bodies are asleep their minds are without power? that their minds are not at all times able to exert themselves even on the same subject, but depend on the state of their bodies? And as for experience proving that the members of the Body can be controlled by the Mind, I fear experience proves very much the reverse.

But it is absurd, they rejoin, to attempt to explain, from the mere laws of Body, such things as pictures, or palaces, or works of art: the Body could not build a church unless the Mind directed it. I have shown, however, that we do not yet know what Body can or can not do, or what would naturally follow from the structure of it; that we experience in the feats of somnambulists something which, antecedently to that experience, would have seemed incredible. This fabric of the human body exceeds infinitely any contrivance of human skill, and an infinity of things, as I have already proved, ought to follow from it.

SPOFFORD, HARRIET ELIZABETH (PRESCOTT), an American author, born at Calais, Maine, in 1835. While she was a child her family removed to Newburyport, Mass., at or near which she has since resided. In 1855 she became the wife of Richard S. Spofford, a lawyer of Boston. About 1850 she began to write stories for periodicals. In 1859 she sent to the *Atlantic Monthly* a story of Parisian life, entitled *In a Cellar*, which was held in abeyance for some time under the impression that it was an unacknowledged translation from the French. This misapprehension was removed: the story was published, and Harriet Prescott soon became a frequent contributor to the best magazines. Some of her numerous pieces have from time to time been collected into volumes. Among her works are: *Sir Rohan's Ghost* (1859), *The Amber Gods, and Other Stories* (1863), *Azarian* (1864), *New England Legends* (1871), *The Thief in the Night* (1872), *Art Decoration applied to Furniture* (1881), *Marquis of Carabas* (1882), *Poems* (1882), *Hester Stanley at St. Mark's* (1883), *The Servant-Girl Question* (1884), *Ballads about Authors* (1888).

Her sister, MARY NEWMARCH PRESCOTT (1849–1888), was a frequent contributor, in prose and verse, to periodicals.

RUTH YETTON'S ART-STUDIES.

Without premeditation or affectation or search Miss Yetton had found an art; an art in which she stood almost alone. As she began to give herself rules, one that she found absolute was to work from nothing but the life. During the winter, and while yet her means were very small, the opposite course had been needful; but even then some little card where a handful of brown stems and ruddy berries from the snowy roadside seemed to have been thrown where she had caught just the topmost tips of the bare tree in the square, lined like any evanescent sea-moss, delicate as the threads of smoke that wander upward, faintly lined in rosy purple and etched upon a calm, deep sky with most exquisite and intricate entanglement of swaying spray and swinging bud; even then things like these commanded twice the price of any copy of her past sketches. Something of this was due to growth, perhaps. Already she felt that she handled her pencil with a swifter decision, and there was a courage in her color.

But when spring came she revelled. She took jaunts deeper among the outlying regions. One day, luncheon in pocket, she went pulling apart old fallen twigs and bits of stone on the edge of a chasm where dark and slumbrous waters forever mantled, and returning the forty miles in the afternoon train, brought home with her bountiful bunches, root and blood-red leaf, downy bud and flaky flower of the purple hepatica—the hepatica whose pristine element, floating out of heaven and sinking into the sod with every star-sown fall of snow, answers the first touch of wooing sunshine, assailed of dazzle, enriched with some tincture of the mould's own strain, and borrowing from the crumbling granites that companion it all winter an atom of fibre, a moment of permanence; breezy bits of gold and purple at last, cuddled in among old gnarls and roots, and calling the wild March sponsor. These before her she wrought patiently on ivory, with all delicate veinery and tender tint, painting in a glossy jet of background, till, rivalling the Florentine, the dainty mosaic was ready for the cunning goldsmith who should shape it to the pin that gathers the laces deep in any lady's bosom.

Then, when the brush had exhausted their last essence, some messenger of the year, some little stir in her pulse, warned her of hurrying May-flowers, and she sped down to the Plymouth woods, within sound of their rustling seashore, to pull up clustered wet trailing masses, flushed in the warmest, wealthiest pink, with the heartsomest flower that blows. And there, in the milder weather, she took her only familiar, her father, that he might plunge his trembling hands deep down among the flowers; or, sitting on a mossy knoll, listen to the wild song of the pines above. Sometimes, too, she stood with him through long reveries in the wide rhodora marshes, where some fleece of burning mist seemed to be falling, and caught and tangled in the filaments upon the bare twigs and sprays that lovingly detained it. At other times she lingered over the blushing wild-honeysuckle, and every tribe of fragrance poured strength and light into her spirit. Always in gathering her trophies from among their natural surroundings she felt half her picture painted. . . . .

At length, when—summer ended and her tramps among pastures on fire with their burning huckleberry-bushes, just begun — there came an order from across the seas for a book of autumn leaves, accompanied by a check for two hundred dollars, Miss Yetton thought her fortune made.—*Azarian.*

A SIGH.

It was nothing but a rose I gave her,
Nothing but a rose ;
Any wind might rob of half its savor,
Any wind that blows.

When she took it from my trembling fingers
With a hand as chill—
Ah, the flying touch upon them lingers,
Stays and thrills them still !

Withered, faded, pressed between the pages,
Crumpled fold on fold—
Once it lay upon her breast, and ages
Cannot make it old !

HAPPY DAY OF HAPPY JUNE.

Ah, happy day, refuse to go !
Hang in the heavens forever so!
Forever in mid afternoon,
Ah, happy day of happy June!
Pour out thy sunshine on the hill
The piny wood with perfume fill,
And breathe across the surging sea
Land-scented breezes that shall be
Sweet as the gardens that they pass
Where children tumble in the grass !

Ah, happy day, refuse to go!
Hang in the heavens forever so !
And long not for thy blushing rest
In the soft bosom of the west ;
But bid gray evening get her back
With all the stars upon her track!
Forget the dark, forget the dew,
The mystery of the midnight blue,
And only spread thy wide, warm wings,
While Summer her enchantment flings!

Ah, happy day, refuse to go!
Hang in the heavens forever so!
Forever let thy tender mist
Lie, like dissolving amethyst,
Deep in the distant dales, and shed
Thy mellow glory overhead !
Yet wilt thou wander—call the thrush,
And have the wilds and waters hush
To hear his passion-broken tune
Ah, happy day of happy June!

SPRAGUE, CHARLES, an American poet born at Boston in 1791; died in 1876. He was engaged in mercantile business until 1825, when he became cashier of the Globe Bank, Boston, a position from which he retired in 1864. A collection of his poems was published in 1850, and a later one in 1876. Besides numerous occasional poems they include the *Shakspeare Ode*, recited in 1823; *Curiosity*, delivered as a Phi Beta Kappa poem at Harvard, in 1829; and the Boston *Centennial Ode* (1830).

THE WINGED WORSHIPPERS.

[*Addressed to two little birds, who flew into a church during service, and remained perched there.*]

Gay, guiltless pair,
What seek ye from the fields of heaven?
Ye have no need of prayer,
Ye have no sins to be forgiven.

Why perch ye here,
Where mortals to their Maker bend?
Can your pure spirits fear
The God ye never could offend?

Ye never knew
The crimes for which we come to weep;
Penance is not for you,
Blest wanderers of the upper deep.

To you 'tis given
To wake sweet Nature's untaught lays;
Beneath the arch of heaven
To chirp away a life of praise.

Then spread each wing
Far, far above, o'er lakes and lands
And join the choirs that sing
In yon blue dome not reared with hands.

Or, if ye stay
To note the consecrated hour,
Teach me the airy way,
And let me try your envied power.

Above the crowd,
On upward wings could I but fly,
I'd bathe in yon bright cloud,
And seek the stars that gem the sky.

'Twere heaven indeed
Through fields of trackless light to soar,
On Nature's charms to feed,
And Nature's own great God adore.

I SEE THEE STILL.

I see thee still!
Remembrance, faithful to her trust,
Calls thee in beauty from the dust.
Thou comest in the morning light,
Thou'rt with me in the gloomy night;
In dreams I meet thee as of old,
Then thy soft arms my neck enfold,
And thy sweet voice is in mine ear.
In every scene to memory dear
I see thee still!

I see thee still!
In every hallowed token round:
This little ring thy finger bound,
This lock of hair thy forehead shaded,
This silken chain by thee was braided;
These flowers, all withered now like thee,
Sweet sister, thou didst cull for me;
This book was thine—here didst thou read,
This picture—ah yes! here indeed
I see thee still!

I see thee still!
Here was thy summer noon's retreat;
Here was thy favorite fireside seat;
This was thy chamber—here, each day,
I sat and watched thy sad decay,
Here on this bed thou last didst lie,
Here on this pillow thou didst die:
Dark hour! once more its woes unfold!
As then I saw thee pale and cold,
I see thee still!

I see thee still!
Thou art not in the grave confined—

Death cannot claim the immortal Mind.
Let earth close o'er its sacred trust,
But goodness dies not in the dust.
Thee, O my sister! 'tis not thee
Beneath the coffin's lid I see;
Thou to a fairer land art gone:
There let me hope, my journey done,
To see thee still!

SHAKSPEARE.

[*From an Ode recited at the Shakspeare Celebration in Boston, in* 1823.]

Then Shakspeare rose!—
Across the trembling strings
His daring hand he flings,
And lo! a new creation glows!
There, clustering round, submissive to his will,
Fate's vassal train his high commands fulfil:—

Madness, with his frightful scream,
Vengeance, leaning on his lance,
Avarice, with his blade and beam,
Hatred, blasting with a glance;
Remorse that weeps, and Rage that roars,
And Jealousy that dotes, but dooms, and murders yet adores;
Mirth, his face with sunbeams lit,
Waking Laughter's merry swell,
Arm in arm with fresh-eyed Wit,
That waves his tingling lash, while Folly Shakes his bell.

Despair, that haunts the gurgling stream,
Kissed by the virgin moon's cold beam,
Where some lost maid wild chaplets wreathes
And, swan-like, there her own dirge breathes,
Then broken-hearted sinks to rest,
Beneath the bubbling wave that shrouds her maniac breast.

Young Love with eye of tender gloom,
Now drooping o'er the hallowed tomb
Where his plighted victims lie,
Where they met, but met to die,
And now, when crimson buds are sleeping

Through the dewy arbor peeping,
Where Beauty's child, the frowning world forgot,
To Youth's devoted tale is listening,
Rapture on her dark lash glistening,
While fairies leave their cowslip cells, and guard the happy spot.

Thus rise the phantom throng
Obedient to their Master's song,
And lead in willing chains the wondering soul along.

For other worlds war's Great One sighed in vain;
O'er other worlds see Shakspeare rove and reign!
The rapt magician of his own wild lay,
Earth and her tribes his mystic wand obey.
Old Ocean trembles, thunder cracks the skies
Air teems with shapes, and tell-tale spectres rise;
Night's fearful hags their fearful orgies keep,
And faithless Guilt unseals the lip of sleep;
Time yields his trophies up, and Death restores
The mouldered victims of his voiceless shores.
The fireside legend, and the faded page,
The crime that cursed, the deed that blest an age.
All, all, come forth, the good to charm and cheer,
To scourge bold Vice, and start the generous tear;
With pictured Folly gazing worlds to shame,
And guide young Glory's foot along the path to fame.

SPRAGUE, WILLIAM BUELL, an American clergyman and author, born at Andover, Conn., in 1795, died at Flushing, N. Y., in 1876. He graduated at Yale in 1815; studied at the Princeton Theological Seminary, and in 1819 was settled as associate pastor of the Congregational Church at West Springfield, Conn. In 1829 he became pastor of the Second Presbyterian Church in Albany, N. Y., retaining this post until his resignation in 1869. Among his numerous writings are: *Letters to a Daughter* (1822), *Letters from Europe* (1828), *Lectures on Revivals* (1832), *Aids to Early Religion* (1847), *Words to a Young Man's Conscience* (1848). His most important work, to which the labor of many years was devoted, was the *Annals of the American Pulpit*, containing biographies of clergymen of all denominations, with Historical Introductions to the biographies of each denomination, the whole being brought down to 1855. The publication of this work was begun in 1857, the ninth and concluding volume was issued in 1867. In the Preface he thus sets forth the plan of the work:

PLAN OF THE "ANNALS OF THE AMERICAN PULPIT."

In the construction of this work I had an eye to the history of the Church, as well as to the biography of its ministers. I have therefore kept each denomination by itself, and have arranged the names under each chronologically, so that the gradual changes of the ministry can be easily traced, and the progress of each denomination also, so far as it is identified with the character and doings of its ministers.

The work is chiefly distinguished by two characteristics. One is that the testimony concerning character is, with very few exceptions, original. It is not only the sentiments but the very language of the individual who could speak from actual knowledge. The other characteristic feature of the work is that it at least claims an exemption from denominational partiality. My only aim has been to present what I supposed to be a faithful outline of the life and character of each individual, without justifying or condemning opinions they have respectively held. . . . . One of the most difficult and delicate things in connection with the work has been the selection of its subjects. The general principle that has controlled me has been the following: to include those who were eminent for their talents, their acquirements, or their usefulness, or who were particularly distinguished in their history.

SPRAT, THOMAS, an English divine, born in 1636; died in 1713. He was one of the foremost London preachers. He took an active part in the politico-ecclesiastical movements of his day; he became chaplain to Charles II., by whom, in 1684, he was made Bishop of Rochester. He gave his support to the government of James II., but embraced the cause of William and Mary, and assisted at their coronation. In 1692 an attempt was made to implicate him in a plot to restore the exiled Stuarts. This utterly failed, and the chief conspirator was put in the pillory, and a few years afterwards was hanged for coining false money, Sprat's works embrace a few *Poems*, several eloquent *Sermons*, and an elaborate *History of the Royal Society of London for the Improving of Natural Knowledge* (1667).

PHILOSOPHY AND FAITH.

We are guilty of false interpretations of providence and wonders when we either make those to be miracles that are none, or when we put a false sense upon those that are real; when we make general events to have a private aspect, or particular accidents to have some universal signification. Though both these may seem at first to have the strictest appearance of religion, yet they are the greatest usurpations of the secrets of the Almighty, and unpardonable presumptions on His high prerogatives of punishment and reward. And now, if a moderating of those extravagances must be esteemed profaneness, I confess I cannot absolve the experimental philosopher. It must be granted that he will be very scrupulous in believing all manner of commentaries on prophetical visions, in giving liberty to new predictions, and in assigning the causes and making out the paths of God's judgments amongst His creatures.

He cannot suddenly conclude all extraordinary events to be the immediate finger of God; because he familiarly beholds the inward working of things, and thence perceives that many effects which used to affright the ignorant are brought forth by the common instruments of nature. He cannot be suddenly inclined to pass censure on men's eternal condition from any temporal judgments that may befall them, because his long converse with all matters, times, and places has taught him the truth of what the Scripture says, that "all things happen alike to all." He cannot blindly consent to all imaginations of devout men about future contingencies, seeing he is so rigid in examining all particular matters of fact. He cannot be forward to assent to spiritual raptures and revelations; because he is truly acquainted with the temper of men's bodies, the composition of their blood, and the power of fancy, and so better understands the difference between diseases and inspirations.

But in all this he commits nothing that is irreligious. 'Tis true that to deny that God has heretofore warned the world of what was to come, is to contradict the very Godhead itself; but to reject the sense which any private man shall fasten to it, is not to disdain the Word of God, but the opinions of men like ourselves. To declare against the possibility that new prophets may be sent from heaven, is to insinuate that the same infinite wisdom which once showed itself in that way is now at an end. But to slight all pretenders that come without the help of miracles is not a contempt of the Spirit, but a just circumspection that the reason of men be not over-reached. To deny that God directs the course of human things, is stupidity; but to hearken to every prodigy that men frame against their enemies, or for themselves, is not to reverence the power of God, but to make that serve the passions, the interests, and revenges of men. . . . .

Let us, then, imagine our philosopher to have all slowness of belief. and rigor of trial, which by some is miscalled a blindness of mind and hardness of heart. Let us suppose that he is most unwilling to grant that anything exceeds the force of nature, but where a full evidence convinces him. Let it be allowed that he is always alarmed, and ready on his guard, at the noise of any miraculous event, lest his judgment should be surprised by the disguises of faith. But does he by this diminish the authority of ancient miracles? or does he not rather confirm them the more, by confining their number, and taking care that every falsehood should not mingle with them? Can he by this undermine Christianity, which does not now stand in need of such extraordinary testimonies from heaven; or do not they rather endanger it who still venture its truth on so hazardous a chance; who require a continuance of signs and wonders, as if the works of our Saviour and his apostles had not been sufficient?

Who ought to be esteemed the most carnally-minded—the enthusiast who perverts religion with his own passions, or the experimenter that will not use it to flatter and obey his own desires, but to subdue them? Who is to be thought the greatest enemy of the gospel—he that loads men's faith by so many improbable things as will go near to make the reality itself suspected, or he that only admits a few arguments to confirm the evangelical doctrines, but then chooses those that are unquestionable? It cannot be an ungodly purpose to strive to abolish all holy cheats, which are of fatal consequence both to the deceivers and those that are deceived:—to the deceivers, because they must needs be hypocrites, having the argument in their keeping; to the deceived, because if their eyes shall ever be opened, and they chance to find that they have been deluded in any one thing, they will be apt not only to reject that, but even to despise the very truths themselves which they had before been taught by these deluders.—*History of the Royal Society.*

SQUIER, EPHRAIM GEORGE, an American author, born at Bethlehem, N. Y., in, 1821; died at Brookyln, N. Y., in 1888. In early life he worked on a farm; afterwards taught school, studied civil engineering, and became a newspaper editor, lastly at Chilicothe, Ohio. Here, in conjunction with Dr. A. H. Davis, he prepared an account of the Ancient Monuments in the Mississippi Valley, which was published in the "Smithsonian Contributions to Knowledge" for 1848, where also was printed in the next year his account of the Aboriginal Monuments in the state of New York. In 1849 he was appointed Special Envoy to the States of Central America. In 1853 he again visited Central America in connection with a projected railway to connect the Atlantic and the Pacific, which occupied his attention for several years. In 1863 he was appointed U. S. Commissioner to Peru, where he made a thorough examination of the existing remains of Inca civilization. For several years thereafter he resided in New York, employed in literary labor. In 1874, his mental faculties, especially his memory, became impaired, so that he became incapable of performing any work which required continuous thought. He, however, so far recovered, as to put in order the extensive material which he had already collected for his work on Peru. Besides several monographs, mainly upon American archæology, his works are: *Nicaragua: its People, Scenery*, etc. (1852), *Notes on Central America* (1854), *Waikna; Adventures on the Mosquito Shore*, a romance published under the pseudonym of Samuel A. Bard (1855), *The States of Central Amer-*

ica (1870), *Peru, the Land of the Incas* (1871).

TIAHUANUCO, THE BAALBEC OF THE NEW WORLD.

Tiahuanuco lies almost in the very centre of the great terrestrial basin of lakes Titicaca and Aullagas, and in the heart of a region which may be characterized as the Thibet of the New World. Here, at an elevation of 12,900 feet above the sea, in a broad, open, and uncultivated plain, cold in the wet, and frigid in the dry season, we find the evidences of an ancient civilization, regarded by many as the oldest and the most advanced of both the American Continents. The first thing that strikes the visitor in the village of Tiahuanuco is the great number of beautifully cut stones built into the rudest edifices, and paving the squalidest courts. They are used as lintels, jambs, seats, tables, and as receptacles for water. The church is mainly built of them; the cross in front of it stands on a stone pedestal which shames the symbol it supports in excellence of workmanship. On all sides are vestiges of antiquity from the neighboring ruins, which have been a real quarry whence have been taken the cut stones not only for Tiahuanuco and all the churches of its valley, but for erecting the cathedral of La Paz, the capital of Bolivia, situated in the deep valley of one of the streams falling into the river Beni, twenty leagues distant. The monuments of the past have furnished most of the materials for the public edifices, the bridges, and highways of the present day.

The ruins of Tiahuanuco have been regarded by all students of American antiquities as in many respects the most interesting and important, and at the same time most enigmatical, of any on the continent. They have excited the admiration and wonder alike of the earliest and the latest travellers, most of whom, vanquished in their attempts to penetrate the mystery of their origin, have been content to regard them as the solitary remains of a civilization that disappeared before that of the Incas began, and was contemporaneous with that of Egypt and of the East. Unique, yet perfect in type, and harmonious in style, they appear to be the work of a people who were thorough masters of an architecture which had no infancy, and passed through no period of growth, and of which we find no other examples. Tradition, which mumbles more or less intelligibly of the origin of many other American monuments, is dumb concerning these. The wondering Indians told the first Spaniards that "they existed before the sun shone in the heavens;" that they were raised by giants; or that they were the remains of an impious people whom an angry Deity had converted into stone because they had refused hospitality to his vicegerent and messenger.—*Land of the Incas.*

SACSAHUAMAN, THE ANCIENT FORTRESS OF CUZCO.

The capital of the Inca empire was not defended by walls, such as protected some of the ancient Inca cities. Its valley, surrounded by high mountains, was itself naturally almost impregnable, and the approaches to it were covered by fortifications. But the city nevertheless had its citadel or fortress. It was built upon the bold headland projecting into the valley of Cuzco, between the rivulets Huatenay and Rodadero, looking from below like a high, abrupt hill, but being really only the spur of a shell or plateau, somewhat irregular in surface which in turn is commanded by higher hills or mountains, themselves the escarpments of remote natural terraces or *puna* lands. This headland is called *Los Altos del Sacsahuaman*, the latter being a compound word signifying "Gorge thyself, Hawk!" Thus metaphorically did the Incas glorify the strength of their fortress: "Dash thyself against its rocky and inpregnable sides, if thou wilt; the hawks will gather up the fragments!" . . . .

The usual ascent to the Sacsahuaman, and which is practicable by horses, is through the gorge of the Rodadero to the right of the eminence, where a road is partly cut out of the hill and partly built up against it—a cliff on one side and a precipice on the other. As we ascend, we observe, high above us, long lines of walls, which are the faces of the eastern terraces of the fortress. These become heavier as we advance, until when we reach the level of the plateau, up the rugged front of which we have been struggling, they cease to be simply retaining walls, and rise in massive independent walls, composed of great blocks of limestone. A gateway, flanked by heavy stones opens on our left. Passing through this gateway, we have our first view of the great Cyclopean walls of the Fortress of Sacsahuaman, the most massive among monuments of this character either in the Old or in the New World. The outline of the eminence, on the side towards the rocks of the Rodadero, is rather concave than otherwise, and it is along this face that the heaviest works of the fortress were built. They remain substantially perfect and will remain so—unless disturbed by a violence which is not to be anticipated—as long as the Pyramids shall last, or Stonehenge and the Colisseum endure, for it is only with these works that the Fortress of the Sacsahuaman can be properly compared. . . . .

The stones composing the walls are massive blocks of blue limestone, irregular in size and shape. One of these stones is 27 feet high, 14 feet broad, and 12 in thickness. Stones of 15 feet in length, 12 in width, and 10 in thickness, are common in the outer walls. They are all slightly bevelled on the face, and near the joints chamfered down sharply to the contiguous faces.—The joints are not now, if they ever were, so perfect as they are represented by the chroniclers. They are neverthless wonderfully close, and cut with a precision rarely seen in modern fortifications.—*Land of the Incas.*

STAËL-HOLSTEIN, ANNE LOUISE GERMAINE NECKER DE, a French author, born at Paris in 1766; died there in 1817. She was the only child of the finance minister, Necker. She early showed literary genius and brilliant conversational gifts. At the age of twenty she was married to the Swedish ambassador, Baron de Staël-Holstein. She was in sympathy with the French revolution, but deplored its excess, and she devised a plan for the safety of the royal family, which was not acted upon, saved Montmorency and others from the guillotine, and in 1793 went to London, where she published an appeal in behalf of Marie Antoinette. She met Talleyrand there, and on his return to France, aided him to enter the ministry. She was conspicuous in Paris as a leader of the constitutional party, but was banished and went to Germany, where she became acquainted with the royal family, and with Goethe and Schiller. On the death of her father, she went to Italy, where she collected material for her story *Corinne*. In 1805 she went to Switzerland, and alternately resided at Geneva and Coppet. *Corinne* was published in France in 1807; but in Germany, the work which had been printed with the approval of the censors, was confiscated. For political reasons Napoleon oppressed Mme. de Staël, and converted her residence at Coppet into a prison. She was forbidden to go two miles from the house, but in 1812 she escaped by taking a walk from which she never returned. She went through Switzerland to Vienna, and, pursued by Napoleon's officers, travelled to Russia, where she was received by the imperial family. She afterwards took refuge in London. During Napoleon's banishment to Elba she resided in Paris. In 1816 she made an unsuccessful attempt to restore her health by a trip to Italy. Her friend Schlegel was with her to the last, and Chateaubriand first met Mme. Recamier at the death-bed of Mme. de Staël. For several years she was separated from her husband, whom she rejoined in his last illness in 1802. In 1811 she was secretly married to Albert Jean de Rocca, a French officer, and military writer. This fact was not known until after her death. Mme. de Staël's versatility was extraordinary. She excelled in every branch of composition, was a linguist, a singer of some talent, and a clever amateur actress, and dramatist. Her works are *Delphine*, a novel, in which she idealizes herself (1802), *Corinne, en l'Italie* (1807), *De l'Allemagne* (1813), all of which have passed through many editions and translations. Her other works include: *Lettres sur les Ecrits et le Caractère de J. J. Rousseau* (1788), *Reflexions sur la Paix* (1794), *De l'Influence des Passions sur le Bonheur des Individus et des Nations* (1796), *De la Littérature considérée dans ses Rapports avec les Institutions Sociales* (1800). *Considérations sur les Principaux Événéments de la Révolution Française* (1818), and *Dix Années d'Exil* (1821). Her complete works were edited by her son, Auguste, with notes by her daughter, Mme. Necker de Saussure (17 vols., 1820–1). This was followed by a new edition supplemented by *Œuvres Diverses* (5 vols., 1828–9). Mme. de Staël's correspondence with the grand duchess, Louisa of Saxe-Weimar, in 1800–17 was published in 1862, and her other letters were published by Saint-René Taillandier in the following year.

CONTRASTED MERITS OF FRENCH AND GERMAN WRITERS.

Perspicuity is in France one of the first merits of a writer; for the first object of a reader is to give himself no trouble, but to catch, by running over a few pages in the morning what will enable him to shine in conversation in the evening. The Germans, on the contrary, know that perspicuity can never have more than a relative merit: a book is clear according to the subject and according to the reader. Montesquieu cannot be so easily understood as Voltaire, and nevertheless he is as clear as the object of his meditations will permit. Without doubt clearness should accompany depth of thought; but those who confine themselve sonly to the graces of wit and the play on words, are much more sure of being understood. They have nothing to do with mystery, why then should they be obscure? The Germans, through an opposite defect, take pleasure in darkness; they often wrap in obscurity what was before clear, rather than follow the beaten road; they have such a disgust for common ideas, that when they find themselves obliged to recur to them, they surround them with abstract metaphysics, which give them an air of novelty till they are found out. German writers are under no restraint with their readers; their works being received and commented upon as oracles, they may envelope them with as many clouds as they like; patience is never wanting to draw those clouds aside; but it is necessary at length to discover a divinity; for what the Germans can least support, is to see their expectations deceived; their efforts and their perseverance render some great conclusion needful. If no new or strong thoughts are discovered in a book, it is soon disdained; and if all is pardoned in behalf of superior talent, they scarcely know how to appreciate the various kinds of address displayed in endeavoring to supply the want of it.

The prose of the Germans is often too much neglected. They attach more importance to style in France than in Germany; it is a natural consequence of the interest excited by words, and the value they must acquire in a country where society is the first object. Every man with a little understanding is a judge of the justness or suitableness of such and such a phrase, while it requires much attention and study to take in the whole compass and connection of a book. Besides, pleasantry finds expressions much sooner than thoughts, and in all that depends on words only, we laugh before we reflect.

It must be agreed nevertheless that beauty of style is not merely an external advantage, for true sentiments almost always inspire the most noble and just expressions; and if we are allowed to be indulgent to the style of a philosophical writing, we ought not to be so to that of a literary composition; in the sphere of the fine arts, the form in which a subject is presented to us is as essential to the mind, as the subject itself.

The dramatic art offers a striking example of the distinct faculties of the two nations. All that relates to action, to intrigue, to the interest of events is a thousand times better combined, a thousand times better conceived, among the French; all that depends on the development of the impressions of the heart, on the secret storms of strong passion, is much better investigated among the Germans.

In order to attain the highest point of perfection in either country, it would be necessary for the Frenchman to be religious, and the German more a man of the world. Piety opposes itself to levity of mind, which is the defect and the grace of the French nation; the knowledge of men and of society would give to the Germans that taste and facility in literature which is at present wanting to them. The writers of the two countries are unjust to each other; the French, nevertheless, are more guilty in this respect than the Germans; they judge without knowing the subject, and examine after they have decided; the Germans are more impartial. Extensive knowledge presents to us so many different ways of beholding the same object, that it imparts to the mind the spirit of toleration which springs from universality.

The French would, however, gain more by comprehending German genius, than the Germans would in subjecting themselves to the good taste of the French. In our days, whenever a little foreign leaven has been allowed to mix itself with French regularity, the French have themselves applauded it with delight. J. J. Rousseau, Bernardin de Saint Pierre, Chateaubriand, etc., are, in some of their works, even unknown to themselves, of the German school; that is to say, they draw their talent only out of the internal sources of the soul. But if German writers were to be disciplined according to the prohibitory laws of French literature, they would not know how to steer amid the quicksands that would be pointed out to them; they would regret the open sea, and their minds would be much more disturbed than enlightened. It does not follow that they ought to hazard all, and that they would do wrong in sometimes imposing limits on themselves; but it is of consequence to them to be placed according to their own modes of perception. In order to induce them to adopt certain necessary restrictions, we must recur to the principle of those restrictions without employing the authority of ridicule, which is always highly offensive to them.

Men of genius in all countries are formed to understand and esteem each other; but the vulgar class of writers and readers, whether German or French, bring to our recollection that fable of La Fontaine, where the stork cannot eat in the dish, nor the fox in the bottle. The most complete contrast is perceived between minds developed in solitude, and those formed by society. Impressions from external objects and the inward recollections of the soul, the knowledge of men and abstract ideas, action and theory, yield conclusions totally opposite to each other. The literature, the arts, the philosophy, the religion of these two nations attest this difference; and the eternal boundary of the Rhine separates two intellectual regions, which, no less than the two countries, are foreign to each other.—*Germany* (*L'Allemagne*).

VESUVIUS.

Leaving Pompeii they proceeded to Portici, whose inhabitants beset them with loud cries of "Come and see the mountain!" thus they designate Vesuvius. Has it need of name? It is their glory; their country is celebrated as the shrine of this marvel. Oswald begged Corinne to ascend in a sort of palanquin to the Hermitage of St. Salvadore, which is half-way up, and the usual resting place for travellers. He rode by her side to overlook her bearers; and the more his heart filled with the generous sentiments such scenes inspire, the more he adored Corinne.

The country at the foot of Vesuvius is the most fertile and best cultivated of the kingdom most favored by Heaven in all Europe. The celebrated Lacryma Christi vine flourishes beside land totally devastated by lava, as if nature here made a last effort, and resolved to perish in her richest array. As you ascend, you turn to gaze on Naples, and on the fair land around it—the sea sparkles in the sun as if strewn with jewels; but all the splendors of creation are extinguished by degrees, as you enter the region of ashes and of smoke, that announces your approach to the volcano. The iron waves of other years have traced their large black furrows in the soil. At a certain height, birds are no longer seen; further on, plants become very scarce; then, even insects find no nourishment. At last all life disappears; you enter the realm of death, and the slain earth's dust alone slips beneath your unassured feet. . . . . . A hermit lives betwixt the confines of life and death. One tree, the last farewell to vegetation, stands before his door, and beneath the shade of its pale foliage are travellers wont to wait the night ere they renew their course; for during the day the fires and lava, so fierce when the sun is set, look dark beneath his splendor. This metamorphose is in itself a glorious sight, which every eve renews the wonder that a continual glare would waken.—*Corinne. Transl. of* ISABEL HILL.

KLOPSTOCK.

Those who have known Klopstock respect as much as they admire him. Religion, liberty, love, occupied all his thoughts. His religious profession was found in the performance of all his duties: he even gave up the cause of liberty when innocent blood would have defiled it; and fidelity consecrated all the attachments of his heart. Never had he recourse to his imagination to justify an error; it exalted his soul without leading it astray. It is said that his conversation was full of wit and taste; that he loved the society of women, particularly of French women, and that he was a good judge of that sort of charm and grace which pedantry reproves. I readily believe it, for there is always something of universality in genius, and perhaps it is connected by secret ties to grace, at least to that grace which is bestowed by nature. How far distant is such a man from envy, selfishness, excess of vanity, which many writers have excused in themselves in the name of the talents they possessed!—*De l'Allemagne.*

STAGNELIUS, ERIK JOHAN, a Swedish poet, born on the island of Oland in 1793; died in 1823 His father became Bishop of Kalmar, and the son was educated at the University of Lund. His reputation as a poet in his native country is second only to that of Tegnér. Many of his poems are in the form of Sonnets, some of which have been translated into English by Edmund Gosse, who says of them: "Though exceedingly mystical, and often obscure, they are certainly the most original in the Swedish language."

THE SIGHS OF THE CREATURES.

What sighs the hill ?
What the North wind through the pine-
wood that blows ?
What whispers the rill,
Whilst through the valley so softly it flows ?
What says the morning,
Golden mists born in ?
What the night's moon all heaven adorning,
Silently garing on valleys below ?
What thinks the red rose ? what the narcisse ?
Or the stern precipice,
Gloomy and threatening, what does it know ?
We know, and we think, and we sigh, and we
speak !
O man, from the trance of thy stupor awake,
And up to the primal-life's region go back !
If thou wilt ascend to the true world ideal,
Into light will transform all the gloomy, the
real,
We also transfigured shall follow thy track.
Thou thyself art in bonds to material powers.
Alas ! The same terrible bondage is ours,
For lead where thou wilt we must still follow
thee ! [under ;
One law, that is common to both, we lie
Unfetter the creatures—thy bonds burst
asunder ;
Unfetter thyself, and thou them settest free !

LUNA.

Deep slumber hung o'er sea and hill and plain;
With pale pink cheek fresh from her watery caves,
Slow rose the sun out of the midnight waves,
Like Venus out of ocean born again;
Olympian blazed she on the dark blue main:
"So shall, ye gods!" hark how my weak hope raves—
"My happy star ascend the sea that laves
Its shores with quiet, and silence all my pain!"
With that, there sighed a wandering midnight breeze
High up among the topmost tufted trees
And o'er the Moon's face blew a veil of cloud;
And in the breeze my Genius spake, and said,
"While thy heart stirred, thy glimmering hope has fled,
And, like the Moon, lies muffled in a shroud."

MEMORY.

O camp of flowers, with poplars girdled round,
The guardians of life's soft and purple bud!
O silver spring, beside whose brimming flood
My dreaming childhood its Elysium found!
O happy hours with love and fancy crowned,
Whose horn of plenty flatteringly subdued
My heart into a trance, whence with a rude
And horrid blast, fate came my soul to hound:
Who was the goddness who empowered you all
Thus to bewitch me?—Out of wasting snow
And lily-leaves her head-dress should be made!
Weep, my poor lute, nor on Astræa call:
She will not smile, nor I who mourn below,
Till I, a shade, in heaven clasp her, a shade.

ETERNITY.

Up through the ruins of my earthy dreams
I catch the stars of immortality

What store of joy can lurk in heaven for me?
What other hope feed those celestial gleams?
Can there be other grapes whose nectar streams
For me, whom earth's vine fails? Oh! can it be
That this most helpless heart again may see
A forehead garlanded, an eye that beams?
Alas! 'tis childhood's dream that vanisheth!
The heaven-born soul that feigns it can return
And end in peace this hopeless strife with fate!
There is no backward step; 'tis only death
Can break those cords of wasting fire that burn,
Can break the chain, the captive liberate.

STANHOPE, Philip Henry, Earl, an English statesman and historian, born in 1805; died in 1875. He succeeded his father in the earldom in 1855, previous to which he was known by his courtesy title of Lord Mahon. He graduated at Oxford in 1827, and entered Parliament in 1830. In 1834–35, he was made Under-Secretary for Foreign Affairs; and Secretary to the Indian Board of Control in 1845–46. He was elected President of the Society of Antiquaries in 1846, and Lord Rector of the University of Aberdeen in 1858. His principal works are: *History of England from the Peace of Utrecht* (1713), *to the Peace of Aix la Chapelle* (1783), *History of the War of the Succession in Spain*, *Life of the Great Condé*, *Life of Belisarius*, *Life of William Pitt*, and a volume of *Miscellanies*.

CHARLES EDWARD STUART, "THE YOUNG PRETENDER."

Charles Edward Stuart is one of those characters that cannot be portrayed at a single sketch, but have so greatly altered as to require a new delineation at different periods. View him in his later years, and we behold the ruins of intemperance—as wasted but not as venerable as those of time. We find him in his anticipated age a besotted drunkard, a peevish husband, a tyrannical master; his understanding debased, and his temper soured.

But not such was the Charles Stuart of 1745. Not such was the gallant Prince, full of youth, of hope, of courage, who, landing with seven men in the wilds of Moidart, could rally a kingdom round his banner, and scatter his foes before him at Preston and at Falkirk. Not such was the gay and courtly host of Holyrood. Not such was he whose endurance of fatigue and eagerness for battle shone pre-eminent even amongst Highland chiefs; while fairer critics proclaimed him the most winning in conversation, the most graceful in the dance.

Can we think lowly of one who could acquire such unbounded popularity in so few months, and over so noble a nation as the Scots; who could so deeply stamp his image on their hearts that even thirty or forty years after his departure, his name, as we are told, always awakened the most ardent praises from all who had known him? The most rugged cheeks were seen to melt at his remembrance, and tears to steal down the furrowed cheeks of the veteran. Let us, then, without denying the faults of his character, or extenuating the degradation of his age, do justice to the lustre of his manhood.—*History of England.*

STANLEY, ARTHUR PENRHYN, an English clergyman and author, born at Alderly in 1815; died in 1881. His father, who was Rector of Alderly, afterwards became Bishop of Norwich, and his *Memoirs* have been written by his son. He was trained at Rugby, where he was the favorite pupil of Dr. Arnold; thence he proceeded to Oxford, and in 1838 was made a Fellow of University College, in which he also became a tutor. He was made Canon of Canterbury in 1851; Professor of Ecclesiastical History at Oxford in 1858; Dean of Westminster in 1864. In 1872 he was elected one of the select preachers before the University of Oxford, notwithstanding the vehement opposition of the High Church party. Among the principal works of Dean Stanley are: *Life and Correspondence of Thomas Arnold* (1844), *Sermons and Essays on the Apostolic Age* (1846), *The Epistles to the Corinthians* (1854), *Sinai and Palestine* (1855), *Lectures on the Eastern Church* (1861), *Lectures on the Jewish Church* (1865), *Lectures on the Church of Scotland* (1871). He also published several series of *Essays* and *Sermons*, preached on various occasions. In 1862 he accompanied the Prince of Wales upon an extended tour in the East. The following is from a sermon preached at Ehden at the foot of the "Mountain of the Cedars."

LESSONS FROM THE CEDARS OF LEBANON.

Our last Sunday in Syria has arrived, and it has been enhanced to us this morning by the sight of these venerable trees which seemed to the Psalmist and the Prophets of old, one of the chief glories and wonders of the creation. Two main ideas were conveyed to the minds of those who then saw them, which we may still bear away with us:

One is that of their greatness, breadth, solidity, vastness. "The righteous," says the Psalmist, "shall flourish like a palm-tree." That is one part of our life; to be upright, graceful, gentle, like that most beautiful of oriental trees. But there is another quality added— "He shall spread abroad like a cedar in Libanus." That is, his character shall be sturdy, solid, broad; he shall protect others as well as himself; he shall support the branches of the weaker trees around him; he shall cover a vast surface of the earth with his shadow; he shall grow, and spread, and endure; he and his works shall make the place where he was planted memorable for future times.

The second feeling is the value of reverence. It was reverence for these great trees which caused them to be employed for the sacred service of Solomon's Temple, and which has ensured their preservation for so long. It was reverence for Almighty God that caused these trees, and these only, to be brought down from this remote situation to be employed for the Temple of Old. Reverence, we may be sure, whether to God or to the great things which God has made in the world, is one of the qualities most needful for every human being, if he means to pass through life in a manner worthy of the place which God has given him in the world.

But the sight of the Cedars, and our encampment here, recall to us that this is the close of a manner of life which, in many respects, calls to mind that of the ancient Israelites, as we read it in the lessons of this and of last Sunday, the Book of Numbers and of Deuteronomy: "How goodly are thy tents, O Jacob, and thy tabernacles, O Israel,"—so unlike our common life, so suggestive of thoughts which can hardly come to us again. It brings us back, even with all the luxuries which surround us, to something of the freshness, and rudeness and simplicity of primitive life, which it is good for us all to feel at one time or other. It reminds us, though in a figure, of the uncertainty and the instability of human existence, so often compared to the pitching and striking of a tent. The spots on which, day after day for the last six weeks we have been encamped, have again become a desolate open waste; "The Spirit of the Desert stalks in," and their place will be known no more. How like the way in which happy homes rise and sink, and vanish, and are lost. . . . .

May I take this occasion of speaking of the importance of this one solemn ordinance of religion, never to be forgotten, wherever we are—morning and evening prayer? It is the best means of reminding ourselves of the presence of God. To place ourselves in His hands before we go forth on our journey, on our pleasure, on our work—to commit ourselves again to him before we retire to rest—this is the best security for keeping up our faith and trust in Him in whom we all profess to believe, whom we all expect to meet after we leave this world. It is also the best security for our leading a good and a happy life. It has been well said twice over by the most powerful delineator of human character (with one exception) ever produced by our country, that prayer to the Almighty Searcher of Hearts is the best check to murmurs against Providence, or to the inroad of wordly passions, because nothing else brings before us so strongly their inconsistency and unreasonableness. We shall find it twice as difficult to fall into sin if we have prayed against it every morning, or if we thank God for having kept it from us that very evening. It is the best means of gaining strength and refreshment and courage and self-denial for the day. It is the best means of gaining content and tranquillity and rest for the night, for it brings us, as nothing else can bring us, into the presence of Him who is the source of all these things, and who gives them freely to those who truly and sincerely ask for them.

STANLEY, Henry Morton (original name John Rowlands), a Welsh-American explorer, born near Denbigh, Wales, in 1840. In 1855, he came as cabin-boy to New Orleans, was befriended by a merchant, served in the Confederate army, and, after capture, in the Federal navy; was newspaper correspondent in Turkey, and with the British army in the Abyssinian war. In 1870 he was sent by the N. Y. *Herald* to find Livingstone, found him, and returned in 1872. His second exploration, beginning 1874, added much to the knowledge of the Victoria and Albert lakes, and ended with his famous descent of a great river which proved to be the Congo. From 1879 to 1884, sent by the King of Belgium, he completed the grand work of founding the Free State of Congo. From 1887, for two years, he went to the relief of Emin Pasha, making a journey of 1,670 miles through the vast central forest of Africa, described in his book *In Darkest Africa* (1890). His previous works are: *How I Found Livingstone* (1872), *My Kalulu* (1872), *Coomassie and Magdala* (1874), *Through the Dark Continent* (1878), and *The Congo, and the Founding of its Free State* (1885).

STANLEY'S MEETING WITH LIVINGSTONE.

I pushed back the crowds, and passing from the rear walked down a long avenue of people until I came to the semi-circle of Arabs, in front of which stood "the white man with the gray beard." As I advanced slowly towards him I noticed he was pale, looked wearied, had a gray beard; wore a bluish cap with a faded gold band round it; had on a red-sleeved waistcoat, and a pair of gray tweed trowsers. I would have run to him, only I was a coward in the presence of such a mob; would have embraced him, only he was an Englishman, and I did not know how he would receive me. So I did what cowardice and false shame suggested was the best thing—walked deliberately up to him, took off my hat, and said—

"Dr. Livingstone, I presume?"

"Yes," said he, with a smile, lifting his cap slightly.

I replace my hat on my head, and he puts on his cap, and we both shake hands, and I then say aloud—"I thank God, Doctor, I have been permitted to see you."

He answered—"I feel thankful that I am here to welcome you."

I turn to the Arabs, take off my hat to them in response to a saluting chorus of "Yambos" I receive, and the Doctor introduces them to me by name. Then, oblivious of the crowds, of the men who shared with me my dangers, we—Livingstone and I—turn our faces towards his *tembe*. He points to the veranda—or, rather, stone platform—under the broad overhanging eaves. He points to his own particular seat, which I see his age and experience in Africa has suggested; namely, a straw mat with a goat-skin over it, and another skin nailed to the wall to protect his back from contact with the cold mud. I protest against taking this seat, which so much more befits him than me; but the Doctor will not yield; I must take it.

We are seated—the Doctor and I—with our backs against the wall. The Arabs take seats on our left. More than a thousand natives are in our front, filling the whole square densely; indulging their curiosity, and discussing the fact of two white men meeting at Ujiji—one of them just come from Manyne'ma, in the west, the other from Unyanyebuke, in the east.

Conversation began. What about?—Oh, we mutually asked questions of each other, such as—"How did you come here?" and "Where have you been all this long time? The world has believed you dead."

Yes, that was the way it began; but whatever the Doctor informed me, and that which I communicated to him, I cannot correctly report; for I found myself gazing at him, conning the wonderful man at whose side I now sat in Central Africa. Every hair of his head, every wrinkle of his face, the wanness of his features, and the slightly wearied look he wore, were all imparting intelligence to me—the knowledge I craved for ever since I heard the words—"Take what you want; but find Livingstone!" What I saw was deeply interesting to me, and unvarnished truth. I was listening and reading at the same time.. What did these dumb witnesses relate to me? Oh, reader, had you been at my side on this day in Ujiji, how eloquently could be told the nature of this man's work! Had you been there, but to see and hear! His lips gave me the details—lips that never lie. I cannot repeat what he said. I was too much engrossed to take my note-book out, and begin to stenograph his story. He had so much to say that he began at the end, seemingly oblivious of the fact that five or six years had to be accounted for. But his account was fast oozing out; it was growing fast into grand proportions—into a most marvellous history of deeds.—*How I Found Livingstone.*

ENTERING THE GREAT FOREST.

This was on the 28th day of June, and until the 5th of December, for 160 days, we marched through the forest, bush and jungle, without ever having seen a bit of greensward of the size of a cottage chamber floor. Nothing but miles and miles, endless miles of forests, in various stages of growth and various degrees of altitude, according to the ages of the trees, with varying thickness of undergrowth according to the character of the trees which afforded thicker or slighter shade. It is to the description of the march through this forest and to its strange incidents I propose to confine myself for the next few chapters, as it is an absolutely unknown region opened to the gaze and knowledge of civilized man for the first since the waters disappeared and were gathered into the seas, and the earth became dry land. . . .

The head of the column arrived at the foot of a broad, cleared road, twenty feet wide and three hundred yards long, and at the further end probably three hundred natives of the town of Yankondé stood gesticulating, shouting, with drawn bows in their hands. In all my experience of Africa I had seen nothing of this kind. The pioneers halted, reflecting, and remarking somewhat after this manner: "What does this mean? The pagans have carved a broad highway out of the bush to their town for us, and yet there they are at the other end, ready for a fight! It is a trap, lads, of some kind, so look sharp."

With the bush they had cut they had banked and blocked all passage to the forest on either side of the road for some distance. But, with fifty pairs of sharp eyes searching around above and below, we were not long in finding that this apparent highway through the bush bristled with skewers six inches long sharpened at both ends, which were driven into the ground half their length, and slightly covered with green leaves so carelessly thrown over them that we had thought at first these strewn leaves were simply the effect of clearing bush.

Forming two lines of twelve men across the road, the first line was ordered to pick out the skewers, the second line was ordered to cover the workers with their weapons, and at the first arrow-shower to fire. A dozen scouts were sent on either flank of the road to make their way into the village through the woods. We had scarcely advanced twenty yards along the cleared way before volumes of smoke broke out of the town, and a little cloud of arrows came towards us, but falling short. A volley was returned. The skewers were fast being picked out, and an advance was steadily made until we reached the village at the same time that the scouts rushed out of the underwood, and as all the pioneers were pushed forward the firing was pretty lively, under cover of which the caravan pressed through the burning town to a village at its eastern extremity, as yet unfired.—*In Darkest Africa.*

LEAVING THE GREAT FOREST.

This, then, was the long promised view and the long expected exit out of gloom! Therefore I called the tall peak terminating the forested ridge, of which the spur whereon we stood was a part, and that rose two miles east of us to a height of 4,600 feet above the sea, Pisgah,—Mount Pisgah,—because, after 156 days of twilight in the primeval forest, we had first viewed the desired pasture lands of Equatoria.

The men crowded up the slope eagerly, with inquiring open-eyed looks, which, before they worded their thoughts, we knew meant "Is it true? Is it no hoax? Can it be possible that we are near the end of this forest hell?" . . .

"Aye, friends, it is true. By the mercy of God we are well nigh the end of our prison and dungeon!" They held their hands far out yearningly towards the superb land, and each looked up to the bright blue heaven in grateful worship, and after they had gazed as though fascinated, they recovered themselves with a deep sigh, and as they turned their heads, lo! the sable forest heaved away to the infinity of the west, and they shook their clenched hands at it with gestures of defiance and hate. Feverish from a sudden exultation, they apostrophized it for its cruelty to themselves and their kinsmen; they compared it to Hell, they accused it of the murder of one hundred of their comrades, they called it the wilderness of fungi and wood beans; but the great forest which lay vast as a continent before them, and drowsy, like a great beast, with monstrous fur thinly veiled by vaprous exhalations, answers not a word, but rested in its infinite sullenness, remorseless and implacable as ever.—*In Darkest Africa.*

STANNARD, Henrietta Eliza Vaughan (Palmer,) ("John Strange Winter" *pseud.*), an English author, born at York in 1856. She is the daughter of Henry V. Palmer, rector of St. Margaret's, York, and she was married to Arthur Stannard in 1884. She began to write at an early age, and contributed to the *Yorkshire Chronicle.* Among her books are: *Regimental Martyrs* (1878), *The Ordeal by Paint* (1879), *Cavalry Life* (1881), *Regimental Legends* (1882), *Mignon: or Bootles' Baby*, on which her fame chiefly rests (1883), *Mignon's Secret* (1887), *Beautiful Jim of the Blankshire Regiment* (1888), and *Mrs. Bob* (1890).

LETTER VERSUS SPIRIT.

For hours after he left the anteroom Bootles kept out of every one's way—indeed until Lacy came to tell him that Gilchrist was dead. Then, it being close upon the hour of eleven, he went and knocked at the door of Mignon's nursery. The nurse opened it a few inches, and seeing who it was, set it open wide.

"Is Miss Mignon asleep?" he asked.

"Yes, sir; hours ago," the woman answered.

He passed into the inner room, where the child was lying. A candle burned on a table beside the cot, casting its light on the fair baby face, now flushed in sleep, and on the tangled coverlet one hand grasping the whip with which he had ridden and won that day, the other holding the card of the races. Bootles bent and scanned her face closely, but not one trace could he discern of likeness to the father—not one—and he drew a deep breath of relief that it was so.

Well he remembered Lacy's puzzled scrutiny of the year-old baby. "There's a likeness to Gilchrist, but I don't know where to plant it." If there had been a likeness then, it had now passed away; and as Bootles satisfied himself that it was so, his love for her, which during the last few hours had hung trembling in the balance, though he would hardly have acknowledged it, even to himself, reasserted itself, and rose up in his heart stronger than ever. Just then she moved uneasily in her sleep.

"Lal, where *is* Bootles?" she asked. Then, after a pause, "Gotted *another* headache?" And an instant later, "Miss Grace said Mignon was to be *very* kind to Bootles."

Bootles bent down and kissed her, and she awoke.

"Bootles," she said, in sleepy surprise; then, imperatively, "take me up."

So Bootles carried her to the fire in the adjoining room, where the nurse was sewing a fresh frill of lace on the pretty velvet frock, with its braidings of scarlet and gold, which she had worn that day.

"Lal said Mignon wasn't to go to Bootles," she said, reproachfully.

"Bootles has been bothered, Mignon," he answered.

"Poor Bootles!" stroking his cheek with her soft hand. "Bootles was vexed; Lal said so. But not with Mignon. Mignon told Lal so," confidently.

"Never with Mignon," answered Bootles, resting his cheek against the tossed golden curls, and feeling as if he had done this faithful baby heart a moral injustice by his hours of anger and doubt.

There was a moment of silence, broken by the nurse. "Have you heard, sir, how Mr. Gilchrist is?" she asked.

Bootles roused himself. "He is dead, nurse. Died half an hour ago."

"Then, if you please, sir," she asks, hesitatingly, "might I ask if it is true about Miss Mignon?"

"Yes, it is true," his face darkening.

"Because, sir, Miss Mignon should have mourning," she began, when Bootles cut her short.

"I shall not allow her to wear mourning for Mr. Gilchrist," he said, curtly; so the nurse dared say no more.

Three days later the funeral took place; and if the facts of the dead man's having acknowledged Miss Mignon as his child, and having admitted to Bootles that he had transferred her that night from his own quarters to Bootles' rooms, created a sensation, it was as nothing to the intense surprise caused by the will, which was read, by the dead man's desire, before all the officers of the regiment.

In it he left his entire property to his daughter Mary Gilchrist, now in the care of Captain Ferrers, and commonly known as Mignon, on condition that Captain Ferrers consented to be her sole guardian and trustee until she had attained the age of twenty-one, or until her marriage, provided it should be with her guardian's sanction, and on the express understanding that Captain Ferrers should not give up the care of the child to her mother, even temporarily. To his wife, Helen Gilchrist, a copy of this testament was to be sent forthwith. Should any of the conditions be violated, the whole property of which he died possessed should go to his cousin, Lucian Gavor Gilchrist; but if the conditions be faithfully observed Captain Ferrers should have the power of applying any or all of the income arising from the estate for the use and maintenance of the said Mary Gilchrist.

"Cwrazy!" murmured Lacy to Bootles, who listened in contemptuous silence, and wondered in no small dismay what kind of a life he should have if Mignon's mother chose to make herself objectionable.

But the will was not crazy at all; far from it. It was only a very cleverly thought out plan for keeping mother and child apart. Bootles would take care not to endanger Mignon's inheritance, and Gilchrist had taken advantage of it to carry out his animosity toward his wife to the bitter end.

But of course there was one contingency he had never thought of or provided for—*marriage.*

It was less than a week after Gilchrist's death that Bootles received a note by hand, signed Helen Gilchrist.

"Already!" he groaned, impatiently.

"May I trouble you to send the child to see me for half an hour during this afternoon?" she said, and that was all.

But Bootles did not see *sending* the child to be quietly stolen away. He forgot quite that since Gilchrist had not left his widow a farthing she would probably be now no better able to provide for the child than she had been when compelled to cast her baby upon the father's mercy. Therefore, immediately after lunch, he drove down to the hotel from which the note had been written. Yes; Mrs. Gilchrist was within—this way. And then—then—Bootles, with the child fast holding his hand, was shown into a room, and there they found—*Miss Grace!*

The truth flashed into his mind instantly. She rose hurriedly, and he saw that she was clad in black, but was not in widow's dress. She fell upon her knees and almost smothered Mignon with kisses.

"Mignon! Mignon!" she cried.

"Mignon has been very kind to Bootles," Mignon explained, not knowing whether to laugh or cry.

"My Mignon! my baby!" the mother sobbed. Bootles watched them—the two things he loved best on earth.

"Have you nothing to say to me?" he asked at last.

"What shall I say?" She had risen from her knees, and now moved shyly away.

"You might say," said Bootles, severely "that you are very sorry that you, a married woman, deceived me and stole my heart away. You might say that, for one thing."

"But I am not sorry," cried Mignon's mother, audaciously.

"Then you might take a leaf out of Mignon's book, and say, as she says when I have a headache, 'Mignon *loves* Bootles.'"

"I wreally do think," remarked Lacy to the fellows, when the astounding news had been told and freely discussed, "that now we must let that poor, malicious, cwrooked-minded chap wrest in his gwrave in peace. Seems to me," he continued, with his most reflective air, "that —er—Solomon was wright, and said a vewry wise thing, when he said, 'Love laughs at locksmiths.'"

"Solomon!" cried a voice, amid a shout of laughter.

"Oh, wasn't it Solomon?" questioned Lacy, mildly. "It's of no consequence; some one said it. But only think of that poor devil spending his last moments wraising a barwrier to keep mother and child apart, and old Bootles fulfills all the conditions to the letter, and bwreaks them all in the spirit by—marwriage!"—*Bootles' Baby*.

STEDMAN, Edmund Clarence, an American poet and critic, born at Hartford, Conn., in 1833. He studied at Yale College about two years. In 1832 he became editor of the *Winsted Herald*, in Litchfield County, Conn., which he conducted until 1855, when he removed to New York. In 1859 he became connected with the New York *Tribune*. In 1860 he put forth his first volume, *Poems, Lyric and Idyllic*, containing many pieces which has already appeared in periodicals. In the same year he became connected with the New York *World*, and during the first two years of the civil war he was the Washington correspondent of that journal. In 1864 he abandoned journalism as a profession, and became a stockbroker in New York, but was active in literary pursuits. His subsequent volumes of poems are: *Alice of Monmouth, and other Poems* (1864), *The Blameless Prince, and other Poems* (1869). As a critic and historian of literature he has attained a foremost place. His principal works in this department are: *The Victorian Poets* (1875), *The Poets of America* (1885), and, in conjunction with Ellen Mackay Hutchinson, *The Literature of the Republic*, an extensive selection from the whole circle of American literature in every department (1888–90).

TOUJOURS AMOUR.

Prithee tell me, Dimple-Chin,
At what age does love begin?
Your blue eyes have scarcely seen
Summers three, my fairy queen,
But a miracle of sweets,
Soft approaches, sly retreats,
Show the little archer there,
Hidden in your pretty hair.

When didst thou learn a heart to win?
Prithee tell me, Dimple-Chin!—
"Oh," the rosy lips reply,
"I can't tell you if I try.
'Tis so long I can't remember:
Ask some younger lass than I."

Tell, O tell me, Grizzled-Face,
Do your heart and head keep pace?
When does hoary love expire?
When do frosts put out the fire?
Can its embers burn below
All that chill December snow?
Care you still soft hands to press,
Bonny heads to smooth and bless?
When does love give up the chase?
Tell, O tell me, Grizzled-Face!—
"Ah!" the wise old lips reply,
"Youth may pass and strength may die;
But of love I can't foretoken:
Ask some older sage than I!"

THE DOOR-STEP.

The conference-meeting through at last,
We boys around the vestry waited
To see the girls come tripping past,
Like snow-birds willing to be mated.

Not braver he that leaps the wall
By level musket-flashes litten
Than I, who stepped before them all
Who longed to see me get the mitten.

But no: she blushed and took my arm!
We let the old folks have the highway,
And started toward the Maple Farm
Along a kind of lover's by-way.

I can't remember what we said—
'Twas nothing worth a song or story;
Yet that rude path by which we sped
Seemed all transformed, and in a glory.

The snow was crisp beneath our feet,
The moon was full, the fields were gleaming;
By hood and tippet sheltered sweet,
Her face with youth and health was beaming.

The little hand outside her muff—
  O sculptor, if you could but mould it!
So lightly touched my jacket-cuff
  To keep it warm I had to hold it.

To have her with me there alone,
  'Twas love and fear and triumph blended,
At last we reached the foot-worn stone
  Where that delicious journey ended.

The old folks, too, were almost home;
  Her dimpled hand the latches fingered;
We heard the voices nearer come,
  Yet on the door-step still we lingered.

She shook her ringlets from her hood
  And with a "Thank you, Ned," dissembled;
But yet I knew she understood
  With what a daring wish I trembled.

A cloud passed kindly overhead,
  The moon was slily peeping through it,
Yet hid its face, as if it said—
  "Come, now or never! do it! *do it.*"

My lips till then had only known
  The kiss of mother and of sister;
But somehow, full upon her own
  Sweet, rosy, darling mouth—I kissed her!

Perhaps 'twas boyish love, yet still—
  O listless woman, weary lover!—
To feel once more that fresh, wild thrill
  I'd give—but who can live youth over?

WHAT THE WIND BRINGS.

"Which is the wind that brings the cold?"—
  The North Wind, Freddy, and all the snow;
And the sheep will scamper into the fold
  When the North begins to blow.

"Which is the wind that brings the heat?"—
  The South Wind, Katy; and corn will grow
And peaches redden for you to eat,
  When the South begins to blow.

"Which is the wind that brings the rain?"—
The East Wind, Arty; and farmers know
That cows come shivering up the lane
When the East begins to blow.

"Which is the wind that brings the flowers?"
The West Wind, Bessy; and soft and low
The birds sing in the summer hours
When the West begins to blow.

THE UNDISCOVERED COUNTRY.

Could we but know
The land that ends our dark, uncertain travel,
Where be those happier hills and meadows low—
Ah, if beyond the spirit's inmost cavil,
Aught of that country could we surely know,
Who would not go?

Might we but hear
The hovering angels' high imagined chorus,
Or catch, betimes, with wakeful eyes and clear,
One radiant vista of the realm before us,
With one rapt moment given to see and hear,
Ah, who would fear?

Were we quite sure
To find the peerless friend who left us lonely,
Or there, by some celestial stream as pure,
To gaze on eyes that here were love-lit only—
This weary mortal coil, were we quite sure,
Who would endure?

THE POET AND THE LAWS OF POETRY.

It is an open question whether a poet need be conscious of the existence and bearing of the laws and conditions under which he produces his work. It may be a curb and detriment to his genius that he should trouble himself about them in the least. But this rests upon the character of his intellect and includes a further question of the effects of culture. Just here there is a difference between poetry and the cognate arts of expression, since the former has somewhat less to do with material processes and effects. The freedom of the minor sculptor's, painter's, or composer's genius is not checked, while scope and precision are increased, by knowledge of the rules of his calling, and of their application in different regions and times. But in the case of the minor poet, excessive culture and wide acquaintance with methods and masterpieces often destroys spontaneity. . . .

Full-throated, happy minstrels like Béranger or Burns, need no knowledge of thorough-bass and the historical range of composition. Their expression is the carol of the child, the warble of the skylark scattering music at his own sweet will. Nevertheless, there is no strong imagination without vigorous intellect, and to its penetrative and reasoning faculty there comes a time when the laws which it has instinctively followed must be apparent; and later still, it cannot blind itself to the favoring or adverse influences of period and place. Should these forces be restrictive, their baffling effect will teach the poet to recognize and deplore them, and to endeavor, though with wind and tide against him, to make his progress noble and enduring.

In regard to the province of the critic there can, however, be no question. It is at once seen to be twofold. He must recognize and broadly observe the local, temporal, and general conditions under which poetry is composed, or fail to render adequate judgment upon the genius of the composer. Yet there always are cases in which poetry fairly rises above the idealism of its day. The philosophical critic, then, in estimating the importance of an epoch, also must pay full consideration to the messages that it has received from poets of the higher rank, and must take into account the sovereign nature of a gift so independent and spontaneous that from ancient times men have united in looking upon it as a form of inspiration.—*Victorian Poets.*

STEELE, RICHARD, a British author, born at Dublin in 1671; died in Wales in 1729. He was educated at Charterhouse School, London, Addison being one of his schoolfellows. He afterwards entered the University of Oxford, but left without taking a degree, and enlisted in the Horse Guards, where he rose to the rank of captain. In 1701 he put forth *The Christian Hero*, a religious treatise, and within a few years produced several fairly successful comedies, the earliest being *The Funeral, or Grief a la Mode* (1702), the last, and best, being *The Conscious Lovers* (1722). He was a gay and clever man about town, and in 1706 was appointed Court Gazetter, and was made Gentleman Usher to Prince George of Denmark, husband of Queen Anne. He advocated Whig principles, and when, in 1711, that party went out of power, he was ousted from his office of Gazetter, and was formally expelled from the House of Commons, to which he had been returned. It was not long, however, before the Whig party again returned to power, and Steele was restored to court favor, and received the honor of knighthood.

Steele was an industrious pamphleteer; but his fame rests upon his Essays on life and manners, rather than upon his dramas or his political writings. In this department he ranks next after Addison, though at a wide interval. In 1709 Steele started *The Tatler*, a tri-weekly periodical devoted to town gossip, domestic and foreign news, and essays upon social topics. Addison, at Steele's request, began early to furnish papers for *The Tatler;* and, said Steele, "I fared like a distressed prince who calls in a powerful neighbor to his aid. I was undone by my auxiliary. When I had once called him in, I could not subsist without him. The paper was advanced indeed. It was raised to a greater thing than I intended it." It was decided, after two years, that the paper should be discontinued, and a new periodical established, embracing the best features of *The Tatler*. This was *The Spectator*, the plan of which was Addison's, though Steele drew up roughly the characters of the Club, who were to be its ostensible conductors. Steele contributed to the first series of *The Spectator* some of his cleverest essays. But Steele had become immersed in political discussions, and Addison went on without him. Steele set up *The Guardian*, and subsequently *The Englishman*, in both which he had some assistance from Addison. The date of these publications falls within the years 1711 and 1714; that is, up to the time when Steele was involved in the temporary ruin caused by the overthrow of the Whig party. They add nothing to the reputation of Steele.

ON CASTLE-BUILDING.

Mr. Spectator: I am a fellow of a very odd frame of mind, as you will find by the sequel; and I think myself fool enough to deserve a place in your paper. I am unhappily far gone in building, and am one of that species of men who are properly denominated Castle-builders, who scorn to be beholden to the earth for a foundation, or dig in the bowels of it for materials; but erect their structures in the most unstable of elements—the air; fancy alone laying the line, marking the extent, and shaping the model. It would be difficult to enumerate what august palaces and stately porticos have grown under my forming imagination, or what verdant meadows and shady groves have started into being by the powerful heat of a strong fancy.

A castle-builder is ever just what he pleases; and as such I have grasped imaginary sceptres, and delivered uncontrollable edicts from a throne to which conquered nations yielded obedience. I have made I know not how many inroads into France, and ravaged the very heart of the kingdom. I have dined in the Louvre, and drank champagne at Versailles; and I would have you to take notice I am not only able to vanquish a people already cowed and accustomed to flight, but I could, Almanzor-like, drive the British general from the field, were I less a Protestant, or had ever been affronted by the confederates.

There is no art or profession whose most celebrated masters I have not eclipsed. Wherever I have afforded my salutary presence, fevers have ceased to burn and agues to shake the human fabric. When an eloquent fit has been upon me, an apt gesture and proper cadence have animated each sentence, and gazing crowds have found their passions worked up into rage, or soothed into a calm. I am short, and not very well made; yet upon the sight of a fine woman I have stretched into proper stature, and killed with a good air and mien.

These are the phantoms that dance before my waking eyes, and compose my day-dreams. I should be the most contented man alive were the chimerical happiness which springs from the paintings of fancy less fleeting and transitory. But alas! it is with grief of mind I tell you, the least breath of wind has often demolished my magnificent edifices, swept away my groves, and left no more trace of them than if they had never been. My exchequer has sunk and vanished by a rap on my door; the salutation of a friend has cost me a whole continent; and in the same moment I have been pulled by the sleeve, my crown has fallen from my head. The ill consequences of these reveries is inconceivably great, seeing the loss of imaginary possessions makes impressions of real woe. Besides, bad economy is visible and apparent in builders of invisible mansions. My tenants' advertisements of ruins and dilapidations often cast a damp on my spirits, even in the instant when the sun, in all his splendor, gilds my eastern palaces. Add to this the pensive drudgery in building, and constant grasping aerial trowels, distracts and shatters the mind and the fond builder of Babels is often cursed with an incoherent diversity and confusion of thoughts. I do not know to whom I can more properly apply myself for relief from this fantastical evil than yourself, whom I earnestly implore to accommodate me with a method how to settle my head and cool my brainpan. A dissertation on Castle-building may not only be serviceable to myself, but all architects who display their skill in the thin element. Such a favor would oblige me to make my next soliloquy not contain the praises of my dear self, but of the Spectator, who shall by complying with this, make me his obliged and humble servant.—*The Spectator*, No. 167.

STEFFENS, HEINRICH, a Norwegian author, born in 1773; died in 1845. He was originally a Lutheran; for a time wandered from that faith, but ultimately went back to it. He describes the process of his re-conversion in his *How I became a Lutheran Once More.* He wrote several scientific works, many Essays, among which is one upon *Scandinavian Myths*, and several imaginative stories, among which are *Walseth and Leith*, *The Four Norwegians*, and *Malcolm.*

PHYSIOGNOMY OF LEGENDS.

Amid my researches in natural history I always had a great curiosity in exploring what I may call the physiognomy of the legends of various districts, or, in other words, the resemblance which these legends bear to the natural scenery amid which they had their birth. Various districts are marked by the prevalence of various kinds of plants and grasses. Granite, limestone, and other rocks give peculiar formations to chasms, hills, and valleys; and these distinctions affect the varieties of trees. The effects of light and shade in the morning and evening, the aspects of waters, and tones of waterfalls are various in differents districts. And, as I have often imagined, the natural characteristics of a district may be recognized in its legends. I know of no better instance to support my supposition than such as may be found on the northern side of the Hartz Mountains, where a marked difference may be found between the legends of the granite regions and those of a neighboring district of slate-rocks. The old stories that may be collected between the Ilse and the Ocker differ in their coloring from the tales preserved among the peasantry in Budethal or Selkethal; while the legend of Hans Heiling in Bohemia is a genuine production of a granite district.

Seeland, the island home of my childhood, is

on the whole a level country, and only here and there hilly; but in some parts it can show prospects of surpassing beauty. The hills are rounded with an indescribable gracefulness; there is a charm in the fresh greenness of the pastures; the beechwoods have an imposing and venerable aspect; the sea winds its arms about amid the verdure of these woodland solitudes; and lakes of silver brightness lie encircled by graceful trees. The leaves rustling, brooks murmuring, the sounds of many insects, the plaintive notes of birds, and the gentle plashing of waves upon the lonely shore are the only sounds which break the silence. While I write of such a scene, I feel a longing to return to the quiet home of my childhood. In such a solitude I have sometimes felt as if I had approached the sacred place of one of the old legends, and in such a solitude we still may feel their power. When twilight gathers over woods, lakes, and pastures, we may see once more the phantom-ships, guided by departed spirits of the olden times, sailing among the green islands; we may hear the melancholy dirges for fallen heroes, or the plaintive song of the forsaken maid; and when the storm is bending all the boughs of the beechwoods, we may hear, blended in the gale, the loud cries of the Wild Huntsman and his followers.

STEPHEN, LESLIE, an English author, born at Kensington in 1832. In 1857 he took his degree of M. A. at Trinity Hall, Cambridge, where he remained several years as Fellow and Tutor. In 1864 he left Cambridge, and engaged in literary work at London. In 1871 he became editor of the *Cornhill Magazine*, retaining the position until 1882, when he relinquished it in order to assume the editorship of the *Dictionary of National Biography* the twenty-fourth volume of which has just appeared in 1890. In 1883 he was elected to the Lectureship of English Literature at Cambridge. His principal works are: *The Playground of Europe* (1871), *Hours in a Library* (three series, 1874. 1876, 1879), *History of English Thought in the Eighteenth Century* (1876), *The Science of Ethics* (1882). He wrote the Lives of Johnson, Pope, and Swift in the "English Men of Letters;" edited the works of Fielding, with a Biographical Sketch, and has been a constant contributor to periodicals.

PERSONAL TRAITS OF JOHNSON.

It was not until some time after Johnson came into the enjoyment of his pension that we first see him through the eyes of competent observers. The Johnson of our knowledge—the most familar figure to all students of English literary history—had already long passed the prime of life, and had done the greatest part of his literary work. His character, in the common phrase, had been "formed" years before; as, indeed, people's characters are chiefly formed in the cradle; and not only his character but the habits which are learned in the great schoolroom of the world, were fixed beyond any possibilities of change. The strange eccentricities which had now become a second nature amazed the society in which he was for twenty years the prominent figure. Unsympathetic observers—those especially to whom the Chesterfieldian type represented the ideal of humanity—were simply disgusted or repelled. The man, they thought, might be in his place in a Grub Street pot-house; but he had no business in a lady's drawing-room. If he had been modest and retiring they might have put up with his defects; but Johnson was not a person whose qualities, good or bad, were of a kind to be ignored. Naturally enough, the fashionable world cared little for the rugged old giant. "The great," said Johnson, "had tried him, and given him up; they had seen enough of him;" and his reason was very much to the purpose: "Great lords and ladies don't love to have their mouths stopped;" especially not, one may add, with an unwashed fist.

It is easy to blame them now. Everybody can see that a saint in beggar's rags is intrinsically better than a sinner in gold lace. But the principle is one of those which serves for judging of the dead much more than for regulating our own conduct. Those, at any rate, may throw the first stone at the Horace Walpoles and Chesterfields who are quite certain that they would ask a modern Johnson to their houses.—*Life of Johnson.*

POPE'S TRANSLATION OF HOMER.

Pope undoubtedly achieved, in some true sense, an astonishing success. . . .

He succeeded in the judgment both of the critics and of the public of the next generation. Johnson calls the Homer "the noblest version of poetry the world has ever seen." Gray declared that no other would ever equal it; and Gibbon that it had every merit except that of faithfulness to the original. This merit of fidelity, indeed, was scarcely claimed by any one. Bentley's phrase, "A very pretty poem, Mr. Pope, but you must not call it Homer," expresses the uniform view taken from the first by those who could read both. Its fame, however, has survived into the present century. Byron speaks—and speaks, I think, with genuine feeling—of the rapture with which he first read Pope as a boy, and says that no one will ever lay him down except for the original. Indeed the testimonies of opponents are as signal as those of admirers. Johnson remarks that the Homer "may be said to have tuned the English tongue;" and that no writer since its appearance has wanted melody. Coleridge virtually admits the fact, though drawing a different conclusion, when he says that the translation of Homer has been one of the main sources of that "pseudo-poetic diction" which he and Wordsworth were trying to put out of credit. Cowper, the earliest representative of the same movement, tried to supplant Pope's Homer by his own; and his attempt proved at least the reputation held in general by his rival. If, in fact, Pope's Homer was a recognized model for near a century, we may dislike the style, but we must admit the power implied in a performance which thus became the accepted standard of style for the best part of a century. —*Life of Pope.*

STEPHENS, Alexander Hamilton, an American statesman, born at Crawfordsville, Georgia, in 1812; died at Atlanta in in 1883. He graduated at Franklin College in 1832; studied law, and was admitted to the bar in 1834. He was elected to Congress in 1843, and held his seat by successive re-elections until 1859, when he resigned. Upon the formation of the Southern Confederacy he was elected Vice-President. After the downfall of the confederacy he was imprisoned for several months at Fort Warren, in Boston harbor, but was released upon his own recognizance. He afterwards lectured upon law, and in 1870 became editor of a newspaper at Atlanta, Georgia. In 1874 he was again elected to the Congress of the United States. He resigned in 1882, and was elected Governor of Georgia. Besides numerous published speeches his principal works are: *Constitutional View of the Late War between the States* (2 vols. 1867–1870), *School History of the United States* (1870), *History of the United States* (1883). The *War between the States* takes the form of a series of imaginary Colloquies between himself and several other persons, held at his residence, "Liberty Hall," near Crawfordsville.

FIRST IMPRESSIONS OF GENERAL GRANT.

I was never so much disappointed in my life in my previously formed opinions either of the personal appearance or bearing of one about whom I had heard and read so much. The disappointment, moreover, was in every respect favorable and agreeable. I was instantly struck with the great simplicity and perfect naturalness of his manners, and the entire absence of everything like affectation, or even the usual military air or mein of men in his position. He was plainly attired, sitting in a log cabin [at City Point near Petersburg, February 1, 1865], busily writing at a small table by a kerosene lamp. It was night when we arrived. There was nothing in his appearance or surroundings which indicated his official rank. There were neither guards nor aids around him.

His conversation was easy and fluent, without the least effort or constraint. In this nothing was so closely noticed by me as the point and terseness with which he expressed whatever he said. He did not seem either to court or avoid conversation; but whenever he did speak, what he said was directly to the point, and covered the whole matter in a few words. I saw, before being with him very long, that he was exceedingly quick in perception and direct in purpose, with a vast deal more of brain than of tongue, as ready as that was at his command. We were with General Grant two days. The more I became acquainted with him, the more I became thoroughly impressed with the very extraordinary combination of rare elements of character which he exhibited. . . . .

Upon the whole, the result of this first acquaintance with General Grant was the conviction on my mind that, taken all in all, he was one of the most remarkable men I had ever met with; and that his career in life, if his days should be prolonged, was hardly entered upon; that his character was not yet fully developed; that he was not aware of his own power; and that if he lived he would in the future exert a controlling influence in shaping the destinies of this country, either for good or for evil. Which it would be, time and circumstances alone could disclose.—*The War between the States,* Colloquy XXII.

STEPHENS, Ann Sophia (Winterbotham), an American author, born at Derby, Conn., in 1813; died at Newport, R. I., in 1886. In 1831 she married Mr. Edward Stephens of Portland, Maine. Mrs. Stephens had already commenced her literary career, which was thenceforth actively pursued almost to the close of her life. She was from time to time connected, as editor or contributor, with various magazines, and also wrote several popular novels. A uniform editon of her writings, was completed in 1886, in twenty-three volumes. The most successful of her novels was *Fashion and Famine* (1854).

THE WAIF AND THE HUCKSTER-WOMAN.

With the earliest group that entered Fulton Market that morning was a girl of perhaps thirteen or fourteen years old, but tiny in her form, and appearing far more juvenile than that. A pretty quilted hood of rose-colored calico was turned back from her face, which seemed naturally delicate and pale; but the fresh air, and perhaps a shadowy reflection from her hood, gave the glow of a rose-bud to her cheeks. Still there was anxiety upon her young face. Her eyes, of a dark violet-blue, drooped heavily beneath their black and curling lashes if any one from the numerous stalls addressed her; for a small splint basket on her arm, new and perfectly empty, was a sure indication that the child had been sent to make purchase; while her timid air, the blush that came and went on her face, bespoke as plainly that she was altogether unaccustomed to the scene, and had no regular place to make her humble bargains.

The child seemed a waif cast upon the market, and she was so beautiful, notwithstanding her humble dress of faded and darned calico, that at almost every stand she was challenged pleasantly to pause and fill her basket. But she only cast down her eyes and blushed more deeply as with her little bare feet she hurried on through the labyrinth of stalls toward that portion of the market occupied by the huckster-women. Here she began to slacken her pace, and to look about her with no inconsiderable interest. . . .

At length the child—for she seemed scarcely more than that—was growing pale, and her eyes turned with a sort of sharp anxiety from one face to another, when suddenly they fell upon the buxom old huckster-woman whose stall we have described. There was something in the good dame's appearance that brought an eager and satisfied look to that pale face. She drew close to the stand, and stood for some seconds, gazing timidly on the old woman.

It was a pleasant face and a comfortable form that the timid girl gazed upon. Smooth and comely were the full and rounded cheeks, with their rich autumn color, dimpled like an over-ripe apple. Fat and good-humored enough to defy wrinkles, the face looked far too rosy for the thick gray hair that was shaded, not concealed by a cap of clear white muslin with a deep border, and tabs that met like a snowy girth to support the firm double-chin. Never did your eyes dwell upon a chin so full of health and good-humor as that. It sloped with a sleek smiling grace down from the plump mouth, and rolled with a soft white wave into the neck, scarcely leaving an outline, or the want of one, before it was lost in the white of that muslin kerchief folded so neatly beneath the ample bosom of her gown. Then the broad linen apron of blue and white check, girdling her waist, and flowing over the rotundity of person, was a living proof of the ripeness and wholesome state of her merchandise. —I tell you, reader, that woman, take her for all in all, was one to draw the attention—aye, and the love—of a child who had come barefooted and alone in search of kindness.—*Fashion and Famine.*

STEPHENS, JOHN LLOYD, an American traveller and author, born at Shrewsbury, N. J., in 1805; died at New York in 1852. He graduated at Columbia College in 1822; studied law, and commenced practise at New York. He subsequently travelled for two years in Egypt, the Holy Land, Greece, European Turkey, and parts of Russia, and upon his return published, *Incidents of Travel in Egypt, Arabia Petræa, and the Holy Land* (1837), and *Incidents of Travel in Greece, Turkey, Russia, and Poland* (1838). In 1839 he was appointed U. S. Minister to the States of Central America, and made explorations of the ancient ruins in that region, and published *Incidents of Travel in Central America, Chiapas, and Yucatan* (1841). In 1842 he again visited Yucatan, and wrote, *Incidents of Travel in Yucatan* (1843). Both these works were profusely illustrated. He became vice-president of the Panama Railroad Company, and in 1849 negotiated a treaty with New Granada by which the right to construct the railroad was granted. Subsequently, as president of the company, he superintended the construction of the railroad up to the time of his death.

THE SLAVE-MARKET AT CAIRO.

One of my first rambles in Cairo was to the slave-market. It is situated nearly in the centre of the city, as it appeared to me, although after turning half-a-dozen corners in the narrow streets of a Turkish city, I will defy a man to tell where he is exactly. It is a large old building enclosing a hollow square with chambers all around, above and below. There were probably five or six hundred slaves sitting on mats in groups of ten or twenty, each group belonging to a different proprietor.

Most of them were entirely naked, though some, whose shivering forms evinced that even there they felt the want of their native burning sun, were covered with blankets. They were mostly from Dongola and Sennaar, but some were Abyssinians with yellow complexions, fine eyes and teeth, and decidedly handsome. The Nubians were very dark, but with oval, regularly-formed, and handsome faces, mild and amiable expression, and no mark of the African except the color of their skin.

The worst spectacle in the bazaar, was that of several lots of sick, who were separated from the rest, and arranged on mats by themselves; their bodies, thin and shrunken, their chins resting upon their knees, their long, lank arms hanging helplessly by their sides, their faces haggard, their eyes fixed with a painful vacancy, and altogether presenting the image of man in his most abject condition. Meeting them on their native sands, their crouching attitudes, shrunken jaws, and rolling eyes might have led one to mistake them for those hideous animals the orang-outang and the ape. Prices vary from twenty to one hundred dollars; but the sick, as carrying with them the seeds of probable death, are coolly offered for almost nothing, as so much damaged merchandise which the seller is anxious to dispose of before it becomes utterly worthless on his hands. There was one—an Abyssinian—who had mind as well as beauty in her face. She was dressed in silk, and wore ornaments of gold and shells, and called me as I passed, and peeped from behind a curtain, smiling and coquetting, and wept and pouted as I went away; and she thrust out her tongue to show me that she was not like those I had just been looking at, but that her young blood ran pure and healthy in her veins.—*Travels in Egypt.*

SUMMARY OF EXPLORATIONS IN YUCATAN.

I have now finished my journey among ruined cities. In our long, irregular, and devious route we have discovered the crumbling remains of forty-four ancient cities, most of them but a short distance apart, though from the great change that has taken place in the country, and the breaking up of the old roads, having no direct communication with each other. With but few exceptions all were lost, buried, and unknown, never before visited by a stranger, and some of them perhaps never looked upon by the eyes of a white man. Involuntarily we turn for a moment to the frightful scenes of which this region now so desolate must have been the theatre; the scenes of blood, agony, and war which preceded the destruction, desolation, or abandonment of these cities. But leaving the boundless space in which imagination might rove, I confine myself to the consideration of facts. If I may be permitted to say so, in the whole history of discoveries there is nothing to be compared with those here presented. They give an entirely new aspect to the great continent on which we live, and bring up with more force than ever the question which I once with some hesitation, undertook to answer—who were the builders of these American cities?—*Travels in Yucatan.*

STEPNIAK, SERGIUS, the pen name of a Russian author, nihilist, and homicide. His real name is said to be Kazcheffsky. It has been given as Michael Dragomanof. In 1878, Aug. 16, while Gen. Mezenbzeff, chief of the Imperial Russian Police, was walking with a friend in a deserted street of St. Petersburg, Kazcheffsky approached him from behind and twice plunged a long surgeon's knife into his back, between the shoulder blades. The assassin escaped; the chief died a few moments later. For some years Kazcheffsky has lived in London. He passes much time in the British Museum making notes, but otherwise in retirement, often writing all night. To the London *Times* he is said to contribute much on Russian topics. He keeps up intercourse with Siberian prisons, and, under him, an association has been formed to publish frequent accounts of atrocities suffered by exiles. He writes English with ease, is an impressive speaker, and is expected to lecture in this country. His works are: *The Russian Peasantry—their Agrarian Condition, Social Life, and Religion*, *Underground Russia*, *Russia under the Tzars*, *The Russian Storm-Cloud*, *or, Russia in Her Relation to Neighboring Countries*, and *The Career of a Nihilist.*

SHOOTING AT THE TZAR.

The great and terrible day had come.

From early dawn Audrey only slumbered, awakened every quarter of an hour by his excessive dread of missing his time. A strip of dazzling light penetrating through a rent in the blind, played upon the wall opposite his couch, announcing a splendid day. When that strip reached the corner of the chest of drawers, he knew that it would be time for him to rise.

But he preferred to get up at once. He pulled the bed-clothes from the leather couch which had served him as bed during his stay at head-quarters, and, carefully folding them up, he put them away in the yellow chest of drawers standing opposite.

"To-night I shall sleep in the cell of the Fortress, if I am not killed on the spot," said he to himself.

He closed the drawers, and proceeded to pull up the blinds of the two windows.

The remark was made in the plainest matter-of-fact tone, just as if he had been merely stating that the weather promised to be fair that day.

He was in a peculiar state of mind this morning, as distant from despondent resignation as from exaltation or from passion of any kind. It was the cold, absolute inward peace of a man who had settled all accounts with life, and had nothing to expect or to fear, or to give. True, there was yet that deed for him to do. But so much had been already overcome towards its completion, and the little which yet remained was now so certain to be carried out, that this great deed of his life he almost considered as accomplished. Whilst still a living man in full command of his mental and physical energy, he had the strange, but perfectly tangible sensation of being already dead, looking upon himself, all those connected with him, and the whole world, with the unruffled, somewhat pitying serenity of a stranger.

The whole of his life was clearly present to his mind, in the minutest details, very clear, the proportions well preserved. He thought of Tania, of the friends he was leaving behind him, of their party, of the country,—but in a calm dispassionate way, as if everything that held him to life had receded to an enormous distance. . . .

The distance to the Palace Square, where the attempt had to take place, was considerable. But Audrey intended to traverse it all on foot:

he would be more independent of chance in walking than in riding, and could easily regulate his pace so as to reach the spot in time, not one minute too soon or too late. Besides, as a foot passenger he would be much less noticeable on approaching the Tzar's promenade ground, which teemed with spies.

In his calm stoical mood Audrey walked along Lafonskaia Street, Transfiguration Square, and a part of Taurida Street, partly with, partly against the human stream, receiving upon his retina the images of faces—young, old, merry, serious; of horses, carriages, shops, policemen —all instantly forgotten as soon as he had passed them, attentive only to keep at his regular pace. Thus he reached the corner of the Taurida Garden, where a chance meeting with two perfect strangers upset his mental equilibrium, and brought disorder and tumult into the mental calm which he thought no longer subject to any disturbance.

These strangers, whose path came so unseasonably across his own, were two young folks, —a girl and a young man, looking like students, and to all appearances lovers. They came from the Greek Street, and were going arm-in-arm talking, along the outer railing of the Taurida Garden, smiling, caressing each other with their eyes. The young man was telling the girl in a low voice something very tender, judging from the radiant face of the girl. The pair went on slowly, almost reluctantly, as if burdened with their happiness, paying no attention to anything around.

But Audrey could not take his eyes off that girl; she was so remarkably like his own Tania. She was a little taller, and the lower part of her face was heavier, but the complexion, the quaint set of the head, the long eyebrows, resembling the outstretched wings of a bird, and that something which gives character to a face and to a figure, were exactly those of Tania. She was even dressed in dark blue, Tania's favorite color. Audrey would have given much to have seen her eyes; he was sure they would be like those he was never to look into again. But the girl's face was turned in profile to him, and she never bestowed one glance in his direction. . . . .

The girl passed, smiling and blushing, little suspecting the emotions she had caused in the stranger against whom she had brushed. The couple turned the corner and disappeared. But Audrey could not at once recover his self-control. The layer of ice, with which by an effort of will he had succeeded in covering up all his feelings, was broken, and the sea of bitter sadness hidden beneath burst forth. The image of his Tania rose before him no longer as a distant shadow, but warm with life, suffering, love, and beauty, as close and real as the girl who had just passed him.

How was the poor child now? How will she be to-night, when the act anticipated has become an accomplished fact? How will she bear it, when all is over with him? . . . .

The Tzar was at this moment a few paces beyond the monument to Alexander I., facing the Palace.

From the window of a house opposite two young men looked upon the scene of the coming encounter with beating hearts.

George was one of them.

He had seen Audrey's coming in collision with the three spies, and had already given him up for lost. Now he saw the master of all the Russias turning the corner, and Audrey, calm, stern as fate, moving towards him. On seeing a stranger in his way the Tzar gave a momentary start, but still went on.

In breathless suspense George watched as the distance between the two diminished step by step until they seemed to him to have come within a few paces of each other, and nothing had yet happened, and they were still advancing.

Why does he wait? What could it mean?. . . But it was a delusion; the distance which appeared in perspective so short was about fifteen yards.

Here, according to regulations, Audrey had to take off his hat and stand bareheaded until his master should pass. But instead of doing that act of obeisance, he plunged his hand into his pocket, drew a revolver, pointed and fired at the Tzar instantaneously.

The ball struck in the wall of the house at the Tzar's back some forty yards off, almost under the cornice. The shot had missed; the revolver kicked strongly, and had to be pointed at the feet for a fatal shot. This Audrey discovered too late. For a moment he stood petrified with consternation, both hands hanging down. The next moment he rushed onward, his brow knitted, his face pale, firing shot after shot. The Tzar, pale likewise, the flaps of his long overcoat gathered up in his hands, ran from him as quickly as he could. But he did not lose his presence of mind; instead of running straight, he ran in zigzags, thus offering a very difficult aim to the man running behind him. That saved him; only one of the shots pierced the cape of his overcoat, the rest missed altogether.

In less than a minute Audrey's six shots were spent. The flock of spies, who at first had made themselves scarce, now appeared from all sides, their numbers growing every moment. George saw Audrey encompassed at all points by the crowd of them, wild at his having eluded their vigilance. For a moment they stood at a distance, cautious, none daring to be the first to approach him. Then seeing him disarmed and making no show of resistance, they rushed on him all at once. But George heard only their fierce shouts and cries, for he had covered his face with both hands, and saw nothing more.

Audrey was thrown into prison, half dead. He recovered, and was in due time tried, condemned, and executed.—*The Career of a Nihilist.*

STERLING, John, an English author, born on the island of Bute in 1806; died at Ventnor, Isle of Wight, in 1844. He was educated at Trinity College, Cambridge, and began the study of law; with the ultimate purpose of entering political life; but in 1834 took orders, and became curate to his friend Julius Charles Hare, the Rector of Hurstmonceaux. After eight months he resigned the curacy, and entered upon a literary life in London, where he was intimate in the best literary society—with Carlyle more than any other man. His health, however, was always delicate, compelling him to pass much of his time in warmer climates. His published works are: *Arthur Coningsby*, a novel (1833), *The Onyx Ring*, a tale which appeared in *Blackwood's Magazine* (1836), *Minor Poems* (collected in 1839), *The Election*, a poem (1841), *Strafford*, a tragedy (1843). A collection of his *Prose Writings* was published in 1848, edited by Archdeacon Hare, who also wrote a *Life of Sterling*. Carlyle in his *Life of Sterling*, introduces extracts from his Letters, which are in fact Essays.

DIOGENES TEUFELSDRÖCKH.

[*From a Letter to Carlyle*—1835.]

What distinguishes Teufelsdröckh not merely from the greatest and the best of men who have been on earth for eighteen hundred years, but from the whole body of those who have been looking forwards toward the good, and have been the salt and the light of the world, is this—that he does not believe in a God. He does not belong to the herd of sensual and thoughtless men, because he does not perceive in all Existence a unity of power; because he does believe that this is a real power external to him, and dominant to a certain extent over him, and does not think that he is himself a shadow in a world of shadows. He has a deep feeling of the beautiful, the good, and the true, and a faith in their final victory.

At the same time how evident is the strong inward unrest, the Titanic heaving of the mountain; the storm-like rushing over land and sea in search of peace. He writhes and roars under the consciousness of the difference in himself between the possible and the actual, the hoped-for and the existent. He feels that duty is the highest law of his own being; and knowing how it bids the waves be stilled into an icy fixedness and grandeur, he trusts (but with a troubled inward misgiving) that there is a principle of order which will reduce all confusion to shape and clearness. But wanting peace himself, his fierce dissatisfaction fixes on all that is weak, corrupt, and imperfect around him; and instead of a calm and steady co-operation with all those who are endeavoring to apply the highest ideas as remedies for the worst evils, he holds himself aloof in savage isolation, and cherishes (though he dare not own) a stern joy at the prospect of that catastrophe which is to turn loose again the elements of man's social life, and give for a time victory to evil; in hopes that each new convulsion of the world must bring us nearer to the ultimate restoration of all things. . . . .

Something of this state of mind I may say that I understand; for I have myself experienced it. And the root of the matter appears to me—a want of sympathy with the great body of those who are now endeavoring to guide and help onward their fellow-men. And on what is this alienation grounded? It is, as I believe, simply in the difference on that point: The strong, deep, habitual recognition of a one Living *Personal* God, essentially wise, good and holy, the Author of all that exists, and in a reunion with whom is the only end of all rational beings.

The following lines are the last written words of Sterling. They were written in pencil and handed to his sister-in-law only a few hours before his sudden but not unexpected death.

THE LAST VERSES OF STERLING.

Could we but hear all Nature's voice,
From Glow-worm up to Sun,
'Twould speak with one concordant sound,
"Thy will, O God, be done!"

But hark, a sadder, mightier prayer
From all men's hearts that live:
"Thy will be done in earth and heaven,
And Thou my sins forgive!"

Sterling's longest poem, *The Sexton's Daughter*, a narrative, contains more than four hundred stanzas. Perhaps the best of all his poems are some of the eighteen *Hymns of a Hermit*, though some of the *Minor Poems* are worthy to stand by their side. The world, indeed, hardly knows how much poorer it is by the early death of John Sterling.

HYMN TO THE DEITY.

O Thou, who strength and wisdom sheddest
O'er all thy countless works below,
And harmony and beauty spreadest
On lands unmoved and seas that flow;
From grains and motes to spheres uncounted,
From deeps beneath to suns above!
My gaze with awe and joy has mounted,
And found in all thy ordering love.

The fly around me smoothly flitting,
The lark that hymns the morning-star,
The swan on crystal water sitting,
The eagle hung on skies afar—
To all their cleaving wings Thou givest,
Like those that bear the seraph's flight;
In all, O perfect Will! Thou livest,
For all hast oped thy world of light.

The grass that springs beside the fountain,
The silver waves that sparkle there
The trees that robe the shadowy mountain,
And, high o'er all,—the limpid air,
Amid the vale each lowly dwelling
Whose hearts with sweet religion shine—
In measure all things round are swelling
With tranquil Being's force divine.

And deep and vast beyond our wonder
The links of power that binds the whole,
While day and dusk, and breeze and thunder,
And life and death unceasing roll;
While all is wheeled in endless motion
Thou changest not, upholding all;
And lifting man in pure devotion,
On Thee thou teachest him to call.

To him, thy child, Thyself revealing,
He sees what all is meant to be;
From him thy secret not concealing,
Thou bid'st his will aspire to Thee.
And so we own in thy creation
An image painting all Thou art;
And crowning all the revelation,
Thy loftiest work, the human heart.

The Will, the Love, the sunlike Reason,
Which Thou hast made the strength of man,
May ebb and flow through day and season,
And oft may mar their seeming plan;
But Thou art here to nerve and fashion
With better hopes our world of care,
To calm each base and lawless passion,
And so the heavenly life repair.

In all the track of earth-born ages
Each day displays thy guidance clear;
And best divined by holiest sages
Makes every child in part a Seer.
Thy Laws are bright with purest glory,
To us Thou givest congenial eyes;
And so in earth's unfolding story
We view thy truth that fills the skies.

But midst thy countless forms of being
One shines supreme o'er all beside,

And man, in all thy wisdom seeing,
  In Him revères a sinless guide.
In Him alone, no longer shrouded
  By mist that dims all meaner things,
Thou dwell'st, O God! unveiled, unclouded,
  And fearless peace thy presence brings.

Then teach my heart, celestial Brightness!
  To know that Thou art hid no more,
To sun my spirit's dear-bought whiteness,
  Beneath thy rays, and upward soar;
In all that is, a law unchanging
  Of Truth and Love may I behold,
And own, 'mid Thought's unbounded ranging,
  The timeless One proclaimed of old.

Hymns of a Hermit, IX.

THE MEASURE OF LIFE.

There are two frequent lamentations which might well teach us to doubt the wisdom of popular opinions: men bewail in themselves the miseries of old age, and in others the misfortunes of an early death. They do not reflect that life is made up of emotions and thoughts, some cares and doubts and hopes and scattered handfuls of sorrow and pleasure, elements incapable of being measured by rule or dated by an almanac. It is not from the calendar or the parish-register that we can justly learn for what to grieve and wherefore to rejoice; and it is rather an affected refinement than a sage instinct, to pour out tears in proportion as our wasting days, or those of our friends, are marked by clepsydra. And even as old age, if it be the fruit of natural and regular existence, is full, not of aches and melancholy, but of lightness and joy; so there are men who perform their course in a small circle of years, whose maturity is to be reckoned not by the number of their springs and summers, but of their inward seasons of greenness and glory, and who by a native kindliness have enjoyed, during a brief and northern period, more sunshine of soul than ever came to the clouded breast of a basking Ethiop.

STERNE, LAURENCE, an English clergyman and author, born of English parents at Clonmel, Ireland, in 1713; died at London in 1768. He was taken to England in his eleventh year, placed at school and afterwards sent to the University of Oxford, where he graduated in 1736. He took orders, and was immediately presented to the living of Sutton, in Yorkshire. Other preferments were bestowed upon him, among which was a prebend in York Cathedral. In 1759 he put forth the first two volumes of *The Life and Opinions of Tristram Shandy;* the succeeding volumes appeared at intervals, the ninth and last in 1767. From 1762 to 1767 he resided partly in London and partly in France, where his way of life was far from being in accordance with his clerical profession. He had written only the first part of the *Sentimental Journey through France and Italy*, when he died somewhat suddenly. At various times he put forth volumes of *Sermons*. A collection of his *Letters* was published in 1775. All of his works were published under the pseudonym of "Mr. Yorick."

ON NAMES.

I would sooner undertake to explain the hardest problem in geometry than to pretend to account for it that a gentleman of my father's great good sense—knowing (as the reader must have observed him), wise also in political reasoning, and curious too in philosophy, and in polemical (as he will find) no way ignorant—could be capable of entertaining a notion so out of the common track, that I fear the reader, when I come to mention it to him, if he is in the least of a choleric temper will immediately throw the book by; if mercurial, he will laugh most heartily at it, and if he is of a grave and saturnine cast, he will, at first sight, condemn it as fanciful and extravagant. And that was in respect to the choice and imposition of Christian names, on which he thought a great deal more depended than what superficial minds were capable of conceiving. His opinion in this matter was that there was a strange kind of magic basis, which good or bad names, as he called them, irresistibly impressed upon our characters and conduct.

The hero of Cervantes argued not the point with more seriousness; nor had he more faith, or more to say, on the powers of necromancy in dishonoring his deeds, or on Dulcinea's name in shedding lustre upon them, than my father had on those of Trismagistus or Archimedes, on the one hand, or of Niky and Simkin, on the other. "How many Cæsars and Pompeys," he would say. "by mere inspiration of the names, have been rendered worthy of them! And how many," he would add, "are there who might have done exceedingly well in the world had not their characters and spirits been totally depressed and Nicodemus'd into nothing!"

"I see plainly, sir, by your looks" (or as the case happened), my father would say, "that you do not heartily subscribe to this opinion of mine, which to those," he would add, "who have not sifted it to the bottom, I own has an air more of fancy than of solid reasoning in it. And yet, my dear sir—if I may presume to know your character—I am morally assured I should hazard little in stating a case to you—not as a party in the dispute, but as a judge—and trusting my appeal upon it to your own good sense and candid disquisition in this matter. You are a person free from as many narrow prejudices of education as most men, and—if I may presume to penetrate farther into you—of a liberality of genius above bearing down an opinion merely because it wants friends. Your son—your dear son—from whose sweet and open temper you have so much to expect—your 'Billy,' Sir—would you for the world have called him 'Judas?' Would you, my dear Sir," he would say, laying his hand upon your breast—and with the genteelest address, and in the soft and irresistible *piano* of voice which the nature of the *argumentum ad hominem* absolutely requires—" would you, Sir, if a Jew of a godfather had proposed the name of your child, and offered you his purse along with it, would you have consented to such a desecration of him? . . . .

"Your greatness of mind in this action, which I admire, with that generous contempt of money which you show me in the whole transaction, is really noble; and what renders it more so is the principle of it: the working of a parent's love upon the truth of this very hypothesis—namely, that was your son called Judas, the sordid and treacherous idea so inseparable from this name would have accompanied him through life like his shadow, and in the end make a miser and a rascal of him in spite, Sir, of your example."—*Tristram Shandy.*

"I CAN'T GET OUT!"

As for the Bastile, the terror is in the word. "Make the most of it you can," said I to myself, "the Bastile is but another word for a tower, and a tower is but another word for a house you can't get out of. Mercy on the gouty! for they are in it twice a year; but with nine lives a day, and pen, ink, and paper, and patience, albeit a man can't get out, he may do very well within, at least for a month or six weeks; at the end of which, if he is a harmless fellow, his innocence appears, and he comes out a better and a wiser man than he went in."

I had occasion—I forget what—to step into the courtyard as I settled this account; and remember I walked downstairs in no small triumph with the conceit of my reasoning. "Beshrew the sombre pencil," said I, vauntingly, for I envy not its powers, "which paints the evils of life with so hard and deadly a coloring. The mind sits terrified at the objects she has magnified herself and blackened. Reduce them to their proper size and hue, and she overlooks them. "'Tis true," said I, correcting the proposition, "the Bastile is not an evil to be despised; but strip it of its towers, fill up the fosse, unbarricade the doors, call it simply a place of confinement, and suppose 'tis some tyrant of a distemper, and not of a man, which holds you in it, the evil vanishes, and you bear the other half without complaint."

I was interrupted in the heyday of this soliloquy with a voice which I took to be of a child, which complained that it "could not get out!" I looked up and down the passage, and seeing neither man nor woman nor child, I went out without further attention. In my return back through the passage I heard the same words repeated twice over; and looking up I saw it was a starling hung in a little cage. "I can't get out! I can't get out!" said the starling. I stood looking at the bird; and to every person that came through the passage, it ran in fluttering to the side towards which they approached it, with the same lamentation of its captivity.

"God help thee!" said I, "but I will let thee out, cost what it will;" so I turned about the cage to get at the door. It was twisted and double-twisted so fast with wire, there was no getting it open without pulling the cage to pieces. I took both hands to it. The bird flew to the place where I was attempting his deliverance, and thrusting his head through the trellis, pressed his breast against it as if impatient. "I fear, poor creature," said I, "I cannot set thee at liberty."—"No," said the starling, "I can't get out! I can't get out!" said the starling.

I vow I never had my affections more tenderly awakened; nor do I remember an incident in my life where the dissipated spirits, to which reason had been a bubble were so suddenly called home. Mechanical as the notes were, yet so true in tune to nature were they chanted, that in one moment they overthrew all my systematic reasonings upon the Bastile; and I heavily walked upstairs, unsaying every word I had said in going down them.

"Disguise thyself as thou wilt," said I, "still slavery is a bitter draught; and, though thousands in all ages have been made to drink of thee, thou art no less bitter on that account. 'Tis thou, thrice sweet and gracious goddess" —addressing myself to Liberty—"whom all in public or in private worship; whose taste is grateful, and ever will be so, till nature herself shall change. No tint of words can spot thy snowy mantle, or chemic power turn thy sceptre into iron. With thee to smile upon him as he eats his crust, the swain is happier than his monarch, from whose court thou art exiled. Gracious Heaven!" cried I, kneeling down upon the last step but one of the ascent, "grant me but health, thou great bestower of it, and give me but this fair goddess as my companion, and shower down thy mitres, if it seems good unto thy divine providence, upon the heads which are aching for them.—*Sentimental Journey.*

STEVENSON, ROBERT LOUIS, a Scottish novelist, essayist and poet, born at Edinburgh, Scotland, in 1850. His father, Thomas S., and two uncles, a grandfather, and great-grandfather, were engineers in the lighthouse service. In the dedication of one of his books to his father, he says, "by whose devices the great sea-lights in every quarter of the globe shine out more brightly." Robert was educated at Cambridge, studied law and was admitted to practice. His literary work began in contributions to magazines; many of the papers have been gathered in book form. In 1879 he came as a steerage passenger to America, and crossed the continent in an emigrant car. He married Mary Van de Grift in California, and she was co-author with him of *The Dynamiter*. Some of his California experiences are recorded in *The Silverado Squatters*. In 1886, he was living in Skerryvore, at Bournemouth, southern England. Returning to this country, in slender health, he spent some time in the wilderness at Lake Saranac, northern New York; and is now voyaging the South Seas, making some stay at the Samoan islands. Of his numerous books, *Dr. Jekyll and Mr. Hyde* (1885) is the one most widely known; next to this are such as *Treasure Island*, *Kidnapped* (1886), *The Black Arrow* (1888), *Prince Otto*, *The Master of Ballantrae* (1889). *Virginibus Puerisque* and *Familiar Studies of Men and Books* (1887) are volumes of essays. A book of poems (1887), bears the title *Underwoods*—crisp in poetic description, and half of the volume in quaint Scottish dialect. Other works are: *An Inland Voyage*, *Travels with a Donkey in the Cévennes*, *The*

Merry Men, *Memoir of Fleming Jenkin*, and *A Child's Garden of Verses.*

THE HOUSE BEAUTIFUL.

A naked house, a naked moor,
A shivering pool before the door,
A garden bare of flowers and fruit
And poplars at the garden foot:
Such is the place that I live in,
Bleak without and bare within.

Yet shall your ragged moor receive
The incomparable pomp of eve,
And the cold glories of the dawn
Behind your shivering trees be drawn;
And when the wind from place to place
Doth the unmoored cloud-galleons chase,
Your garden gloom and gleam again,
With leaping sun, with glancing rain.
Here shall the wizard moon ascend
The heavens, in the crimson end
Of day's declining splendor; here
The army of the stars appear.
The neighboring hollows, dry or wet,
Spring shall with tender flowers beset;
And oft the morning muser see
Larks rising from the broomy lea,
And every fairy wheel and thread
Of cob-web dew-bediamonded.
When daisies go, shall winter time
Silver the simple grass with rime;
Autumnal frosts enchant the pool
And make the cart-ruts beautiful;
And when snow-bright the moor expands,
How shall your children clap their hands!

To make this earth, our hermitage,
A cheerful and a changeful page,
God's bright and intricate device
Of days and seasons doth suffice.

Underwoods.

REQUIEM.

Under the wide and starry sky,
Dig the grave and let me lie.

Glad did I live and gladly die,
And I laid me down with a will.

This be the verse you grave for me:
Here he lies where he longed to be;
Home is the sailor, home from sea,
And the hunter home from the hill.

Underwoods.

THE TWO PHILOSOPHERS.

On one of the posts before Tentaillon's carriage entry he espied a little dark figure perched in a meditative attitude, and immediately recognized Jean-Marie.

"Aha," he said, stopping before him humorously, with a hand on either knee. "So we rise early in the morning, do we? It appears to me that we have all the vices of a philosopher."

The boy got to his feet and made a grave salutation.

"And how is our patient?" asked Deprez.

It appeared the patient was about the same.

"And why do you rise early in the morning?" he pursued.

Jean-Marie, after a long silence, professed that he hardly knew.

"You hardly know?" repeated Deprez. "We hardly know anything, my man, until we try to learn. Interrogate your consciousness. Come, push me this inquiry home. Do you like it?"

"Yes," said the boy slowly; "yes, I like it."

"And why do you like it?" continued the Doctor. "(We are now pursuing the Socratic method). Why do you like it?"

"It is quiet," answered Jean-Marie; "and I have nothing to do; and then I feel as if I were good."

Doctor Deprez took a seat on the post at the opposite side. He was beginning to take an interest in the talk, for the boy plainly thought before he spoke, and tried to answer truly.

"It appears you have a taste for feeling

good," said the Doctor. "Now, then, you puzzle me extremely; for I thought you said you were a thief; and the two are incompatible."

"Is it very bad to steal?" asked Jean-Marie.

"Such is the general opinion, little boy," replied the Doctor.

"No; but I mean as I stole," exclaimed the other. "For I had no choice. I think it is surely right to have bread; it must be right to have bread, there comes so plain a want of it. And then they beat me cruelly if I returned with nothing," he added. "I was not ignorant of right and wrong; for before that I had been well taught by a priest, who was very kind to me." (The Doctor made a horrible grimace at the word "priest.") "But it seemed to me, when one had nothing to eat and was beaten, it was a different affair. I would not have stolen for tartlets, I believe; but any one would steal for bread."

"And so I suppose," said the Doctor, with a rising sneer, "you prayed God to forgive you, and explained the case to Him at length."

"Why, sir?" asked Jean-Marie. "I do not see."

"Your priest would see, however," retorted Deprez.

"Would he?" asked the boy, troubled for the first time. "I should have thought God would have known."

"Eh?" snarled the Doctor.

"I should have thought God would have understood me," replied the other. "You do not see; but then it was God that made me think so, was it not?"

"Little boy, little boy," said Deprez, "I told you already you had the vices of philosophy; if you display the virtues also, I must go. I am a student of the blessed laws of health, an observer of plain and temperate nature in her common walks; and I cannot preserve my equanimity in presence of a monster. Do you understand?"

"No, sir," said the boy.

"I will make my meaning clear to you," replied the Doctor. "Look there at the sky—behind the belfry first, where it is so light, and then up and up, turning your chin back, right to the top of the dome, where it is already as blue as at noon. Is not that a beautiful color? Does it not please the heart? We have seen it all our lives, until it has grown in with our familiar thoughts. Now," changing his tone, "suppose that sky to become suddenly of a live and fiery amber, like the color of clear coals, and growing scarlet towards the top—I do not say it would be any the less beautiful; but would you like it as well?"

"I suppose not," answered Jean-Marie.

"Neither do I like you," returned the Doctor, roughly. "I hate all odd people, and you are the most curious little boy in all the world."

Jean-Marie seemed to ponder for a while, and then he raised his head again and looked over at the Doctor with an air of candid inquiry. "But are you not a very curious gentleman?" he asked.

The Doctor threw away his stick, bounded on the boy, clasped him to his bosom, and kissed him on both cheeks. "Admirable, admirable imp!" he cried.

"What a morning, what an hour for a theorist of forty-two! No," he continued, apostrophizing heaven, "I did not know that such boys existed; I was ignorant they made them so; I had doubted of my race; and now! It is like," he added, picking up his stick, "like a lover's meeting. I have bruised my favorite staff in that moment of enthusiasm. The injury, however, is not grave." He caught the boy looking at him in obvious wonder, embarrassment, and alarm. "Hello!" said he, "Why do you look at me like that? Egad, I believe the boy despises me. Do you despise me, boy?"

"O, no," replied Jean-Marie, seriously; "only I do not understand."

"You must excuse me, sir," returned the Doctor, with gravity; "I am still so young. O, hang him!" he added to himself. And he took his seat again and observed the boy sardonically. "He has spoiled the quiet of my morning," thought he. "I shall be nervous all day, and have a febricule when I digest. Let me compose myself." And so he dismissed his pre-occupations by an effort of the will which he had long practised, and let his soul roam abroad in the contemplation of the morning. He inhaled the air, tasting it critically as a connoisseur tastes a vintage, and prolonging the expiration with hygienic gusto. He counted the little flecks of cloud along the sky. He followed the movements of the birds around the church tower—making long sweeps, hanging poised, or turning airy somersaults in fancy, and beating the wind with imaginary pinions. And in this way he regained peace of mind and animal composure, conscious of his limbs, conscious of the sight of his eyes, conscious that the air had a cool taste, like a fruit, at the top of his throat; and at last, in complete abstraction, he began to sing. The Doctor had but one air—"Malbrouck s'en va-t-en guerre;" even with that he was on terms of mere politeness; and his musical exploits were always reserved for moments when he was alone and entirely happy.

He was recalled to earth rudely by a pained expression on the boy's face. "What do you think of my singing?" he inquired, stopping in the middle of a note; and then, after he had waited some little while and received no answer, "What do you think of my singing?" he repeated, imperiously.

"I do not like it," faltered Jean-Marie.

"Oh, come!" cried the Doctor. "Possibly you are a performer yourself?"

"I sing better than that," replied the boy.

The Doctor eyed him for some seconds in stupefaction. He was aware that he was angry, and blushed for himself in consequence, which made him angrier.

"If this is how you address your master!" he said at last, with a shrug and a flourish of his arms.

"I do not speak to him at all," returned the boy. "I do not like him."

"Then you like me?" snapped Doctor Deprez, with unusual eagerness.

"I do not know," answered Jean-Marie.

The Doctor rose. "I shall wish you a good morning," he said. "You are too much for me. Perhaps you have blood in your veins, perhaps celestial ichor, or perhaps you circulate nothing more gross than respirable air; but of one thing I am inexpugnably assured:—that you are no human being. No, boy"—shaking his stick at him—"you are not a human being. Write, write it in your memory—'I am not a human being—I have no pretension to a human being—I am a dive, a dream, an angel, an acrostic, an illusion—what you please, but not a human being.' And so accept my humble salutations and farewell!"

And with that the Doctor made off along the street in some emotion, and the boy stood, mentally gaping, where he left him. . . . .

"Never!" cried Madame. "Never, Doctor, with my consent. If the child were my own flesh and blood, I would not say no. But to take another person's indiscretion on my shoulders—my dear friend, I have too much sense."

"Precisely," replied the Doctor. "We both had. And I am all the better pleased with our wisdom, because—because——" He looked at her sharply.

"Because what?" she asked, with a faint premonition of danger.

"Because I have found the right person," said the Doctor firmly, "and shall adopt him this afternoon."—*The Treasure of Franchard (Merry Men).*

TRUTH OF INTERCOURSE.

Among sayings that have a currency in spite

of being wholly false upon the face of them, for the sake of a half-truth upon another subject which is accidentally combined with the error, one of the grossest and broadest conveys the monstrous proposition that it is easy to tell the truth and hard to tell a lie. I wish heartily it were. But the truth is one; it has first to be discovered, then justly and exactly uttered. Even with instruments specially contrived for such a purpose—with a foot rule, a lever, or a theodolite—it is not easy to be exact; it is easier, alas! to be inexact. From those who mark the divisions on a scale to those who measure the boundaries of empires or the distance of the heavenly stars, it is by careful method and minute, unwearying attention that men rise even to material or to sure knowledge, even of external and constant things. But it is easier to draw the outline of a mountain than the changing appearance of a face; and truth in human relations is of this more intangible and dubious order: hard to seize, harder to communicate. . . .

"It takes," says Thoreau, in the noblest and most useful passage I remember to have read in any modern author, "two to speak truth—one to speak and another to hear." He must be very little experienced, or have no great zeal for truth, who does not recognize the fact. A grain of anger or a grain of suspicion produces strange acoustical effects, and makes the ear greedy to remark offence. Hence we find those who have once quarrelled carry themselves distantly, and are ever ready to break the truce. To speak truth there must be moral equality or else no respect; and hence between parent and child intercourse is apt to degenerate into a verbal fencing bout, and misapprehensions to become ingrained. And there is another side to this, for the parent begins with an imperfect notion of the child's character, formed in early years or during the equinoctial gales of youth; to this he adheres, noting only the facts which suit his preconception; and wherever a person fancies himself unjustly judged, he at once and finally gives up the effort to speak truth. With our chosen friends, on the other hand, and still more between lovers (for mutual understanding is love's essence), the truth is easily indicated by the one and aptly comprehended by the other. A hint taken, a look understood, conveys the gist of long and delicate explanations: and where the life is known even *yea* and *nay* become luminous. In the closest of all relations—that of a love well founded and equally shared—speech is half discarded, like a roundabout, infantile process or a ceremony of formal etiquette; and the two communicate directly by their presences, and with few looks and fewer words contrive to share their good and evil and uphold each other's hearts in joy. For love rests upon a physical basis; it is a familiarity of nature's making and apart from voluntary choice. Understanding has in some sort outrun knowledge, for the affection perhaps began with the acquaintance; and as it was not made like other relations, so it is not, like them, to be perturbed or clouded. Each knows more than can be uttered; each lives by faith, and believes by a natural compulsion; and between man and wife the language of the body is largely developed and grown strangely eloquent. The thought that prompted and was conveyed in a caress would only lose to be set down in words, ay, although Shakespeare himself should be the scribe.

Yet it is in these dear intimacies, beyond all others, that we must strive and do battle for the truth. Let but a doubt arise, and alas! all the previous intimacy and confidence is but another charge against the person doubted. —*Virginibus Puerisque.*

STEWART, DUGALD, a Scottish philosopher, born at Edinburgh in 1753; died in 1828. He studied at the University of Edinburgh, where his father was Professor of Mathematics, until 1771, when he entered the University of Glasgow. In 1772 he was invited by his father to teach the mathematical classes at Edinburgh; was made joint-professor in 1775, and in 1780 became Professor of Moral Philosophy, retaining the chair until 1810, when he withdrew from its active duties. His lectures were highly popular. They covered the subjects of Psychology. Metaphysics, Logic, Ethics, Natural Theology, Politics, Political Economy, and the Principles of taste. His principal philosophical works are: *Elements of the Philosophy of the Human Mind* (Vol. I. 1793; Vol. II. 1814), *Philosophical Essays* (1810), *Dissertation on the History of Ethical Philosophy* (1821), *Philosophy of the Active and Moral Powers* (1828).

THE MEMORY.

It is generally supposed that of all our faculties Memory is that which nature has bestowed in the most unequal degrees on different individuals; and it is far from being impossible that this opinion may be well founded. If, however, we consider that there is scarcely any man who has not memory sufficient to learn the use of language, and to learn to recognize, at the first glance, the appearance of an infinite number of familiar objects, besides acquiring such an acquaintance with the laws of nature, and the ordinary course of human affairs, as is necessary for directing his conduct in life, we shall be satisfied that the original disparities among men in this respect are by no means so immense as they seem to be at first view; and that much is to be ascribed to different habits of attention, and to a difference of selection among the various events presented to their curiosity. It is worthy of remark, also, that those individuals who possess unusual powers of memory with respect to any one class of objects, are commonly as remarkably deficient in some of the other applications of that faculty.

A similar observation, I can almost venture to say, will be found to apply to by far the greater number of those in whom this faculty seems to exhibit a preternatural or anomalous degree of force. The *varieties* of memory are indeed wonderful, but they are not to be confounded with the *inequalities* of memory. One man is distinguished by a power of recollecting names and dates and genealogies; a second by the multiplicity of speculations and of general conclusions treasured up in his intellect, a third by the facility with which words and combinations of words—the *ipsissima verba* of a speaker or of an author—seem to lay hold of his mind; a fourth by the quickness with which he seizes and appropriates the sense and meaning of an author, while the phraseology and style seem altogether to escape his notice; a fifth by his memory for poetry; a sixth by his memory for music; a seventh by his memory for architecture, statuary, and painting, and all the other objects of taste which are addressed to the eye. All these different powers seem miraculous to those who do not possess them; and as they are apt to be supposed by superficial observers to be commonly united in the same individuals, they contribute much to encourage those exaggerated estimates concerning the original inequalities among men in respect to this faculty, which I am now endeavoring to reduce to their first standard.

As the great purpose to which this faculty is subservient is to enable us to collect and to retain for the future regulation of our conduct the results of our past experience, it is evident that the degree of perfection which it attains in the case of different persons must vary—first, with the facility of making the original acquisition; secondly, with the permanence of the acquisition; and, thirdly, with the quickness or readiness with which the individual is able, on particular occasions, to apply it to use.

The qualities of a good memory are—in the first place, to be susceptible; secondly to be retentive; and, thirdly, to be ready. It is but rarely that these three qualities are united in the same person. We often indeed, meet with a memory which is at once susceptible and ready; but I doubt much if such memories be commonly very retentive: for the same set of habits which are favorable to the first two qualities are adverse to the third.

Those individuals, for example, who with a view to conversation make a constant business of informing themselves with respect to the popular topics, or of turning over the ephemeral publications subservient to the amusement or to the politics of the times, are naturally led to cultivate a susceptibility and readiness of memory, but have no inducement to aim at that permanent retention of select ideas which enables the scientific student to combine the most remote materials, and to concentrate at will on a particular object all the scattered lights of his experience and of his reflections. Such men (as far as my observation has reached) seldom possess a familiar or correct acquaintance even with those classical remains of our early writers which have ceased to furnish topics of discourse to the circles of fashion. A stream of novelties is perpetually passing through their minds, and the faint impressions which it leaves soon vanish to make way for others, like the traces which the ebbing tide leaves upon the sand. Nor is this all. In proportion as the associating principles which lay the foundation of susceptibility and readiness predominate in the memory, those which form the basis of our more solid and lasting acquisitions may be expected to be weakened.—*Elements of the Philosophy of the Human Mind.*

STIMSON, FREDERIC JESUP ("J. S. of Dale," *pseud.*), an American novelist and author of law books. He was born at Dedham, Mass., in 1855, graduated at Harvard in 1876, and from the Law School two years later. In 1884–85 he was Assistant Attorney-General of Massachusetts. His works in the line of his profession are a *Law Glossary* (1881), and *Am. Stat. Law* (1886); his novels are: *Guerndale* (1882), *The Crime of Henry Vane* (1884), *The King's Men* (co-author and same date), *The Sentimental Calendar* (1886), *First Harvests*, a satire on New York high life, and *The Residuary Legatee*, both published in 1888. One of the stories in the *Sentimental Calendar* is that of a bridegroom who fell into a glacier crevasse, in 1837, and (the rate of motion and length of time having been computed) was sought, not in vain, by his aged widow at the foot of the glacier forty-five years afterwards.

THE BRIDEGROOM IN THE GLACIER.

In the summer of 1882, the little Carinthian village of Heiligenblut was haunted by two persons. One was a young German scientist, with long hair and spectacles: the other was a tall English lady slightly bent, with a face wherein the finger of time had deeply written tender things. Her hair was white as silver, and she wore a long black veil. Their habits were strangely similar. Every morning, when the eastern light shone deepest into the ice-cavern at the base of the great Pasterzen glacier, these two would walk thither; then both would sit for an hour or two and peer into its depths. Neither knew why the other was there. The woman would go back for an hour in the late afternoon; the man, never. He knew that the morning light was necessary for his search.

The man was the famous young Zimmermann, son of his father, the old doctor, long since dead. But the Herr Doctor had written a famous tract, when late in life, refuting all Splüthners, past, present, and to come; and had charged his son, as a most sacred trust, that he should repair to the base of the Pasterzen glacier in the year 1882, where he would find a leaden bullet, graven with his father's name, and the date A. U. C. 2590. All this would be a vindication of his father's science. Splüthner, too, was a very old man, and Zimmermann the younger (for even he was no longer young) was fearful lest Splüthner should not live to witness his own refutation. The woman and the man never spoke to each other.

Alas, no one could have known Mrs. Knollys in the young days of the century; not even the inkeeper, had he been there. But he, too, was long since dead. Mrs. Knollys was now bent and white-haired; she had forgotten, herself, how she looked in those old days. Her life had been lived. She was now like a woman of another world; it seemed another world in which her fair hair had twined about her husband's fingers, and she and Charles stood upon the evening mountain, and looked in one another's eyes. That was the world of her wedding-days, but it seemed more like a world she had left when born on earth. And now he was coming back to her in this. Meantime the great Pasterzen glacier had moved on, marking only the centuries; the men upon its borders had seen no change; the same great waves lifted their snowy heads upon its surface; the same crevasse was still where he had fallen. At night, the moonbeams, falling, still shivered off its glassy face; its pale presence filled the night, and immortality lay brooding in its hollows.

Friends were with Mrs. Knollys, but she left them at the inn. One old guide remembered her, and asked to bear her company. He went with her in the morning, and sat a few yards from her, waiting. In the afternoon she went alone. He would not have credited you, had you told him that the glacier moved. He thought it but an Englishwoman's fancy, but he waited with her. Himself had never forgotten that old day. And Mrs. Knollys sat there silently, searching the clear depths of the ice, that she might find her husband.

One night she saw a ghost. The latest beam of the sun, falling on a mountain opposite, had shone back into the ice-cavern; and seemingly deep within, in the grave azure light, she fancied she saw a face turned towards her. She even thought she saw Charles's yellow hair, and the self-same smile his lips had worn when he bent down to her before he fell. It could be but a fancy. She went home, and was silent with her friends about what had happened. In the moonlight she went back, and again the next morning before dawn. She told no one of her going; but the old guide met her at the door, and walked silently behind her. She had slept, the glacier ever present in her dreams.

The sun had not yet risen when she came; and she sat a long time in the cavern, listening to the murmur of the river, flowing under the glacier at her feet. Slowly the dawn began, and again she seemed to see the shimmer of a face—such a face as one sees in the coals of a dying fire. Then the full sun came over the eastern mountain, and the guide heard a woman's cry. There before her was Charles Knollys! The face seemed hardly pale; and there was the same faint smile—a smile like her memory of it, five and forty years gone by. Safe in the clear ice, still unharmed, there lay —O God! not her Charles; not the Charles of her own thought, who had lived through life with her and shared her sixty years; not the old man she had borne thither in her mind—but a boy, a boy of one and twenty, lying asleep, a ghost from another world coming to confront her from the distant past, immortal in the immortality of the glacier. There was his quaint coat, of the fashion of half a century ago; his blue eyes open; his young, clear brow; all the form of the past she had forgotten; and she, his bride, stood there to welcome him, with her wrinkles, her bent figure, and thin white hairs. She was living, he was dead; and she was two and forty years older than he.

Then at last the long, kept tears came to her and she bent her white head in the snow. The old man came up with his pick, silently, and began working in the ice. The woman lay weeping, and the boy, with his still, faint smile, lay looking at them, from the clear ice-veil, from his open eyes.

I believe that the professor found his bullet; I know not. I believe that the scientific world rang with his name and the thesis that he published on the glacier's motion, and the changeless temperature his father's lost thermometer had shown. All this you may read. I know no more.

But I know that in the English church-yard there are now two graves, and a single stone, to Charles Knollys and Mary, his wife; and the boy of one and twenty sleeps there with his bride of sixty-three; his young frame with her old one, his yellow hair beside her white. And I do not know that there is not some place, not here, where they are still together, and he is one and twenty and she is eighteen. I do not know this; but I know that all the pamphlets of the German doctor cannot tell me it is false.

Meantime the great Pasterzen glacier moves on, and the rocks with it; and the mountain flings his shadow of the planets in its face.—*Sentimental Calender.*

STOCKTON, Francis Richard, an American author, born at Philadelphia in 1834. After graduating at the Central High School, he became an engraver, but soon abandoned art for literature; becoming connected with periodicals in Philadelphia, New York, and Boston. He has written several novels, and numerous short stories, which have been collected into separate volumes, among which are: *Ting-a-ling Stories* (1870), *Rudder Grange* (1879), *The Lady or the Tiger?* (1884), *The Late Mrs. Null* (1886), *Christmas Week, and Other Tales* (1887), *The Bee-Man of Orne, and Other Fanciful Tales* (1887), *The Casting Away of Mrs. Lecks and Mrs. Aleshine* (1887), *The Dusantes* (1888), *Amos Kilbright* (1888), *Personally Conducted* (1889), *The Great War Syndicate* (1889), *The Merry Chanter* (1890), and *Ardis Claverden* (1890).

THE LADY OR THE TIGER?

In the very olden time there lived a semi-barbarous King whose ideas, though somewhat polished and over-sharpened by the progressiveness of distant Latin neighbors, were still large, florid, and untrammelled, as became the half of him which was barbaric. He was a man of exuberant fancy, and withal of an authority so irresistible that at his will he turned his various fancies into facts. Among the borrowed notions by which his barbarism had been semified was that of the Public Arena in which, by exhibitions of manly and beastly valor, the minds of his subjects were refined and colored. But even here the exuberant and barbarous fancy of the king asserted itself.

The Arena of the king was built, not to give the people an opportunity of hearing the rhapsodies of dying gladiators, nor to enable them to view the inevitable conclusion of a conflict between religious opinions and hungry jaws, but for purposes far better adapted to widen and develop the mental energies of the people. This vast amphitheatre, with its encircling galleries, its mysterious vaults, and its unseen passages, was an agent of poetic justice, in which vice was punished, or virtue rewarded, by the decision of an impartial and incorruptible Chance. When a subject was accused of a crime of sufficient importance to interest the King, public notice was given that on an appointed day the fate of the accused person would be decided in the King's Arena. . . . .

When all the people had assembled in the galleries, and the King, surrounded by his court, sat high upon his throne of royal state on one side of the arena, he gave a signal; a door beneath him opened, and the accused subject stepped out into the amphitheatre. Opposite him, on the other side of the enclosed space, were too doors exactly alike, and side by side. It was the duty and the privilege of the person on trial to walk directly to these doors, and open one of them. He could open either door at pleasure; he was subject to no guidance or influence but that of the afore-mentioned and impartial Chance. If he opened the one door, there came out of it a hungry Tiger, the fiercest and most cruel that could be procured, which immediately sprang upon him and tore him in pieces, as a punishment for his guilt. But if he opened the other door, there came forth from a Lady, the most suitable to his years and station that his Majesty could select among his fair subjects; and to this Lady he was immediately married, as a reward of his innocence. It mattered not that he might already possess a wife and family, or that his affections might be engaged upon an object of his own selection. The King allowed no such subordinate arrangements to interfere with his great scheme of retribution and reform. . . . .

This was the King's semi-barbaric method of administering justice. Its perfect fairness is obvious. The criminal could not know out of which door would come the Lady. He opened either he pleased, without having the slightest idea whether in the next instant he was to be devoured or married. On some occasions the Tiger came out of one door, and on some occasions out of the other. The decisions of this tribunal were not only fair, they were positively determinate. The accused person was instantly punished if he found himself guilty; and if innocent, he was rewarded on the spot, whether he liked it or not. There was no escape from the judgments of the King's Arena. . . .

This semi-barbaric King had a daughter, as blooming as his most florid fancies, and with a soul as fervent and imperious as his own. As is usual in such cases, she was the apple of his eye, and was loved by him above all humanity. Among his courtiers was a young man of that fineness of blood and lowness of station common to the conventional heroes of romance who love royal maidens. This royal maiden was well satisfied with her lover, for he was brave and handsome to a degree unsurpassed in all this Kingdom; and she loved him with an ardor that had enough of barbarism in it to make it exceedingly warm and strong. This love-affair moved on happily for many months, until one day the King happened to discover its existence. He did not hesitate or waver in regard to his duty in the premises. The youth was immediately cast into prison, and a day was appointed for his trial in the King's Arena. . . . .

Of course everybody knew that the deed of which the accused had been charged had been done. He had loved the Princess; and neither he, nor she, nor any one else, thought of denying the fact. But the King would not think of allowing anything of this kind to interfere with the workings of the tribunal in which he took such great delight and satisfaction. No matter how the affair turned out, the youth would be disposed of; and the King would take an æsthetic pleasure in watching the course of events, which would determine whether or not the young man had done wrong in allowing himself to love the Princess. . . . .

As the youth advanced into the arena, he turned, as the custom was, to bow to the King; but he did not think at all of that royal personage. His eyes were fixed upon the Princess, who sat to the right of her father. Had it not been for the moiety of barbarism in her nature it is probable that the lady would not have been there; but her intense and fervid soul would not allow her to be absent on an occasion in which she was so deeply interested. From the moment the decree had gone forth that her lover should decide his fate in the King's Arena she had thought of nothing, night or day, but the great event, and the various subjects connected with it. Possessed of more power, influence, and force of character than any one who had ever before been interested in such a case, she had done what no other person had done, she had possessed herself of the secret of the doors. She knew in which of the rooms that lay behind those doors stood the cage of the Tiger, with its open front, and in which waited the Lady. . . . .

And not only did she know in which room stood the Lady, ready to emerge should her door be opened, but she knew who the lady was. It was one of the fairest and loveliest of the damsels of the Court who had been selected as the reward of the accused youth, should he be proved innocent of aspiring to one so far above him; and the Princess hated her. Often had she seen—or imagined that she had seen—this fair creature throwing glances of admiration upon the person of her lover; and sometimes she thought these glances were perceived and returned. Now and then she had seen them talking together. It was but for a moment; but much can be said in a brief space. It may have been on most unimportant topics; but how should she know that? The girl was lovely, but she had dared to raise her eyes to the loved one of the Princess; and with all the intensity of the savage blood transmitted to her through long lines of barbaric ancestors, she hated the woman who blushed and trembled behind that silent door.

When her lover turned and looked at her, and his eye met hers, as she sat there, paler and whiter than any one else in the vast ocean of anxious faces about her, he saw, by that quick power of perception given to those whose souls are one, that she knew behind which door crouched the Tiger, and behind which stood the Lady. He had expected her to know it. He understood her nature, and his soul was assured that she would never rest until she had made plain to herself this thing, hidden to all other lookers-on—even to the King. The only hope of the youth in which there was any element of certainty was based upon the success of the Princess in discovering this mystery; and the moment he looked upon her he saw that she had succeeded.

Then it was that his quick and anxious glance asked the question—"*Which?*" It was as plain to her as if he had shouted it from where he stood. There was not a moment to be lost. The question was asked in a flash; it must be answered in another. Her right hand lay on the cushioned parapet before her. She raised her hand and made a slight, quick movement to the right. No one saw her. Every eye but hers was fixed on the man in the arena. He turned, and with a firm and rapid step walked across the empty space. Every heart stopped beating, every breath was held, every eye was fixed immovably upon that man. Without the slightest hesitation he went to the door on the right, and opened it.

Now the point of the story is this: Did the Tiger come out of that cage, or did the Lady?

The more we reflect upon this question, the harder it is to answer. It involves a study of the human heart, which leads us through mazes of passion out of which it is difficult to find our way. Think of it, fair reader, not as if the decision depended upon yourself, but upon that hot-blooded, semi-barbaric Princess—her soul at a white heat beneath the combined fires of despair and jealousy. She had lost him: but who should have him? Her decision had been indicated in an instant; but it had been made after days and nights of anxious deliberation. She had known she would be asked; she had decided what she would answer; and without the slightest hesitation she had moved her hand to the right. The question of her decision is not one to be lightly considered, and it is not for me to set myself up as the one person able to answer it. And so I leave it with all of you: Which came out of the opened door—the Lady or the Tiger?

STODDARD, CHARLES WARREN, an American poet and journalist, born at Rochester, N. Y., in 1843. He was educated in New York City and in California, his father removing westward in 1855. At an early age he wrote poetry and was engaged in newspaper work, In 1864, he visited the Hawaiian Islands, and from 1873 to 1878, traveled extensively as correspondent of the San Francisco *Chronicle.* He was Professor of English Literature in Notre Dame College, Indiana, in 1885–6. To the *Century Magazine*, he has contributed descriptive verse. His volume of poems is dated 1867, and his prose contributions to periodicals, collected in book form, are *South-Sea Idyls* (1873), *Mashallah: a Flight into Egypt* (1881), and *Lepers of Molokai* (1885)—the last two being notes of travel, and the *Idyls* a mixture of fact and fancy in prose.

A SURF-SWIMMER.

There was a break in the reef before us; the sea knew it, and seemed to take special delight in rushing upon the shore as though it were about to devour sand, savages, and everything. Kahéle and I watched the surf-swimmers for some time, charmed with the spectacle. Such buoyancy of material matter I had never dreamed of. Kahéle, though much in the flesh, could not long resist the temptation to exhibit his prowess, and having been offered a surf-board that would have made a good lid to his coffin, and was itself as light as cork and as smooth as glass, suddenly threw off his last claim to respectability, seized his sea-sled, and dived with it under the first roller which was then about to break above his head, not three feet from him. Beyond it, a second roller reared its awful front, but he swam under that with ease; at the sound of his "open sesame," its emerald gates parted and closed after him. He seemed some triton, playing with the elements, and dreadfully "at home" in that very wet place. The third and mightiest of the waves was gathering its strength for a charge upon the shore. Having reached its outer ripple, again Kahéle dived and reappeared on the other side of the watery hill, balanced for a moment in the glassy hollow, turned suddenly, and, mounting the towering monster, he lay at full length on his fragile raft, using his arms as a bird its pinions,—in fact, soaring for a moment with the wave under him. As it rose, he climbed to the top of it, and there, in the midst of seething like champagne, on the crest of a rushing sea-avalanche about to crumble and dissolve beneath him, his surf-board hidden in spume, on the very top bubble of all, Kahéle danced like a shadow. He leaped to his feet and swam in the air, another Mercury, tiptoeing a heaven-kissing hill, buoyant as vapor, and with a suggestion of invisible wings about him.—Kahéle transformed for a moment, and for a moment, only; the next second my daring sea-skater leaped ashore, with a howling breaker swashing at his heels. It was something glorious and almost incredible; but I saw it with my own eyes, and I wanted to double his salary on the spot.—*South-Sea Idyls.*

AT NIGHT.

It was still night; the sea was again moaning; the cool air of the mountain rustled in the long thatch at the doorway; a ripe breadfruit fell to the earth with a low thud. I rose from my mat and looked about me. The room was nearly deserted; some one lay swathed like a mummy in a dark corner of the lodge, but of what sex I knew not,—probably one who had outlived all sensations, and perhaps all desires; a rush, strung full of oily *kukui* nuts, flamed in the centre of the room, and a thread of black smoke climbed almost to the peak of the roof; but, falling in with a current of fresh air, it was spirited away in a moment.

I looked out of the low door: the hour was such a one as tinges the stoutest heart with superstition; the landscape was complete in two colors,—a moist transparent gray, and a thin, feathery silver, that seemed almost palpable to the touch. Out on the slopes near the stream reclined groups of natives, chatting, singing, smoking, or silently regarding the moon. I passed them unnoticed; dim paths led me through guava jungles, under orange groves, and beside clusters of jasmine, overpowering in their fragrance. Against the low eaves of the several lodges sat singers, players upon rude instruments of the land, and glib talkers, who waxed eloquent, and gesticulated with exceeding grace. Footsteps rustled before and behind me; I stole into the thicket, and saw lovers wandering together, locked in each other's embrace, and saw friends go hand-in-hand conversing in low tones, or perhaps mute, with an impressive air of the most complete tranquillity. The night-blooming cereus laid its ivory urn open to the moonlight, and a myriad of crickets chirped in one continuous jubilee. Voices of merriment were wafted down to me; and, stealing onward toward the great meadow by the stream, where the sleepless inhabitants of the valley held high carnival, I saw the most dignified chiefs of Méha sporting like children, while the children capered like imps, and the whole community seemed bewitched with the glorious atmosphere of that particular night.—*South-Sea Idyls.*

STODDARD, ELIZABETH DREW (BARSTOW), an American author, born at Mattapoisett, Mass., in 1823. In 1851 she became the wife of Richard H. Stoddard. Besides not unfrequent contributions, in prose and verse, to periodicals, she has published three strong novels, *The Morgesons* (1862), *Two Men* (1865), and *Temple House* (1867), and *Lolly Dinks's Doings*, a story for children (1874). A new edition of her novels was published in 1888.

ON THE CAMPAGNA.

Stop on the Appian Way
In the Roman Campagna :
Stop at my tomb—
The tomb of Cecilia Metella !
To-day as you see it
Alaric saw it ages ago,
When he, with his pale-visaged Goths
Sat at the gates of Rome
Reading his Runic shield.—
Odin, thy curse remains !

Beneath these battlements
My bones were interred with Roman pride,
Though centuries before my Romans died :
Now my bones are dust; the Goths are dust;
The river-bed is dry where sleeps the king :
My tomb remains.
When Rome commanded the earth
Great were the Metelli ;
I was Metellus's wife ;
I loved him—and I died.
Then with slow patience built he this memorial;
Each century marks his love.

Pass by on the Appian Way
The tomb of Cecilia Metella.
Wild shepherds alone seek its shelter;
Wild buffaloes tramp at its base ;
Deep in its desolation,
Deep as the shadow of Rome.

THE HOUSE OF YOUTH.

The rough north winds have left their icy caves
To growl and group for prey
Upon the murky sea ;
The lonely sea-gull skims the sullen waves
All the gray winter day.

The mottled sand-bird runneth up and down,
Amongst the creaking sedge,
Along the crusted beach,
The time-stained houses of the sea-walled town
Are tottering on its edge.

An ancient dwelling in this ancient place,
Stands in a garden drear,
A wreck with other wrecks ;
The Past is there, but no one sees a face
Within, from year to year.

The wiry rose trees scratch the window-pane ;
The window rattles loud ;
The wind beats at the door,
But never gets an answer back again,
The silence is so proud.

The last that lived there was an evil man ;
A child the last that died
Upon its mother's breast.
It seemed to die by some mysterious ban ;
Its grave is by the side
Of an old tree whose notched and scanty leaves
Repeat the tale of woe,
And quiver day and night,
Till the snow cometh, and a cold shroud weaves,
Whiter than that below.

This time of year a woman wanders there—
They say from distant lands :
She wears a foreign dress,
With jewels on her breast, and her fair hair
In braided coils and bands.

The ancient dwelling and the garden drear
At night know something more ;
Without her foreign dress
Or blazing gems, this woman stealeth near
The threshold of the door.

The shadow strikes against the window-pane;
    She thrusts the thorns away,
        Her eyes peer through the glass,
And down the glass her great tears drip like
        rain
    In the gray winter day.

The moon shines down the dismal garden track,
    And light's the little mound ;
        But when she ventures there,
The black and threatening branches wave her
        back,
    And guard the ghastly ground.

What is the story of this buried Past ?
    Were all its doors flung wide.
        For us to search its rooms,
And we to see the race, from first to last,
    And how they lived and died :—

Still would it baffle and perplex the brain,
    But teach this bitter truth ;
        Man lives not in the past:
None but a woman ever comes again
    Back to the house of Youth !

STODDARD. LAVINIA (STONE), an American poet, born at Guilford, Conn., in 1787; died at Blakely, Ala., in 1820. She was the eldest daughter of Elijah and Lavinia Fairchild Stone. While she was yet an infant. her parents removed to Patterson, New York. In 1811 she was married to Dr. William Stoddard. and with him established an academy at Troy. N. Y. The failure of her health led to their removal to Blakely, Alabama, where they both died.

Mrs. Stoddard wrote many poems, of which some were published anonymously, others under her name. They were never published collectively, but one of them, *The Soul's Defiance*, is included in most of the anthologies published in the United States.

THE SOUL'S DEFIANCE.

I said to Sorrow's awful storm,
  That beat against my breast,
Rage on—thou mayst destroy this form,
  And lay it low at rest;
But still the spirit that now brooks
  Thy tempest, raging high,
Undaunted on its fury looks,
  With steadfast eye.

I said to Penury's meagre train,
  Come on—your threats I brave;
My last poor life-drop you may drain,
  And crush me to the grave;
Yet still the spirit that endures
  Shall mock your force the while,
And meet each cold. cold grasp of yours
  With bitter smile.

I said to cold Neglect and Scorn,
  Pass on—I heed you not;
Ye may pursue me till my form
  And being are forgot;

Yet still the spirit, which ye see
  Undaunted by your wiles,
Draws from its own nobility
  Its highborn smiles.

I said to Friendship's menaced blow,
  Strike deep—my heart shall bear;
Thou canst but add one bitter woe
  To those already there;
Yet still the spirit that sustains
  This last severe distress,
Shall smile upon its keenest pains,
  And scorn redress.

I said to Death's uplifted dart,
  Aim sure—oh, why delay?
Thou wilt not find a fearful heart—
  A weak, reluctant prey;
For still the spirit firm and free,
  Unruffled by this last dismay,
Wrapt in its own eternity,
  Shall pass away.

STODDARD, RICHARD HENRY, an American poet, and litterateur, born at Hingham, Mass., in 1825. He came to New York when a boy, and entered an iron-foundry, where he worked as a moulder for several years. He began to write for periodicals while under age, and in 1849 put forth *Footprints*, his first volume of poems. Some three years afterwards he was appointed to a clerkship in the New York Custom House, a position which he retained many years, when he resigned in order to devote himself wholly to literary labor. Among his many volumes of poems are: *Songs of Summer* (1857), *The King's Bell* (1863), *The Book of the East* (1871), *The Lion's Cub* (1890). In 1880 was published a collected edition of his poems up to that date. Since that time he has been a frequent contributor, in verse and prose, to periodicals. He is the literary editor of the New York *Mail and Express*. Among his prose works are, *Life, Travels, and Books of Alexander von Humboldt*, *The Loves and Heroines of the Poets*, and *Adventures in Fairy Land*. He has put forth, as compiler, *Melodies and Madrigals, from Old English Poets*, and *The Late English Minor Poets*. He also prepared, with additions, new editions of Griswold's *Poets and Poetry of America*, and *The Female Poets of America*. A collection of Mr. Stoddard's later poems is (1890) in preparation for the press.

The Ode *Mare Victum*, "The Conquered Sea," was composed on occasion of laying the first Atlantic cable, connecting the two continents. The first message was transmitted August 6, 1858. But defects occurred in the cable: and though several messages were sent and received each way, these grew fainter and fainter, until September 1st, when they ceased altogether. This attempt was practically a failure except in so far as it demonstrated the practicability of laying a cable across the Atlantic. The "Victory over the Sea" was not really won until eight years afterwards.

MARE VICTUM.

I.

What means this clamor in the summer air,
These pealing bells, the firing of these guns?
What news is this that runs
Like lightning everywhere?
And why these shouting multitudes that meet
Beneath our starry flags that wave in every
street?
Some mighty deed is done,
Some victory is won!
What victory? No hostile Power, or Powers,
Dare pour their slaves on this free land of ours;
What could they hope to gain, beyond their
graves?
It must be on the waves;
It must be o'er the race of ocean-kings,
Whose navies plough a furrow o'er the Earth.
The same great Saxon Mother gave us birth,
And yet, as brethren will, we fight for little
things.
I saw her battle-ships, and saw our own,
Midway between the Old World and the New;
I feared there was some bloody work to do,
And heard, in thought, the sailor-widows' moan.
Triumphant waved their fearless flags: they
met,
But not with lighted match or thundering
gun;
They met in peace, and part in peace, and yet
A victory is won!
Unfold the royal battle-rolls of Time
In every land, a grander cannot be:
So simple, so sublime:
A victory o'er the Sea!

II.

What would they think of this, the men of old
Around whose little world its waters rolled
Unmeasurable, pitiless as Fate,
A thing to fear and hate?
Age after age they saw it flow, and flow,
Lifting the weeds, and laying bare the sands;
Whence did it come, and whither did it go?
To what far isles, what undiscovered lands?
Who knoweth? None can say, for none have
crossed
That unknown sea; no sail has ventured there
Save what the storms have driven, and those are
lost;
And none have come—from where?
Beyond the straits where those great Pillars
stand
Of Hercules, there is no solid land;
Only the fabled Islands of the Blest,
That slumber somewhere in the golden West:
The Fortunate Isles, where falls no winter
snow,
But where the palm-trees wave in endless
Spring,
And the birds sing,
And balmy west-winds blow!
Beyond this bright Elysium all is sea;
A plain of foam that stretches on and on,
Beyond the clouds, beyond the setting sun,
Endless and desolate as Eternity! . . . .
Who shall explore its bounds, if bounds there
be?
Who shall make known to man the secrets of
the sea?
The Genoese! His little fleet departs,
Steered by the prospering pilot of the wind:
The sailors crowd the stern with troubled
hearts,
Watching their homes that slowly drop behind;
His looms before, for by the prow he stands,
And sees in his rapt thoughts the undis-
covered lands. . . . .
Day follows day; night, night; and sea and
sky

Still yawn beyond, and fear to fear succeeds.
At last a knot of weeds goes drifting by,
And then a sea of weeds.
The winds are faint with spice, the skies are bland,
And filled with singing-birds, and some alight,
And cheer the sailors with the news of land,
Until they fly at night.
At last they see a light!
The keen-eyed Admiral sees it from his bark,
A little dancing flame that flickers through the dark.
They bed their rusty anchors in the sand,
And all night long they lie before the land,
And watch, and pray for day.
When morning lifts the mist, a league away
Like some long cloud on ocean's glittering floor,
It takes the rising sun—a wooded shore,
With many a glassy bay.
The first great footstep in that new-found world
Is his who plucked it from the sea. . . . .
But thousands followed to the lands he won;
They grew as native to the waves, as free
As sea birds in the sun.
Their white sails glanced in every bay and stream;
They climbed the hills, they tracked the pathless woods;
And towns and cities o'er the solitudes
Rose as in a dream!
The happy Worlds exchanged their riches then;
The New sent forth her tribute to the Old,
In galleons full of gold,
And she repaid with men!
Thus did this grand old sailor wrest the key
From Nature's grasp, unlocking all the Past:
And thus was won at last
A victory o'er the sea.

III.

The victory of to-day
Completes what he began
Along the dark and barren watery way,
And in the Mind of Man!

He did but find a world of land, but we
What worlds of thought in land, and air, and
sea! . . . .
The worlds are nearer now, but still too far;
They must be nearer still! to Saxon men
Who dare to think, and use the tongue and pen,
What can be long a bar?
We rob the lightning of its deadly fires,
And make it bear our words along the wires
That run from land to land. Why should we
be
Divided by the Sea?
It shall no longer be! A chain shall run
Below its stormy waves, and bind the Worlds
in One!
'Tis done!
The Worlds are One! [Race
And lo! the chain that binds them binds the
That dwell on either shore;
By Space and Time no more
Divided; for to-day there is no Time or Space!
We speak—the lightnings flee,
Flashing the thoughts of man across the Con-
quered Sea.

IV.

Ring jubilant bells! ring out a merry chime
From every tower and steeple in the land;
Triumphant music for the march of time,
The better days at hand!
And you, ye cannon, through your iron lips,
That guard the dubious peace of warlike
Powers,
Thunder abroad this victory of ours,
From all your forts and ships!
We need your noisy voices to proclaim
The Nation's joy to-day from shore to shore;
The grim protection of your deathful flame
We hope to need no more;
For, save our English brothers, who dare be
Our foes, or rivals, on the land or sea?
Nor dare we fight again as in the past;
For now that we are One contention ends;
We are, we must be, friends:
This victory is the last!

HOW SONGS ARE BEGOT AND BRED.

How are songs begot and bred?
  How do golden measures flow?
From the heart or from the head?
  Happy Poet! let me know.

Tell me first how folded flowers
Bud and bloom in vernal bowers;
How the south-wind shapes its tune—
The harper he of June!

None may answer, none may know;
Winds and flowers come and go,
And the self-same canons bind
Nature and the Poet's mind.

THE COUNTRY LIFE.

Not what we would, but what we must,
  Makes up the sum of living;
Heaven is both more and less than just
  In taking and in giving.
Swords cleave to hands that sought the plough,
And laurels miss the soldier's brow.

Me, whom the city holds, whose feet
  Have worn its stony highways,
Familiar with its loneliest street—
  Its ways were never my ways.
My cradle was beside the sea.
And there, I hope, my grave will be.

Old homestead! in that gray old town
  Thy vane is seaward blowing,
The slip of garden stretches down
  To where the tide is flowing;
Below they lie, their sails all furled,
The ships that go about the world.

Dearer that little country house,
  Inland, with pines beside it;
Some peach-trees, with unfruitful boughs,
  A well, with weeds to hide it,
No flowers, or only such as rise
Self-sown, poor things, which all despise.

Dear country home! Can I forget
  The least of thy sweet trifles?
The window-vines that clamber yet,
  Whose bloom the bee still rifles?
The roadside blackberries, growing ripe!
And, in the woods, the Indian Pipe?

Happy the man who tills his field,
  Content with rustic labor;
Earth does to him her fullness yield,
  Hap what may to his neighbor.
Well days, sound nights—Oh, can there be
A life more rational and free?

Dear country life of child and man!
  For both the best, the strongest,
That with the earliest race began,
  And has outlived the longest.
Their cities perished long ago;
Who the first farmers were we know.

Perhaps our Babels too will fall:
  If so, no lamentations,
For Mother Earth will shelter all
  And feed the unborn nations;
Yes, and the swords that menace now
Will then be beaten to the plough.

THE SKY.

The sky is a drinking cup that was overturned
  of old,
And it pours in the eyes of men its wine of airy
  gold!
We drink of that wine all day, till the last
  drop is drained up,
And are lighted off to bed by the jewels in the
  cup.

SINGING BIRDS UNCAUGHT.

Birds are singing round my window,
  Tunes the sweetest ever heard,
And I hang my cage there daily,
  But I never catch a bird.

So with thoughts my brain is peopled,
  And they sing there all day long;
But they will not fold their pinions
  In the little cage of song.

THE FLIGHT OF YOUTH.

There are gains for all our losses,
  There are balms for all our pain,
But when Youth, the dream, departs,
It takes something from our hearts,
  And it never comes again.

We are stronger, we are better,
  Under Manhood's sterner reign,
Still we feel that something sweet
Followed Youth, with flying feet,
  And will never come again.

Something beautiful has vanished,
  And we sigh for it in vain;
We behold it everywhere,
In the earth and in the air,
  But it never comes again.

WIND AND RAINS.

Rattle the window, Winds!
  Rain, drip on the panes!
There are tears and sighs in our hearts and eyes,
  And a weary weight on our brains.

The gray sea heaves and heaves
  On the dreary flats and sand
And the blasted limb of the churchyard yew,
  It shakes like a ghostly hand.

The dead are engulfed beneath it,
  Sunk in the glassy waves;
But we have more dead in our hearts to-day
  Than the Earth in all her graves.

STODDARD, WILLIAM OSBORNE, an American author, born at Homer, N. Y., in 1835. He graduated at the University of Rochester in 1858, edited successively the Chicago *Daily Ledger* and the *Central Illinios Gazette*, and in 1861 became President Lincoln's private secretary. For two years after the rebellion he was United States Marshal for Arkansas. He has published numerous books, and is one of the best American writers for young people. Among his works are: *Royal Decrees of Scandenberg* (1869), *Verses of Many Days* (1875), *Dismissed* (1878), *Dab Kinzer* (1881), *Esau Harding* (1882), *Saltillo Boys* (1882), *Talking Leaves* (1882), *Among the Lakes* (1883), *Life of Abraham Lincoln* (1884), *Two Arrows* (1886), *The Volcano under the City* (1887), *Lives of the Presidents* (1886–88), *Crowded out o' Crofield*, and *Chuck Purdy* (1890).

THE PRAIRIE PLOVER.

The dim mists heavily the prairies cover
And, through the gray,
The long-drawn, mournful whistle of the plover
Sounds, far away.

Slowly and faintly now the sun is rising
Fog-blind and grim,
To find the chill world 'neath him sympathizing
Bluely with him.

Upon the tall grass where the deer are lying
His pale light falls,
While, wailing like some lost wind that is dying,
The plover calls.

Ever the same disconsolate whistle only,
No loftier strains;—
To me it simply means, "Alas, I'm lonely
Upon these plains."

No wonder that these endless, dull dominions
Of roll and knoll
Cause him to pour forth thus, with poised pinions,
His weary soul.

Could I the secret of his note discover,
Sad, dreary strain,—
I'd sit and whistle, all day, like the plover,
And mean the same.

Verses of Many Days.

EVADING THE ENEMY.

All the old men said, one after another, that they knew just how many Apaches there were in that war party. Had they known how very strong it was, they might have been even worse puzzled, but Long Bear was really a clear-headed leader, and he decided the whole matter promptly and finally. He told his gathering braves that the place where they were was a bad one to fight in, while their pale-face friends had selected a peculiarly good one. They themselves had but twenty-three warriors armed with rifles, and nearly as many more young men and well-grown boys around with bows and arrows. That was no force with which to meet Apaches, nobody knew how many, and all sure to be riflemen. To go back through the pass was to die of sure starvation, even if they were not followed and slaughtered among the rocks. The Apaches were plainly making for that very pass, he said; and he was only a keen-eyed chief, and not at all a prophet, when he read the matter correctly and said:

"'Pache run away from blue-coats. All in a hurry. Not stop. Nez Percé hide and let them go by. Not fight. Keep pony. Keep hair. Good. Ugh!". . . .

Long Bear finished his speech of explanation, and then, without a moment's pause, he gave the order to break up camp and prepare to march, carrying with them every pound of provisions. Not one moment was to be lost in gaining such protection as might be had from the good position of the miners, and from the fact that they were pale-faces of some importance, and from the other great fact that they were all good riflemen. There was hardly anybody in the band, old enough to understand what an Apache was, who did not fully appreciate the force of the chief's argument, and every squaw did her best to hasten the departure. Lodges came down, ponies were packed, children were gathered, warriors and braves and boys completed their preparations for fighting; the Big Tongue declared his readiness to kill a large number of Apaches, and One-eye was compelled to abandon forever all the bones he had buried since the people he barked for had settled upon the bank of that river.

There was a good deal of quiet and sober efficiency in spite of the excitement. Two Arrows had further questions to answer from quite a number of his elders. He was furnished with one of the best ponies in the drove in acknowledgment of his services. He was now, also, to figure as a kind of guide, and he did not once think of or mention the fatigue of his long hard ride. He very willingly ate, however, the whole of a buffalo steak, broiled for him by one of the squaws, and felt a good deal better afterward. He almost felt that he had earned a rifle, or at least a pistol, but well knew that it was in vain to ask for one when the supply was insufficient to arm all the braves who were a full head taller than himself.

Still it was a magnificent thing at last, to ride out at the head of the cavalcade, by the side of a tall warrior, as the one boy of all that band who was on first-rate terms with the pale-faces and knew perfectly the trail leading to them. As for that, any red man of them all could have followed the tracks of the wagon wheels, even at night, but Two Arrows had no idea of surrendering that part of his growing importance. It would have done Na-tee-kah's proud heart good to have seen him, and it would have been well worth the while of almost anybody else to have had a good look at the whole affair, as the motley array poured out into the moonlight from under the shadowy cover of the primeval forest.

There were no sleepy ones except the pappooses, and they could sleep under the tightly-drawn blankets upon the backs of their mothers as well as anywhere else. All the rest were more or less hardened to the quick changes and migrations of the kind of life into which they had been born. They were not likely to be injured by being kept up pretty late for one night, and there was no need that anybody should walk, now that their four-footed wealth had returned. . . . .

The Nez Percé camp had been broken up with great celerity, and no time had been lost, but, after all, the summons to move had come upon them most unexpectedly. There had been a great deal to do, and but a dim light to do it by, and so it was pretty late before the picturesque caravan was in motion. It took a line of march toward the mountains until its head struck the well-marked tracks of the loaded wagons, and from that point forward its course required little guiding. By a stern command from Long Bear, the utmost silence was maintained, and, after the moon went down, the movement might fairly be said to have been performed in secret. There was no danger that any small squad of Apache scouts would assail so strong a party. Even the squaws and children felt pretty safe, but it was very hard upon the Big Tongue, for that great brave soon found himself in an advanced party, commanded by Long Bear himself, and after that he was under an absolute necessity of not saying anything during the whole march.—*Two Arrows.*

STOLBERG, FRIEDRICH LEOPOLD, COUNT, a German diplomat and litterateur, born 1750; died in 1819. He was born at Bramstadt, Holstein, and educated at Halle and Göttingen. During much of his life he was minister or embassador at the courts of Lubeck, Berlin, St. Petersburg and Copenhagen. He was the author of many poems and of a classical drama, *Theseus.* Among his translations from Greek to German are the Iliad, the discourses of Socrates, and the dialogues of Plato. Other works are a romance, *The Island*, *Travels in Germany, Switzerland and Italy*, and a history of the Christian religion in fifteen volumes, written after he became a Catholic. His travels, which contain some of his poems, were translated into English by Thomas Holcroft, London, 1797.

RAPHAEL.

How was my soul o'erwhelmed, immortal man!
When, first, entranced, fired by thy mighty mind,
Filled with thy genius, motionless I stood!
Through all the Vatican thy spirit breathed!
The dead, called up by thee, before me rose,
Moving, living, breathing; discoursing themes
Of heaven and earth; of angels, martyrs, men;
Of sinners and of saints; of apostles and gods.

Of what pure æther did the Eternal frame
Thy soul, from which streamed, flooding, Nature's first
Great Cause! He that made, he that saved, and he
That will eternally reward his best,
Most admirable workman! Yes, 'twas he
That did inspire thy genius, guide thy hand,
And purify thy spirit! Chased far off

Each thought that glowed not with celestial fire,
And fitted thee to fill the mighty task;
That, daring else, audacious, rash, had been.

Thy course on earth is run! Ages have rolled
Over thy peaceful grave! like as the youth
Howling laments, who with his virgin bride
Is by the raging torrent swept away;
So suffering Art, with wails, and tears, and cries
Impatient calls, with anguish clamorous now,
And now supplicating her own Raphael,
Her to re-visit, and her sons impel
Again to seize the pencil, bold and free,
And emulate the mighty master's fire.

Behold the Grecian muse, with dusty train,
Erst by Apelles wooed, won, and enjoyed!
Lo, mid the wrecks of Time, she weeping stands;
Ever and anon, glancing at thy tomb,
And bitterly rememb'ring days long past
I hear her murmurs now, in dead of night;
The chaste Diana present, though half veiled,
The blast of darkness chasing now, and now
Admitting! Terror struck, I hear her sigh
For her departed sons! And last Raphael!
Mournful as the widowed Spring over her
Blighted fruits! Or as the bleak Winter's winds
Howl through the ruins of the houseless Gods,
Thus fearfully, thus plaintively, she grieves!

"Pride of my heart! Delight of eye! Where!
Oh where art thou fled? Laurel crowned by me,
And by my sister Muses, thee we caught,
While yet an infant, in our arms; and fed
Thee with immortal sweets! Homer not more
Our nursling; nor Plato our more delight!
On thy forehead beamed the morning dawn;
Thine eyes shot fire; bright as meridian day
Thy visage shone; while manna dropt from Heaven,

And fruits that Paradise alone can yield,
Here proffered to thy lips! Wisdom thine ear
Saluted; and Nature, in all her bloom,
Splendid in charms, first met thy infant eye;
Prolific shed her roseate dews around,
And, in one large bequest, poured out her stores,
Gave all she had, and taught thee all she knew.

"Where art thou now, my son? Too like the flower,
Which the tender virgin rears, tempest swept,
The moment of maturity beheld
Thee blighted, in the fulness of thy bloom."
Thus mourned the Muse! And thus, with sighs of deep
Regret, pensive I homeward bent my way.

Travels.

TO THE SEA.

The boundless shining, glorious sea,
With ecstasy I gaze on thee;
Joy, joy to him whose early beam
Kisses thy lip, bright Ocean-stream;
Thanks for the thousand hours, old Sea,
Of sweet communion held with thee;
Oft as I gazed, thy billowy roll
Woke the deep feelings of my soul.
Drunk with the joy, thou deep-toned Sea,
My spirit swells to heaven with thee;
Or, sinking with thee, seeks the gloom
Of nature's deep, mysterious tomb.

At evening, when the sun grows red,
Descending to his watery bed,
The music of thy murmuring deep
Soothes e'en the weary earth to sleep.
Then listens thee the evening star;
So sweetly glancing from afar;
And Luna hears thee, when she breaks
Her light in million-colored flakes.

Oft when the noonday heat is o'er,
I seek with joy the breezy shore,
Sink on thy boundless, billowy breast,
And cheer me with refreshing rest.

The poet, child of heavenly birth,
Is suckled by the mother Earth;
But thy blue bosom, holy Sea,
Cradles his infant fantasy.

The old blind minstrel on the shore
Stood listening thy eternal roar,
And golden ages, long gone by,
Swept bright before his spirit's eye.
On wing of swan the holy flame
Of melodies celestial came,
And Iliad and Odyssey
Rose to the music of the Sea.

TO NATURE.

Holy Nature, sweet and free,
Let me ever follow thee,
Guide me with thy hand so mild,
As in leading strings a child!

And when weary, then will I
Sweetly on thy bosom lie,
Breathing Heaven's joys, so blest,
Clinging to a mother's breast.

Ah! with thee 'tis sweet to dwell,
Ever will I love thee well;
Let me ever follow thee,
Holy Nature, sweet and free

Transl. of ALFRED BASKERVILLE.

STONE, William Leete, an American journalist and author, born at New Paltz, N. Y., in 1792; died at Saratoga Springs in 1844. After learning the trade of a printer he became the editor of several newspapers, lastly, in 1821, of the New York *Commercial Advertiser*. Besides several works of local and temporary interest he wrote the *Life of Joseph Brant* (1838), *Life and Times of Red-Jacket* (1840), *Border Wars of the Revolution* (1839), *Poetry and History of Wyoming* (1841), *Life of Uncas and Miantonomo* (1842). At the time of his death he was engaged upon *The Life and Times of Sir William Johnson*. This work was in 1865 completed by his son, William Leete Stone, Jr., born in 1835 who also wrote the Life of his father, and several works relating mainly to incidents in American history.

THE "MASSACRE" AT WYOMING.

The Provincials pushed rapidly forward; but the British and Indians were prepared to receive them, their line being formed a small distance in front of their camp in a plain thinly covered with pine, shrub-oaks, and undergrowth, and extending from the river to a marsh at the foot of the mountain. On coming in view of the enemy, the Americans, who had previously marched in a single column, instantly deployed into a line of equal extent, and attacked from right to left at the same time. The right of the Americans was commanded by Col. Zebulon Butler, opposed to Col. John Butler commanding the enemy's left. Col. Dennison commanded the left of the Americans, and was opposed by Indians forming the enemy's right. The battle commenced at about forty rods' distance, without much execution at the onset, as the brushwood interposed obstacles to the sight. The militia stood the fire well for a time, and as they pressed forward there was some giving way on the enemy's right.

Unluckily just at this moment the appalling war-whoop of the Indians rang in the rear of the American left—the Indian leader having conducted a large party of his warriors through the marsh, and succeeded in turning Dennison's flank. A heavy and destructive fire was simultaneously poured into the American ranks; and amidst the confusion Col. Dennison directed his men to "fall back," to avoid being surrounded, and to gain time to bring his men into order again. This direction was mistaken for an order to "retreat," whereupon the whole line broke, and every effort of their officers to restore order was unavailing.

At this stage of the battle, and while thus engaged, the American officers, mostly fell. The flight was general. The Indians, throwing alway their rifles, rushed forward with their tomahawks, making dreadful havoc, answering the cries for mercy with the hatchet, and adding to the universal consternation those terrific yells which invest savage warfare with tenfold horror. So alert was the foe in this bloody pursuit that less than sixty of the Americans escaped either the rifle or the tomahawk. Some of the fugitives escaped by swimming the river, and others by flying to the mountains. As the news of the defeat spread down the valley, the greater part of the women and children, and those who remained behind to protect them, likewise ran to the woods and the mountains; while those who could not escape thus, sought refuge in Fort Wyoming. The Indians, apparently wearied with pursuit and slaughter, desisted; and betook themselves to secure the spoils of the vanquished. . . .

On the morning of the day after the battle, Col. John Butler, with the combined British and Indians, appeared before Fort Wyoming, and demanded its surrender. Articles of capitulation were entered into, by which it was stipulated that the settlers should be disarmed, and the garrison demolished; that all the prisoners and the public stores should be given up; that the property of "the people called Tories" should be made good, and they be permitted to remain peaceably upon their farms. In behalf of the settlers it was stipulated that they should be left in the unmolested occupation of their farms.

Unfortunately, however, the British commander either could not or would not enforce the terms of the capitulation, which were to a great extent disregarded, as well by the Tories as Indians. Instead of finding protection, the valley was again laid waste; the houses and improvements were destroyed by fire, and the country plundered. Families were broken up and dispersed, men and their wives separated, and some of them carried into captivity; while far the greater number fled to the mountains, and wandered through the wilderness to the older settlements. Some died of their wounds, others from want and fatigue; while others still were lost in the wilderness, or were heard of no more. Several perished in a great swamp in the neighborhood which from that circumstance acquired the name of "The Shades of Death," and retains it to this day. But it does not appear that anything like a "massacre" followed the capitulation. . . . .

. There is an important correction to be made in reference to every account of this battle extant. This correction regards the name and just fame of Joseph Brant, whose character has been blackend with all the infamy—both real and imaginary—connected with this bloody expedition. Whether Brant was at any time in company of this expedition is doubtful; but it is certain, in the face of every historical authority, British and American, that so far from being engaged in the battle, he was many miles distant at the time of its occurrence. Such has been the uniform testimony of the British officers engaged in that expedition, and such was always the word of Brant himself.—*Life of Brant.*

STORRS, RICHARD SALTER, an American pulpit orator and lecturer, born at Braintree, Mass., in 1821. He is the fourth of a family series of preachers, his grandfather having been a chaplain in the Revolutionary army. He was graduated at Amherst in 1839, taught in the Munson and Williston academies, studied law with Rufus Choate, and theology at Andover. After a year's pastorate in Brookline, Mass., he was called in 1846, to the new church of the Pilgrims, Brooklyn, N. Y. His Brooklyn Institute lectures on *The Constitution of the Human Soul* (1855), his Union Theological Seminary lectures on *The Divine Origin of Christianity* (1881), and the like, have been published in book form; and many addresses on important public occasions have been printed in pamphlet form, such as his Phi Beta Kappa address at Harvard on *The Supernatural in Letters and Life*, etc. His latest publication is *The Puritan Spirit* (1890). He has long been recognized as unexcelled in culture and oratory, and especially as marked by a magnificence of speech that is the very body, not the mere raiment, of his thought. In 1887, he received the highest honor in the gift of his denomination, the presidency of the American Board of Foreign Missions.

THE SUPERNATURAL IN POETRY AND ART.

Even the beauty which picturesque verse loves to celebrate depends for its tender and supreme recognition on such spiritual insight. It is a recent notion of physicists that beauty is never an end in itself, in the outward and evident scheme of things, but exists only to serve utilities. The notion, I must think, has its root in another—that the system has originated, not in intelligence and beneficent purpose, but in the development of mechanical forces. The apprehension of a prescient ordaining mind, behind all phenomena, loving beauty for its own sake, and delighting to lodge it in the curl of the wood or the sheen of the shell, as well as in the petals and perfume of flowers, the crest of waves, or the prismatic round of the rainbow — this is indispensable to the clear recognition, or the sympathetic rendering, of even the outward beauty of nature. Then only does this stand in essential correlation with spiritual states, which find images in it; while then alone does it knit the present, on which it casts its scattered lights, with vanished paradises, and spheres of beauty unapproached.

There is a transcendent mood of the spirit wherein the meanest flower that blows awakens thoughts too deep for tears; when the grass blade is oracular, and the common bush seems afire with God, and when the splendors of closing day repeat the flash of jasper and beryl. It is when the soul is keenly conscious of relations to systems surpassing sense, and to a creative personal Spirit by whom all things are interfused. Aside from that, the yellow primrose is nothing more; and the glory of the sunset—seen from Sorrento or seen from Cambridge—fails from the hues of lucid gold or glowing ruby, because there fall no more suggestions, from all their splendors, of realms beyond the fading vision.

But if this be true of outward nature, how much more clearly of the spirit of man! Then only can this be manifested to us in the mystery of verse, with any just interpretation of what is profound and typical in it, when it is recognized as personal, moral, of divine origin and divine affiliations, with unsounded futures waiting for it; when, in other words, it is set in relation with immense and surpassing realms of life. I may not properly illustrate from the living, but one example irresistibly suggests itself. Hawthorne's genius did not utter itself in rhyme, but how solitary, high-musing, it moves in this atmosphere of the essential mystery of life, as in the tenebrous splendor of sombre clouds, all whose edges burn with gold!

Without something of this, poetry always is commonplace. Outward action may be vividly pictured. Tragical events may find fit memorial. The manifold pageants, popular or imperial, may march before us, through many cantos, as on a broad and brilliant stage. But these, alone, are as the paltry plumes of fireweed, taking the place of the burned forest, whose every tree-stem was "the mast of some great ammiral." The grand and imperative intuitions of the soul, which affirm the ideal, and are prophetic of things above nature—the "thoughts that wander through eternity," the love, prayer, passion, hope, which have no ultimate consummation on earth, and which in themselves predict immortality—these, which must furnish the substance of poetry, are only represented, in the most ductile and musical verse, upon the basis of the spiritual philosophy. Poets differ, as do the colors which astronomy shows in the radiant suns—blue, purple, gold—bound in the firm alliances of the heavens. But a sun black in substance, and shooting bolts of darkness from it, were as easily conceivable as a Comtist Shakespeare or an agnostic Wordsworth.—*Recognition of the Supernatural in Letters and in Life.*

STORY, Joseph, an American jurist and author, born at Marblehead, Mass., in 1779; died at Cambridge in 1845. He graduated at Harvard in 1798; studied law, was admitted to the bar in 1801, and commenced practice at Salem. For some years he took an active part in political affairs, supporting the general policy of the administrations of Jefferson and Madison, and in 1809 was elected to Congress by the Democratic (then known as the Republican) party. In 1811 he was appointed an Associate Justice of the Supreme Court of the United States. In 1829 he was made Dane Professor of Law at Harvard, in accordance with the express stipulation of the founder of that chair; his instructions being given during the vacations of the Supreme Court. His Inaugural Address was on the "Value and Importance of the Study of Law." The following is a portion of this address:—

THE IMPORTANCE OF CLASSICAL STUDIES.

The importance of classical learning to professional education is so obvious, that the surprise is that it could ever have become matter of disputation. I speak not of its power in refining the taste, in disciplining the judgment, in invigorating the understanding, or in warming the heart with elevated sentiments; but of its power of direct, positive, necessary instruction. Until the eighteenth century the mass of science, in its principal branches, was deposited in the dead languages, and much of it still reposes there. To be ignorant of these languages is to shut out the lights of former times, or to examine them only through the glimmerings of inadequate translations. What should we say of the jurist who never aspired to learn the maxims of law and equity which adorn the Roman Codes? What of the physician who could deliberately surrender all the knowledge heaped up for so many centuries in the Latinity of continental Europe? What of the minister of religion who should choose not to study the Scriptures in the original tongue, and should be content to trust his faith and his hopes, for time and for eternity, to the dimness of translations which may reflect the literal import, but rarely can reflect with unbroken force the beautiful spirit of the text?

I pass over all consideration of the written treasures of antiquity which have survived the wreck of empires and dynasties, of monumental trophies and triumphal arches, of palaces of princes and temples of the gods. I pass over all consideration of those admired compositions in which wisdom speaks as with a voice from heaven; of those sublime efforts of poetical genius which still freshen, as they pass from age to age, in undying vigor; of those finished histories which still enlighten and instruct governments in their duty and their destiny; of those matchless orations which roused nations to arms, and chained senates to the chariot-wheels of all-conquering eloquence. These all may now be read in our vernacular tongue. Ay! as one remembers the face of a dead friend by gathering up the broken fragments of his image; as one listens to a tale of a dream twice told; as one catches the roar of the ocean in the ripple of a rivulet; as one sees the blaze of noon in the first glimmer of twilight.

Mr. Justice Story delivered many popular speeches and addresses, and contributed to the *North American Review* and other publications several papers on literary topics. A collection of some of these *Miscellaneous Writings* was published in 1835. But the bulk of his works are of a strictly professional character, consisting of reports of the Supreme Court, judgments pronounced by him, and treatises upon important legal questions. Among the treatises which still rank as authority are: *Commentaries on the Conflict of Laws* (1834), *Commentaries on Equity Jurisprudence* (1836), *Equity Pleadings* (1838), *On Promissory Notes* (1846). But of more general interest are the *Commentaries on the Constitution of the United States*, published in 1833, followed soon afterwards by an Abridgment, designed especially as a text-book in colleges and academies. The following are the concluding paragraphs of this Abridgment:—

DANGERS THAT THREATEN THE REPUBLIC.

The fate of other republics—their rise, their progress, their decay, and their fall—are written but too legibly on the pages of history, if, indeed, they were not continually before us in the startling fragments of their ruins. These republics have perished, and have perished by their own hands. Prosperity has enervated them, corruption has debased them, and a venal populace has consummated their destruction. The People, alternately the prey of military chieftains at home and of ambitious invaders from abroad, have been sometimes cheated out of their liberties by servile demagogues, sometimes betrayed into a surrender of them by false patriots, and sometimes they have willingly sold them for a price to a despot who had bidden the highest for his victims. They have disregarded the warning voice of their best statesmen, and have persecuted and driven from office their truest friends. They have listened to the counsels of fawning sycophants, or base calumniators of the wise and good. They have reverenced power more in its high abuses and summary movements than in its calm and constitutional energy, when it dispensed blessings with a liberal hand. They have surrendered to faction what belonged to the common interests and common rights of the country. Patronage and party, the triumph of an artful popular leader, and the discontents of a day, have outweighed, in their view, all solid principals and institutions of government. Such are the melancholy lessons of the past history of republics down to our own. . . . .

If our Union should once be broken up, it is impossible that a new Constitution should ever be formed, embracing the whole territory. We shall be divided into several nations or confederacies, rivals in power, pursuits, and interests; too proud to brook injury, and too near to make retaliation distant or ineffectual. Our very animosities will, like those of all other kindred nations, become the more deadly, because our lineage, laws, and institutions are the same. Let the history of the Grecian and Italian republics warn us of our dangers. The National Constitution is our last and our only security. United, we stand; divided, we fall.

Let, then, the rising generation be inspired with an ardent love for their country, and an unquenchable thirst for liberty, and a profound reverence for the Constitution and the Union. Let the American youth never forget that they possess a noble inheritance, bought by the toils and sufferings and blood of their ancestors; and capable, if wisely improved and faithfully guarded, of transmitting to their latest posterity all the substantial blessings of life, the peaceful enjoyment of liberty, of property, of religion, and of independence. The structure has been erected by architects of consummate skill and fidelity, its foundations are solid; its compartments are beautiful as well as useful; its arrangements are full of wisdom and order; and its defences are impregnable from without.

Story was buried in Mount Auburn Cemetery, and a sum of money was raised to erect a statue of him there, the execution of which was confided to his son, William W. Story, who has raised another monument to his father in the *Life and Letters of Joseph Story* (1851).

STORY, William Wetmore, an American sculptor and author, son of Joseph Story, born at Salem, Mass., in 1819. He graduated at Harvard in 1838, studied law under his father, entered upon practice, and put forth *Reports of Cases argued before the Circuit Court of the United States for the First Circuit* (1842), and a treatise on the *Law of Contracts not under Seal* (1844). He was also a frequent contributor, in prose and verse, to periodicals, and published a volume of *Poems* in 1847. He had developed a high talent for sculpture; and about 1850 abandoned the legal profession, and took up his residence in Rome, devoting himself to Art and Literature. His principal works are: *Life and Letters of Joseph Story* (1851), a volume of *Poems* (1856), *Roba di Roma, or Walks and Talks about Rome* (1862), *Proportions of the Human Figure* (1866), *Graffiti d'Italia*, consisting of dramatic poems (1869), *The Roman Lawyer in Jerusalem, at the Time of Our Saviour* (1870), *Nero, an Historical Play* (1875), *Castle St. Angelo* (1877), *He and She, or a Poet's Portfolio* (1883), *Fiammetta* (1885), *Conversations in a Studio* (1890). A revised and enlarged edition of *Roba di Roma* appeared in 1887, and his *Poetical Works*, in two volumes, in 1886.

THE UNEXPRESSED.

Strive not to say the whole! the Poet in his
  Art
Must intimate the whole, and say the smallest
  part.

The young moon's arc her perfect circle tells;
The limitless within Art's bounded outline
  dwells.

Of every noble work the silent part is best ;
Of all expressions, that which cannot be expressed.

Each Act contains the life, each work of Art the world,
And all the planet-laws are in each dew-drop pearled.

MIDNIGHT.

Midnight in the sleeping city ! clanking hammers beat no more ;
For a space the hum and tumult of the busy day are o'er.

Streets are lonely and deserted, where the sickly lamp lights glare,
And the steps of some late passer only break the silence there.

Round the grim and dusky houses, gloomy shadows nestling cower ;
Night hath stifled life's deep humming into slumber for an hour.

Sullen furnace-fires are glowing over in the suburbs far,
And the lamp in many a household shineth like an earthly star.

O'er the hushed and sleeping city, in the cloudless sky above,
Never-fading stars hang watching in eternal peace and love.

Years and centuries have vanished, change hath come to bury change,
But the starry constellations on their silent pathway range.

Great Orion's starry girdle, Berenice's golden hair,
Ariadne's crown of splendor, Cassiopeia's shining chair,

Saggitarius and Delphinus, and the clustering Pleiad train,
Aquila and Ophiucus, Pegasus and Charles's Wain,

Red Antares and Capella, Aldebaran's mystic light,
Alruccabah and Arcturus, Sirius and Vega white :—

They are circling calm as ever on their sure but hidden path,
As when mystic watchers saw them with the reverent eye of Faith.

So unto the soul benighted lofty stars there are, that shine
Far above the mists of error, with a changeless light divine.

Lofty souls of old beheld them, burning in life's shadowy night ;
And they still are undecaying 'mid a thousand centuries' flight.

Love and Truth, whose light and blessing every reverent heart may know,
Mercy, Justice, which are pillars that support this life below ;

These in sorrow and in darkness in the inmost soul we feel,
As the sure, undying impress of the Almighty's burning seal.

Though unsolved the mighty secret which shall thread the perfect whole,
And unite the finite number unto the Eternal Soul,

We shall one day clearly see it ; for the soul a time shall come,
When, enfranchised and unburdened, Thought shall be its only home ;

And Truth's fitful intimations, glancing on our fearful sight,
Shall be gathered to the circle of one mighty disk of light.

THE PROCESSION OF THE CRUCIFIXION.

Among the celebrations which take place throughout Italy during Holy Week is one which though not peculiar to Rome, deserves record here for its singularity. On Good Friday it is the custom of the people of Prato, a little town near Florence, to celebrate the occasion by a procession, which takes place after nightfall, and is intended to represent the procession to the cross. The persons composing it are mounted on horseback, and dressed in fantastic costumes borrowed from the theatrical wardrobe, representing Pontius Pilate, the centurions, guards, executioners, apostles, and even Judas himself. Each one carries in one hand a flaring torch, and in the other some emblem of the Crucifixion—such as the hammer, pincers, shears, sponge, cross, and so on. The horses are all unshod, so that their hoofs may not clatter on the pavement; and, with a sort of mysterious noiselessness, the singular procession passes through all the principal streets, illuminated by torches that gleam picturesquely on their tinsel-covered robes, helmets, and trappings.

This celebration only takes place once in three years; and on the last occasion but one, a tremendous thunderstorm broke over the town as the procession was passing along. The crowd thereupon incontinently dispersed, and the unfortunate person who represented Judas, trembling with superstitious fear, fell upon his knees, and—after the fashion of Nick Bottom, the weaver, who relieved the Duke Theseus by declaring that he was only a lion's fell, and not a veritable lion—cried out to the Madonna, "*Misericordia per me!* I am not really Judas, but only the cobbler at the corner, who is representing him—all for the glory of the blessed Bambino!" And in consideration of this information the Madonna graciously extended him her potent aid; but he henceforth rejoiced in the popular nickname of Judas.—*Roba di Roma.*

STREET, ALFRED BILLINGS, an American poet, born at Poughkeepsie, N. Y., in 1811; died in 1881. After having been admitted to the bar he was made State Librarian at Albany. In 1859 he published *The Council of Revision of the State of New York, with Biographical Sketches of its Members*, and in 1863 *A Digest of Taxation*, embracing the principal tax-laws of all the states of the Union. Mr. Street commenced his literary career with a volume entitled, *The Burning of Schenectady, and other Poems* (1842), then followed *Drawings and Paintings* (1844), and *Frontenac, a Metrical Romance* (1849). He was a frequent contributor to periodicals, and collections of his *Poems* were several times made. His principal prose sketches are: *Woods and Waters, or Summer in the Saranacs Lake and; Mountain, or Autumn in the Adirondacks; Eagle Pine, or Sketches of a New York Frontier Village; The Indian Pass.*

A FOREST WALK.

A lovely sky, a cloudless sun,
  A wind that breathes of leaves and flowers,
O'er hill and dale my steps have won
  To the cool forest's shadowy bowers;
One of the paths all round that wind,
  Traced by the browsing herds, I choose,
And sights and sounds of human kind
  In nature's own recesses lose.
The beech displays its marbled bark,
  The spruce its green tent stretches wide,
While scowls the hemlock, grim and dark,
  The maple's scalloped dome beside;
All weave a high and verdant roof,
That keeps the very sun aloof,
Making a twilight soft and green
Within the columned, vaulted scene.

Sweet forest-odors have their birth
From the closed boughs and teeming earth;
  Where pine-cones dropped, leaves piled and
    dead,
Long tufts of grass, and stars of fern,
With many a wild-flower's starry urn,
  A thick, elastic carpet spread.
Here, with its mossy pall, the trunk,
Resolving into soil, is sunk;
  There, wrenched but lately from its throne
By some fierce whirlwind circling past,
  Its huge roots massed with earth and stone,
One of the woodland kings is cast.

Above, the forest-tops are bright
With a broad blaze of sunny light;
  But now a fitful air-gust parts
The screening branches, and a glow,
  Of dazzling, startling radiance darts
Down the dark stems, and breaks below;
The sylvan floor is bathed in gold;
Low sprouts and herbs, before unseen,
Display their shades of brown and green;
Tints brighten o'er the velvet moss,
Gleams twinkle in the laurel's gloss;
The robin, brooding on her nest,
Chirps, as the quick ray strikes her breast;
And, as my shadow prints the ground,
I see the rabbit upward bound;
With pointed ears and earnest look
Then scamper to the darkest nook,
Where, with crouched, limb and staring eye,
He watches while I saunter by.

A narrow vista, carpeted
With rich green grass, invites my tread.
Here showers the light in golden dots,
There sleeps the shade in ebon spots,
So blended that the very air
Seems net-work as I enter there.
  The partridge whose deep-rolling drum
Afar has sounded on my ear,
  Ceasing his beatings as I come,
Whirrs to the sheltering branches near;
The little milk-snake glides away,

The brindled marmot dives from day;
And now between the boughs, a space.
Of the blue, laughing sky I trace,
On each side shrinks the bowery shade,
Before me spreads an emerald glade;
The sunshine steeps its grass and moss,
That couch my footsteps as I cross;
Merrily hums the tawny bee,
The glittering humming-bird I see;
Floats the bright butterfly along,
The insect choir is loud in song:
A spot of light and life; it seems
A fairy haunt for fancy's dreams.

Here stretched, the pleasant turf I press
In luxury of idleness.
Sun-streaks, and glancing wings, and sky,
Spotted with cloud-shapes, chain my eye;
While murmuring grass and waving trees—
Their leaf-harps sounding to the breeze—
And water-tones that tinkle near,
Blend their sweet music to my ear;
And by the changing shades alone
The passage of the hours is known.

ON THE SUMMIT OF TAHÀWAS.

I chanced to look up: and lo! a rocky dome, a dark pinnacle, an awful crest, scowled above my head, apparently impending over it, as if to fall and crush me. What was it? It was the stately brow of old Tahawas, the Piercer of the Sky! Throned in eternal desolation, its look crushing down the soaring forest into shrubs, there it towered, the sublime King of the Adirondacks, its forehead furrowed by the assaults of a thousand centuries. There it towered, beating back the surges of a million tempests! There it stood—and—by Jove, if there isn't a lizard crawling up there! Or stop, let me see! Upon my modesty, if the lizard, by the aid of my glass, doesn't enlarge itself into Bob Blin! and there is Merrill following. And so I followed too.

Showers of stones, loosened by my guide rattled past. Still up I went. Over the precipitous rocks by clambering its cracks and crannies, through its tortuous galleries, along the dizzy edges of the chasms. A score of times I thought the summit was just in front, but no. On still went my guides, and on still I followed. But at last Merrill and Robert both became stationary—in fact, seated themselves—their figures sharply relieved against the sky. Surmounting a steep acclivity, then turning into a sort of winding gallery, and passing a large mass of rock, I placed myself at their side; and lo! the summit! Famished with thirst, I looked around, and basins of water, hollowed in the stern granite, met my gaze: real jewels of the skies—rain-water—and truly delicious it was.

Next my eye was sweetly startled by one of the most delicate flowers—a harebell—that ever grew: sweet as Titania, blue as Heaven, and fragile as Hope—here on the bald tip-top of old Tahawas. I looked around for humming-birds and butterflies! It was a beautiful sight, that little blossom trembling at the very breath, yet flourishing here. Here, where the tawny grass sings sharp and keen in the wrathful hurricane that the eagle scarce dares to stem; where even the pine-shrub cannot live, and the wiry juniper shows not even its wiry wreath; here, where the bitter cold lingers nearly all the year, and the snowflake dazzles the June sun with its golden glitter; here on the summit of a peak to which the lightning lowers its torch, and at whose base the storm-cloud crouches. . . .

Clear and bright shines the prospect below; and herein we are lucky. Old Tahawas ofttimes acts sulky; he will not allow his vassal landscape to show itself, but shrouds it in a wet, clinging mist. To-day, however, he permits it to appear in his presence, and lo, the magic! A sea of mountain-tops! a sea frozen at its wildest tumults!—*The Indian Pass.*

STRICKLAND, Agnes, an English author, born in 1806; died in 1874. She wrote several books of verse and fiction before entering upon her career as a writer of historical biography. Her principal works in this department are: *Lives of the Queens of England*, in which she was assisted by her sister, Elizabeth Strickland (12 vols. 1840-1849), *Lives of the Queens of Scotland* (8 vols., 1840-1849), *Lives of the Seven Bishops* (1866.) In 1871 she received a pension of £100.

QUEEN MARY'S RESIGNATION OF THE SCOTTISH CROWN.

The conspirators, calling themselves the Lords of Secret Council, having completed their arrangements for the long-meditated project of depriving her of her crown, summoned Lord Lindsay to Edinburgh, and on the 23d of July, 1567, delivered to him and Sir Robert Melville three deeds, to which they were instructed to obtain her signature, either by flattering words or by absolute force. The first contained a declaration, as if from herself, that "being in infirm health, and worn out with the cares of government, she had taken purpose voluntarily to resign her crown and office to her dearest son, James, Prince of Scotland." In the second her "trusty brother, James, Earl of Moray," was constituted Regent for the Prince, her son, during the minority of the royal infant. The third appointed a provisional Council of Regency, consisting of Morton and the other Lords of Secret Council, to carry on the government until Moray's return, or, in case of his refusing to accept it, till the Prince arrived at the legal age for exercising it himself.

Aware that Mary would not be easily induced to execute such instruments, Sir Robert Melville was especially employed to cajole her into this political suicide. That ungrateful courtier, who had been employed and trusted by his unfortunate sovereign ever since her return from France, and had received nothing but benefits from her, undertook this office. Having obtained a private interview with her, he deceitfully entreated her to "sign certain deeds that would be presented to her by Lindsay, as the only means of preserving her life, which, he assured her, was in the most imminent danger. Then he gave her a turquoise ring, telling her it was sent to her from the Earls of Argyle, Huntly, and Athole, Secretary Lethington, and the Laird of Grange, "who loved her Majesty," and had by that token accredited him to exhort her to avert the peril to which she would be exposed if she ventured to refuse the requisition of the Lords of Secret Council, whose designs they well knew were to take her life, either secretly or by means of a mock trial among themselves.

Finding the Queen impatient of this insidious advice, Melville produced a letter from the English ambassador, Throckmorton, out of the scabbard of his sword, telling her he had concealed it there at the peril of his own life, in order to convey it to her—a paltry piece of acting, worthy of the parties by whom it had been devised, for the letter had been written for the express purpose of inducing Mary to accede to the demission of her regal dignity; telling her, as if in confidence, that it was the Queen of England's sisterly advice that she should not irritate those who had her in their power, by refusing the only concession that could save her life; and observing that "nothing that was done under her present circumstances could be of any force when she regained her freedom." Mary, however, resolutely refused to sign the deeds; declaring with truly royal courage, that she would not make herself a party to the treason of her own subjects, by acceding to their lawless requisition, which, as she truly alleged, "proceeded only of the ambition of a few, and was far from the desire of her people."

The fair-spoken Melville having reported his ill

success to his coadjutor Lord Lindsay, Moray's brother-in-law, the bully of the party, who had been selected for the honorable office of extorting by force from the royal captive the concession she denied, that brutal ruffian burst rudely into her presence, and, flinging the deeds violently upon the table before her, told her to sign them without delay, or worse would befall her. "What!" exclaimed Mary. "Shall I set my hand to a deliberate falsehood; and, to gratify the ambition of my nobles, relinquish the office God hath given me to my son—an infant a little more than a year old, incapable of governing the realm—that my brother Moray may reign in his name?" She was proceeding to demonstrate the unreasonableness of what was required of her, but Lindsay contemptuously interrupted her with scornful laughter; then, scowling ferociously upon her, he swore, with a deep oath, that if she would not sign these instruments, he would do it with her heart's blood, and cast her into the lake to feed the fishes. . . .

Her heart was too full to continue the unequal contest. "I am not yet five-and-twenty," she pathetically observed. Somewhat more she would have said, but her utterance failed her, and she began to weep with hysterical emotion. Sir Robert Melville, affecting an air of the deepest concern, whispered in her ear an earnest entreaty for her to save her life by signing the papers, reiterating that "whatever she did would be invalid because extorted by force."

Mary's tears continued to flow, but sign she would not till Lindsay, infuriated by her resolute resistance, swore that, "having begun the matter, he would also finish it then and there," forced the pen into her reluctant hand; and, according to the popular version of this scene of lawless violence grasped her arm in the struggle so rudely as to leave the prints of his mail-clad fingers visibly impressed. In an access of pain and terror, with streaming eyes and averted head, she affixed her regal signature to the three deeds, without once looking at them.—*Queens of Scotland.*

STROTHER, DAVID HUNTER, an American author, born at Martinsburg Virginia, in 1816; died at Charlestown, West Virginia, in 1888. In 1840, after studying art at Philadelphia and New York, he went to Europe, where he remained five years. After his return to America he passed some years in New York, where he acquired skill as a designer and a draughtsman on wood for engravers. He returned to Virginia in 1848; and in 1852, under the pseudonym of "Porte Crayon," he began in *Harper's Magazine* a series of articles illustrative of life and scenery in Virginia. Not only were these papers written by him, but the numerous illustrations were designed and drawn upon wood by himself. In fact, he tells his story by means of both pencil and pen. These papers were in 1857 collected into a volume entitled *Virginia Illustrated.* Immediatly after the breaking out of the civil war he entered the Union service, as captain, and rose to the rank of colonel in the West Virginia cavalry. He resigned his commission in 1864, and in 1865 received the brevet rank of brigadier-general of Volunteers. After the close of the war, although his time was mainly occupied in the care of his estate, he occasionally contributed illustrated articles to periodicals. From 1879 to 1885 he was U. S. Consul-general in Mexico.

LITTLE MICE.

One morning a huge negro made his appearance in the hall, accompanied by all the negro servants, and all in a broad grin.

"Sarvant, master," said the giant, saluting, cap in hand, with the grace of a hippotamus. I'se a driver, sir."

"Indeed!" said Porte, with some surprise. "What is your name?"

"Ke! hi!" snickered the applicant for office, and looked toward Old Tom.

"He's name Little Mice," said Tom; and there was a general laugh.

"That's a queer name, at least, and not a very suitable one; has he no other?" inquired Porte.

"Why, d'ye see, Mass' Porte," said Tom, "when dis nigga was a boy his ole Miss tuck him in de house to sarve in de dinin'-room. Well, every day she look arter her pies an' cakes, an' dey done gone. 'Dis is onaccountable,' say ole Miss. 'Come here, boy. What goes wid dese pies?'—He says, 'Spec, missus, little mice eats 'em.'—'Very well,' says she; 'maybe dey does.'—So one mornin' arter she come in onexpected like, an' she see dis boy, pie in he's mouf.—'So,' says she, 'I cotch dem little mice at last, have I?'—an' from dat day, sir, dey call him nothin' but Little Mice; an' dat been so long dey done forgot his oder name, if he ever had any."

The giant during this narrative rolled eyes at Old Tom, and made menacing gestures in an underhand way; but being unable to stop the story, he joined in the laugh that followed, and then took up the discourse.

"Mass' Porte, never mind dat ole possum. Anyhow I ben a-drivin' horses all my life; an' I kin wait on a gemplum fuss rate. To be sure it sounds sort a foolish 'mong strangers; but you can call me Boy, or Hoss, or Pomp, or anyting dat suits; I comes all the same!"

Having exhibited a permit to hire himself, Crayon engaged him on the spot; moved thereto, we suspect, more by the fun and originality indicated in Mice's humorous phiz than by any particular fact or consideration. The newly appointed dignitary bowed himself out of the hall, sweeping the floor with his cap at each reverence. But no sooner was he clear of the respected precinct, than the elephantine pedals commenced a spontaneous dance, making a clatter on the kitchen-floor like a team of horses crossing a bridge. During this performance he shook his fists—in size and color like an old ham—alternately at Old and Young Tom.

"Heh, ye ole turkey-buzzard! I take you in dar to recommend me, an' you tell all dem lies. You want to drive yourself, heh! An' you black calf, you sot up to drive gemplum's carriage, did you? Mass' Porte too smart to have any sich 'bout him!"

Old Tom's indignation at this indecorous conduct knew no bounds. He pitched into Mice incontinently, and bestowed a shower of kicks and cuffs upon his carcass. Tom's honest endeavors were so little appreciated that they only served to increase the monster's merriment "Yah, yah! lame grasshopper kick me!" shouted he, escaping from the kitchen; and making a wry face through the window at Tom, he swung himself off to the stables to "look arter his critters."

A couple of pipes with some tobacco, and a cast-off coat, soothed the mortification of the senior and junior Tom to such an extent that they were both seen the next morning actually assisting Mice in getting out the carriage.—*Virginia Illustrated.*

STUBBS, William, an English clergyman and historian, born at Knaresborough in 1825. He graduated at Christ Church, Oxford, taking a first-class in classics, and a third-class in mathematics. He was ordained in 1848, and became Vicar of Neverstock in 1850. In 1862 he received the appointment of Librarian to the Archbishop of Canterbury at his palace at Lambeth. From 1860 to 1866 he was Inspector of Schools for the diocese of Rochester. In 1866 he was appointed Regius Professor of Modern History at Oxford. In 1869 he was made Curator of the Bodleian Library at Oxford. In 1875 he was presented to the Rectory of Cholderton; but resigned in 1879, on being appointed Canon Residentiary of St. Paul's. He has put forth several works relating mainly to the ecclesiastical and political archæology of England. His principal works in the department of English history are: *Chronicles and Memorials of Richard I.* (1865), *Select Charters, and Other Illustrations of English Constitutional History* (1870), *The Constitutional History of England in its Origin and Development* (3 vols., 1874, 1875, 1878), *History of the University of Dublin* (1890).

ENGLAND UNDER THE HOUSE OF LANCASTER.

The history of the three Lancastrian reigns (Henry IV., Henry V., and Henry VI.—1399-1461) has a double interest. It contains not only the foundation, consolidation, and destruction of a fabric of dynastic power, but parallel with it, the trial and failure of a great constitutional experiment; a premature testing of the strength of the parliamentary system. The system does not indeed break under the strain, but it bends and warps so as to show itself unequal to the burden; and instead of arbitrating between the other forces of the time, the parliamentary constitution finds itself either superseded altogether, or reduced to the position of a mere engine which these forces can manipulate at will. The sounder and stronger elements of English life seem to be exhausted, and the dangerous forces avail themselves of the weapons with equal disregard to the result. Although the deposition of Richard II. and the accession of Henry IV. were not the pure and legitimate result of a series of constitutional workings, there were many reasons for regarding the revolution of which they were a part as only slightly premature; the constitutional forces appeared ripe, although the particular occasion of their exertion was to a certain extent accidental, and to a certain extent the result of private rather than public causes.

Richard's tyranny deserved deposition had there been no Henry to revenge a private wrong; Henry's qualifications for sovereign power were adequate, even if he had not a great injury to avenge and a great cause to defend. The experiment of governing England constitutionally seemed likely to be fairly tried. Henry could not, without discarding all the principles which he had ever professed, even attempt to rule as Richard II. and Edward III. had ruled. He had great personal advantages. If he were not spontaneously chosen by the nation, he was enthusiastically welcomed by them; he was in the closest alliance with the clergy, and of the greater baronage there was scarcely one who could not count cousinship with him. He was reputed to be rich, not only on the strength of his great inheritance but in the possession of the treasures which Richard had amassed to his own ruin. He was a man of high reputation for all the virtues of chivalry and morality; and possessed in his four young sons a pledge to assure the nation that it would not soon be troubled with a question of succession, or endangered by a policy that would risk the fortunes of so noble a posterity. Yet the seeds of future difficulties were contained in every one of the advantages of Henry's position—difficulties that would increase with the growth and consolidation of his rule, grow stronger as the dynasty grew older, and in the end prove too great both for the men and the system.—*Constitutional History of England.*

HENRY IV. OF ENGLAND.

The character of Henry IV. has been drawn by later historians with a definiteness of outline altogether disproportioned to the details furnished by contemporaries. Like the whole period on which we are entering, the portrait has been affected by controversial views and political analogies. If the struggle between Lancaster and York obscured the lineaments of the man in the view of the partisans of the fifteenth century, the questions of legitimacy, usurpation, divine right, and indefeasible royalty obscured them in the minds of later writers. There is scarcely one in the whole line of our kings of whose personality it is so difficult to get any definite idea. The impression produced by his earlier career is so inconsistent with that derived from his later life, and from his conduct as a king, that they seem scarcely reconcilable as traits of one life. We are tempted to think that, like other men who have taken part in great crises, or in whose life a great crisis has taken place, he underwent some deep change of character at the critical point.

As Henry of Derby he is the adventurous, chivalrous Crusader; prompt, energetic, laborious; the man of impulse rather than of judgment; led sometimes by his uncle Gloucester, sometimes by his father; yet independent in action, averse to bloodshed, strong in constitional belief. If with Gloucester and Arundel he is an appellant in 1388, it is against the unconstitutional position of the favorites; if against Gloucester and Arundel in 1397 he takes part with John of Gaunt and Richard, it is because he believes his old allies have crossed the line which separates legal opposition from treason and conspiracy. On both these critical occasions he shows good faith and honest intent rather than policy or foresight. As king we find him suspicious, cold-blooded, and politic; undecided in action, cautious and jealous in private and public relations; and if not personally cruel, willing to sanction and profit by the cruelty of others. . . . .

Although he was a great king and the founder of a dynasty, the labor and sorrow of his task were ever more present to him than the solid success which his son was to inherit. Always in deep debt, always kept on the alert by the Scotch and the Welsh; wavering between two opposite lines of policy with regard to France; teased by the Parliament, which interfered with his household, and grudged him supplies; worried by the clergy, to whom he had promised more than he could fulfil; continually alarmed by attempts on his life, disappointed in his second marriage, bereft by treason of the aid of those whom he had trusted in his youth, and dreading to be supplanted by his own son; ever in danger of becoming the sport of Court factions which he had failed to extinguish or reconcile—he seems to us a man whose life was embittered by the knowledge that he had taken on himself a task for which he was unequal; whose conscience, ill-informed as it may have been, had soured him; and who felt that the judgments of men, at least would deal hardly with him when he was dead.—*Constitutional History of England.*

STURGIS, JULIAN, an English novelist, published in 1879 *English Life in Venice*, highly finished and analytical; in 1880, *Little Comedies*, some of them favorites in private theatricals; in 1882, *Dick's Wandering*, the heroine an American girl, with an English lover; in 1885, *John Maidment*, a political novel; in 1887, *Thraldom*, a study of personal magnetism. Besides these are his *My Friends and I*, *An Accomplished Gentleman*, and *John-a-Dreams*. His work is carefully and delicately done, often with much quiet, satirical humor.

MISS FALCONHURST.

During the first days of his visit to us Gentle Geordie had declined with his usual air of laziness to go to the Castle or to know its inmates. At first he said, as he generally said, that it was too much trouble; he maintained languidly that his constitution required complete repose after his journey. When he had reposed for eight-and-forty hours he passed easily to a new excuse. . . .

For a full week George Effingham declined to accompany us on our daily walk. He smiled on our start; and said he asked nothing but to be let alone—to be left on the sofa and to the labors necessary for his schools. At the end of a week he rose and stretched himself.

"I find," he said smiling, "that I am not quite good enough for the hermit's life. As you fellows keep all your conversation for the people on the hill, I must go thither too, or consent to forego the voice of man."

We thought that this was intended for a jest, for we had long ceased to urge him to accompany us; but when we climbed to the terrace on the afternoon of that day we found him in close conversation with General Falconhurst. The General held him by the button, and Gentle Geordie, with amiable nods and brief speeches, was confirming his new acquaintance in all his false ideas of University life. It was annoying to some of us to find that Geordie immediately became the General's favorite. He smiled pleasantly when the elderly gentleman talked; it was never any trouble to him to smile. As usual, he smiled himself into favor.

But though George Effingham with usual luck delighted the father, his smiling and his soft lazy speech seemed to produce a precisely opposite effect in the daughter. Miss Falconhurst had the air of being irritated by the very first word George Effingham spoke in her presence. . . .

Before their acquaintance was an hour old she had begun to throw darts at Geordie. Each time they met, the darts were sharper and more frequent. She seemed bent on rousing him from his invincible good temper. It was well-nigh impossible. The more energetic her attack, the more languid his defence. He surrendered every position with a light heart; and with a light heart he reöccupied them all when the engagement was over. The sharper her tongue, the more pleasure appeared in his smile. He seemed to take a gentle interest in his own wounds, in wondering when the next dart was coming, and where it would strike him. So were all his powers concentrated into pure exasperation. Every day he carried to her home a small offering of sentiments which were calculated to annoy the lady. He not only shaped his speech, but also his life, to the same good end. He delighted to come lounging in the character which would most surely irritate her. He discovered at once her love of heroism and self sacrifice; therefore he plumed himself ostentatiously on selfishness and cowardice. He would do nothing but sit in the sun. when it was warm enough on the terrace, or by the fire when the mists crept up from the sea. He refused a mount on the ground that he was afraid of horses; he said that his nerves could not bear the sound of a gun;

he lisped forth his opinions, that it was too much trouble to play games. Now, none of these reasons were true, as I very well knew. They are reasons which I might have urged in my own case, with far more truth; since I confess that I join in the sports and pastimes of young men less from any natural inclination than from a strong desire to be with the young men themselves—to see what they are doing, to find out what they are thinking. But George Effingham is not like me. He is a very pretty horseman, and was one of the best tennis-players in our time at Oxford. Indeed he is one of those men who do most things well, and with the crowning grace of apparent ease. He seems to sit well on a horse, because it would be an effort to him to sit otherwise; to place a ball in the right place, because his racquet so willed it, and he would not balk his racquet. In short, there seemed to be but one true reason for Gentle Geordie's conduct at the castle—the desire to irritate Honoria Falconhurst. He was very polite in manner, always sweet-tempered as a cherub; and when he begged that his attendance might be excused, he would plead with a childlike look the meanest motives. It was too much trouble; or he was frightened; or he didn't see what good *he* could get out of it. Such were his excuses, and so the young lady was moved to looks of scorn and to hasty speech. She shot arrows into him, whereat he smiled as if tickled; she threw caps in his way, which, though to her eye they fitted him to a nicety, he would by no means wear. It was a very pretty game for the spectators; and yet I could see that it afforded no pleasure to Michael Horatio Belbin. . . .

"Oh, why did you neglect your opportunity?" I said, almost blaming him in my vexation. "Why didn't you go to her fresh from saving George Effingham—from your heroic action—then you would have won the whole thing."

"It was too late."

"Too late!"

"The second time that Geordie went to the castle, I knew what would be."

"They did nothing but quarrel."

Michael looked at me, and even smiled as he said, "I have eyes."

I knew that he had eyes. But had I not eyes too?

"Effingham's luck is something which defies calculation," I said crossly; for I was annoyed.

"He deserves it," said Michael; "and no man could take it better; he has the sweetest temper in the world, and yet she may trust him; he will make her happy." His voice had dropped, and he seemed to be speaking to himself. Then he looked at me again and smiled.

"The ever-victorious Geordie," he said softly. —*My Friends and I.*

SUCKLING, Sir John, an English dramatist and lyrical poet; born in 1608, at Whitton, parish of Twickenham, Middlesex, died in 1642. His father held high royal offices, and his maternal uncle became Earl of Middlesex. He is interesting chiefly as a typical courtier and wit in the time of Charles I., and as author of airy verse, a few of his songs being remarkably free from the libertinism and petty conceits of the rest and of his age. In 1623 he entered Trinity College, Cambridge, and five years later travelled on the continent. As an attendant of the Marquis of Hamilton, he served in the army of Gustavus Adolphus of Sweden. Against the Scottish Covenanters, he equipped at his own great expense the most conspicuous troop of cavaliers, clad in scarlet and white. In 1660, he entered the Long Parliament. As a conspirator for the rescue of the Earl of Strafford from the Tower he was obliged to flee to France, where he died a bachelor in 1642.

SONG.

When, dearest, I but think of thee,
Methinks all things that lovely be
Are present, and my soul delighted:
For, beauties that from worth arise
Are like the grace of deities,
Still present with us, though unsighted.

Thus while I sit, and sigh the day
With all his borrowed lights away,
Till night's black wings do overtake me,
Thinking on thee,—thy beauties then,
As sudden lights do sleeping men,
So they by their bright lights awake me.

Thus absence dies, and dying proves
No absence can subsist with loves
That do partake of fair perfection;
Since in the darkest night they may

By love's quick motion find a way
To see each other by reflection.

The waving sea can with each flood
Bathe some high promont that hath stood
Far from the main up in the river :
O, think not then but love can do
As much, for that's an ocean too,
Which flows not every day, but ever.

TO AN HONEST LOVER.

Honest lover whatsoever,
If in all thy love there ever
Was one wavering thought; if thy flame
Were not still even, still the same:
Know this,
Thou lov'st amiss,
And to love true,
Thou must begin again and love anew

If when she appears i' th' room,
Thou dost not quake, and are struck dumb,
And in striving this to cover,
Dost not speak thy words twice over,
Know this,
Thou lov'st amiss,
And to love true,
Thou must begin again and love anew.

If fondly thou dost not mistake,
And all defects for graces take,
Persuad'st thyself that jests are broken,
When she hath little or nothing spoken,
Know this,
Thou lov'st amiss,
And to love true,
Thou must begin again and love anew. . .

If by this thou dost discover
That thou art no perfect lover,
And desiring to love true,
Thou dost begin to love anew,
Know this,
Thou lov'st amiss,
And to love true,
Thou must begin again and love anew.

SUE, Eugène, a French novelist, born at Paris in 1804; died in 1857. He was the son of Jean Joseph Sue, from whom he inherited wealth. He was named after the son of the empress Josephine, Eugène de Beauharnais. For a time he was surgeon in the army, then gave himself to painting, and finally became an author. From 1830 to 1833, he wrote stories of the sea; these were followed by historical romances—*Jean Cavalier*, *The Count of Létorières*, and *The Commander of Malta*. *The Mysteries of Paris* appeared in 1842, and *The Wandering Jew* in 1846. Other works are *Mathilde* and *Thérèse Dunoyer*. He was elected to the National Assembly in 1850.

THE WANDERING JEW AT PARIS.

It is night. The moon shines and the stars glimmer in the midst of a serene but cheerless sky; the sharp whistlings of the north-wind, that fatal, dry and icy breeze, ever and anon burst forth in violent gusts. With its harsh and cutting breath, it sweeps Montmartre's Heights. On the highest point of the hills, a man is standing. His long shadow is cast upon the stony, moonlit ground. He gazes on the immense city, which lies outspread beneath his feet. Paris—with the dark outline of its towers, cupolas, domes, and steeples, standing out from the limpid blue of the horizon, while from the midst of the ocean of masonry, rises a luminous vapor, that reddens the starry azure of the sky. It is the distant reflection of the thousand fires, which at night, the hour of pleasures, light up so joyously the noisy capital.

"No," said the wayfarer; it is not to be. The Lord will not exact it. Is not *twice* enough?

"Five centuries ago, the avenging hand of the Almighty drove me hither from the uttermost confines of Asia. A solitary traveller

I had left behind me more grief, despair, disaster, and death, than the innumerable armies of a hundred devastating conquerors. I entered this town, and it, too, was decimated. "Again, two centuries, ago the inexorable hand, which leads me through the world, brought me once more hither; and then, as the time before, the plague, which the Almighty attaches to my steps, again ravaged this city, and fell first on my brethren, already worn out with labor and misery.

"My brethren—mine?—the cobbler of Jerusalem, the artisan accused by the Lord, who, in my person, condemned the whole race of workmen, ever suffering, ever disinherited, ever in slavery, toiling on like me without rest or pause, without recompense or hope, till men, women, and children, young and old, all die beneath the same iron yoke—that murderous yoke, which others take in their turn, thus to be borne from age to age on the submissive and bruised shoulders of the masses.

"And now, for the third time in five centuries, I reach the summit of one of the hills that overlook the city. And perhaps I again bring with me fear, desolation, and death.

"Yet this city, intoxicated with the sounds of its joys and its nocturnal revelries, does not know—oh! does not know that *I* am at its gates.

"But no, no! my presence will not be a new calamity. The Lord, in his impenetrable views, has hitherto led me through France, so as to avoid the humblest hamlet; and the sound of the funeral knell has not accompanied my passage.

"And, moreover, the spectre has left me—the green, livid spectre, with its hollow, blood-shot eyes. When I touched the soil of France, its damp and icy hand was no longer clasped in mine—and it disappeared.

"And yet—I feel that the atmosphere of death is around me. The sharp whistlings of that fatal wind cease not, which, catching me in their whirl, seem to propagate blasting and mildew as they blow

"But perhaps the wrath of the Lord is appeased, and my presence, here is only a threat—to be communicated in some way to those whom it should intimidate.

"Yes; for otherwise he would smite with a fearful blow, by first scattering terror and death here in the heart of the country, in the bosom of this immense city!

"Oh! no, no! the Lord will be merciful. No! he will not condemn me to this new torture.

"Alas! in this city, my brethren are more numerous and miserable than elsewhere. "And should I be their messenger of death?

"No! the Lord will have pity. For, alas! the seven descendants of my sister have at length met in this town. And to them likewise should I be the messenger of death, instead of the help they so much need?

"For that woman, who like me wanders from one border of the earth to the other, after having once more rent asunder the nets of their enemies, has gone forth upon her endless journey.

"In vain she foresaw that new misfortunes threatened my sister's family. The invisible hand, that drives me on, drives *her* on also.

"Carried away, as of old, by the irresistible whirlwind, at the moment of leaving my kindred to their fate, she in vain cried with supplicating tone:

"'Let me at least, O Lord, complete my task!' —'Go ON!'—'A few days, in mercy, only a few poor days!'—'Go ON!'—'I leave those I love on the brink of the abyss!'—'Go ON! Go ON!'

"And the wandering star again started on its eternal round. And her voice, passing through space, called on me to the assistance of mine own.

"When that voice reached me, I knew that

the descendants of my sister were still exposed to frightful perils. Those perils are even now on the increase.

"Tell me, O Lord! will they escape the scourge, which for so many centuries has weighed down our race?

"Wilt thou pardon me in them? wilt thou punish me in them? Oh, that they might obey the last will of their ancestor!

"Oh, that they might join together their charitable hearts, their valor and their strength, their noble intelligence, and their great riches!

"They would then labor for the future happiness of humanity—they would thus, perhaps, redeem me from my eternal punishment!

"The words of the Son of Man, LOVE YE ONE ANOTHER, will be their only end, their only means."—*The Wandering Jew.*

SUETONIUS, CAIUS TRANQUILLUS, a Roman biographer, born about A. D. 70. He was the son of a tribune of the army, practiced law, and held office under the emperor Hadrian. For character and various learning he was held in high esteem in his time and since. But few of his many works have been preserved, and these are of great value, viz., the *Lives of the Twelve Cæsars*, and brief lives of "grammarians," (literati) and of "rhetoricians" (orators). Of the emperors, may be selected Titus, the destroyer of Jerusalem (though he would have saved the Temple) and the builder of the Coliseum,—a man who was wonderfully reformed and humanized by accession to power, not brutalized, or corrupted like many of the emperors.

THE EMPEROR TITUS.

He was by nature extremely benevolent: for whereas all the emperors after Tiberius, according to the example he had set them, would not admit the grants made by former princes to be valid, unless they received their own sanction, he confirmed them all by one general edict, without waiting for any applications respecting them. Of all who petitioned for any favor, he sent none away without hopes. And when his ministers represented to him that he promised more than he could perform, he replied, "No one ought to go away downcast from an audience with his prince." Once at supper, reflecting that he had done nothing for any that day, he broke out into that memorable and justly admired saying, "My friends, I have lost a day." More particularly, he treated the people on all occasions with so much courtesy, that, on his presenting them with a show of gladiators, he declared, "He should manage it, not according to his own fancy, but that of the spectators," and did accordingly. He denied them nothing, and very frankly encouraged them to ask what they pleased. Espousing the cause of the Thracian party among the gladiators, he frequently joined in the popular demonstrations in their favor, but without compromising his dignity or doing injustice. To omit no opportunity of acquiring popularity, he sometimes made use of the baths he had erected, without excluding the common people. There happened in his reign some dreadful accidents; an eruption of Mount Vesuvius, in Campania, and a fire at Rome, which continued three days and three nights, besides a plague, such as scarcely ever was known. Amidst these many great disasters, he not only manifested the concern which might be expected from a prince, but even the affection of a father for his people; one while comforting them by his proclamations and another while relieving them to the utmost in his power. He chose by lot, from among the men of consular rank, commissioners for repairing the losses in Campania. The estates of those who had perished by the eruption of Vesuvius, and who had left no heirs, he applied to the repairs of the ruined cities. With regard to the public buildings destroyed by fire in the City, he declared that nobody should be a loser but himself. Accordingly, he applied all the ornaments of his palaces to the decoration of the temples, and purposes of public utility, and appointed several men of the equestrian order to superintend the work. For the relief of the people during the plague, he employed, in the way of sacrifice and medicine, all means, both human and divine. Amongst the calamities of the times were informers and their agents; a tribe of miscreants who had grown up under the license of former reigns. These he frequently ordered to be scourged or beaten with sticks in the forum, and then, after he had obliged them to pass through the amphitheatre as a public spectacle, commanded them to be sold for slaves, or else banished to some rocky islands. And to discourage such practices in the future, amongst other things he prohibited actions to be successively brought under different laws for the same cause, or the state of the affairs of deceased persons to be inquired into after a certain number of years.

Having declared that he accepted the office of Pontifex Maximus for the purpose of preserving his hands undefiled, he faithfully adhered to his promise. For after that time he was neither directly nor indirectly concerned in the death of any person, though he sometimes was justly irritated. He swore "that he would perish himself rather than prove the destruction of any man." Two men of patrician rank being convicted of aspiring to the empire, he only advised them to desist, saying "that the sovereign power was disposed of by fate," and promised them that if there was anything else they desired of him, he would grant it. He also immediately sent messengers to the mother of one of them, who was at a great distance, and in deep anxiety about her son, to assure her of his safety. Nay, he not only invited them to sup with him, but next day, at a show of the gladiators, purposely placed them close by him; and handed to them the arms of the combatants for inspection. It is said likewise, that having had their nativities cast, he assured them "that a great calamity was impending on both of them, but from another hand, and not from his." Though his brother was continually plotting against him, almost openly stirring up the armies to rebellion, and contriving to get away, yet he could not endure to put him to death, or to banish him from his presence; nor did he treat him with less respect then before. But, from his first accession to the empire, he constantly declared him his partner in it, and that he should be his successor; and begging of him sometimes in private, with tears in his eyes, "to return the affection he had for him." Amidst all these favorable circumstances, he was cut off by an untimely death, more to the loss of mankind than himself.

SULLIVAN, T. R., an American novelist, poet, and dramatist; born at Boston, in 1849. He was fitted for Harvard College, but did not enter, beginning instead a business life in Boston, 1866–1870; then in Paris, 1870–1873. Returning to Boston, he pursued business by day and literature by night, till 1888, when he retired from business. His principal works are many dramatic adaptations from the French, and (in collaboration) two original plays (1876–1880), poems in the *Century*, *Lippincott*, *Life*, etc. (1880–1885), *Roses in Shadow*, a novel (1885), dramatization of Stevenson's *Dr. Jekyll and Mr. Hyde* (1886), *Day and Night Stories* (1890).

NEW ENGLAND GRANITE.

"Your happy household is your best argument," said Luxmore; "but think of the risk they run in saying 'yes.' Look around you at the unhappy marriages."

"Nonsense. The man runs his risk, doesn't he? Why not the woman? Because she is too self-centered; she will not let herself go a single instant. . . . Look at the case in point. Here is Sylvia Belknap, young, lovely, rich beyond reckoning. She has no near relatives; she lives alone with her servants and her companion, Miss Winchester. It is the most selfish and limited of lives. She writes her checks, studies her art and her philosophy, cuts the leaves of her review, dines, dances, and her day is done. Unluckily her coldness, that should repel, attracts. More than one better man than she deserves to get, has dangled after her and come to grief. She cannot understand it, she has improved all antiquated ideas away. I have no patience with such a temperament. Her smile makes me think of a vein of quartz in its granite setting. She is like the reef out there,—the waves rush at it and the biggest can only dash itself to pieces. What are you laughing at now?"

"Only to think that the gods made Mordaunt poetical."

It was the following autumn that Luxmore's "Circe and Ulysses,"—his first great picture,—made him suddenly famous. Long before the summer there came rumors that he was bent, at last, upon that higher flight from which his self-distrust had hitherto deterred him. The world saw less of him than of old. And though he looked pale and worn, his air of hopeful determination showed that he was dealing with a problem which hard work would solve. Mordaunt and one or two other friends saw the work in progress and promised great things. Great things, therefore, were expected. And the result, given to the public, surpassed expectation.

He had chosen the moment of the king's first meeting with the enchantress, when, armed with the sprig of moly, he draws his sword defiantly, declining to become a brute at her command. The figures, of life-size, were superbly modelled; the composition was original and fine, the color fully worthy of it. His triumph proved in every way complete. An English amateur pounced upon the picture, paying without a murmur the sum he demanded for it, carrying it off to London. Hard upon this followed an order for a pendant at his own price. His long apprenticeship had not been served in vain. His reputation rose at last; he had but to sustain the bubble, now soaring into sight of all the world.

From misfortune, fortune. There can be no doubt that to what, in technical phrase, may be termed heart-failure Luxmore's first success was due. In that memorable winter twilight he had broken down utterly at the sight of Sylvia's roses still surviving the desolation of his home. Home! He had hoped for one, and the echo of that hope, resounding in the lonely place, brought him hours of anguish,—

days and nights of it, scoring themselves like years. For age is measured more by lost illusions than by actual flight of time. One or two intimate friends saw the change in him and remarked upon it; but they invited no confidences, and he made none. He met the world's glance without flinching, walked erect with a firm step, hugging to himself his "gnarling sorrow" as bravely as a Spartan. Mordaunt alone suspected the truth; but even to him it remained always a mere suspicion. He became, none the less, a model of discreet and devoted friendship. Various were the devices he employed to change the current of his comrade's thoughts, to shorten his hours of solitude. . . .

The stupor slowly wore itself away, to be succeeded by a fierce reaction. An hour came when Luxmore woke and said: "She has ruined one man; she shall be the making of another. I cannot hate her. I will forget her. I am not like Selden." He plunged into work, wearily enough at first. Day by day, however, gaining strength from this healthful stimulus, he applied himself more closely, grew more and more at one with his difficult task, found to his delight that something better than his old self had taken possession of him. This it was to live; no earthly joy that he had ever known was comparable to it. Leaving noble work behind them, men were more than men. And if not the fulfilment, the endeavor; to that end men were endowed with souls,—"to strive, to seek, to find, and not to yield."

The last fumes of the alembic had cleared away. He knew now that they had lent their colors to an air-drawn shape, a creature of his own mind, totally unreal, perhaps too perfect for material existence. That lovely soul, divine in its perceptions, could never consciously or unconsciously have so betrayed two men; for her there would have been no second victim to dismiss with an allusion to the first. She would have been unselfish and considerate, quick to interpret a silence that every look and every act of his had contradicted, eager to avert the merest possibility of danger. With all the weakness of her sex she would have proved herself the strongest and noblest of women,—an angel with a human heart, not a cold abstraction. How well he remembered Mordaunt's warning, when he had fatally disregarded it. She had only to reveal herself, to bring home to him the cleverness of that description. . . .

"I see. Your work absorbs you; you have no other end in life."

"None."

"And does it make you happy?"

"I do not ask so much of it. I have lost a hope, but I have gained a virtue,—the virtue of contentment. In this life we are all servants and not masters; the rewards come after. I serve to win them. I live only for a few letters in high relief upon a tombstone,—for a statue, perhaps; for fame, immortality, who knows? for happiness elsewhere."

He looked not at her, but straight before him, through the half-empty rooms, towards the Mexican minister who had just risen to take leave. A star glittered upon his breast. The light of it flashed in Luxmore's eyes.

At a slight sound beside him he turned his head. One of the slender sticks of her fan had broken in Miss Belknap's hands. "It is nothing," she said, rising. "As you were saying, you have grown older, if not wiser. All your ideas are completely changed."

He rose too. "No," he said. "My ideal,—that is all."

"And nothing can change that?"

"Nothing in the world."

She held out her hand once more. "Since you will go, then, I wish you all possible success."

"It is to you that I shall owe it," he replied, looking at her now, as their hands clasped. He could hardly believe his own eyes, for hers were full of tears.

"They are going," he said. "Shall I take you to our hostess?"

"No. I shall stay a little longer. Good-night."

"Good-night,—until we meet again!"

On his way home he reviewed their talk lightly, laughing to himself. "And yet," he thought, "she would have flung me over. I would not have trusted her even then." That was his conclusion. To his last hour he will never doubt it.

"Until we meet again!" We toss a ball into the air perchance to catch, to return or not, at pleasure. In this case it was returned, but only after twenty years, throughout which Luxmore remained true to his ideal, winning honors, orders, stars as brilliant as the Mexican's. The better to enjoy them he went through the form of denization, and became a British subject. He grew gray and rich and stout and comfortable,—but alone. He never married.—*Day and Night Stories.*

SUMNER, CHARLES, an American statesman and scholar, born at Boston in 1811; died at Washington in 1874. He graduated at Harvard in 1830; studied at the Cambridge Law School, and in 1834 commenced practice at Boston. He was appointed Reporter to the Circuit Court, and put forth three volumes known as *Sumner's Reports*. and other legal works. In 1837 he went to Europe, where he remained three years. In 1844 he edited *Vesey's Reports*, in 20 volumes, to which he appended much original matter. He also lectured in the Cambridge Law School, and began to take an active part in politics, especially in opposition to the extension of slavery in the Territories. In 1851 he was elected to the U. S. Senate, succeeding Daniel Webster. On May 22, 1856, he was violently assaulted, while seated at his desk in the Senate Chamber, by Mr. Preston Brooks, a member of Congress from South Carolina, and so severely beaten with a bludgeon that his life was thought to be endangered. It was seven years before his health was fully restored, a considerable part of the interval being passed in Europe. In 1857 he was re-elected to the Senate; but was not able to take his seat permanently until 1859. During the civil war, and afterwards, he was chairman of the Senate Committee on Foreign Relations. He was re-elected Senator in 1862, again in 1869, and died near the conclusion of his third consecutive senatorial term.

During the whole of his active life Mr. Sumner, besides his speeches and reports in Congress, delivered numerous public addresses on political and literary topics. A collection of his earlier *Addresses and*

Essays, in three volumes, was published in 1850. An edition of his *Complete Works*, comprising about 15 volumes, was commenced in 1870. His *Life* has been written by Charles A. Phelps.

JUDICIAL INJUSTICES.

I hold Judges, and especially the Supreme Court of the country, in much respect, but I am too familiar with the history of judicial proceedings to regard them with any superstitious reverence. Judges are but men, and in all ages have shown a full share of human frailty. Alas! alas! the worst crimes of history have been perpetrated under their sanction. The blood of martyrs and of patriots, crying from the ground, summons them to judgment.

It was a judicial tribunal which condemned Socrates to drink the fatal hemlock, and which pushed the Saviour barefoot over the pavements of Jerusalem, bending beneath his cross. It was a judicial tribunal which, against the testimony and entreaties of her father, surrendered the fair Virginia as a slave; which arrested the teachings of the great Apostle to the Gentiles, and sent him in bonds from Judea to Rome; which, in the name of the Old Religion, adjudged the Saints and Fathers of the Christian Church to death in all its most dreadful forms; and which afterwards, in the name of the New Religion, enforced the tortures of the Inquisition, amidst the shrieks and agonies of its victims, while it compelled Galileo to declare, in solemn denial of the great truth he had disclosed, that the earth did not move round the sun.

It was a judicial tribunal which in France during the long reign of her monarchs lent itself to be the instrument of every tyranny, as during the brief Reign of Terror it did not hesitate to stand forth the unpitying accessary of the unpitying guillotine.

It was a judicial tribunal in England, surrounded by all the forms of law, which sanctioned every despotic caprice of Henry the Eighth, from the unjust divorce of his queen to the beheading of Sir Thomas More; which lighted the fires of persecution that glowed at Oxford and Smithfield over the cinders of Latimer, Ridley, and John Rogers; which, after deliberate argument, upheld the fatal tyranny of Ship-Money, against the patriot resistance of Hampden, which, in defiance of justice and humanity, sent Sidney and Russell to the block; which persistently enforced the laws of Conformity that our Puritan Fathers persistently refused to obey; and which afterwards, with Jeffreys on the bench, crimsoned the page of English history with massacre and murder—even with the blood of innocent women.

Ay, Sir, and it was a judicial tribunal, in our country, surrounded by all the forms of law, which hung the witches at Salem; which affirmed the constitutionality of the Stamp-Act while it admonished "jurors and the people" to obey; and which now in our day, lent its sanction to the unutterable atrocity of the Fugitive Slave Bill.—*Speech, September*, 1854.

THE KANSAS-NEBRASKA BILL.

From the depths of my soul, as a loyal citizen and as Senator, I plead, remonstrate, protest against the passage of this Bill. I struggle against it as against death; but as in death itself corruption puts on incorruption, and this mortal body puts on immortality, so from the sting of this hour I find assurance of that triumph by which freedom will be restored to her immortal birthright in the Republic.

The Bill you are about to pass is at once the worst and the best on which Congress ever acted. Yes, Sir, worst and best at the same time.

It is the worst Bill, inasmuch as it is a present victory of Slavery. In a Christian land, and in an age of civilization, a time-honored statute of freedom is struck down, opening the way to all the countless woes and wrongs of human bondage. Among the crimes of history another is soon to be recorded, which no tears can blot out, and which in better days will be read with universal shame. The Tea-Tax and the Stamp-Act, which aroused the patriot rage of our fathers, were virtues by the side of this transgression; nor would it be easy to imagine at this day any measure which more openly and wantonly defied every sentiment of justice, humanity, and Christianity. Am I not right, then, in calling it the worst Bill on which Congress ever acted?

There is another side to which I gladly turn. It is the best Bill on which Congress ever acted, for it annuls all past compromises with slavery, and makes any future compromise impossible. Thus it puts Freedom and Slavery face to face, and bids them grapple. Who can doubt the result? It opens wide the door of the future, when at last there will really be a North and the slave-power will be broken; when this wretched despotism will cease to dominate over our Government; when the National Government will be divorced in every way from slavery, and, according to the true intention of our fathers, freedom will be established everywhere—at least beyond the local limits of the States. . . . .

Thus, standing at the very grave of freedom in Nebraska and Kansas, I lift myself to the vision of that happy resurrection by which freedom will be assured, not only in these Territories, but everywhere under the National Government. More clearly than ever before, I now penetrate that great future when slavery must disappear. Proudly I discern the flag of my country, as it ripples in every breeze, at last in reality, as in name, the flag of freedom—undoubted, pure, and irresistible. Am I not right, then, in calling this Bill the best on which Congress ever acted? Sorrowfully I bend before the wrong you commit. Joyfully I welcome the promises of the future.—*In the Senate, May,* 1854.

SWEDENBORG, Emanuel, a Swedish theosophist, born at Stockholm in 1688; died at London in 1772. He completed his course at the University of Upsala in 1709; travelled for two years, and resided abroad until 1716, when he returned to Sweden. Between 1717 and 1722 he put forth several treatises on philosophical topics, and was engaged in public affairs. In 1722 he was appointed Assessor of Mines. Between 1722 and 1745 he wrote several important works on physical science, among which are: *Opera Philosophica et Mineralia*, *Œconomia Regni Animalis* and *De Cultu et Amore Dei*, the last being an allegorical presentation of his theory of the creation. When he had reached his fifty-fifth year he believed himself divinely commissioned to enunciate a new system of religious truth, and permitted to have frequent intercourse with angelic intelligences. He resigned his assessorship, and devoted himself to the study of the Bible, especially of the Old Testament, and to the writing and publication of works setting forth the principles of his new faith. Of these works the principal are: *The Heavenly Arcana*, put forth at different periods from 1749 to 1756, and *The True Christian Religion*, published in the last year of his life, which sets forth the dogmatic system of his teachings. *The Heavenly Arcana* is primarily an exposition of the Books of Genesis and Exodus, interspersed with sections in which are narrated, "the wonderful things seen and heard in Heaven and Hell." The exposition of Genesis, the first thirty-one chapters, occupies in the English translation four large closely-printed volumes.

There can be no question that Swedenborg was thoroughly convinced of the verity of the revelations which he enunciated. It is related that on his death-bed, and only two days before he breathed his last, a Swedish clergyman who was with him solemnly adjured him to tell the truth in regard to his teachings: to which Swedenborg replied: "As true as you see me before you, so true is everything I have written. I could have said much more had I been permitted. When you come into eternity, you will see all things as I have stated and described them, and we shall have much to say concerning them to each other."—Swedenborg made no attempts to gain proselytes except by the writing of his books, and their publication, which was done at his own expense. The association commonly designated as the Swedenborgian Church, but styling itself "The Church of the New Jerusalem," was organized at London in 1788.

THE INTERNAL SENSE OF THE OLD TESTAMENT.

That the Word of the Old Testament includes arcana of Heaven, and that all its contents, to every particular, regard the Lord and his Heaven, the Church, Faith and the things relating to Faith, no man can conceive who only views it from the Letter. For the Letter, or literal sense, suggests only such things as respect the externals of the Jewish Church, when, nevertheless, it everywhere contains internal things, which do not in the least appear in those externals, except in a very few cases where the Lord revealed and unfolded them to the Apostles: as, that Sacrifices are significative of the Lord; and that the Land of Canaan and Jerusalem are significative of Heaven; and that Paradise has a like signification.

But that all and every part of its contents—even to the most minute, not excepting the smallest jot and tittle—signify and involve spiritual and celestial things is a truth to this day deeply hidden from the Christian world; in consequence of which little attention is paid to the Old Testament. This truth, however, might appear plainly from this single circumstance, that the Word being of the Lord could not possibly be given without containing interiorly such things as relate to Heaven, to the Church and to Faith. For if this be denied, how can it be called the Word of the Lord, or be said to have any Life in it? For whence is its Life but from those things which possess life? that is, except from hence, that all things in it, both general and particular, have relations to the Lord, who is the very Life itself. Wherefore, whatsoever does not interiorly regard Him, does not live; nay, whatsoever expression in the Word does not involve Him, or in some measure relate to Him is not divine.

It is impossible, while the mind abides in the literal sense only, to see that it is full of such spiritual contents. Thus, in the first chapters of Genesis nothing is discoverable from the literal sense but that they treat of the creation of the world, and of the garden of Eden, which is called Paradise, and also of Adam, as the first created man; and scarcely a single person supposes them to relate to anything besides. But that they contain arcana which were never heretofore revealed will sufficiently appear from the following pages; where it will be seen that the first chapter of Genesis, in its interior sense, treats of the New-Creation of Man, of his Regeneration, in general, and specifically of the most ancient Church; and this in such a manner that there is not a single syllable which does not represent, signify, and involve something spiritual.

That this is really the case in respect to the Word, it is impossible for any mortal to know except from the Lord. Wherefore it is expedient here to premise that of the Lord's divine mercy it has been granted to me, now for several years, to be constantly and uninterruptedly in company with Spirits and Angels, hearing them converse with each other, and conversing with them. Hence it has been permitted me to hear and see things in another life which are astonishing, and which have never before come to the knowledge of any man, nor entered into his imagination. I have been instructed concerning different kinds of Spirits, and the state of souls after death; concerning Hell, or the lamentable state of the unfaithful; concerning Heaven, or the most happy state of the faithful; and particularly concerning the doctrine of Faith which is acknowledged throughout all Heaven.—*The Heavenly Arcana.*

SOME REVELATIONS OF THE HEAVENLY STATE.

In order that I might be acquainted with the nature and quality of Heaven, it was frequently and for a long continuance granted me by the Lord to perceive the delights of heavenly joys; in consequence of which, being convinced by sensible experience, I can testify to them, but by no means describe them. However, a word should be spoken on the subject for the sake of conveying some idea of it, however imperfect.

It is an affection of innumerable delights and joys which form one simultaneous delight in which common delights and affections are the harmonies of innumerable affections, not perceived distinctly, but obscurely, the perception being most general. Still it is given to perceive that there are innumerable delights within it, arranged in such admirable order as can never be described; those innumerable things being such as flow from the order of Heaven. Such an order obtains in the most minute things of affection, which are only presented as one general thing, and are perceived according to the capacity of him who is their subject.

In a word, every general contains infinite particulars arranged in a most orderly form, every one of which has life, and affects the mind, and that from the inmost ground or centre. Indeed, all heavenly joys proceed from inmost principles. I perceived also that this joy and delight issued, as it were, from the heart, diffusing itself gently and sweetly through all the inmost fibres, and from them to the compound fibres, and that with so exquisite and inward a sense of pleasure as if every fibre were a fountain of joyous perceptions and sensations, in comparison with which gross corporeal pleasures are but as the muddy waters of a putrid lake compared with the wholesome ventilations of pure, refreshing breezes.—*The Heavenly Arcana.*

SWIFT, JONATHAN, a British ecclesiastic, politician, and author, born at Dublin in 1667; died there in 1745. His father, an Englishman of good family, who had recently come over to Ireland, died before the birth of his son; and an uncle took charge of the boy who, in his fourteenth year was entered at Trinity College, Dublin, where he was chiefly remarkable for irregularities and breaches of college discipline; and received the degree of Bachelor of Arts "by special favor"—a term used to indicate lack of merit. The state of affairs in Ireland was then in nowise encouraging to English adventurers or their descendants, and in his twenty-first year Swift went over to England, and sought the assistance of the veteran statesman, Sir William Temple, who was a distant kinsman by marriage. Temple took him into his service, as private secretary; but treated him with little consideration.

After a couple of years Swift, who had seriously devoted himself to the improvement of his mind, solicited Temple to procure for him some public employment. The request not being complied with, Swift resigned his situation, and in 1694 went back to Ireland, with the design of entering the Church. Before he could be admitted to Holy Orders it was required by the Bishop that he should present a certificate of good conduct while residing with Sir William Temple. Sir William not only gave the certificate, but recommended Swift so highly that immediately after his ordination he received the prebend of Kilroot, in Ireland. Here his conduct was such as to excite some scandal among the neighboring gentry, and he grew weary of the position. Temple, moreover, was desirous to get back a secretary whose capacities he had come to appreciate. He wrote to Swift, urging his return, and promising to make strenuous efforts for his promotion. In 1696 Swift resigned his prebend, and returned to Temple's residence at Moor Park, near London.

Swift now began his political career, to narrate which would require an account of English parties and factions for several disgraceful years. He became a noted character in clubs and coffee-houses, among men of letters and political leaders. At first he was a zealous Whig, and wrote bitterly against the Tories. In 1708 Lord Wharton was made Lieutenant of Ireland, and Swift procured an earnest recommendation from Lord Somers, to which Wharton is said to have made answer— "Oh, my Lord, we must not prefer or countenance these fellows; we have not character enough ourselves."

About 1710 Swift was introduced to Harley, Lord of Oxford, who was rising into political importance, as a person who had been injuriously treated by the Whig Cabinet, and one who might be won over to do good service to the other side. Swift went over, and put forth several pamphlets, which were highly serviceable to the new Ministry. For these services he claimed an adequate reward. He demanded an English bishopric, which Harley was quite willing to grant, provided it could be done without offending his clerical supporters. But this could not be done. Archbishop Sharpe, in the name of his brethren, urged Queen Anne not to bestow the episcopal dignity upon a person whose belief in

Christianity was suspicious, who had written *The Tale of a Tub*, and who had moreover lampooned the Duchess of Somerset, one of the Queen's favorites. The Queen declared that Swift should never be made a prelate: and it was impossible to induce her to change her determination. The best that could be done for Swift was to make him Dean of St. Patrick's, in Dublin, whither he went in 1713.

For a large part of the subsequent thirty-two years of his life Swift mingled largely in political affairs; but his career as Dean of St. Patrick's was for the most part fairly creditable. It is inexpedient here to enter upon that part of his personal history connected with the names of Hester Johnson ("Stella") and Mrs. Vanhomrigh ("Vanessa"). Notwithstanding all that has been written on the subject, very little has been made absolutely certain. About all that is positively proven is that Swift and "Stella" were privately married in 1716, both of them verging upon fifty; that they never lived together as man and wife; that seven years later "Vanessa" pressed Swift to make her his wife so urgently that he was obliged to confess that he was already legally married to "Stella;" that "Vanessa" died not long after, having revoked a will which she had executed, leaving her large fortune to Swift.

As Swift advanced in years all the worst elements in his nature—as in the case of his own Struldbrugs—became aggravated. He had long been subject to fits of giddiness; these now became more frequent and more violent, and the acerbity of his temper increased with them. He occasionally put forth a tractate or an epigram as keen and bitter as anything he had ever written in his best days. In 1736, while engaged in writing a stinging lampoon on the Irish House of Commons, he was seized with a fit of giddiness so severe and long-continued, that he never afterwards attempted any work requiring thought or labor. In 1741 his mental condition became such that it was necessary to appoint legal guardians of his person and property. He gradually sank into a profound lethargy. "He went off," says the servant who attended upon him, "like the snuff of a candle." He had bequeathed all his property to found a hospital for idiots and lunatics. Years before he had written a sort of epitaph upon himself, in which he says:—

"He gave the little wealth he had
To build a house for fools and mad,
To show, by one satiric touch,
No nation wanted it so much."

Swift's writings form a bulky collection. As edited by Sir Walter Scott they comprise nineteen large volumes. His *Life* has been written, or attempted, by many hands, notably by Scott. It is succinctly given by Leslie Stephen in the "English Men of Letters" series. He wrote much verse, none of it of high poetic excellence. Though it abounds in clever hits, it is frequently marked by gross indecency. His numerous political productions were important in their day; but they relate to matters of little interest to after times. Few wittier things have ever been written than *The Tale of a Tub*, intended as a satire upon Catholicism and Lutheranism. The fame of Swift as an English classic, rests mainly upon his *Gulliver's Travels*, which appeared anonymously in 1727; although its authorship soon became an open secret.

It was originally designed to form part of a satire to be written conjointly by Swift, Arbuthnot, and Pope, to ridicule the abuses of human learning, and the extravagant stories of travellers. Viewed simply as a marvellous tale, told with the appearance of simple veracity, the work is hardly inferior to *Robinson Crusoe.* The account of the Struldbrugs indeed stands by itself: one might almost fancy it to be a prophecy by Swift of his own last sad years. Swift so far departed from the original design, as to make the work a satire upon English institutions and customs of his own time; but we doubt whether, with rare exceptions, the interest of the reader is greatly enhanced by being told who were intended by the characters introduced.

THE EMPEROR OF LILLIPUT.

The Emperor is taller by almost the breadth of my nail than any of his court, which alone is sufficient to strike an awe into the beholders. His features are strong and masculine, with an Austrian lip, and arched nose; his complexion olive, his countenance erect, his body and limbs well-proportioned, all his movements graceful, and his deportment majestic. He was then past his prime, being twenty-eight years and three-quarters old, of which he had reigned seven in great felicity, and generally victorious. For the better convenience of beholding him, I lay on my side, so that my face was parallel to his, and he stood but three yards off. However, I have had him since many times in my hand, and therefore cannot be mistaken in my description. His dress was very plain and simple, and the fashion of it between the Asiatic and the European; but he had on his head a light helmet of gold, adorned with jewels, and a plume on the crest. He held his sword drawn in his hand, to defend himself if I should happen to break loose. It was almost three inches long; the hilt and scabbard were gold, enriched with diamonds. His voice was shrill, but very clear and articulate; and I could distinctly hear it when I stood up. His Imperial Majesty spoke often to me, and I returned answers; but neither of us could understand a syllable.—*Voyage to Lilliput.*

DIVERSIONS AT THE COURT OF LILLIPUT.

The Emperor had a mind, one day, to entertain me with several of the country shows, wherein they exceeded all the nations I have known, both for dexterity and magnificence. I was diverted by none so much as that of the rope-dances, performed upon a slender white thread, extended about two feet and twelve inches from the ground. This diversion is only practiced by those persons who are candidates for great employments and high favor at court. They are trained in this art from their youth, and are not always of noble birth or liberal education. When a great office is vacant, either by death or disgrace (which often happens), five or six of these candidates petition the Emperor to entertain his Majesty and the court with a dance on the rope, and whoever jumps the highest without falling, succeeds in the office.

Very often the chief Ministers themselves are commanded to show their skill, and to convince the Emperor that they have not lost their faculty, Flimnap the Treasurer, is allowed to cut a caper on the straight rope at least an inch higher than any other lord in the whole empire. I have seen him do the summerset several times together upon a trencher fixed on a rope, which is no thicker than common pack-thread in England. My friend Reldresal, principal Secretary for Private Affairs, is in my opinion, the second after the Treasurer; the rest of the court officers are much on a par.

These diversions are often attended with fatal accidents, whereof great numbers are on record. I myself have seen two or three candidates break a limb. But the danger is much greater when the Ministers themselves are commanded to show their dexterity; for by contending to excel themselves and their fellows they strain so far that there is hardly one of them who has not received a fall, and some of them two or three. I was assured that a year or two before my arrival Flimnap would infallibly have broken his neck if one of the King's cushions, that accidentally lay on the ground, had not weakened the force of his fall.

There is likewise another diversion which is only shown before the Emperor and the Empress, and the First Minister, upon particular occasion.* The Emperor lays on the table three fine silken threads of six inches long; one is blue, the other red, and the third green. These threads are proposed as prizes for those persons whom the Emperor has a mind to distinguish by a peculiar mark of his favor. The ceremony is performed in his Majesty's great chamber of state where the candidates are to undergo a trial of dexterity, very different from the former, and such as I have not observed in any other country of the New or Old World. The Emperor holds a stick in his hands, both ends parallel to the horizon, while the candidates, advancing one by one, sometimes leap over the stick, sometimes creep under it, backward and forward, several times, according as the stick is advanced or depressed. Sometimes the Emperor holds one end of the stick and the First Minister the other; sometimes the Minister has it entirely to himself. Whoever performs his part with the most agility, and holds out the longest in leaping and creeping, is rewarded with the blue-colored silk; the red is given to the next, and the green to the third, which they all wear girt twice about the middle, and you see few great

*[This satirizes the three great British Orders. *Blue* is the Cognizance of the Order of the Garter; *red* of the Bath; *green* of the Thistle.]

persons about this court who are not adorned with one of these girdles.—*Voyage to Lilliput.*

THE GREAT ACADEMY OF LAGADO.

This Academy is not an entire single building, but a continuation of several houses on both sides of a street which, growing waste, was purchased and applied to that use. I was received very kindly by the Warden, and went for many days to the Academy. Every room had in it one or more Projectors; and I believe I could not be in fewer than five hundred rooms.

The first man I saw was of a meagre aspect, with sooty hands and face; his hair and beard long, ragged, and singed in several places. His clothes, shirt, and skin were all of the same color. He had been eight years upon a project of extracting sunbeams from cucumbers, which were to be put in phials hermetically sealed, and let out to warm the air in raw, inclement summers. He told me he did not doubt that in eight years more he should be able to supply the Governor's garden with sunshine at a reasonable rate; but he complained that his stock was low, and entreated me to give him something as an encouragement to ingenuity, especially as this had been a very dear season for cucumbers. . . . .

I saw another at work to calcine ice into gunpowder; who likewise showed me a treatise he had written concerning the malleability of fire, which he intended to publish. There was a most ingenious architect who had contrived a new method for building houses, by beginning at the roof and working downward to the foundation; which he justified to me by the like practice of those prudent insects, the bee and the spider. . . . .

We crossed a walk to the other part of the Academy, where the projectors in Speculative Learning resided. The first Professor I saw was in a very large room, with forty pupils around him. After salutation, observing me to look earnestly upon a frame which took up the greatest part of the length and breadth o. the room, he said: "Perhaps I might wonder to see him employed in a project for improving Speculative Knowledge by practical and mechanical operations. But the world would soon be sensible of its usefulness; and he flattered himself that a more noble, exalted thought never sprang into any other man's head. Every one knew how laborious the usual method is of attaining to art and sciences; whereas by his contrivance the most ignorant person, at a reasonable charge, might write books in philosophy, poetry, politics, laws, mathematics. and theology without the least assistance from genius or study."

He then led me to the frame, about the sides whereof all his pupils stood in ranks. It was twenty feet square, placed in the middle of the room. The superficies was composed of several bits of wood about the bigness of a die, but some larger than others. They were all linked together by slender wires. These bits of wood were covered on every square with paper pasted on them; and on these papers were written all the words of their language, in their several moods, tenses, and declensions, but without any order. The Professor then desired me to observe, for he was going to set his engine at work. The pupils, at his command, took each of them hold of an iron handle, whereof there were forty fixed around the edges of the frame; and giving them a sudden turn, the whole disposition of the words was entirely changed. He then commanded six-and-thirty of the lads to read the several lines softly, as they appeared upon the frame; and where they found three or four words together that might make part of a sentence, they dictated to the four remaining boys, who were scribes. This work was repeated three or four times; and at every turn the engine was so contrived that the words shifted into new places, as the square bits of wood moved up and down.

Six hours a day the young students were

employed in this labor; and the Professor showed me several volumes in large folio, already collected, of broken sentences, which he intended to piece together, and out of these rich materials to give the world a complete body of all the arts and sciences; which, however, might be still improved and much expedited, if the public would raise a fund for making and employing five hundred such frames in Lagado, and oblige the managers to contribute in common their several collections. He assured me that this invention had employed all his thoughts from his youth; that he had emptied the whole vocabulary into his frame, and made the strictest computation of the general proportion there is in books between the numbers of particles, nouns, and verbs, and other parts of speech. . . . .

I was at the Mathematical School, where the Master taught his pupils after a method scarcely imaginable to us in Europe. The proposition and the demonstration were fairly written on a thin wafer, with ink composed of cephalic tincture. This the student was to swallow upon a fasting stomach, and for three days to eat nothing but bread and water. As the wafer digested, the tincture mounted to his brain, bearing the composition along with it. But the success has not hitherto been answerable, partly by some error in the *quantum* or proportion, and partly by the perverseness of the lads, to whom this bolus is so nauseous that they generally steal aside and discharge it upwards before it can operate; neither have they been yet persuaded to use so long an abstinence as the prescription requires.—*Voyage to Laputa.*

THE STRULDBRUGS.

One day, in much good company, I was asked by a person of quality whether I had seen any of their *Struldbrugs*, or "Immortals." I said I had not; and desired he would explain to me what he meant by such an appellation, applied to a mortal creature. He told me that sometimes a child happened to be born in a family with a red circular spot in his forehead, directly over the left eyebrow, which was an infallible mark that it should never die. The spot, as he described it, was about the compass of a silver threepence, but in the course of time grew larger, and changed its color ; for at twelve years old it became green, so continued till five-and-twenty, then turned to a deep blue ; at five and forty it grew coal-black, and as large as an English shilling ; but never admitted any further alteration. He said these births were so rare that he did not believe there could be above eleven hundred Struldbrugs of both sexes in the whole empire ; of which he computed about fifty in the metropolis ; and among the rest a young girl born about three years ago ; that these productions were not peculiar to any family, but a mere effect of chance ; and the children of the Struldbrugs themselves were equally mortal with the rest of the people. . . . .

After this preface he gave me a particular account of the Struldbrugs among them. He said they commonly acted like mortals till about thirty years old ; after which by degrees they grew melancholy and dejected, increasing in both till they came to fourscore. This he learned from their own confession ; for otherwise, there not being above two or three of that species born in an age, they were too few to form an observation by.

When they came to fourscore years—which is reckoned the extremity of living in this country—they had not only all the follies and infirmities of other old men, but many more which arose from the dreadful prospect of never dying. They were not only opinionative, peevish, covetous, morose, vain, talkative ; but incapable of friendship, and dead to all natural affection, which never descended below their grandchildren. Envy and impotent desires are their prevailing passions. But those objects against which their envy seems principally directed are the vices of the younger sort and the deaths of the old. By reflecting on the former they find themselves cut off from all possibility of pleasure; and whenever they see a funeral they lament and repine that others have gone to a harbor of rest to which they themselves can never hope to arrive. They have no remembrance of anything but what they learned and observed in their youth and middle age, and even that is very imperfect; and for the truth or particulars of any fact it is safer to depend on common tradition than upon their best recollections. The least miserable among them appear to be those who turn to dotage, and entirely lose their memories; these meet with more pity and assistance because they want many bad qualities which abound in others.

If a Struldbrug happens to marry one of his own kind, the marriage is dissolved, of course, by the courtesy of the kingdom, as soon as the younger of the two comes to be fourscore; for the law thinks it a reasonable indulgence that those who are condemned, without any fault of their own, to a perpetual continuance in the world should not have their misery doubled by the load of a wife. As soon as they have completed the term of eighty years they are looked on as dead in law; their heirs immediately succeed to their estates; only a small pittance is reserved for their support, and the poor ones are maintained at the public charge. After that period they are held incapable of any employment of trust or profit; they cannot purchase lands or take leases; neither are they allowed to be witnesses in any cause, either civil or criminal—not even for the decision of metes and bounds.

At ninety they lose their teeth and hair. They have at that age no distinction of taste, but eat and drink whatever they can get, without relish or appetite. The diseases they were subject to still continue, without increasing or diminishing. In talking, they forget the common appellation of things and the names of persons, even those who are their nearest friends and relations. For the same reason, they never can amuse themselves with reading, because their memory will not serve to carry them from the beginning of a sentence to the end; and by this defect they are deprived of the only entertainment whereof they might otherwise be capable. The language of the country being always upon the flux, the Struldbrugs of one age do not understand those of another; neither are they able after two hundred years to hold any conversation (farther than by a few general words) with their neighbors the mortals; and thus they lie under the disadvantage of living like foreigners in their own country.

This was the account given me of the Struldbrugs, as near as I can remember. I afterwards saw five or six of different ages, the youngest not above two hundred years old, who were brought to me at several times by my friends; but although they were told that I was a traveller, and had seen all the world, they had not the least curiosity to ask me a question; only desired I would give them *slumdark*, or a token of remembrance; which is a modest way of begging, to avoid the law which strictly forbids it, because they are provided for by the public, although indeed with a very scanty allowance.—*Voyage to Laputa.*

SWINBURNE, ALGERNON CHARLES, an English poet, born near Henley-on-the Thames in 1837. He was the son of a British Admiral, was educated partly in France, and partly at Eton. In his twentieth year he was entered at Balliol College, Oxford, but left without taking a degree. His principal works are: *The Queen Mother* and *Rosamund*, both dramas (1860), *Atalanta in Calydon* a dramatic poem constructed after Grecian models (1864), *Chastelard* (1865), *Poems and Ballads* (1866), *A Song of Italy* (1867), *Siena, a Poem* (1868), *Ode on the Proclamation of the French Republic* (1870), *Songs before Sunrise* (1871), *Bothwell, a Tragedy* (1874), *Essays and Studies* (1875), *Poems and Ballads*, second series (1878), *A Study of Shakspeare* (1879), *Studies in Song*(1881), *Tristram of Lyonesse* (1882), *A Century of Roundels* (1883), *Songs of the Spring-tides* (1880), *Locrine, a Tragedy* (1887), *Poems and Ballads*, third series (1889), *A Study of Ben Jonson* (1889).

CHORUS FROM "ATALANTA IN CALYDON."

Before the beginning of years
  There came to the making of man
Time, with a gift of tears;
  Grief, with a glass that ran;
Pleasure, with pain for leaven;
  Summer, with flowers that fell;
Remembrance, fallen from heaven;
  And madness, risen from hell;
Strength, without hands to smite;
  Love that endures for a breath;
Night, the shadow of light;
  And Life, the shadow of death.

And the high gods took in hand
  Fire, and the falling of tears,

And a measure of sliding sand
  From under the feet of years,
And froth and drift of the sea,
  And dust of the laboring earth,
And bodies of things to be,
  In the houses of death and of birth;
And wrought with weeping and laughter,
  And fashioned with loathing and love,
With life before and after,
  And death beneath and above;
For a day and a night and a morrow,
  That his strength might endure for a span
With travail and heavy sorrow,
  The holy spirit of man.

From the winds of the north and the south
  They gathered as unto strife;
They breathed upon his mouth,
  They filled his body with life;
Eyesight and speech they wrought
  For the veils of the souls therein;
A time for labor and thought,
  A time to serve and to sin.
They gave him a light in his ways,
  And love, and a space for delight;
And beauty and length of days,
  And night, and sleep in the night.
His speech is a burning fire,
  With his lips he travaileth;
In his heart is a blind desire,
  In his eyes foreknowledge of death;
He weaves, and is clothed with derision;
  Sows, and he shall not reap;
His life is a watch or a vision
  Between a sleep and a sleep.

THE HOUNDS OF SPRING.

When the Hounds of Spring are on Winter's traces,
  The mother of months in meadow or plain
Fills the shadows and windy places
  With lisp of leaves and ripple of rain,
And the brown bright nightingale, amorous,
Is half assuaged for Itylus,

For the Thracian ships and the foreign faces;
The tongueless vigil, and all the pain:

Come with bows bent and with emptying of quivers,
Maiden most perfect, Lady of Light,
With a noise of winds and many rivers,
With a clamor of waters, and with might;
Bind on thy sandals, O thou, most fleet,
Over the splendor and speed of thy feet!
For the faint east quickens, the wan west shivers,
Round the feet of the day and the feet of the night.

Where shall we find her, how shall we sing to her,
Fold our hands round her knees and cling?
Oh that man's heart were fire and could spring to her
Fire, or the strength of the streams that spring!
For the stars and the winds are unto her
As raiments, as songs of the harp-player;
For the risen stars and the fallen cling to her,
And the southwest wind and the west wind sing.

For Winter's rains and ruins are over,
And all the season of snows and sins;
The days dividing lover and lover,
The light that loses, the night that wins;
And time remembered is grief forgotten,
And frosts are slain and flowers begotten,
And in green underwood and cover
Blossom by blossom the Spring begins.

The full streams feed on flower of rushes,
Ripe grasses trammel a travelling foot;
The faint fresh flame of the young year flushes
From leaf to flower and flower to fruit;
And fruit and leaf are as gold and fire,
And the oat is heard above the lyre,
And the hoofed heel of a Satyr crushes
The chestnut-husk at the chestnut root.

And Pan by noon and Bacchus by night,
Fleeter of foot than the fleet-foot kid,
Follows with dancing and fills with delight
The Mænad and the Bassaria;
And soft as lips that laugh and hide,
The laughing leaves of the trees divide,
And screen from seeing and leave in sight
The God pursuing, the maiden hid.
Atalanta in Calydon.

THE INTERPRETERS.

I.

Days dawn on us that make amends for many
Sometimes,
When heaven and earth seem sweeter even than any
Man's rhymes.
Light had not all been quenched in France, or quelled
In Greece,
Had Homer sung out, or had Hugo held
His peace.
Had Sappho's self not left her word thus long
For token,
The sea round Lesbos yet in waves of song
Had spoken.

II.

And yet these days of subtler air and finer
Delight,
When lovelier looks the darkness, and diviner
The light—
The gifts they give of all these golden hours,
Whose urn
Pours forth reverberate rays or shadowing showers
In turn—
Clouds, beams, and winds that make the live day's track
Seem living—
What were they did no spirit give them back
Thanksgiving?

III.

Dead air, dead fire, dead shapes and shadows telling
Time nought;
Man gives them sense and soul by song, and dwelling
In thought.
In human thought their being endures, their power
Abides:
Else were their life a thing that each light hour
Derides.
The years live, work, sigh, smile, and die, with all
They cherish;
The soul endures, though dreams that fed it fall
And perish.

IV.

In human thought have all things habitation;
Our days
Laugh, lower, and lighten past, and find no station
That stays.
But thought and faith are mightier things than time
Can wrong,
Made splendid once with speech, or made sublime
By song.
Remembrance, though the tide of change that rolls
Wax hoary,
Gives earth and heaven, for song's sake and the soul's
Their glory.

Poems and Ballads. Third Series.

IN A GARDEN.

Baby, see the flowers!
—Baby sees
Fairer things than these,
Fairer though they be than dreams of ours.

Baby, hear the birds!
—Baby knows
Better songs than those,
Sweeter though they sound than sweetest words.

Baby, see the moon!
—Baby's eyes
Laugh to watch it rise,
Answering light with love and night with noon.

Baby, hear the sea!
—Baby's face
Takes a graver grace,
Touched with wonder what the sound may be.
Baby, see the star!
—Baby's hand
Opens warm and bland,
Calm in claim of all things fair that are.

Baby, hear the bells!
—Baby's head
Bows, as ripe for bed,
Now the flowers curl round and close their cells.

Baby, flower of light,
Sleep and see
Brighter dreams than we,
Till good day shall smile away good night.

Poems and Ballads. Third Series.

SWING, David, a popular American preacher born in Cincinnati in 1830. He graduated at Miami University, Ohio, in 1852, and was Professor of Languages there for twelve years. Since 1866 he has been in Chicago, first as Presbyterian pastor. Since his famous trial for heresy, which did not result in condemnation, he has from preference taken an independent position, preaching for many years past in Music Hall. He has published in book form two series of discourses, entitled *Truths of To-Day*, and another under the titles of *Motives of Life*, all marked by geniality, individuality of expression, and wholesomeness.

INTELLECTUAL PROGRESS.

No doubt the human race has sought gold too ardently, and does so still, but we must not suffer that passion to conceal from us the fact that in all the many civilized centuries, this same race has with equal zeal asked the universe to tell man its secrets. We have been not only a money-making race, but we have been rather good children, and have studied hard the lessons on the page of science and art and history. If, when you look out and see millions rushing to and fro for money, you feel that man is an idolater, you can partly dispel the painful thought if you attempt to count the multitude who in that very hour are poring over books, or who in meditation are seeking the laws of the God of nature. Millions upon millions of the young and the old are in these days seeking, at school or at home, in life's morn or noon or evening, the facts of history and science and art and religion. In order to be ourselves properly impelled or enticed along life's path, we must make no wrong estimate of the influences which are impelling mankind, for if we come to think that all are worshiping gold, we too, despairing of all else, will soon degrade ourselves by bowing at the same altar. It is necessary for us always to be just. We must be fully conscious of the fact that there are many feet hurrying along through the places of barter, intent on more gold, but so must we be conscious that there is a vast army of young and old who are asking the great world to come and tell them its great experience, and to lead them through its literature and arts, and down the grand avenues of histor. You saw the fortune, you read the will of the last millionaire when he died, but did you with equal zeal mark how our scholars hurried to the far West to study the last eclipse of the sun, and how a score of new sciences met on that mountain summit to ask the shadow to tell them something more about the star depths and the throne of the Almighty? When the Chaldean men of science attempted to learn the truths of the heavens, they were compelled to look up with the eye only. All they had was the eye and a loving heart. They filled seventy volumes with their imperfect studies. A comet they were compelled to designate as a star that carried a train behind and a crown in front. When the time of our late eclipse drew near, what a procession of arts and of instruments moved far out to where the shadow would fall! And others had marked just where the darkness would come and the second of its coming. As man can measure the width of a river, and find through what spaces it flows, so modern learning marked out that river of shade and built up its banks, and along came the brief night and flowed in them most carefully. But the astronomer went not alone; the science which can analyze a flame millions of miles distant, and tell what is being consumed; the science which can announce in a second a fall of heat; the science which can convey the true time two thousand miles while the excited heart beats once—these, and that grandest science which can see the rings of Saturn and the valleys of the Moon, assembled on that height in the very summer when we are lamenting most that mankind knows no pursuit except that of gold. That Rocky Mountain scene only faintly illustrates the intellectual activity of an era. If the passion for money is great in our day, it is also true that the intellectual power of the same period is equally colossal. No reader, be he ever so industrious, can keep pace with the issue of good books, and money itself is alarmed lest the new thoughts and invention of to-morrow may overthrow its investment of yesterday. Stocks tremble at the advance of intellect. A glory of this intellectual passion may be found in the fact that it is not confined to a group of scholars, as old inquiry and education were confined, but like liberty and property, it has passed over to the many. Not all the multitude of the world are gold-seekers, but on the opposite there are tens of thousands of men, and women too, who are lovers of truth more than of money, and are standing by the fountains of knowledge with no thought or expectation of ever being rich. Education and knowledge, the power to think and to enjoy the thought of others, have long since transformed a cottage into a palace. Thus, although society seeks too fondly the money-prize, yet he will do great injustice to our land who fails to see what an immense motive of life this pursuit of knowledge has always been and remains. If then, we could go through our years aright, we must not believe that the air around us is all poisonous with the incense burned to Mammon, but that there is also a sweetness in the wind coming from the altars where the millions of truth-lovers kneel.—*Motives of Life.*

SWINTON, WILLIAM, an American author, born in Scotland in 1838. He came to America at an early age, studied at Toronto, Canada, with a view to the Presbyterian ministry. He, however, adopted the profession of a teacher, and in 1853 became Professor of Ancient and Modern Languages in a female seminary at Greensborough, N. C., where he wrote a series of magazine articles which were subsequently published collectively under the title, *Rambles among Words* (1859). He afterwards came to New York, where he engaged in teaching, and became editorially connected with the *New York Times*, of which he was correspondent with the Army of the Potomac during the early part of the civil war. From 1869 to 1874 he was Professor of Belles-Lettres in the University of California. Returning to New York, he prepared a series of educational text-books. His principal works in the department of military history are: *Campaigns of the Army of the Potomac* (1866), *The Twelve Decisive Battles of the War* (1867), *History of the New York Seventh Regiment during the War of the Rebellion* (1870).

THE BATTLE OF GETTYSBURG.

Gettysburg was the battle the greatest in its proportions, and the greatest in respect to the issue involved, of all the actions waged during four years between the mighty armies of the East. In point of losses alone it deserves to rank with the first-class battles of history; for on the Union side the casualties were nearly 24,000, and on the Confederate side they exceeded 27,000, killed, spoiled, or taken. The circumstances under which Lee initiated the campaign authorized him to expect the most important results from the invasion of the North.

Having many times before defeated the Army of the Potomac with a much inferior force, it was not unwarrantable for him to assume that he would again triumph now that he had an army equal in strength to that of his adversary. . . .

It must be conceded that the plan of operations devised by Lee, while wonderfully bold, was yet thoroughly methodical and well-matured. For if the march removed his army to an indefinite distance from his base, he yet had an easy-guarded line of communications, by way of the Cumberland and Shenandoah Valley, to his dépôts at Winchester and Gordonsville, whence he could readily draw ammunition. And in the matter of supplies he was in nowise dependent on Virginia; for the well-peopled and productive soil of Pennsylvania affords ample resources for the subsistence of an army, for a time, and whilst moving, without the use of magazines, by the European method of requisitions at the cost of the inhabitants. The proof of this is furnished in the fact that the Confederate army not only subsisted on the country during the campaign, but that, in addition, it forwarded to the Potomac great quantities of cattle and corn that served to eke out their meagre larder until such time as the maturing crops furnished fresh supplies.

Being thus easy in respect to that part on which Frederick the Great has said that armies like serpents, move—to wit, the belly—Lee, leading a powerful, valiant, and enthusiastic army, confidently moved to an anticipated victory. His aim was the capture of Washington, the defeat of the Army of the Potomac, and the retention of a footing long enough on loyal soil to so work upon the North that, under the combined pressure of its own fears, the uprising of the reactionary elements at home, and perhaps the influence of the Powers abroad, it might be disposed to sue for peace. He had ample means for the conduct of the enterprise. which was of itself not extravagant;

and it is rare that any military operation presents greater assurance of success than Lee had of attaining his end of conquering a peace on Northern soil.

In tracing out the causes of Lee's defeat we shall find that something was due to the faults of that commander himself, something to the good conduct of General Meade, much to the valor of the Army of the Potomac, and much again to Fortune, "that name for unknown combinations of infinite power," which, maugre every seeming assurance of success, was wanting to the Confederates. It was not by the prevision nor by the manœuvres of either general that the forces were brought into collision on July 1, though the Union commander is certainly entitled to great credit for the promptitude with which, accepting the issue accidentally presented, he threw forward his army to Gettysburg. Here nature, as well as circumstances, and the unusual temerity of Lee, favored the Union army. Elated by the success of the first day, the Confederate commander, contrary to his intent and promise, determined to attack. But while the position might readily be turned, it was impregnable by direct assault, if maintained with skill and firmness. And it was so maintained; for the Army of the Potomac, realizing the tremendous issue involved, feeling that it stood there for the defense of its own soil, fought with far more determination than it had ever displayed in Virginia.

The experiment of the Pennsylvania campaign gave a complete and final quietus to the scheme of Southern invasion of the loyal States, and the enterprise was never more attempted. Nor indeed was the Army of Northern Virginia ever again in condition to undertake such a movement. This was not alone due to the shock which it received in its *morale* from so disastrous a blow, but to its material losses, the portentous sum of which exceeded the aggregate of its casualties in the whole series of battles which Grant delivered from the Rapidan to the James River. This subtraction of force, viewed merely in numerical count, was most grave, considering the great exhaustion of the fighting resources of the Confederates; while, when we take into account the quality of the men the loss was irreparable; for the 30,000 put *hors de combat* at Gettysburg were the very flower and *élite* of that incomparable Southern infantry which, tempered by two years of battle, and habituated to victory, equalled any soldiers that ever followed the eagles to conquest.—*The Twelve Decisive Battles.*

SYMONDS, JOHN ADDINGTON, an English author, born at Bristol in 1840. He was educated at Harrow School and at Oxford. In 1862 he obtained a College Fellowship, but soon vacated it by marriage. Delicate health has for many years compelled him to reside in a warm climate, principally in Italy and Switzerland, and most of his works—the earliest of which appeared in 1872—are upon Italian subjects. In verse he has published: *Sonnets of Michelangelo and Campanella*, a volume of *Sonnets on the Thought of Death*, *Many Moods, New and Old*. His prose works are: *Introduction to the Study of Dante; Studies of the Greek Poetry*, *Renaissance in Italy*, *Sketches in Italy and Greece*, *Italian By-Ways*, and the lives of *Shelley* and *Sir Philip Sidney*, in the "English Men of Letters." The seventh and last volume of his work on the Italian Renaissance was published in 1886.

IN THE MENTONE GRAVEYARD.

Between the circling mountains and the sea
  Rest thou! Pure spirit whose work is done,
Here to the earth whate'er was left of thee
  Mortal, we render. But beyond the sun
  And utmost stars, who know what life begun
Even now nor ever to be ended, bright
With clearest effluence of unclouded light,

Greets thee undazzled?—Lo! this peace of tombs
  With rose-leaf and with clematis and vine,
And violets that smile in winter, blooms,
  Sun, moon, and stars in sweet procession shine
  Above thy shadeless grave; the waves divine
Gleam like a silver shield beneath; the bare
Broad hills o'erhead, defining the free air,

Enclose a temple of the sheltering skies
  To roof thee. Noon and eve and lustrous
    night,
The sunset thou didst love, the strong sunrise
  That filled thy soul erewhile with strange
    delight,
  Still on thy sleeping clay shed kisses bright;
But thou—Oh, not for thee these waning powers
Of morn and evening, these poor paling flowers,

These narrowing limits of sea, sky, and earth!
  For in thy tombless City of the dead
Sunrising and sunsetting, and the mirth
  Of Spring-time and of Summer, and our red
  Rose-wreaths are swallowed in the streams
    that spread
Supreme of Light ineffable from Him,
Matched with whose least of rays our sun is
    dim.

Oh, blessed! It is for us, not thee, we grieve!
  Yet even so, ye voices, and you tide
Of souls innumerous that panting heave
  To rhythmic pulses of God's heart, and hide
  Beneath your myriad booming breakers wide
The universal Life invisible,
Give praise! Behold, the void that was so still

Breaks into singing, and the desert cries—
  Praise, praise to Thee! praise for Thy servant
    Death,
The healer and deliverer! from his eyes
  Flows life that cannot die; yea with his
    breath
  The dross of weary earth he winnoweth,
Leaving all pure and perfect things to be
Merged in the soul of Thine immensity!

Praise, Lord, praise for this our brother Death!
  Though also for the fair mysterious veil
Of life that from thy radiance severeth
  Our mortal sight; for these faint blossoms
    frail
  Of joy on earth we cherish, for the pale
Light of the circling years, we praise Thee too;
Since thus as in a web Thy Spirit through

The phantom world is woven! Yet thrice praise
For him who frees us! Surely we shall gain,
A guerdon for the exile of these days,
Oneness with Thee; and as the drops of rain,
Cast from the throbbing clouds in Summer's pain,
Resume their rest in ocean, even so we,
Lost for awhile, shall find ourselves in Thee.

SAVONAROLA.

As Savonarola is now launched upon his vocation of prophecy, this is the right moment to describe his personal appearance and his style of preaching. We have abundant material for judging what his features were, and how they flashed beneath the storm of inspiration. Fra Bartolommeo, one of his followers, painted a profile of him in the character of S. Peter Martyr. This shows all the benignity and grace of expression which his stern lineaments could assume. It is a picture of the sweet and gentle nature latent within the fiery arraigner of his nation at the bar of God. In contemporary medals the face appears hard, keen, uncompromising, beneath its heavy cowl. But the noblest portrait is the intaglio engraved by Giovanni della Corniole, now to be seen in the Uffizzi at Florence. Of this work Michael Angelo, himself a disciple of Savonarola, said that art could go no further. We are therefore justified in assuming that the engraver has not only represented faithfully the outline of Savonarola's face, but has also indicated his peculiar expression. A thick hood covers the whole head and shoulders. Beneath it can be traced the curve of a long and somewhat flat skull, rounded into extraordinary fullness at the base and side. From a deeply sunken eyesocket emerges, scarcely seen, but powerfully felt, the eye that blazed with lightning. The nose is strong, prominent, and aquiline, with wide nostrils, capable of terrible dilation under the stress of vehement emotion. The mouth has full, compressed, projecting lips. It is large, as if made for a torrent of eloquence; it is supplied with massive muscles, as if to move with energy and calculated force and utterance. The jawbone is hard and heavy; the cheekbone emergent: between the two the flesh is hollowed, not so much with the emaciation of monastic vigils as with the athletic exercise of wrestlings in the throes of prophecy. The face, on the whole, is ugly, but not repellent; and in spite of its great strength, it shows signs of feminine sensibility. Like the faces of Cicero and Demosthenes, it seems the fit machine for oratory. But the furnace hidden away behind that skull, beneath that cowl, have made it haggard with a fire not to be found in the serener features of the classic orators. Savonarola was a visionary and a monk. The discipline of the cloister left its trace upon him. The wings of dreams have winnowed and withered that cheek as they passed over it. The spirit of prayer quivers upon those eager lips. The color of Savonarola's flesh was brown; his nerves were exquisitely sensitive yet strong; like a network of steel, elastic, easily overstrained, they recovered their tone and temper less by repose than by the evolution of fresh electricity. With Savonarola fasts were succeeded by trances, and trances by tempests of vehement improvisation. From the midst of such profound debility that he could scarcely crawl up the pulpit steps, he would pass suddenly into the plenitude of power, filling the Dome of Florence with denunciations, sustaining his discourse by no mere trick of rhetoric that flows to waste upon the lips of shallow preachers, but marshaling the phalanx of embattled arguments and pointed illustrations, pouring his thought forth in columns of continuous flame, mingling figures of sublimest imagery with reasonings of severest accuracy, at one time melting his audience to tears, at another freezing them with terror, again quickening their souls with prayers and pleadings and blessings that had in them the sweetness of the very spirit of Christ. His sermons began with scholastic exposition; as they advanced, the ecstasy of inspiration fell upon the preacher, till the sympathies of the whole people of Florence gathered round him, met and attained, as it were, to single consciousness in him. He then no longer restrained the impulse of his oratory, but became the mouthpiece of God, the interpreter to themselves of all that host. In a fiery crescendo, never flagging, never losing firmness of grasp or lucidity of vision, he ascended the altar steps of prophecy, and, standing like Moses on the mount between the thunders of God and the tabernacles of the plain, fulminated period after period of impassioned eloquence. The walls of the church re-echoed with sobs and wailings dominated by one ringing voice. The scribe to whom we owe the fragments of these sermons, at times breaks off with these words: Here I was so overcome with weeping that I could not go on! Pico della Mirandola tells us that the mere sound of Savonarola's voice, startling the stillness of the Duomo, thronged through all its space with people, was like a clap of doom; a cold shiver ran through the marrow of his bones, the hairs of his head stood on end as he listened. Another witness reports: "These sermons caused such terror, alarm, sobbing and tears that every one passed through the streets without speaking, more dead than alive.—*Renaissance in Italy.*

TACITUS, Caius Cornelius, a Roman historian, born about 55 A. D.; died about 117 A. D. He was eminent as an orator and pleader; married a daughter of Julius Agricola; held important positions under Vespasian, Domitian, and Nero (69–98 A. D.), after which nothing definite is recorded of his personal history. He wrote *A Dialogue Concerning Orators*, which was held in high esteem. His *Life of Agricola*, his father-in-law, is of great value for its information concerning the early inhabitants of Britain. His *Germania* gives nearly all the knowledge which we have of the ancient Germans. His *History of Rome* narrated the events from 69 to 96 A. D.; but the greater part of this has been lost, only the portions relating to the years 69 and 70 being extant. His *Annals* narrated the events from the year 14 to 68; but of the sixteen Books only nine, and portions of three others, are now known to exist. Our extracts are from the translation of Brodribb and Church.

THE DEATH OF TIBERIUS.

The bodily powers of Tiberius were now leaving him, but not his skill in dissembling. There was the same stern spirit; he had his words and his looks under strict control; and occasionally would try to hide his weakness, evident as it was, by a forced politeness. After frequent changes of place, he at last settled down on the promontory of Misenum, in a country-house once owned by Lucius Lucullus. It was there discovered that he was drawing near his end; and thus there was a physician of the name of Charicles usually employed, not indeed to have the direction of the Emperor's varying health, but to put his advice at his immediate disposal. This man, as if he was leaving on business of his own, clasped his hand with a show of homage, and touched his pulse. Tiberius noticed it. Whether he was displeased, and strove the more to hide his anger, is a question. At any rate, he ordered the banquet to be resumed, and sat at the table longer than usual, apparently by way of showing honor to his departing friend. Charicles, however, assured Macro that his breath was failing, and that he would not last more than two days. All was at once hurry; there were conferences among those on the spot, and dispatches to the generals and armies. On the 15th of March [37 A. D.] his breath failing, he was believed to have expired; and Caius Cæsar was going forth, with a numerous throng of congratulating followers, to take first possession of the empire, when suddenly news came that Tiberius was recovering his voice and sight, and calling for persons to bring him food to recover him from his faintness. Then ensued a universal panic; and while the rest fled hither and thither, every one feigning grief or ignorance, Caius Cæsar, in silent stupor, passed from the highest hopes to the extremity of apprehension. Macro, nothing daunted, ordered the old Emperor to be smothered under a huge heap of clothes, and all to quit the entrance-hall.—*Annals*, VI. 50.

THE CAREER AND CHARACTER OF TIBERIUS.

And so died Tiberius, in the seventy-eighth year of his age. His father was Nero, and he was on both sides descended from the Claudian house, though his mother passed, by adoption, first into the Livian, then into the Julian family. From earliest infancy perilous vicissitudes were his lot. Himself an exile, he was the companion of a proscribed father; and on being admitted as a step-son into the house of Augustus, he had to struggle with many rivals so long as Marcellus and Agrippa, and subsequently Caius and Lucius Cæsar, were in their glory. Again, his brother Drusus enjoyed in a greater degree the affection of the citizens. But he was more than ever on dangerous ground after his marriage with Julia, whether he tolerated or escaped from his wife's profligacy. On his return from Rhodes he ruled the Emperor's now heirless house for twelve years, and the Roman world, with absolute sway, for twenty-three. His character, too, had its distinct periods. It was a bright time in his life and reputation when, under Augustus, he was a private citizen or held high offices; a time of reserve and crafty assumption of virtue as long as Germanicus and Drusus were alive. Again, while his mother lived he was a compound of good and evil. He was infamous for his cruelty, though he veiled his debaucheries while he loved or feared Segnus. Finally he plunged into every wickedness and disgrace when fear and shame being cast off, he simply indulged his own inclinations.—*Annals.* VI. 51.

THE CONFLAGRATION OF ROME UNDER NERO.

A disaster followed (whether accidental or treacherously contrived by the Emperor is uncertain, as authors have given both accounts) worse, however, and more disastrous than any, which have happened to the city, by the violence of fire. It had its beginning in that part of the Circus which adjoins the Palatine and Cælian hills, where, amid the shops containing inflammable wares, the conflagration both broke out and instantly became so fierce and so rapid from the wind, that it seized in its grasp the entire length of the Circus. For here there were no houses fenced in by solid masonry, or temples surrounded by walls, or any other obstacle to interpose delay. The blaze in its fury ran first through the level portion of the city; then rising to the hills, while it again devastated every place below them, it outstripped all preventive measures, so rapid was the mischief, and completely at its mercy the city, with those narrow winding passages and irregular streets which characterized old Rome.

Added to this were the wailings of terror-stricken women, the feebleness of age, the helpless inexperience of childhood, the crowds who sought to save themselves or others, dragging out the infirm or waiting for them, and by their hurry in the one case, by their delay in the other exaggerating the confusion. . . . At last, doubting what they should avoid, or whither betake themselves, they crowded the streets or flung themselves down in the fields; while some who had lost their all, even their very daily bread, and others, out of love for their kinsfolk whom they had been unable to rescue, perished, though escape was open to them. And no one dared to stop the mischief, because of incessant menaces from a number of persons who forbade the extinguishing of the flames; because others again openly hurled brands, and kept shouting that there was one who gave them authority: either seeking to plunder more freely, or obeying orders.

Nero at this time was at Antium, and did not return to Rome until the fire approached his house which he had built to connect the palace with the gardens of Mæcenas. It could not, however be stopped from devouring the palace, the house, and everything around it. However, to relieve the people, driven homeless as they were, he threw open to them the Campus Martius and the public buildings of Agrippa, and even his own gardens, and raised temporary structures to receive the destitute multitude. Supplies of food were brought up from Ostia and the neighboring towns, and the price of corn was reduced to three *sestertii* [sixpence] a peck. These acts, though popular, produced no effect, since a rumor had gone forth everywhere that, at the very moment when the city was in flames, the Emperor appeared on a private stage, and sang of the destruction of Troy, comparing present misfortunes with the calamities of antiquity.—*Annals*, XV. 38, 39.

www.ingramcontent.com/pod-product-compliance
Lightning Source LLC
Chambersburg PA
CBHW031814270326
41932CB00008B/420

* 9 7 8 3 3 3 7 2 2 0 1 8 1 *